Poverty Policy and Poverty Research

Poverty Policy and Poverty Research

The Great Society and
the Social Sciences

Robert H. Haveman

THE UNIVERSITY OF WISCONSIN PRESS

Published 1987

The University of Wisconsin Press
114 North Murray Street
Madison, Wisconsin 53715

The University of Wisconsin Press, Ltd.
1 Gower Street
London WC1E 6HA, England

First printing

Printed in the United States of America

For LC CIP information see the colophon

ISBN 0-299-11150-4

Contents

Tables and Figures

Tables

Figures

Preface

The idea for a volume such as this was born a number of years ago, during, as I can best recall, a conversation in 1978 with the committee appointed by the National Academy of Sciences to review the state of "poverty research." That committee studied this research area thoroughly and diligently, and concluded that the next stage must include an emphasis on synthesizing what had been learned during the previous decade's basic research effort. Here is how they put it:

Well-chosen, well-executed syntheses . . . can prove of high value in generating understanding of the research frontier and the possibilities of extending it. They would be particularly useful if they were cross-disciplinary syntheses organized around behavioral and policy issues, so that they would more naturally draw attention to future work judged necessary by a standard of policy usefulness rather than solely by disciplinary interest (National Academy of Sciences, 1979, p. 58).

This view, as I remember it, came from the belief that scholarship in the social sciences was too discipline-oriented, too myopic, and too motivated by the need for individual scholars to publish in the major journals if they were to become successful economists or sociologists in their own right. As a result, it was felt that the evolution of the overall poverty research enterprise was too insular and fragmented. Potential gains from assessing what was known, what wasn't known, and what should be known were not being realized, and these gains were large.

Why no one followed the recommendation of the committee is no mystery. Synthesis and assessment are not the types of scholarship that the main journals in the separate disciplines encourage. No new research findings are thereby generated. There is no identifiable audience seeking reflections on the state of a field of research and directions for new efforts. In fact, such reflections are likely to be inconsistent with the current fashions in the separate disciplines—and it is in swimming with these tides that academics build reputations and careers.

The seed planted by the committee germinated until the end of the decade, when another development occurred. During the presidential campaign of 1980 it became clear that the era of the War on Poverty had ended, regardless of who gained the presidency. Growth and defense and investment had replaced concerns with social and human problems on the nation's list of priorities. It seemed time to stand back a bit from the poverty research enterprise, to organize thoughts on what had come before and what it amounted to, and what should come next.

It was in conversations with my colleagues Eugene Smolensky and Sheldon Danziger that I took the next step toward committing myself to this project. They convinced me that after many years of involvement in poverty research, I could undertake the effort with smaller costs than many, and that it was a worthwhile enterprise. This advice, I would note, was not universal; several of my colleagues questioned the wisdom of an effort which they regarded as having a doubtful benefit-cost ratio, from my own point of view.

One of these conversations took place in 1981 in the office of Marshall Robinson and Peter de Janosi, who were then president and vice-president of the Russell Sage Foundation. The purpose of our visit to Sage was to explore the possibility of foundation support for the Institute for Research on Poverty, whose life at that time seemed fragile. Robinson and de Janosi were, consistent with the charter of the foundation, interested more in the effects of the War on Poverty on the social science research enterprise than in poverty research per se. The potential for support to pursue a line of work which I had become convinced had importance sealed the case—I submitted a proposal and received a generous grant.

This volume is the result of the five years of work that the grant initiated. As with all research enterprises, the time from start to finish was about three times as long as expected and for which support was received.

A number of people contributed to this effort both directly and indirectly; the entire list is too long to include here. The Institute for Research on Poverty, its directors—Smolensky and Danziger—and staff deserve most recognition. As it had during the previous decade, the Institute provided the intellectual home and stimulation necessary for this project.

Several persons commented on the various drafts of the manuscript, and its final form reflects their insights. My colleague and wife, Barbara Wolfe, read several drafts and helped me develop a meaningful organization for the volume. She deserves special thanks. Irwin Garfinkel commented on at least two rewritings, and his remarks forced a more critical perspective onto the work. Robert Lampman's wisdom and insights have always been of great value to me and, through my response to his comments, they are once again represented here. Other readers whose comments improved the manuscript are James Morgan, John Palmer, and Harold Watts.

Help with the editing and typing was a crucial part of the entire endeavor. Catherine Cameron did the final typing of the manuscript and, even more important, the editing, tracking down, and collating of the large number of entries in the bibliography. Elizabeth Evanson edited the entire manuscript and caused the catalogue quality of some of its parts to acquire a "story" and a theme. That the volume still does not read as a novel is no fault of hers. Others at the Institute also deserve to be mentioned: John Sorenson, who helped keep the financing of the project on track; Joyce Collins, who regularly greased the wheels of administration; and Cathy Esser, Nancy Rortvedt, and Sue Sticha, who bore a part of the typing load. Betty Reininger efficiently handled proofreading.

The Russell Sage Foundation was the main sponsor of the project. Its grant formed the financial backbone of the effort. I hope Marshall Robinson, Peter de Janosi, and Patricia Lewis are pleased with the result. Other support came from Erasmus University at Rotterdam, the Netherlands Institute of Advanced Study, and the Graduate School of the University of Wisconsin–Madison, all of which made possible a pleasant and productive year in the Netherlands.

Portions of some chapters have appeared in earlier forms as follows: "The War on Poverty and Social Science Research, 1965–1980," in *Research Policy*, 1986, 15:53–66, North-Holland Publishing Co., Amsterdam; "*Social Experimentation* and Social Experimentation," in *Journal of Human Resources*, 1986, 21:586–605; "Methods for Correcting Selectivity Bias: A Legacy of War on Poverty Research," in *Sociology and Social Research*, 1986, 71:4–10; and "Microdata Simulation Modeling after Twenty Years," in *Evaluation Review*, 1986, 10:411–434.

Robert H. Haveman
November 1986

Poverty Policy and Poverty Research

1

Public Policy and Poverty Research: An Overview

In his State of the Union address in January 1964 Lyndon Johnson declared "unconditional war on poverty" in America, and in June he announced plans to create a Great Society through a series of new social programs. Congress concurred shortly thereafter, when it gave legislative embodiment to those programs by passing the Economic Opportunity Act. These policy initiatives of the mid-1960s marked a discrete change in the federal government's willingness to intervene for the purpose of improving the economic situation of poor Americans. The policy change came quickly. In part because of the surge of feeling after President Kennedy's death, Lyndon Johnson was able to develop, propose, and secure passage of a major legislative package of policy interventions with considerable speed. Within two years, a commitment presented in a emotional speech had been transformed into programs in urban ghettos and the rural back country. These early efforts stimulated still other policy changes designed to improve the condition of the poor, and together those measures dominated federal policy-making in the following fifteen years. The period from 1965 to 1980 constitutes the postwar "liberal era" of federal social policy.

In 1980, with the election of President Reagan, that era came to an end. This election partly reflected the electorate's judgment that the interventions begun in 1965 had become too costly, had crowded out needed

defense spending, and had generated adverse effects on economic performance. Since 1981, there has been no War on Poverty—it is as if
victory had been declared, when in fact there was no such conquest. The
reductions in social spending urged by the Reagan administration did
occur, and many of them were targeted precisely on those antipoverty
measures that had been spawned in 1964 and flourished over the intervening years.[1]

The 1965–80 period of the federal War on Poverty is the focus of this
volume. The end of this era in 1981 prompted the writing of the book. A
great deal had happened because of the antipoverty initiative—to the
poor, to the composition of public spending, to the public's perception of
the proper role and responsibility of government, to economic performance, and to the relationships between classes and races. Many of these
changes have been described, examined, and assessed in detail
elsewhere.[2]

Yet a major impact of the Great Society programs has gone largely
unnoticed and certainly undocumented. The initiation of these social
interventions occurred in an intellectual void: the president could call for
a War on Poverty, but nobody—economists, sociologists, social critics,
and least of all policymakers—knew how to wage it effectively. Along
with antipoverty programs, then, came an unprecedented flow of public
spending for research on "the nature and causes of, and the cures for,
poverty."[3] Social scientists became actively involved in the making of
antipoverty policy. These developments changed the social sciences,
altering the choice of topics on which research was undertaken, the
methods of research, and ultimately the state of knowledge in the field. It
is to describe, examine, and assess the impact of that era on the efforts of
social scientists that this book was written.

Several things about the book should be noted at the outset. First, it is
not a comprehensive review and assessment of the impact of the antipoverty policy era on all of the social sciences. It emphasizes developments in
the economics of poverty, though the boundaries between economics,
demography, and sociology in this area are frequently blurred. Two
reasons account for its emphasis. For better or for worse, the fact is that
most of the social science research which was stimulated by the War on
Poverty was in economics.[4] Economists were central in the early planning

---

1. See Bawden (1984) for detailed discussions of this policy shift.
2. See the descriptions and assessments in Plotnick and Skidmore (1975); Haveman
(1977); and Danziger and Weinberg (1986).
3. The quotation was the announced purpose of the Institute for Research on Poverty
when it was established at the University of Wisconsin in 1966.
4. As a sociologist who read an early draft of the manuscript of this book put it: "As much
as we would wish it had been otherwise, the War on Poverty was the playground of

of the War on Poverty; economists directed the research offices of the Office of Economic Opportunity during its lifetime; the economics of poverty became a recognized subdiscipline in the field as early as 1969.[5] The other reason is more pragmatic: the author is an economist, and his disciplinary background has colored judgments regarding the relative importance of areas and topics.

Second, even in the coverage of these largely economic topics, the book is selective. Its subjects are those closely related to policy initiatives which emanated from the agencies centrally involved in the War on Poverty—the Office of Economic Opportunity and what was then the Department of Health, Education, and Welfare. Policy initiatives sponsored by the Department of Housing and Urban Development and the Department of Labor are given much less—in some cases no—attention. Hence, those contributions to knowledge (Chapters 4–7) and methodology (Chapters 8–11) that I have chosen to describe and discuss reflect an explicit judgment regarding both the importance of the contribution and its proximity to antipoverty policy.

Third, while the coverage of the volume is broad, substantial attention is given to the research contributions of scholars who, at one time or another, were affiliated with the federally sponsored Institute for Research on Poverty at the University of Wisconsin–Madison. At first blush this may appear to reflect institutional chauvinism; however, from 1965 to the present that institute has been a focal point for scholars in several disciplines and from numerous universities and institutions who were interested in poverty research issues and antipoverty policy. Many, if not most, of this set of over two hundred people have spent some time at the Institute and have contributed to its research program. The record of poverty research by Institute-affiliated scholars speaks for itself. Established in 1966, by 1980 the Institute had published 35 books, 650 discussions papers, and 18 special reports, and had spent about $20 million, most of them federal dollars, on poverty research. It would be surprising if any review of poverty research during the 1965–80 period did not devote substantial attention to the work of these scholars.

The focus of this volume, then, is the relationship between the making of public policy and the development of social science, or what Henry Aaron termed "politics and the professors."[6] In most analyses of this

economists, not sociologists. . . . It *was* economists who led the War on Poverty, it was economic criteria that were used to assess it. . . . The viewpoint of those who brought the coffee is less central."

5. The *Journal of Economic Literature* first identified the Economics of Poverty as a distinct field of research in 1969, when it began bibliographic referencing of papers in that category.

6. This is the title of his book dealing with the subject (Aaron, 1978).

relationship, it is the impact of science and scientists (in this case, social science and social scientists) on the making of public policy that has been at issue. Aaron concluded that the academy responds to, rather than leads, policy developments. He consequently finds that the work of social scientists has typically contributed little to the formation of public policy. Ernst Stromsdorfer, who has also studied this interaction, found cases in which science contributed to policy developments and other instances where the knowledge and advice of social scientists were ignored by policymakers. Social research studies, he concluded, are part of an adversary process in which "policy makers, while not totally subjective and nonrational, will use whatever data are at hand to support their case, regardless of the methodological purity by which it has been developed" (Stromsdorfer, 1985, p. 258). After sorting through the evidence from a number of case studies of the impact of social science on public policy in the United States, the author of the Introduction to a major study of this interaction stated: "Success or failure in the application of social science [to the policy process] depends on a mesh between the scientific skills *and* political interests of the social scientists on the one side, and the political skills *and* scientific interests of the policy-makers on the other" (Berger, 1980, p. vii). In a few of the cases studied, these skills and interests coincided; in many others they did not.

This volume, however, reverses the question regarding the relationship of policy and social research. Rather than inquiring about the impact of social science and social scientists on public policy decisions, it asks how developments in public policy have affected the evolution of social research. In particular, what has been the impact of the War on Poverty and Great Society initiatives of the 1965–80 period, and of the research support which accompanied these initiatives, on the method and content of the disciplines most heavily affected—primarily economics, but also sociology and political science?

That there should be some causal connection between the War on Poverty and the development of social science knowledge and methods is not surprising. It is not uncommon in the United States for new policy efforts to be accompanied by the expenditure of research monies on topics of relevance to the initiative. As documented in Chapter 2, the War on Poverty was an extreme example of this pattern. Not only were the early designers of that effort painfully aware of the lacunae in knowledge surrounding the effort on which they were embarking, but the federal government's new planning-programming-budgeting system encouraged a strong program of research, demonstration, and evaluation in the new Office of Economic Opportunity. The research support which accompanied the War on Poverty altered the agendas of social researchers.

Another link between policy and the academy concerns the heavy involvement of social science scholars and researchers in the policy-making, policy-development process surrounding the War on Poverty. The development of the idea of such a war, as well as the formulation of the plans and programs which ultimately constituted it, was heavily influenced by social scientists—mainly economists—who came to be closely associated with and influential in the major planning efforts associated with this venture. The high degree of the involvement by economists and other social scientists in the antipoverty effort has often been noted.[7] The research and writings of these scholars, their students, and their colleagues were no doubt influenced by their direct involvement in the policy process.

Finally, more than any other policy initiative in the postwar period—perhaps with the exception of the space program, but surely in the social policy area—the attempt to create a Great Society was accompanied by extensive publicity and news coverage. The intense interest of economists and other social scientists was akin to a "cause." The breadth and depth of this interest influenced the subjects to which scholars and analysts turned their attention.

Books of the sort represented by this volume are not standard fare. It is not a research monograph, in the common sense of that term. No new theoretical propositions are set forth, no new body of data is analyzed, no explicit hypothesis is tested, no scientific conclusions are reached. Moreover, because the War on Poverty was a unique episode in U.S. policy-making, any attempt to develop from the experience general propositions regarding the impact of policy on the content and methods of science would be misguided.

Yet this volume is a research book. It represents an effort to meet the needs for review and synthesis of research, as urged in a report from a committee of the National Academy of Sciences.[8] The report stated that reviews and syntheses of research would serve as an antidote to the narrowing forces within individual disciplines and the centrifugal forces among them. In noting that the disciplines reserve their primary rewards for those who contribute to new developments of knowledge or method rather than those who tell about these developments, the committee spoke of the need "to turn the attention of . . . researchers away from questions defined by the needs of their disciplines" (p. 34), and argued that synthetic work which organizes and appraises the state of knowledge on particular questions "can prove of high value in generating under-

---

7. See, for example, Yarmolinsky (1969), Kershaw (1970), Levine (1970), and Brauer (1982).

8. The recommendation appears in detail in National Academy of Sciences (1979).

standing of the research frontier and the possibilities of extending it" (p. 58).

The volume is not designed for the casual reader, since it is a description and assessment of basic research contributions on the poverty issue. Nor is it designed to be a guide or instructional manual for understanding the details of the research examined. It will not allow researchers and scholars who wish to know the basis for research findings or to appraise the methods on which they are based to bypass the original papers and monographs. The book is intended to be of interest to anyone who wishes an answer to the two-part question, What have been the major advances in poverty research since the inception of the War on Poverty in the United States, and what is the significance and status of these advances? As such it is written to serve as a basic reference for the large number of social policy researchers for whom the poverty issue is of concern, as well as the smaller number of those interested in understanding the linkage between policy-making and social research during the fifteen-year era covered here. Perhaps as important, the volume is designed to meet the needs of analysts desiring an overview and assessment of recent poverty research accomplishments in the United States. Both the contents of the chapters and the bibliography at the end should serve, for example, as an aid to the social research community in Western Europe, where interest in the poverty problem and poverty research is of recent vintage, but growing rapidly.

The overarching theme that runs through the volume is that developments in society and politics have substantial influence on the nature and direction of progress in the social sciences. The message is that social scientists do not live in ivory towers; and that in their efforts to influence society and policy, they themselves are influenced and the course of their disciplines affected. The story that this volume tells adds substance to the assertions of Aaron:

The subjects on which analysts do research are influenced by prevailing political interests and preconceptions. One need not be cynical to recognize that research agendas are influenced by the flow of money from government and foundations, which in turn try to use research budgets at least in part to improve decisions on current issues of public policy. They are not immune to currents of intellectual fashion, which are related to prevailing political moods (1978, p. 157).

The book has three parts. The first discusses the effort to build a Great Society, documents the changes in financial support for poverty research which accompanied this initiative, and measures the impact of this research spending on the absolute and relative levels of poverty research output before and after 1965. The second describes and assesses the contributions to knowledge of a variety of research investigations, ranging from the measurement of poverty to new understanding of the process of status attainment and operation of the labor market. The final part examines advances in the methods of social research stimulated by the War on Poverty.

I

The War on Poverty, 1965–1980: Policy and Research

This part of the volume sets the background for our examination of the contributions to knowledge and to method in economics and sociology that accompanied the antipoverty initiative. Chapter 2 presents a brief overview of the new social programs and recounts their origins and objectives. It describes the magnitude of the shift in federal government spending priorities which accompanied the War on Poverty, and examines the extent to which federal spending targeted on the poor population grew over the succeeding years. The shift in national priorities represented by Great Society programs is unique in magnitude and emphasis. It should not be surprising that economists and other social scientists were affected by both the new flow of research support and the receptivity of policymakers to new knowledge of relevance to antipoverty measures.

Chapter 3 offers a definition of poverty research and research related to poverty issues, and attempts to indicate the growth of resources devoted to this activity over the 1965–80 period. Expenditures on these categories of research are measured and compared with spending in other research areas. These expenditures are also related to aggregate spending on federal antipoverty programs and social welfare activities in general. The poverty research enterprise is seen to be large in absolute terms, but small relative to some of the public expenditures to which it relates. It is also small relative to the aggregate national research enterprise.

Chapter 3 also addresses the relationship of expenditures on poverty and poverty-related research in about 1980 to aggregate social science research spending, both public and private. Through these comparisons, the contribution of poverty and poverty-related research to the size and growth of the overall social science research enterprise is estimated.

While data on poverty research spending provide some evidence on the relationship of that research to social science knowledge and methods, they provide no overall assessment of how social science *without* anti-poverty policy efforts might have differed from social science *with* these efforts. In the final section of Chapter 3, I present the results of a survey of the prominent social science literature before and after the War on Poverty. The goal is to determine the absolute and relative role of poverty-related research in the social science disciplines, as indicated by articles published in the various disciplines preceding and following 1965, and through this means to obtain a rough overall assessment of the impact of these social initiatives on the contribution of poverty research to aggregate social research.

2

The War on Poverty and the Great Society: Motivation, Social Spending, and Results

The war was declared in 1964, and its initial strategy was outlined in the *Economic Report of the President* of that year. As it evolved, the effort consisted of several policy initiatives rather than a single orchestrated attack. Education, job training, and community participation and development were important components. Although income support was not a central feature of the policies that were planned, income redistribution efforts did figure prominently in antipoverty efforts during subsequent years.

The origins, evolution, and impact of the War on Poverty have been described, discussed, and analyzed by several authors (among them Moynihan, 1969; Kershaw, 1970; Levine, 1970). All observers agree that announcement of the war was the catalyst for numerous government activities and initiatives, some within the Office of Economic Opportunity (OEO), others associated with neither OEO nor efforts to aid the poor. Regardless of sponsor, government programs in the social policy area began to merge an antipoverty objective into their preexisting goals.

The purpose of this chapter is not to retell that story, but to set the context for analyses in subsequent chapters. Only with a basic understanding of antipoverty efforts can the important developments in social science knowledge and methods which accompanied these initiatives be clearly seen.

Motivations and Programs

The origins of the War on Poverty have been examined from several viewpoints, and a number of motivations for it have been suggested: compassion stemming from abysmal hardship evident in pockets of the population identified by geography, culture, and race; embarrassment over the inconsistency of this hardship with the image of U.S. affluence; fear regarding the potential for violence and disruption inherent in such inequality; excitement stimulated by the call for progressive new policies from an administration with "liberal" inclinations (or at least rhetoric); the regular and persistent demonstrations of inequity, discrimination, and poverty by an increasingly militant civil rights movement; the perception that the tax cut of 1964 failed to benefit the poor; and faith in the efficacy of social planning held by social scientists and other academics whose influence in government was at its zenith. To disentangle these forces—or to order them—is an impossible task; all were, however, present in some degree. Interestingly, except for general concern with the social status and economic position of blacks generated by the civil rights movement, there was no organized interest group demanding new programs for the poor (see Friedman, 1977). Nor had the platforms of the major political parties assigned this problem particularly high priority. And there was no apparent surge of public opinion designating poverty to be the primary domestic policy priority.[1]

It was owing in part to the nature of these origins that the antipoverty campaign developed as it did. Perhaps because no organized interest group representing the poor was there to demand direct subsidization, and perhaps also because of the domination of OEO policy-planning efforts by social scientists (see Yarmolinsky, 1969; Brauer, 1982), the strategy adopted was premised on the view that the problem was ultimately one of low labor market productivity. The poor were viewed as being in that state because they did not work enough, or because they did not work hard enough, or because their meager skills and qualifications were insufficient to raise them out of poverty even if they did work hard. This condition was in turn attributed to several factors—the lagging state of the economy, the characteristics of the poor, and discrimination against them by those who controlled access to jobs or goods and ser-

1. This is not to imply that there was no support for such an effort in the climate of public opinion prevailing at that time. The book by Michael Harrington (1962) and the article on the invisible poor by Dwight MacDonald (1963) were widely read and discussed. They did appear to motivate intellectuals and other, largely upper-middle class, individuals who read literature of that sort. In some sense these writers built upon the earlier case for public-sector action against poverty made a few years earlier by Galbraith (1958).

vices. All of these factors represented fundamental problems of the American economy. Hence it was argued that any truly effective policy would have to strike at these root causes. Policy to reform or expand the system of income transfers might reduce the maldistribution of income and improve the economic welfare of the poor; they would not, however, alter these structural deficiencies. The remedy required overt policy measures by the federal government designed to improve the performance of the economy, the productivity characteristics of the poor, and the attitudes (or at least the behavior) of those who hired or sold to the poor.

Revitalization of the nation's economy was given high priority on the government's list of antipoverty measures. Unwilling to concede that the poor had a weaker desire to work than did the nonpoor, policy planners viewed the high unemployment and low labor force participation of the poor as the contribution of a lagging economy to the problem of poverty. It was at this time that "the full employment gap" and "fiscal drag" became a part of the president's vocabulary, the time at which fiscal stimulus in the form of the massive tax cut of 1964 was viewed as the way to increase the nation's rate of economic growth, reduce unemployment, and shrink the gap in hours worked (and perhaps wage rates) between the poor and nonpoor. The policy-generated increase in aggregate demand and income would, it was hoped, "trickle down" to the poor, even if the tax cut itself did not benefit them directly (see Gallaway, 1965; Heller, 1966; Aaron, 1967).

To gauge the progress made in securing this improvement in the welfare of poor families, research was supported to measure the extent of poverty and the composition of the poor population. A measure of income poverty developed at the Social Security Administration established a set of absolute income cutoffs, adjusted annually to account for price-level changes, for households of various sizes and locations. In 1964, about 13 percent of all U.S. families and 19 percent of all citizens were found to be in income poverty: a reduction in this indicator was a key objective of the mid-1960s aggregate demand policy.[2]

Stimulating the demand for goods and services would not by itself, however, be sufficient. The problems inherent in the characteristics of the poor would require more specific policies directed toward the poor themselves. The gap in work skills between poor and nonpoor would have to be corrected. Manpower training, both institutional and on the

2. In 1964, the report of the president's Council of Economic Advisers employed for the first time an income-based poverty measure and related it to proposed macroeconomic policies. The official definition and measurement of income poverty was first spelled out in 1965; see Orshansky (1965). The Social Security Administration measure was formally adopted by OEO in 1969. See also Lampman (1971a).

job, was required. Hence the Job Corps, the Neighborhood Youth Corps, programs stemming the Manpower Development and Training Act (MDTA) of 1962, and the Work Incentive program were either established or scheduled for rapid expansion. In addition to a lack of skills, the poor had a good deal less education in general than did the nonpoor. Whereas little could be done to correct the disparity among those cohorts that had already reached working age, better preparation for school, better schooling, and more schooling—all targeted on the children of the poor—would ensure that this deficiency would not afflict the children of this generation's poor as it had those of past generations. Hence Head Start, Upward Bound, Follow Through, the Teacher Corps, and programs under Title I of the Elementary and Secondary Education Act of 1965 were launched. To the extent that low performance in school and on the job was due to deficiencies in diet, Emergency Food Aid and a school lunch program were established. The debilitating effects of illness and disability on job performance could, it was hoped, be reduced by subsidizing medical care for the poor to improve their access to the health care system. For this objective, and also because medical care was becoming viewed as a service not to be allocated on the basis of ability to pay, Neighborhood Health Centers, Medicaid, and to a lesser extent Medicare were set into place to subsidize the medical expenses of welfare recipients, the aged, and the "medically indigent."

Finally, there were programs that were more concerned with restructuring the social institutions by which the poor gained access to jobs and goods and services, and less concerned with the personal traits of the poor. The Community Action program was established ostensibly to coordinate the wide range of social services being provided by state, local, and private organizations. In fact, its establishment served to reduce the political poverty of low-income groups and racial minorities. By granting the poor increased participation in the decisions of agencies that allocated goods and services, their access to these services would be increased. Moreover, this increased participation would enable the poor to alter the composition of services available to them in order to perceive more clearly how institutional change can be encouraged by political action (see Peterson and Greenstone, 1976). Similarly, the Legal Services program was established both to enhance the flow of services to the poor and to enable the poor and their advocates to influence the structure of institutions dispensing goods, services, and jobs. Legislation to ensure equal opportunity in employment and housing—although somewhat belated—was also viewed as an effort to alter the behavior, if not the attitudes, of institutions controlling access to markets for jobs, goods, and services.

This menu of programs can be thought of as the direct outcome of the plans developed as part of the War on Poverty. Taken as a whole, they reflected the judgment that public measures could alter both the performance of the economy and the characteristics of the poor and thereby improve their economic status. Nearly every hypothesis regarding why the poor performed weakly in the labor market was reflected in some program. More labor demand, combined with a socially augmented increase in earnings capacity, was the primary strategy. Increased political participation and advocacy leading to the restructuring of political and social institutions was a second strategy. Not included in the legislation forming the antipoverty campaign was any proposal to overhaul and extend the income transfer and welfare system of the nation, or to institute a system of demogrants (payments to individuals, in some cases varying in amount according to such demographic characteristics as age), family allowances, or negative income taxes. Nor were any new measures proposed by the president or implemented by Congress to alter directly the income distribution.[3] Furthermore, no direct attack on structural weaknesses in the labor market was proposed or implemented. Legislation to ensure equal opportunity in employment stands as the only measure designed to increase the employment and earnings of the poor by explicitly increasing the demand for their services.

Parallel with the direct attack on poverty was another set of efforts. While these measures were not an explicit part of the War on Poverty, they were related to, and to some extent perhaps induced by it. One result of the war was that no government agency and no congressional committee was free from the persistent query regarding policies under their jurisdiction: "What does it do for the poor?" (Lampman, 1974). Indeed, asking this question became an important function of OEO, located as it was in the Executive Office of the President. As a result, the political viability of any proposed measure was enhanced if advocates could demonstrate that it would contribute to the antipoverty objective. Social program advocates in a large number of areas employed this rationale to good advantage.

Over the course of the following decade, the benefits and coverage of the social security program were extended on several occasions, and the structure of the program was modified to increase its antipoverty impact. In 1965, one-third of all elderly persons were poor, and expansion of coverage and benefits to them had a substantial antipoverty effect. To

3. In the first antipoverty planning document prepared by OEO in 1965, a negative income tax was proposed as an important complement to the other policy approaches. This strategy was not accepted by the president and no explicit policy proposal was submitted to the Congress.

some, these modifications of social security compromised the social insurance principle on which the program was founded because they provided more general income support. By 1980 the Food Stamp program—begun in 1964 as a program designed primarily to stabilize and support farm commodity prices—had become a $10 billion program of assistance to all low-income families, regardless of their work status or the cause of their meager income. It became, in effect, a negative income tax for food. Similarly, the evolution of health policy took on an antipoverty character. In 1965 a long-debated program of health care for the aged, Medicare, was passed, and Medicaid, a program reimbursing the health care costs of welfare recipients and those declared "medically indigent," was introduced. Housing assistance for low-income families, a relatively small program before 1965, grew to an annual budget of nearly $5 billion in 1980. Of the in-kind programs that blossomed during this decade, only one, Legal Services, was an integral part of the planned War on Poverty. While the passage and rapid growth of these programs were facilitated by the national antipoverty objective, they were neither initially conceived as part of the war, nor were they within the jurisdiction of OEO.

In addition to these programs and the legislated growth of others justified in part on antipoverty grounds, a third set of policy developments affected the poor. Before 1965, a number of public assistance programs provided cash support to particular categories of poor people: Aid to Families with Dependent Children (AFDC) and Aid to the Aged, Blind, and Disabled were the primary ones. Although many changes were made in these programs during the 1965–80 period, few were intended by either the president or Congress to generate increases in program coverage, in real benefit levels, or in the proportion of citizens eligible to receive benefits.[4] Nevertheless, these welfare programs grew enormously after 1965. This expansion, primarily in AFDC and Aid to the Aged, Blind, and Disabled, was neither planned nor anticipated. Federal cash transfers from these two programs increased from $2 billion in 1965 to over $15 billion in 1980, while total program costs rose from about $5 billion to nearly $23 billion. In the aggregate, federal public assistance expenditures rose from about $3 billion in 1965 to over $63 billion in 1980.

The sources of this growth were complex. The primary one was demo-

4. An exception is the Supplemental Security Income program, which, beginning in 1974, combined the programs for poor aged, blind, and disabled citizens and increased benefit levels. A second possible exception was the 1967 AFDC amendments which, by seeking to increase work incentives, increased the number of families eligible for program benefits. The main motivation of this legislation, however, was to reduce welfare costs and caseloads.

graphic; the number of female-headed families in the United States increased at an unprecedented rate during the 1960s and 1970s. Program changes also encouraged increases in both expenditures and recipients. Those changes included, among other things, increased leniency on the part of welfare administrators, expanded rights and entitlements stemming from the initiatives of organized groups of recipients and legal rights activists, more liberal court interpretations of beneficiary rights and entitlements, the raising of state supplemental benefits, and reduced stigma attached to being on welfare. While the demographic factor worked in the direction of increasing poverty incidence, the program changes contributed to the reduction of income poverty. It can hardly be claimed, however, that these changes were a part of the vision of anti-poverty planners.

As a result of both planned and unplanned developments, then, the economic status of the poor had improved substantially by the early 1970s. Those gains held until 1980, in spite of some increases in poverty incidence as a result of recession in the mid-1970s. Moreover, even though serious inequality remained, the gap between blacks and whites in education and income in 1980 was narrower than in the early 1960s, and the participation of blacks and other groups of the poor in the political process had increased markedly. The volume of cash and, in particular, of in-kind transfers targeted on the poor experienced unprecedented growth. Although only the former contributes to a reduction in officially measured poverty, both have augmented the economic well-being of those at the bottom of the income distribution. Indeed, if family income is defined to include the recipient value of in-kind benefits,[5] the nation in 1980 could be said to have come a considerable distance in reducing income poverty.

Public Social Spending, 1960–1980

The test of "What does it do for the poor?" had a variety of impacts—on the federal budget, on the poor, and on the social sciences. This section addresses three questions: To what extent did social initiatives alter the structure of the federal budget? How was the resulting shift in national priorities reflected in changes in aggregate social welfare spending targeted on the poor from 1965 to 1980? To what extent have the poor been affected by these changes?

---

5. There are several methods for valuing in-kind transfers. "Recipient value" is the amount of cash which the recipient views as being equivalent to the benefit.

Changing Composition of the Federal Budget

One test, admittedly crude, of the proposition that the concerns which led to the War on Poverty also changed government decisions and priorities is the extent to which the allocation of federal expenditures to social welfare and antipoverty goals versus other goals changed after 1965. Table 2.1 presents the structure of the federal budget in 1965 and 1980. Between these two years federal outlays (less interest) grew from 17 percent of gross national product to 20 percent, nearly doubling in real terms, from $271 to $524 billion in 1980 prices. These aggregates, however, mask an important shift in priorities. Income security expenditures (all of the social security programs, Unemployment Insurance, AFDC, and other programs that provide cash transfers or access to essentials)

Table 2.1. The Composition of the Federal Budget, 1965 and 1980 (as percentage of total outlays less interest on debt)

	Fiscal Year	
Category	1965	1980
National defense, international affairs, and veterans' benefits and services	53.2	32.0
Transportation, community and regional development, and revenue sharing	7.5	9.1
Natural resources and environment, energy, and agriculture	6.5	4.8
Income Security	23.4	36.8
Health	1.6	10.5
Education, training, employment, and social services	1.9	5.9
General government, general science, space and technology, other	7.0	2.8
Offsetting receipts	−1.3	−1.9
Total	100.0	100.0
Total outlays less interest as a percentage of GNP	16.7	20.0
Total outlays less interest (billions of current dollars)	$109.8	$524.2
Total outlays less interest (billions of real 1980 dollars)[a]	$271.0	$524.2

Source: Compilations from various tables in U.S. Bureau of the Census, *Statistical Abstract of the United States, 1984* (Washington, D.C.: GPO, 1983).
Note: Small errors may occur owing to reclassification of categories between 1965 and 1980.
[a]The consumer price index (all items) is employed as the deflator.

increased from 23 to 37 percent of the budget. In percentage terms, the growth in health expenditures—due largely to growth in the Medicare and Medicaid programs—was even more rapid, from 1.6 to 10.5 percent. Similarly, the share of the budget devoted to education, training, employment, and social services increased from almost 2 to nearly 6 percent. Taken together, the budget share of these three categories of social programs doubled, from 27 to 53 percent, in the fifteen years after 1965.

Whereas the budget in 1965 could have been characterized as defense-oriented, by 1980 it was clearly oriented toward social welfare concerns. Its share devoted to national defense, international affairs, and veterans' benefits and services declined from 53 to 32 percent. In spite of the Vietnam War, solutions to the problems of poverty, inequality, urban decay, and limited access to health care and education by the poor were the focal points of a concerted federal effort in these years. During this period the "welfare state" made major advances in the United States. The concerns and sentiments which motivated the Great Society efforts also caused a major reordering of national priorities, as reflected in the budget.

Growth of Social Welfare Spending

A second indicator of the focus of national policy on the poor is the growth of total social welfare spending in the United States after 1965. These expenditures are compiled annually by the Social Security Administration to indicate the growth in a set of public measures implicitly designated to represent the U.S. welfare state.

Table 2.2 shows social welfare expenditures for the years 1965, 1970, 1975, and 1980. These expenditures, by both federal and state governments, grew from $77 billion in 1965 to $493 billion in 1980. This sixfold increase represents an average rate of growth (in current dollars) of over 12 percent, a rate double that of the economy as a whole. The largest category of spending is for social insurance, which in 1965 accounted for 36 percent of total social welfare expenditures and rose to nearly 47 percent by 1980. Expenditures on social insurance grew at a rate of 14 percent per year over this period. While much of that growth is attributable to such demographic factors as the aging of the population and earlier ages of voluntary retirement, program coverage was expanded during the period, benefits were made more generous in response to the perception that the aged were a needy group worthy of assistance, and the benefit structure tilted increasingly toward the poor.

Housing (largely public housing) and public aid experienced the most rapid growth over the period. Public housing expenditures increased from $.2 billion to $5.2 billion, growing at an average annual rate of over

Table 2.2. Federal and State Social Welfare Expenditures under Public Programs, 1965–1980 (millions of current dollars)

	1965	1970	1975	1980	Average Annual Percentage Rates of Change
Social Insurance	*28,123*	*54,691*	*123,013*	*229,552*	*14.0*
OASDI	16,998	29,686	63,649	117,118	12.9
Medicare	—	7,149	14,781	34,992	10.6
Unemployment Insurance	3,003	3,820	13,836	18,326	12.1
Workers' Compensation	1,859	2,950	6,479	13,253	13.1
Other	6,263	11,086	24,268	45,863	13.3
Public Aid	*6,284*	*16,487*	*41,308*	*71,602*	*16.2*
Public assistance[a]	4,508	9,220	13,858	17,298	9.0
Medicaid	1,367	5,213	13,502	27,394	20.0
Supplemental Security Income	—	—	6,092	8,226	6.0
Food stamps	36	577	4,694	9,083	36.9
Other	373	1,477	3,162	9,601	21.7
Health Programs	*6,246*	*9,907*	*17,788*	*28,119*	*10.0*
Maternal and Child Health	227	431	567	798	8.4
Other	6,019	9,476	17,221	27,321	10.1
Veterans' Programs	*6,031*	*9,078*	*17,020*	*21,466*	*8.5*
Pensions and compensation	4,141	5,394	7,579	11,306	6.7
Health and medical care	1,229	1,784	3,517	6,204	10.6
Welfare	186	379	934	890	10.4
Other	475	1,521	4,990	3,066	12.4
Education	*28,038*	*50,683*	*80,571*	*120,239*	*9.7*
Elementary and secondary	22,358	38,632	59,746	86,773	9.0
Higher	4,826	9,907	16,384	26,091	11.3
Vocational/Adult	854	2,144	4,441	7,375	14.4
Housing	*319*	*701*	*3,172*	*7,209*	*20.8*
Public housing	235	460	1,456	5,246	20.7
Other	84	241	1,716	1,963	21.0
Other Social Welfare	*2,066*	*4,145*	*6,447*	*14,006*	*12.8*
Vocational rehabilitation	211	704	1,036	1,251	11.9
Institutional care	790	202	296	482	− 3.3
Child nutrition	617	896	2,518	5,259	14.3
Child welfare	354	585	597	800	5.4
Other	94	1,758	2,000	6,214	27.9
Total	77,175	145,784	290,081	493,355	12.4

Source: Tabulated from *Social Security Bulletin, Annual Statistical Supplement*, for each year.

[a]Includes Aid to Families with Dependent Children; General Assistance; and Aid to the Aged, Blind, and Disabled until 1974, when the Supplemental Security Income program began.

22

20 percent. Public aid grew at a rate of 16.2 percent per year over the period. In 1965 these programs, both highly targeted on the poor, accounted for nearly 8.5 percent of total social welfare spending. By 1980, public housing and public aid attracted nearly 16 percent of the nation's public social welfare expenditures. Spending on Medicaid, food stamps, and public housing—all directed toward the poor—grew at a rate in excess of 20 percent per year.

Table 2.3 presents the same series, but in constant (1965) dollars. In real terms, the entire social welfare system grew at a 6.1 percent annual rate from 1965 to 1980. Of the three programs experiencing the most rapid growth, Medicaid and public housing had *real* growth rates of about 14 percent per year, and food stamps expanded by over 30 percent per year.

Although neither of these two tables provides the state-federal breakdown of social welfare expenditures, allocation of spending between the two levels of government is available for each of the years shown. By and large, this allocation indicates that federal spending in most categories grew at a more rapid pace than state expenditures. In 1965, federal expenditures accounted for 49 percent of total social welfare spending; by 1980, 61 percent of social welfare expenditures were undertaken by the federal government. The numbers in parentheses in the 1965 and 1980 columns of Table 2.3 indicate the percentage of the total expenditures in each category accounted for by the federal government in those years. For each of the broader categories except veterans' programs, the federal share increased, often markedly. This is especially true in the program areas most targeted on the low-income population: public aid (from 57 to 68 percent), housing (85 to 92 percent), and other social welfare programs (39 to 63 percent). The rapid growth in public spending targeted on the poor during the 1965–80 period was fueled by policy changes at the national government level.

Growth of the Antipoverty Public Budget

While the expenditures shown in Tables 2.2 and 2.3 constitute all public social welfare expenditures, clearly not all of them represent expenditures on behalf of the poor. It is possible, however, to estimate in rough fashion the dollar benefits from social welfare expenditures which were received by pretransfer-poor families and individuals—those whose incomes before receipt of public income transfers were below the official poverty lines. Such estimates are available for the 1965–72 period, and have been presented in detailed "antipoverty budgets" for 1965, 1968, and 1972 (Plotnick and Skidmore, 1975). Analysis of these "budgets" indicates that the percentage of total public social welfare expenditures

Table 2.3. Federal and State Social Welfare Expenditures under Public Programs, 1965–1980 (millions of 1965 dollars)

	1965[a]		1970	1975	1980a	Average Annual Percentage Rates of Change
Social Insurance	*28,123*	*(78)*	*45,330*	*74,630*	*89,827* *(83)*	*7.7*
OASDI	16,998		24,605	38,615	45,830	6.6
Medicare	—		5,925	8,967	13,693	8.4
Unemployment Insurance	3,003		3,166	8,394	7,171	5.8
Workers' Compensation	1,859		2,445	3,931	5,186	6.8
Other	6,263		9,189	14,723	17,947	7.0
Public Aid	*6,284*	*(57)*	*13,665*	*25,062*	*28,019* *(68)*	*10.0*
Public assistance[b]	4,508		7,642	8,408	6,769	2.7
Medicaid	1,367		4,321	8,192	10,720	13.7
Supplemental Security Income	—		—	3,696	3,219	−2.8
Food stamps	36		478	2,848	3,554	30.6
Other	373		1,224	1,918	3,757	15.4
Health Programs	*6,246*	*(45)*	*8,211*	*10,792*	*11,003* *(47)*	*3.8*
Maternal and Child Health	227		357	344	312	2.1
Other	6,019		7,854	10,448	10,691	3.8
Veterans' Programs	*6,031*	*(100)*	*7,525*	*10,326*	*8,400* *(99)*	*2.2*
Pensions and compensation	4,141		4,471	4,598	4,424	0.4
Health and medical care	1,229		1,479	2,134	2,428	4.5
Welfare	186		314	567	348	4.2
Other	475		1,261	3,027	1,200	6.2

which went to the pretransfer poor hovered between 40 and 43 percent during these years.

In Table 2.4, this analysis is updated and extended by presenting estimates of public social welfare expenditures on the pretransfer poor over the entire 1965–80 period. The data for 1965 and 1970 were adapted from those presented earlier. For 1975 and 1980, two estimates are presented. The first is based on a linear extrapolation to 1975 and 1980 of the program-specific percentage of expenditures going to the pretransfer poor in the 1965, 1968, and 1972 antipoverty budgets. This procedure assumes that the trend in the target effectiveness of each program in the 1965–72 period was maintained until the end of the 1970s. Because the percentage of any single program's benefits going to the pretransfer poor depends upon the size of the pretransfer poverty population, program eligibility rules, program benefit levels, and participation in the program,

Table 2.3. (*continued*)

	1965[a]		1970	1975	1980[a]	Average Annual Percentage Rates of Change
Education	*28,038*	*(9)*	*42,008*	*48,881*	*47,051* (11)	*3.5*
Elementary and						
secondary	22,358		32,020	36,247	33,955	2.8
Higher	4,826		8,211	9,940	10,210	5.0
Vocational/adult	854		1,777	2,694	2,886	8.1
Housing	*318*	*(85)*	*581*	*1,924*	*2,821* (92)	*14.5*
Public housing	235		381	*883*	2,053	14.4
Other	84		200	*1,041*	768	14.8
Other Social Welfare	*2,066*	*(39)*	*3,436*	*4,215*	*5.493* (63)	*6.5*
Vocational rehabili-						
tation	211		584	629	490	5.6
Institutional care	790		167	180	189	−9.5
Child nutrition	617		743	1,528	2,070	8.1
Child welfare	354		485	362	313	−0.8
Other	94		1,457	1,213	2,432	21.7
Total	77,175	(49)	120,823	175,988	193,449 (61)	6.1

Source: Tabulated from *Social Security Bulletin, Annual Statistical Supplement*, for each year.

[a]Number in parentheses designates percentage of federal spending in this category.

[b]Includes Aid to Families with Dependent Children; General Assistance; and Aid to the Aged, Blind, and Disabled until 1974, when the Supplemental Security Income program began.

this extrapolation assumes that the composite of the 1965–72 trends in these factors continued until 1980. The second estimate for each program is based on the percentage of program expenditures going to the poor in 1972, the last year for which an estimate is available. The implicit assumption here is that the level of "target efficiency" within each program remained constant at its 1972 level, and that changes in overall targeting arose only from changes in the composition of the budget. These estimates are crude, and are required because of the absence of program-specific antipoverty allocations beyond 1972.

Table 2.4 indicates that, regardless of the estimate used, the level of real (constant 1965 dollar) expenditures going to the poor increased from $34 billion to between $85 and $94 billion over the 1965–80 period, a nearly threefold increase. The last row of the table indicates that the *proportion* of social welfare expenditures going to the pretransfer poor

Table 2.4. Federal and State Social Welfare Expenditures on Benefits to the Pretransfer Poor, 1965–1980 (billions of 1965 dollars)

Program	1965	1970	1975		1980		Average Annual Percentage Rate of Growth	
Social Insurance	15.0[a]	22.7[a]	35.1[b]	36.4[c]	40.7[b]	45.9[c]	6.7	7.5
OASDI	10.5	14.3	21.8	22.7	24.3	28.2	5.6	6.6
Medicare	—	2.9	4.4	4.3	6.9	6.8	8.6	8.5
Unemployment Insurance	.7	.6	1.6	1.6	1.3	1.4	4.1	4.6
Workers' Compensation	.5	.8	1.5	1.3	2.1	1.7	9.6	8.2
Other	3.3	4.1	5.8	6.5	6.1	7.8	4.1	5.7
Public Aid	5.8	11.4	19.9	21.1	20.5	23.5	8.4	9.3
Public Assistance[d]	4.0	6.5	7.3	7.2	5.7	5.8	2.4	2.5
Medicaid	1.4	3.4	5.3	6.3	6.0	8.2	9.7	11.8
Supplemental Security Income	—	—	3.2	3.2	2.7	2.9	−3.4	−2.0
Food stamps	.04	.4	2.3	2.6	2.7	3.1	28.1	29.0
Other	.4	1.1	1.8	1.8	3.4	3.5	14.3	14.5
Health Programs	3.8	4.6	5.5	5.9	5.1	6.0	2.0	3.0
Maternal and child health	.2	.4	.3	.3	.3	.3	2.7	2.7
Other	3.6	4.2	5.2	5.6	4.8	5.7	1.9	3.1
Veterans' Programs	2.8	3.0	3.5	4.1	2.6	3.2	−.5	0.9
Pensions and compensation	2.1	2.0	1.8	2.1	1.4	1.9	−2.7	−.7
Health and medical care	.2	.3	.5	.5	.6	.5	7.3	6.1
Welfare	.2	.3	.5	.5	.3	.3	2.7	2.7
Other	.3	.4	.7	1.0	.3	.5	0.0	3.4

also increased from 1965 to 1980. Using the extrapolation estimate, expenditures devoted to the pretransfer poor as a percentage of the total were about 44 percent in the 1975–80 period, compared to 42 to 43 percent in the 1965–70 period. The estimate based on the 1972 program-specific percentages suggests that nearly 49 percent of social welfare expenditures were devoted to the poor in the latter half of the 1970s.

This rough estimate of the increase in the percentage of social welfare expenditures on the poor is accounted for by the differential rates of increase in the component program expenditures. Those expenditures that are distributed among the general population grew at relatively moderate rates over the period (see Table 2.3). Those programs include education (3.5 percent), veterans' benefits (2.2 percent), health programs (3.8 percent) and Unemployment Insurance (5.8 percent). On the other hand, welfare programs and others targeted on the poor grew at a much higher rate. Examples include Medicaid (13.7 percent), food stamps (30.6 percent), and public housing (14.4 percent). These differ-

Table 2.4. (*continued*)

Program	1965	1970	1975		1980		Average Annual Percentage Rate of Growth	
Education	5.0	8.7	10.6	9.8	10.7	9.3	5.1	4.1
Elementary and secondary	4.5	6.8	7.2	7.3	6.5	6.8	2.5	2.8
Higher	.3	.9	1.5	1.1	1.8	1.1	11.9	8.7
Vocational/Adult	.2	1.0	1.9	1.4	2.4	1.4	16.6	13.0
Housing	.2	.4	1.4	1.4	2.6	2.0	17.1	15.4
Public housing	.1	.3	.8	.7	2.1	1.5	20.3	18.1
Other	.1	.1	.6	.7	.5	.5	10.7	10.7
Other Social Welfare	1.0	2.2	2.3	2.3	3.4	3.4	8.2	8.2
Vocational rehabilitation	.1	.4	.4	.4	.3	.3	7.3	7.3
Institutional care	.4	.1	.1	.1	.1	.1	−9.2	−9.2
Child nutrition	.1	.2	.9	.5	1.7	.7	18.9	13.0
Child welfare	.3	.3	.2	.3	.2	.3	−2.7	0.0
Other	.1	1.2	.7	1.0	1.1	2.0	16.0	20.0
Total	33.6	51.5	78.3	82.3	85.6	93.8	6.2	6.8
As percentage of total SWE	43.5	42.2	43.9	47.1	44.3	48.6		

[a]This column adapted from Plotnick and Skidmore (1975).

[b]Estimates in this column are based on a linear extrapolation of the percentage of spending in each program going to the pretransfer poor in 1965, 1968, and 1972, found in Plotnick and Skidmore (1975).

[c]Estimates in this column are based on the 1972 percentage of spending in each program category going to the pretransfer poor.

[d]Includes Aid to Families with Dependent Children; General Assistance; and Aid to the Aged, Blind, and Disabled until 1974, when the Supplemental Security Income program began.

ences in growth rates indicate that welfare-type program benefits going to the poor increased as a proportion of the total social welfare expenditures directed toward the poor. The programs to build a Great Society had a distinct "welfare" cast.

Social Spending and Progress against Poverty, 1965–1980

The legislated changes in social welfare programs—especially income security and health programs—after 1965 had a powerful redistributive and antipoverty impact.[6] Because of these program expansions, both the

6. This section's brief summary of the trends and patterns over the 1965–80 period is based on several more detailed accounts. See Plotnick and Skidmore (1975), Haveman (1977), Bawden (1984), Danziger, van der Gaag, et al. (1984), Lampman (1984), and Danziger and Weinberg (1986, Chaps. 1 and 3).

number of beneficiaries and the size of the average benefit increased substantially. By 1980, payments were received by a greater percentage of households than is usually recognized: over 80 percent of poor households and 45 percent of all households received a cash or in-kind transfer in that year. From 1965 to 1980, the average inflation-adjusted cash transfer for all recipient households increased by 55 percent, while mean income for all households increased by only 20 percent. This occurred in spite of the fact that real benefits under AFDC declined in the latter half of the 1970s, because they did not keep pace with inflation. By 1980, the average cash transfer ranged from about $4000 per year for social security recipients to about $2500 per year for AFDC recipients. Access to medical care services also expanded, and by 1980 the poor were visiting physicians almost as often as the nonpoor.

One explanation for the rapid growth in transfers is the relationship between benefit levels and the rate of inflation. During the early 1970s, social security (Old Age, Survivors, and Disability Insurance, OASDI), Supplemental Security Income (SSI), and Food Stamp benefits were tied to the consumer price index, which grew faster than the index of wages over the period. Similarly, Medicare and Medicaid pay the fees charged by health care providers, and thus expand as rapidly as medical care costs. The medical care price index has been one of the most rapidly increasing components of the total price index. A third explanation is the apparently conscious policy of relaxing eligibility requirements for several of these benefits. Finally, demographic forces have caused those groups on which social welfare programs are targeted—primarily the aged and female-headed families—to expand more rapidly than the total population.

The incidence of official poverty declined from about 17 percent of all persons in 1965 to 13 percent in 1980. If the value of in-kind transfers is added to the cash incomes used to measure poverty officially, and adjustments are made to account for taxes and underreporting, the incidence falls by an even greater amount, from about 13 percent in 1965 to about 6 percent in 1979. These changes are shown in Table 2.5. A disproportionate share of the increased transfers has gone to the aged, who, on average, had a high poverty rate in 1965 but who by 1980 were no poorer than the population as whole.

As suggested by the "welfare" character of the growth of public spending targeted on the poor, these reductions in poverty did not result primarily from programs that provided assistance for the poor to earn their way out of poverty. If only market income—referring to earned and other personal income before transfers—is considered, the aggregate incidence of poverty (i.e., pretransfer poverty) increased slightly, from

Table 2.5. Percentage of Persons in Poverty under Different Income Measures, 1965–1980

Year	Pretransfer Poor[a]	Poor after Receipt of Cash Transfers[b]	Poor after Receipt of Cash and In-Kind Transfers[c]
1965	21.3	17.3	13.4
1968	18.2	12.8	9.9
1970	18.8	12.6	9.3
1972	19.2	11.9	6.2
1974	20.3	11.6	7.2
1976	21.0	11.8	6.7
1978	20.2	11.4	n.a.
1979	20.5	11.7	6.1
1980	21.9	13.0	n.a.
Percentage changes, 1965–80	+2.8	−24.9	−54.5[d]

Source: Unless noted otherwise, the data are tabulations from the Survey of Economic Opportunity (for 1965) and various March Current Population Survey computer tapes. Adapted from Danziger and Weinberg (1986, p. 54).

Note: n.a. = not available.

[a]Those whose personal income excluding all government cash transfers lies below the poverty line.

[b]Those whose income including wages and salaries, self-employment and property income, government cash transfers, and all other forms of cash income, before taxes, lies below the poverty line. The official measure of poverty is based on this definition of income. In 1965, the poverty line for a nonfarm family of four was $3,223; in 1980, it was $8,841.

[c]In-kind transfers include food stamps, school lunches, public housing, Medicare, and Medicaid. Income in this column is also adjusted to take account of taxes and underreporting. See Danziger and Weinberg (1986, p. 54) for a detailed explanation of calculations.

[d]Covers years 1965–79.

about 21 to 22 percent over the period. This is not to say, however, that the economic growth and expanded employment opportunities of the 1960s and early 1970s had no effect on market-income poverty. General economic growth had a substantial impact, especially for some groups, notably the families of married black men and persons living in the South. This impact is difficult to observe in the aggregate figures, however, because of contemporaneously offsetting developments: the 1965–80 period witnessed substantial increases in the proportion of the population living in families that are relatively immune to general economic growth, in particular female-headed families and those headed by the aged.

Nevertheless, while the expansion of government income security programs has been the primary force behind the decline in incidence of poverty, many families remain at high risk of becoming poor. In 1980, about one-fifth of all persons living in households headed by black women, one-ninth of all persons living in households headed by white women, and one-tenth of all persons living in households headed by black men remained poor. The 20 percent of all persons who lived in households headed by nonaged women or nonaged black men accounted for about half of the poverty population.

This chapter has provided the background to put in perspective our ensuing examination of the nature of developments in poverty research over the 1965–80 period. These developments, I will claim, reflect the response of economists and other social science researchers to the increased research support that was a part of antipoverty spending, to the new analytical problems which the government's fight against poverty confronted and uncovered, and to the same political drive and enthusiasm which fueled the growth of social spending on the poor during those years.

3

The Dimensions of Poverty Research, 1965–1980

The antipoverty efforts of the mid-1960s led to major reallocations in the federal budget and a significant increase in public spending for both research on the nature of social problems and evaluations of programs designed to remedy them. This chapter addresses the extent to which the social science research community responded to this initiative. It uses two indicators of the quantity of poverty and poverty-related research in the social sciences in the 1960s and 1970s. The first is an "input indicator"— the increase in federal financial support for poverty and poverty-related research which was supplied to (and accepted by) social science researchers after declaration of the War on Poverty. To the extent that this research support paid for services supplied by these researchers, the indicator describes the resources of the social science community that were turned to this issue in the 1960s and 1970s as a result of the new federal undertaking. The second is an "output indicator." Relying on an analysis of the content of journals in economics and sociology, I measure the extent to which poverty-related research is represented in these outlets before and after announcement of the War on Poverty.

The results show that the post-1965 period witnessed a substantial increase in the volume of research on the poverty issue, both in absolute terms and relative to the increase in the pre-1965 period. For several reasons, this finding is not unexpected. First, as the federal government

31

embarked on the effort to reduce poverty and social inequalities, it confronted enormous gaps in the knowledge and understanding that were essential for attainment of its objectives. Who are the poor, and how many of them are there? How is poverty to be defined and measured in the first place? What are the causes of poverty—cultural factors, poor education, discrimination, lack of motivation, workings of the market system, poor macroeconomic performance? What policy instruments are available to government, and which are likely to be the most cost effective? The knowledge available to policy planners on these issues was extremely limited, and insights were sought.

Second, the politics of federal antipoverty policy made research spending an attractive option. Research support was clearly less controversial and risky than, say, community action or a guaranteed income program. And given the uncharted nature of the terrain on which policy was embarking, poverty research expenditures grew rapidly, both in those agencies directly involved in the antipoverty campaign and in a variety of other federal agencies concerned with social policy.

Third, in addition to the War on Poverty, the mid-1960s witnessed the movement to place government on a more rational and analytic basis, a movement which resulted in establishment of the planning-pro-gramming-budgeting system (PPBS) in the Executive Office of the President in 1965, described in more detail below. In response to the PPBS directive, both OEO and the two other agencies most heavily involved in poverty issues, the Department of Labor and the Department of Health, Education, and Welfare, established active and substantial research and evaluation offices. Analysts in these offices perceived the serious lack of knowledge regarding the nature of the poverty problem and the efficacy of policies designed to reduce it; in response, these agencies sponsored substantial antipoverty research during the period following 1965.

Background to the Beginning of Poverty Research

Before 1965, it is doubtful that the term "poverty research" was ever used with any consistency, certainly not to describe a coherent body of research findings, or a particular research methodology, or even an area of study. To be sure, individual researchers in each of the social science disciplines had studied and written about the social and economic characteristics of the low-income population, the factors that caused some people to have low incomes and others high incomes, and the behavioral implications of poverty. By and large, however, these articles and books stood as isolated contributions to the subfields of "social stratification" (in sociology) and "income and wealth" (in economics).

Beginning with announcement of the War on Poverty in 1964, the term "poverty research" came into regular usage. The date of the announcement is an important factor in understanding the origin and meaning of the term.

The early 1960s, it will be recalled, was the era of "McNamaraism" in the federal government. Robert McNamara, President Kennedy's Secretary of Defense, came to that position from the presidency of the Ford Motor Company, where he had become convinced that applying modern management and "systems analysis" techniques to public choices could make contributions to public-sector efficiency. Relying heavily on military analysts from the Rand Corporation in California, a government-supported research and analytic "think tank," McNamara created the Office of Assistant Secretary for Planning and Evaluation, which became a small-scale think tank within the department itself.[1]

That office and its contributions have been described before (Novick, 1965; Wildavsky, 1979). For our purpose, its importance was that its presence and the publicity accompanying it signaled a new approach to doing business in government. Systematic evaluations of the impacts of various policy options were to be made, and these evaluations were to guide the choices made by decision makers. Cost-effectiveness studies were to buttress policy proposals supported by the Defense Department in its deliberations within the administration and the Congress. This was a new and businesslike approach to making public policy.

The novel decision-making strategy was seized on by the press and other observers of the political process because of the revolutionary idea which underlay it—logic, data, and systematic thinking were to compete with, if not dominate, "politics" in the making of public decisions. With Secretary McNamara as the internal advocate for such a procedure within the executive branch—and with Defense Department "whiz kids" finding their way into other governmental agencies—the idea that policy research and program evaluation could serve to increase the standing of executive branch leaders and blunt the extent to which they were buffeted by political pressures found widespread support within the executive branch. This effort culminated in the endorsement of the PPBS by President Johnson in a news conference on August 25, 1965. An executive order was issued requiring all federal agencies to apply benefit-cost

---

1. While the Department of Health, Education, and Welfare and the Department of Labor had created offices with similar titles in the early 1960s, neither had adopted so fully the concept of applying systems analysis and other policy analysis techniques to government decisions as had the Assistant Secretary's office in the Defense Department. See U.S. Congress, Joint Economic Committee (1969).

analysis, cost-effectiveness analysis, and program evaluation techniques to executive branch decisions.

The date on which the executive order was signed was one year after the signing of the Economic Opportunity Act, which began implementation of the War on Poverty and established the OEO as part of the Executive Office of the President. The OEO was created to plan and propose strategies for mounting a governmental attack on the poverty problem. Taking the military analogy seriously, Sargent Shriver, the first director of the OEO, appointed Joseph Kershaw and Adam Yarmolinsky, both of whom had Rand-type analytical backgrounds (Kershaw had been head of the economics department of Rand), to lead formation of the OEO. The staff appointed by them was heavily populated by economists with either Rand Corporation or Defense Department backgrounds. If economic analysis could guide defense-related decisions, and if a conscious PPBS approach would improve the effectiveness of government decisions in all areas, surely that approach would be essential in planning for and mounting a campaign against poverty.

In large part because of the character of the early directors of the Office of Planning, Research, and Evaluation (PR&E) at OEO and the heavily economics-oriented professional staff in this office, it embodied the philosophy of the PPBS. An early discussion of the research at OEO stated: "The Office of Economic Opportunity . . . was one of the first agencies outside the national security area to attempt to adopt the new management philosophy, and its PR&E office has since enjoyed the reputation not only of being one of the earliest agency offices of that type but also one of the best" (National Academy of Sciences, 1971, p. 6).

From the very inception of planning for the War on Poverty, then, the presumption that research and evaluation should guide social policy decisions was a principal tenet. Even during the earliest days of OEO, its PR&E office played an important, if not dominant, role in guiding policy decisions. And central to the activities of that office was the belief that the making of sound antipoverty policy required answers to questions on the nature of poverty and on the effectiveness of measures to reduce it:

- How is poverty to be defined? Given an appropriate definition, how many poor people are there? And if the poor can be counted, what are their characteristics?
- What factors have caused poverty, and which have led to its persistence over time? Is there a vicious circle of poverty which must somehow be broken? Is there a culture of poverty? To what extent does poverty have a racial basis?
- What are the possible options for reducing poverty, and what is the likely effectiveness of each? Which, among manpower training, educa-

tion, community action, rural development, and direct cash transfers is the superior approach to combating poverty?

Questions such as these are basically social scientific in character. They are questions on which social scientists—primarily economists and sociologists—should be able to shed light.

A Working Definition of Poverty Research

The research component of OEO, its PR&E office, evolved as a part of the nation's antipoverty program. There is no evidence that OEO was ever given, or explicitly stated, a clear definition of what poverty research was to be, either for its own use or for that of the research community. Two pieces of evidence suggest, however, what the government planners had in mind.

The first is the mandate given by OEO to the research institute which it established at the University of Wisconsin–Madison. In the agreement between OEO and the university, an institute was to be established with the purpose of conducting research on "the nature and causes of, and cures for, poverty." The agreement stipulated as well that the staff of the Institute for Research on Poverty would comprise many disciplines (the initial staff members were in fact drawn from economics, sociology, psychology, law, political science, and related fields), and that, underlining the uncertain nature of this research domain, the Institute staff would itself decide the kinds of problems to be researched, although it would at the same time be responsive to the research suggestions and requests of OEO.

Issues involving the investigation of poverty span a wide range. Portions of traditional subfields in economics, sociology, and psychology could immediately be included in this definition: the study of income distribution in economics, social stratification in sociology, and social psychology are examples. Clearly, however, OEO planners had something in mind that extensions of these traditional academic areas would not encompass.

The second piece of evidence stems from the topics that the PR&E office of OEO supported and encouraged in its own research program. These priorities were revealed in an extended report submitted in 1968 to the Joint Economic Committee of the Congress by Robert Levine, the second director of PR&E (Levine, 1969). He distinguished between traditional research and "direct program and policy related analysis" (p. 1181). While the former sort of analysis "is both older and more dignified"(p. 1181), the latter involves "the Federal use of economists and economics for policy analysis of problems in which major variables are not economic in nature (e.g., deterrence, educational techniques, health organization); as well as for economic problems previously slighted, such as those associated with special segments of the income distribution (e.g., the poor)" (p. 1182). His emphasis, it should be noted, was on the application of the economist's concern with efficiency and effectiveness to noneconomic problems.

In describing the research and analysis efforts of OEO, Levine established the following categories: (1) general systems analysis—the application of cost-benefit thinking to policy alternatives; (2) evaluation of the impacts of a program on the problem to which it is addressed—measuring the extent to which a program has a payoff in terms of its objectives (namely, poverty reduction) that justifies its costs; (3) analysis of economic and noneconomic phenomena related to poverty. He gave examples of work sponsored by OEO in each of these areas. For the first, general systems analysis, he cited analyses of changes in the socioeconomic composition of the poverty population (designed to guide the allocation of funds between income maintenance versus manpower training programs), legal services versus other services to the poor, and adult versus youth training programs. In the program impact evaluation area, he mentioned studies of the Work-Experience program, the Small Business Development Corporation, and the Community Action program. Projects that fell in the area of longer-term studies of poverty-related phenomena included sponsorship of the Survey of Economic Opportunity, to gain detailed data to assist in program evaluation; a study undertaken at the Institute for Research on Poverty of the relationship of Selective Service to the War on Poverty; the negative income tax experiment (described in Chapter 9 below); and the study of migration from rural to urban areas, including the adjustment problems of rural black migrants, the effect of migration on socioeconomic status, the extent to which poor families who move or change jobs can break the cycle of poverty, and the effects of rural-to-urban migration on urban problems.

From these pieces of evidence, a working definition of poverty research—at least as viewed by those first instrumental in sponsoring it—would run something as follows.[2]

---

2. See also National Academy of Sciences (1979), which described poverty research as follows: "The work of researchers who claim to be studying poverty has struck us as being generally defensible by the criterion of relevance to the situation of poor people and to public policies concerning them. There seems to be little quarrel with this criterion for the center of the field, even though there may be less clear agreement on boundaries. Major general areas of past research that frequently have some bearing on the poor are studies on economic status and inequality; unemployment; underemployment; the operation of labor

Poverty-related research consists of both theoretical and empirical analyses concerned with the measurement of economic well-being, poverty, and inequality; the processes of generation and perpetuation of poverty; the effects of poverty on individual behavior; the design and impacts of alternative policy measures designed to reduce poverty; and the social and political processes affecting the well-being of low-income persons.

Federal Spending on Poverty and Poverty-Related Research, 1965–1980

Given this definition of poverty research, the next question concerns the level of support for it and the growth in support over time. The only data available on which estimates can rely concern support by the federal government.[3] Those data suit our purpose best, in any case, because our main concern is with the impact of federal policy on the social sciences. Moreover, it appears that the overwhelming proportion of support for poverty research during the 1965–80 period came from the federal government.

Estimating the magnitude of the federal poverty research support is difficult, however, as the definition of what is and what is not *research* is not clear. Both narrow and broad definitions have been formulated and used in gathering data. Here we proceed from the narrow to the broad. In interpreting the estimates provided in this section, the distinction between research (R) and research and development (R&D) will be emphasized. The former refers to systematic and basic study aimed at improving

---

markets; public income transfer programs; status attainment; social mobility; education; household decision making; demographic behavior; race; segregation and discrimination; legal, political, and administrative systems; disability; health; aging; housing; evaluation of social programs; cross-national poverty policy; and the collection of data in support of any of these areas of research. We do not intend this to be a complete listing, only an indication of the center of the field. And we would include not only studies of the poor themselves but also studies of the systematic social processes that tend to cause or perpetuate poverty" (p. 6).

While this definition includes a number of standard sociological and economic research areas, it is clearly a broader and more catholic definition than that which apparently guided the early planners of the War on Poverty.

3. A comprehensive estimate of the value of resources devoted to poverty research would include the support of private foundations, state governments, private interest groups, and the nonteaching time and associated academic resources devoted to poverty research unsupported by outside funds. Funding of poverty research by numerous private foundations is difficult to ascertain, as it is nowhere tabulated. Moreover, it is difficult to separate support for research on poverty or poverty-related issues from action and service provision. Similarly, the use by scholars of their own time for research on poverty or poverty-related issues is impossible to determine, but is likely to be substantial.

Table 3.1. Federal Expenditures on Research and Development Related to Antipoverty Programs, 1965–1977 (millions of dollars)

	Current Dollars	1966 Dollars[a]
1965	2.5	2.6
1968	6.4	6.1
1971	23.0	19.0
1976	141.0	83.9
1977	160.0	88.2

Sources: *1965*: A judgmental estimate based on fragmented evidence and trends from the remainder of the years. *1968, 1971*: External expenditures for research by the PR & E Office of OEO. *1976*: A tabulation assembled from data in Abramson (1978). *1977*: A tabulation from the 14 federal agencies most closely involved in antipoverty efforts (data in Covello, 1979) yields an estimate of $89.6 million (current) expended on poverty research, defined to include research plus a portion of demonstration and program evaluation estimates of these agencies. Making rough adjustments from similar data for 1976 from all federal agencies, and taking account of the underestimation in the 1977 estimates due to the inclusion of only 14 agencies, yields the $160 million figure.

[a]Adjusted for inflation by the Consumer Price Index (1966 = 100).

knowledge; the latter includes, in addition, demonstration, evaluation, collection of statistics, development of materials, and dissemination.[4]

The concept of research (or R&D) on *poverty* can also be defined broadly and narrowly. A narrow definition would include research (or R&D) supported only by War on Poverty programs. We call this "poverty research" ("poverty R&D"). A broader definition would include all research (or R&D) on the poor, or on social programs related to the poverty problem, sponsored by the federal government. We call this "poverty-related research" ("poverty-related R&D"). Both definitions will be used here.

A variety of figures are available to shed some light on the extent of financial support for research (or R&D) by the federal government on the poverty problem. Assembling data from a number of sources, and inserting a good amount of judgment, one arrives at the post-1965 series of federal government spending on "poverty R&D" shown in Table 3.1, giving expenditure estimates for those agencies closely involved in anti-

4. See National Academy of Sciences (1978). The academy's Study Project on Social Research and Development, which dealt with R&D on social problems, distinguished seven categories of "social R&D." The two basic categories are (1) knowledge production, and (2) knowledge application. Research is one component of the knowledge production category. These definitions differ somewhat from those used by the National Science Foundation and the Office of Management and Budget. Because data from all three sources are used here, some inconsistencies may arise.

Table 3.2. The Composition of Federal Antipoverty, Poverty-Related, and Social R&D Expenditures, 1976 (millions of dollars)

	Research	Demonstrations	Evaluation	Statistics	Total R&D
R&D expenditures on antipoverty programs[a]	$60	$55	$16	$10	$141
R&D expenditures on poverty-related programs	251	168	52	24	495
Expenditures for social R&D[b]	655	204	61	294	1214

[a]From Abramson (1978).
[b]Tabulated from National Academy of Sciences (1978) and Abramson (1978).

poverty efforts. There is a discontinuity between 1971 and 1976, because the estimates for 1968 and 1971 refer to external expenditures for R&D by the OEO office of Planning, Research, and Evaluation, whereas those for subsequent years relate to a more comprehensive list of antipoverty programs.

From these and related statistics, it seems reasonable to conclude that federal R&D spending on programs to alleviate poverty grew from less than $3 million in 1965 to approximately $200 million per year by 1980.

The composition of poverty R&D expenditures by categories of basic research, demonstration, etc. is available only for 1976. Table 3.2 shows expenditures in these categories under three different concepts of poverty R&D: that used in Table 3.1 (i.e., R&D sponsored by federal antipoverty programs); the broader concept that includes R&D expenditures on all "poverty-related" programs;[5] and all federal "social R&D" (see note 4) expenditures. In each case, about half of the total expendi-

5. The more comprehensive definition assumes that supported R&D contained in "poverty-related programs" is, by definition, poverty-related R&D. "Poverty-related programs" comprise (1) those initiated as part of the War on Poverty (the expenditure data in Table 3.1); (2) longer-standing social programs assigned an antipoverty mission upon inception of the War on Poverty (e.g., community health services and labor market programs for low-skilled workers); (3) programs focusing on social problems which are correlates of poverty (e.g., drug abuse, juvenile delinquency, school-work transition programs); and (4) traditional income support programs which took on an antipoverty objective in the 1960s and 1970s (e.g., social security retirement and disability). The distinctions made among the categories of poverty-related programs are clearly judgmental. They reflect an effort to proceed from a narrow definition of the term "poverty" (taken to imply a direct connection with War on Poverty programs) to a broader definition (taken to imply research sponsored by programs which are concerned with the low-income population or with problems closely associated with that population).

tures were for research, most of the remainder being allocated to demonstration projects.

A few additional figures will put these expenditures in perspective. In 1976, total federal R&D spending was nearly $22 billion. Hence, federal social R&D spending was about 5.5 percent ($1.214 billion/$22 billion) of total federal R&D, while federal poverty R&D and poverty-related R&D were .65 percent ($.141 billion/$22 billion) and 2 percent ($.495 billion/$22 billion) of total federal R&D spending, respectively.

Even these figures are likely to exaggerate the amount of federal expenditures that supported poverty research in the social sciences. A relatively small share of the expenditures for demonstrations, evaluations, and statistics—the "development" component of R&D—are likely to have supported the work of social science researchers, particularly those contributing to the major research journals in the disciplines. Only the research component of this R&D spending is likely to represent expenditures affecting social scientists—$60 million for the narrow definition of poverty research, $251 million for the broader definition of poverty-related research (see Table 3.2).

While the absolute magnitude of these annual amounts of research support may seem large, their size compared to other aggregates in 1976 is revealing. Table 3.3 presents some of these comparisons. While the

Table 3.3. Federal Poverty and Poverty-Related Research Spending as a Proportion of Other Research Expenditure Aggregates, 1976

	Federal Poverty Research	Federal Poverty-Related Research
Spending in 1976	$60 million	$251 million
1. As percentage of total national R&D spending	.15	.64
2. As percentage of total national research spending	.41	1.72
3. As percentage of total federal research spending	.76	3.17
4. As percentage of total national research spending on social sciences	7.23	30.12
5. As percentage of total public social welfare spending	.05	.20
6. As percentage of total social welfare spending on the poor	.10	.43

Source: Calculated by author from data supplied by the National Science Foundation, the National Academy of Sciences, and available in *Social Security Bulletin, Annual Statistical Supplement.* The detailed calculations are available on request.

narrow definition of federal poverty research spending—that by federal antipoverty agencies—suggests that poverty research spending was about 7 percent of total national social science research spending, it was less than one-half percent of the total national research budget. The broader definition of federal poverty-related research spending—i.e., contained in all federal programs related to the poverty problem—indicates that poverty-related research accounted for about 30 percent of total social science research spending in 1976 and about 2 percent of national research spending. The bottom two rows suggest that federal poverty (or poverty-related) research expenditures are trivial proportions of public social welfare spending or of public social welfare expenditures on behalf of pretransfer-poor people—those poor before receipt of a government benefit. The broad definition of federal poverty research spending was less than one-half of one percent of all public expenditures on the pretransfer poor population by the late 1970s.

A final calculation seems relevant. We have seen that federal R&D expenditures contained in antipoverty programs grew rapidly over the 1965–80 period (Table 3.1). Based on this trend in R&D spending, a reasonable estimate is that that research spending (the R component of R&D spending) in antipoverty programs grew from, say, $1 million in 1965 to $75 million by 1980. Using the broader definition—research spending in federal poverty-related programs—poverty-related research is likely to have grown from about $30 million in 1965 to about $300 million in 1980. During this same period, total federal research spending in the social sciences grew from about $160 million in 1965 to about $700 million in 1980.[6] About 15 percent of this $540 million increase in social science research spending over those fifteen years is accounted for by the increase in federal poverty research spending; the increase in federal poverty-related research spending accounts for about 50 percent of the growth in social science research spending.

Poverty Research before and after the War on Poverty Began

The post-1965 period saw a burst of policy measures enacted by the federal government on behalf of the poor. It also saw unprecedented growth on research spending sponsored by antipoverty programs and by programs related to the poverty problem. A natural question regarding this flurry of political action and research spending concerns its effect on the output of the social sciences. How much substance is there in Henry Aaron's statement, quoted earlier, that "one need not be cynical to recognize that research agendas are influenced by the flow of money from

---

6. Tabulations available from the author upon request.

government and foundations, which in turn try to use research budgets at least in part to improve decisions on current issues of public policy" (1978, p. 157)?[7] To what extent has the content and nature of research in the social sciences been altered by concern with antipoverty issues? How extensive was the increased emphasis on poverty-related research, and has it persisted?

These questions are difficult to answer. My procedure has been to study the research output of the social science disciplines over time, in an attempt to identify the change in the level of poverty-related work. I have focused on economics and sociology,[8] because these are the major fields that have been affected by concern with "the nature and causes of, and cures for poverty." The concept of poverty-related research which we have used is that defined earlier in this chapter.

To assess the quantitative role of poverty-related research within these disciplines, three approaches were taken. First, I selected five leading journals in each discipline, and analyzed the extent of poverty-related research in each over time. This provides an indicator of the extent to which such research penetrated the highest and most prestigious outlets within each discipline. Second, to gain an indicator of breadth, I tabulated the poverty-related content of articles in a set of ten economics journals (other than the leading five) over the 1963–80 period, and in all relevant economics journals that existed in 1980 over the same time period.

Tables 3.4 and 3.5 summarize the extent of poverty-related research in five leading journals in economics and sociology. The selection of the journals was, of course, guided by my own judgment, but the final choice was made only after consulting scholars in both of the disciplines.

With the exception of *Econometrica*, the pattern is similar across all of

7. Aaron went on to assert the following regarding the impact on the social sciences of this policy and research support: "Much of this research was the direct result of the legislation itself, which required that a stipulated fraction of appropriations be spent on research and evaluation. Much was undertaken independently by hordes of academics issuing forth from graduate schools motivated not only by the ethics of scholarship but also by the desire to publish rather than perish. The products of this effort consisted of evaluation reports prepared under government contracts, journal articles prepared by academic scholars—often under government grants or contracts—books, magazine and newspaper articles, and an enormous amount of conversation about the new programs, how they worked and whether they were effective, all couched in a language that literally did not exist in prior decades and that those untrained in the social sciences could not understand. Even those who did not understand the language tried to speak it or write it" (p. 170).

8. For purposes of comparison, a similar tabulation was made for political science. In the 1962–64 period, poverty articles accounted for about .4 percent of the total. After 1965, the percentage increased only to approximately 2 percent in political science, staying at about that level until 1980.

Table 3.4. Poverty-Related Research in Five Leading Economics Journals,
Selected Years, 1962–1980

	Number of Poverty-Related Articles	Poverty-Related Articles as Percentage of Total	Poverty-Related Pages as Percentage of Total
American Economic Review			
1962–64	0	0	0
1971–73	21	6.8	6.5
1978–80	14	4.0	3.3
Econometrica			
1962–64	0	0	0
1971–73	4	2.2	2.1
1978–80	12	4.8	4.4
Journal of Political Economy[a]			
1962–64	1	.6	.3
1971–73	19 (8)	10.0 (4.4)	11.2 (4.3)
1978–80	7 (3)	3.6 (1.6)	5.2 (1.6)
Quarterly Journal of Economics			
1962–64	2	2.1	2.1
1971–73	5	5.0	4.9
1978–80	3	2.2	2.1
Review of Economics and Statistics			
1962–64	0	0	0
1971–73	10	7.1	5.3
1978–80	4	2.5	2.4
Total[a]			
1962–64	3	.4	.5
1971–73	59 (48)	6.4 (5.3)	6.5 (4.6)
1978–80	40 (36)	3.6 (4.0)	3.8 (3.0)

[a]Numbers in parentheses include articles in the regular issues of the *Journal of Political Economy*, excluding special supplements.

the economics journals. Before 1965, almost no poverty-related research was published in them; in the 1971–73 period (taken to be representative of the post–War on Poverty period), a large increase is observed. During this immediate "postwar" period, up to 6.5 percent of the articles and pages published in the journals focused on the problem of poverty. By the late 1970s, a significant tailing off, down to 3.5–4.0 percent of journal content, is evident. The largest increase after the announcement of the War on Poverty occurred in the *Journal of Political Economy*.[9] Four of

9. Some of this increase is due to the publication of a special issue in 1972 on "Investment in Education," of which several papers were classified as poverty-related research.

Table 3.5. Poverty-Related Research in Five Leading Sociology Journals,
Selected Years, 1962–1980

	Number of Poverty-Related Articles	Poverty-Related Articles as Percentage of Total	Poverty-Related Pages as Percentage of Total
American Journal of Sociology			
1962–64	2	1.5	1.5
1971–73	6	12.6	12.8
1978–80	11	10.2	10.5
American Sociological Review			
1962–64	0	—	—
1971–73	14	8.2	8.6
1978–80	17	12.1	12.1
Social Forces			
1962–64	9	6.3	7.0
1971–73	8	6.5	5.5
1978–80	10	5.3	4.8
Sociology and Social Research			
1962–64	4	4.0	3.9
1971–73	6	6.0	6.2
1978–80	7	8.9	9.1
Sociological Quarterly			
1962–64	0	—	—
1971–73	7	6.6	5.9
1978–80	3	2.4	2.2
Total			
1962–64	15	2.6	2.4
1971–73	41	6.2	8.8
1978–80	48	7.5	7.8

the five journals showed a rapid decrease in the intensity of their poverty-related publishing from the early to the late 1970s; only *Econometrica*, whose tie to policy-related concerns is probably the least among these journals, showed a persistent increase over the entire period.

As in economics, poverty research represented in the five sociology journals increased rapidly after 1965. Here, however, the 1962–64 base level was substantially higher than in economics—2.4 percent of articles and pages, as compared to .5 percent. And the level of poverty research in the peak 1971–73 period was greater in sociology than in economics—6 percent in terms of articles, and 9 percent in terms of pages, compared to about 5 percent in economics. The persistence of sociological interest in poverty research is clearly greater than in economics: in the later period, almost 8 percent of material in these sociology journals was devoted to poverty research, compared to somewhat less than 4 percent in economics.

Both economics and sociology, then, experienced a rapid increase in poverty research from the 1962–64 period to the 1971–73 period. This interest continued in sociology, but in economics had tapered off substantially by 1980.

Given the general difficulty of publishing material on highly topical issues in the leading scholarly journals, it could be claimed that the pattern shown in these two tables is not representative of the composition of research activities in the disciplines as a whole. As a check, in economics I made an effort to obtain a more global assessment of the incidence of poverty-related research over time. For several reasons this calculation is difficult. First, whereas the five leading journals constitute a fixed pool from which to observe the incidence of poverty-related research over time, there is no such pool for the discipline as a whole. Over time, journals are both initiated and phased out. In fact, over the 1960–80 period there was a surge in the number of economics journals.[10] Moreover, the set of journals included in the major bibliographic sources in the discipline has changed over time, with a general tendency toward increased coverage. Second, once one moves from the leading journals in a particular discipline to a wider selection of journals, the boundaries of the discipline become less clear.[11] Finally, as the set of journals becomes more inclusive, the sheer number of articles on which a judgment must be made regarding inclusion or noninclusion under the rubric of poverty research grows rapidly.

To obtain this more comprehensive view, I have taken the ten journals (other than those in Table 3.4) whose contents were indexed and abstracted in the 1963 *Journal of Economic Abstracts* and which were either general economics journals in English published in the United States, or international journals in English in special fields closely related to the poverty problem.[12] I tabulated the number of poverty-related articles and the percentage of the total number of articles in these journals that were

---

10. In 1963 the *Journal of Economic Abstracts* listed articles from a total of 15 U.S., Canadian, and British journals; by 1980 its successor, the *Journal of Economic Literature*, listed articles from over 125 U.S., Canadian, and British journals.

11. For example, the 1980 *Journal of Economic Literature* lists articles from the *American Historical Review*, the *American Political Science Review*, and *Social Research*.

12. The journals are *American Journal of Economics and Sociology, Industrial and Labor Relations Review, Industrial Relations, Journal of the American Statistical Association, Journal of Law and Economics, Land Economics, Monthly Labor Review, National Tax Journal, Southern Economic Journal*, and *Western Economic Review*.

Table 3.6. Poverty-Related Research in Ten Economics Journals,
Selected Years, 1963–1980[a]

	Total Number of Articles Published	Number of Poverty-Related Articles	Poverty-Related Articles as Percentage of Total
1963	457	20	4.3
1968	323	27	8.4
1973	444	31	7.0
1980	391	30	7.7

[a]Excludes journals listed in Table 3.4.

poverty related. The results are shown in Table 3.6. In this 1963 base set of journals, the incidence of poverty-related articles is about 3 to 4 percentage points higher than for the five leading journals throughout the period. The pattern of increase in incidence and in the number of articles from the period before to that after the War on Poverty is similar across both sets of journals, although the persistence of poverty-related research appears to be greater in these ten journals than in the five leading ones: after dropping from over 8 percent of the total in 1968 to 7 percent in 1973, the incidence (and the absolute number) of poverty-related articles in the ten journals had again increased by 1980.

A final tabulation, again for economics, is presented in Table 3.7. This analysis includes all journals listed in the 1980 *Journal of Economic Literature* (other than those in Table 3.4) which were either general economics journals in English published in the United States, or international journals in special fields closely related to the poverty problem.[13] A content analysis for 1963, 1968, 1973, and 1980 shows that over this period the number of journals meeting that specification increased substantially. Several of those identified in 1980 did not exist in the previous years. As a result the time series yielded by this tabulation reflects (1) changes in the size (number of pages) of a fixed population of journals; (2) incidence of poverty-related research in these journals, and (3) changes in the number of journals and their poverty-related content. This series, then, reflects the change in the incidence of poverty-related articles in the entire pool of outlets (other than those shown in Table 3.4) in each of the years for which the tabulation was made.

The figures for 1963 are the same as those in Table 3.6, since the ten

13. The journals are, in addition to those listed in the preceding note, *Atlantic Economic Journal, Brookings Papers on Economic Activity, Journal of Economic Theory, Journal of Human Resources, Journal of Labor Research, Journal of Public Economics, Journal of Urban Economics, Public Choice, Public Finance Quarterly, Quarterly Review of Economics and Business,* and *Review of Income and Wealth.*

Table 3.7. Poverty-Related Research in Economics Journals, Selected Years, 1963–1980[a]

	Number of Journals	Total Number of Articles Published	Number of Poverty-Related Articles	Poverty-Related Articles as Percentage of Total
1963	10	457	20	4.3
1968	14	473	55	11.6
1973	17	887	96	9.2
1980	21	945	104	11.0

[a]Includes all journals listed in the 1980 *Journal of Economic Literature*, except those in Table 3.4.

journals listed in the 1963 *Journal of Economic Abstracts* still existed in 1980. The subsequent growth in both the absolute number and the incidence of poverty-related articles is greater in Table 3.7 than in Table 3.6. The new journals added in the 1963–80 period included a number which related specially to the poverty issue (e.g., the *Journal of Human Resources* and the *Journal of Urban Economics*). From an incidence rate of 4.3 percent in 1963, before the War on Poverty, the share of poverty-related articles rose to 11.6 percent in 1968, dipped slightly to 9.2 percent in 1973, and rose again to 11 percent in 1980. Over the period, the annual number of poverty-related articles increased from 20 to over 100.

Conclusion

Whether measured by indicators of inputs (federal R and R&D spending) or outputs, the antipoverty policy initiative has clearly had substantial impact on the social sciences. Federal R&D spending under antipoverty programs grew from a few million dollars at the inception of the War on Poverty to about $200 million by 1980 (Table 3.1). The poverty research (as opposed to R&D) component of this spending grew from about $1 million in 1965 to about $75 million in 1980. Although these amounts are small relative to aggregate federal research spending, they came to equal about 10 percent of all federal social science research spending by 1980. Indeed, the increase of federal spending on poverty research over the 1965–80 period accounts for over 15 percent of the growth in total social science research spending in those years. A broader definition of research on poverty issues—what I have termed poverty-related research—stood at about 40 percent of total federal social science research by 1980, and equaled about one-half of the growth in federal social science research spending over the years 1965 to 1980.

The output indicators tell much the same story. Poverty-related research has come to occupy an increased share of journal space. This is true in both the leading journals of both economics and sociology, and (at least in economics) in all of the relevant journals. From 1962 and 1963 to 1980, poverty-related research increased from about .5 percent to about 4 percent of the space in the leading economics journals and from 2 to about 8 percent of the space in the leading sociology journals. In economics, the incidence of poverty-related research is even greater in journals other than the five leading ones: 11 percent of articles in these journals were poverty related in 1980, up from about 4 percent in 1963. The proportion of journal output in these disciplines in 1980 corresponds rather closely to the 10 percent of all federal social science research spending which was accounted for by poverty research in 1980. Whether measured by input or by output, poverty research has come to occupy an important place in the social science disciplines.

II
Poverty Research and Its Contribution to Knowledge

The four chapters in this part of the book describe the advances in knowledge within general areas of academic interest that were tied to the Great Society initiative and to the research support that it generated. The selection of the areas treated in these chapters is my own. It rests on an appraisal of both the importance of the issue and the magnitude of the gain in knowledge since 1965.

Basic to understanding the problem of poverty is the measurement of economic well-being and the nature of its distribution in the population, the topic of Chapter 4. By definition, those who are poor fall at the bottom of this distribution. While the annual cash income of an individual or a household is often used as a proxy for its well-being—and, indeed, stands as the basis for the official definition of who is and who is not poor—all who use it recognize the inadequacy of this measure. Since 1965 there have been major contributions in this area, all of which seek a more comprehensive indicator of economic position. Because of this work, the extent and character of poverty in the United States is much better understood, and the basis for designing policies to alleviate poverty is better informed. Similarly, the perceived degree of economic inequality and the source of it are now more solidly based than in the early days of the antipoverty effort. Perhaps because of this, the expected results of policies intended to reduce poverty and inequality are now more realistically perceived.

The basis for choosing the second area, the design and impacts of income transfer policies, is less obvious. In terms of poverty research, more work was done and writing published in this area than perhaps any other. Although that consideration served as an important basis of this choice, it was not the only factor. A second was the potential for social scientists to contribute to policy-making through the gains in knowledge and the understanding that resulted from this line of research. As Chapter 2 indicated, the major instrument of the antipoverty effort since 1965 has been income transfer policy. The enormous growth of this form of public expenditure, from 3 percent of GNP in 1965 to over 10 percent in 1980, attests to the potential of this policy instrument in redistributing income and altering economic status. Its growth reflects a large shift in national priorities, embodied in the restructuring of the composition of the national budget. As a result of this change, the economic position of many people was altered and individual behavior was modified in a number of dimensions. Such changes are grist for the social scientist's mill. First, in an environment in which such major shifts in policy are occurring, the potential for the work of social scientists to have an impact on the design of policy is substantial. Social scientists, for the most part economists, responded to this environment by proposing, designing, and evaluating the consequences of a wide variety of new or altered policy measures. Second, by implementing new policies, the government in essence created a natural laboratory in which individual behavioral responses to changes in social structure and in incentives could be observed and measured. Knowledge regarding these responses to incentives and policy changes were viewed as important in improving the design and the form of policy measures. Hence, choice of this topic also reflects the response of social scientists to the policy ferment which characterized so much of the 1965–80 period.

Selection of the topics of social mobility and social stratification (Chapter 6) has a different rationale. One of the most important developments in the 1960s and 1970s in the social sciences has been greater understanding of the processes of social movement between and within classes and, in particular, the role of schooling, race, and parental background in accounting for this movement (or lack of it). Few would doubt that the discipline of sociology has been advanced and restructured because of the conceptual and empirical work done in this area. Its tie to the problem of poverty and its motivation by the national antipoverty campaign is attested to by the primary researchers in this field.

Chapter 7 is a potpourri. Poverty research has spanned a variety of areas other than those discussed in Chapters 4–6, and in each has left its mark. This chapter attempts to give at least a flavor of the contributions of that research to a sampling of these areas, including education, segregation and discrimination, and the operation of the labor market. Discussion of the contribution of poverty research in these areas must, of necessity, be sketchy and impressionistic. The bibliographic references form an important component of the discussion.

A few additional points are in order. First, it would be inappropriate to view the topics discussed in Part II as representing the sum and substance—or even the majority—of additions to knowledge contributed by poverty researchers during the period. A wide variety of other contributions were also made, among them the following:

- Research on the "culture of poverty" by sociologists and anthropologists, leading to improved understanding regarding the lifestyles, outlooks, and persistence of a poverty class.
- Research on community action and political participation by political scientists and sociologists, focusing on the mechanisms by which poor and minority groups became organized and active in managing the communities in which they lived.
- Research on the "new home economics" by economists and demographers, which provided a variety of insights into the decisions concerning fertility, marriage, migration, and family structure of both poor and nonpoor families.
- The development of the economics of education and the economics of health as coherent fields of research, with emphasis on the well-being of the poor population.
- Research by sociologists, social psychologists, and lawyers on welfare administration and the public bureaucracy, which aided our understanding of the plight of the poor in their required dealings with welfare, school, and policy administrators and bureaucrats, noting the inadequacy of their access to legal resources in these dealings.

All of these research contributions could have been the subject of a chapter—they were all stimulated by and received support from the War on Poverty—but none was judged to have made as substantial a contribution to knowledge, in particular to policy-relevant knowledge, as those chosen.

It should also be noted that all of the chapters except Chapter 6 emphasize topics with a strong economic content. As Chapters 1 and 2 indicated, from the outset the War on Poverty was conceived of as an economic war; the designs, the debates, and the evaluations were all conducted in economic terms. Economics was the central discipline in both the action and the research components of the war, and that fact is reflected in these chapters.

Finally, although the main focus of each chapter is on the primary research contributions in an area and the nature of the contribution to knowledge which they represent, an attempt to assess what it all adds up to is also a component of each chapter. This assessment is a personal one, and not all readers will agree with it. It is offered as one person's effort to draw the implications for the next generation of poverty research by looking back at the accomplishments of the last generation.

4

Measuring Economic Well-Being, Poverty, and Inequality

The literature concerning measurement of economic position, poverty, and equality derives directly from the federal antipoverty effort; its story therefore deserves to be told first. This chapter discusses the immediate response from the research and policy-analysis community to declaration of a war against poverty, and in particular to the data needs of policymakers responsible for planning that war. The initial effort to measure poverty was widely perceived to be inadequate and produced a body of research designed to improve the measurement of economic status and its distribution over the population as a whole.

Initial Estimates of Poverty

Even before President Johnson announced the war in 1964, data collection and analysis designed to establish the need for antipoverty policies were under way. Some of this early work took place in universities, but most was carried out by researchers and analysts in the federal government during the early 1960s. The first official document to make the case for eradication of poverty was the 1964 *Economic Report of the President*. It offered a definition of poverty and made the first attempt to determine how much existed and who the poor were. Its definition was economic: insufficient money income. The extent of the problem was established by

declaring all families—households of two or more related persons—
"poor" if their annual cash income fell below $3,000. In the *Economic
Report* of the following year, $3,000 was used for families and an arbitrary
figure of $1,500 was designated the cut-off for individuals. Admittedly
crude, these efforts nonetheless served to establish the existence of
poverty in the United States and to indicate roughly who fell into that
category.

The measures provided statistical support for the president's declaration, but encountered substantial criticism; both official and unofficial
efforts to improve on them followed. The measure that was officially
adopted by the government in 1969 was developed at the Social Security
Administration (SSA) in 1965 and was largely the work of a staff researcher, Mollie Orshansky.[1] Like the president's economic report, the
Orshansky definition began with the presumption that economic well-
being is related to the ability to consume goods and services, and that this
ability is best indicated by income, stated in dollar terms. Income was
defined to be the pretax, posttransfer annual cash income of a family,
excluding capital gains or losses. This value was compared with a
threshold designed to represent a minimum level of well-being, adjusted
to account for the varying needs of several family types (according to size,
age, farm or nonfarm residence, male or female head). This level was the
estimated minimum income that would permit a nonfarm family of three
to purchase the U. S. Department of Agriculture's "economy diet,"
assuming that one-third of income went for food. The one-third figure
was taken from household budget studies which typically indicated that
food absorbed about a third of the posttax income of families over a wide
range of incomes (see Plotnick and Skidmore, 1975). For families not
containing three persons, the economy diet for the appropriate family
size was again multiplied by three to obtain the poverty threshold.[2] This
set of poverty lines was then adjusted annually by the consumer price
index (CPI) so that the purchasing power they represented would not
change over time.[3]

A significant improvement on prior measures, the official definition is
nevertheless arbitrary. Among many ensuing criticisms, the following are
the more cogent:

---

1. See Orshansky (1965) and, for further early discussion of the Orshansky measure and
alternatives t. it, Mahoney (1976).

2. Except for couples, for which the multiplier was 3.88, and single individuals, for which
it was 5.92. For farm families, the threshold was set at 85 percent of that for nonfarm
families, to reflect the availability of home-grown food.

3. The poverty lines developed by Orshansky were originally updated by Department of
Agriculture revisions of the food plans. The CPI adjustments were incorporated in 1969 and
applied retroactively.

- The economy food budget on which the thresholds are based came from a study that was out of date by the time the lines became official and, given large changes in tastes, food-purchase options, and income over the intervening period, that basis is unrealistic today.
- The "one-third-of-income-for-food" rule on which the multipliers are based may be relevant for some families but clearly not for a large number of family sizes and structures. Far more adequate and accurate equivalence scales are available than these crude multipliers.
- Whereas the "one-third-of-income-for-food" rule was based on posttax cash income, the SSA applied it to pretax income. Moreover, the "economy budget" was a truly stringent, bare-bones budget, not one on which the one-third pattern was observed.
- Because the official definition is limited to cash income, it neglects the receipt by families of in-kind transfers and therefore exaggerates estimates of poverty. This problem became increasingly severe as the volume of in-kind transfers grew over the years. The same bias results from failure to include the value of government services—e.g., education, highways, etc.—in income.
- The official measure takes no account of assets—physical, financial, or human—or of difference in access to housing of various qualities and costs. A wealthy family with little current income might be classified as poor, as would a final-year medical student. Similarly, a migrant-worker family with money income above the poverty line but little access to housing above substandard levels would be classified as nonpoor, yet an equivalent family with slightly less income but a spacious, rent-controlled apartment would be defined as poor.
- Because the official measure is based on current income, it does not account for the difference between transitory and permanent income: those with temporarily low incomes are counted as poor, even though their permanent income level may be well above the poverty threshold.
- Annual adjustment of the poverty line by the CPI adjusts for inflation, but does not account for rising real income standards.

Not withstanding these weaknesses, the 1965 study was a milestone in the field of poverty analysis, and adoption of "the Orshansky line" as the official measure of poverty represents an important example of the effect of research, combined with a certain amount of political compromise, on policy-making. Its adoption is in fact viewed by many as one of the more lasting and significant achievements of the War on Poverty. James Tobin wrote in 1970:

The Federal "war on poverty," whatever else it has accomplished, established an official measure of the prevalence of poverty in the United States. Adoption of a specific quantitative measure, however arbitrary and debatable, will have durable and far-reaching political consequences. Administrations will be judged by their success or failure in reducing the officially measured prevalence of poverty. So long as any families are found below the official poverty line, no politician will be able to claim victory in the war on poverty or ignore the repeated solemn acknowledgements of society's obligation to its poorer members (p. 83).

Research Responses to the Measurement of Poverty

Any proposed measure of poverty must rest on some reliable and generally accepted indicator by which the well-being or economic status of a set of households can be ranked. Once a ranking is achieved, some line must be drawn to separate the poor from the nonpoor. In each of these two steps, judgment plays a role, and no proposed measure will ever be free of criticism.

The concept of poverty, like those of unemployment, disability, and well-being, is elastic, multidimensional, nonobjective, and culturally determined. No objective measure of it can be either totally satisfying or accommodate more than a few notions of what it means to be "poor."[4] In that sense, efforts devoted to defining and measuring poverty are doomed before they begin. Dorothy Brady argued the futility of the enterprise almost fifteen years before the antipoverty campaign got under way: "When faced directly with the problem of determining [poverty] for a given time and place, the theorist will deny the possibility of a unique answer and the propagandist will settle for one of many solutions if the result suits his purposes" (1951, p. 30).

Nonetheless, the effort to assess economic well-being and poverty has occupied a good deal of the time and resources of social scientists, for the most part economists. The measurement of economic well-being, poverty, and inequality are conceptually quite different enterprises, yet progress in all three areas has taken place simultaneously. Some of the major studies addressed all three issues, moving from revisions in the measurement of economic status to the implications of these revisions for the analysis of poverty and inequality. The literature on measuring

---

4. Robert Lampman described the difficulty of dealing with the concept of poverty as follows: "Poverty is a condition that is difficult to define or characterize. It is relative rather than absolute; it is essentially qualitative rather than quantitative; it is to a certain extent subjective rather than objective; it refers to the general condition of man rather than a specific facet of his existence. We might agree that by some very broad definitions we are all poor (perhaps in spirit) and that even the most fortunate among us miss something of the abundant life which both secular and religious teachings hold out as ideal" (1971a, p. 53).

inequality and poverty is voluminous and has been reviewed elsewhere;[5] our discussion will feature the major contributions.

Measuring Economic Well-Being

If the early measures of poverty put forth by the president's Council of Economic Advisers and the Social Security Administration encountered criticism on several scores, the academic literature which might have guided the analysts who devised these estimates was a virtual wasteland.

In the 1930s a number of pioneering studies of family living and consumption standards in a variety of cultures and nations had been written, principally by Carle C. Zimmerman (1935, 1936), but until 1960 little economic research had focused on the measurement of economic well-being, the distribution of that well-being among individuals or households, or the size and composition of the population with less than acceptable well-being. A small number of postwar studies concerned the degree of inequality in the income distribution, the determinants of the observed level of disparities among the individuals and households within that distribution, and the distribution of tax burdens among various classes.[6] However, the emphasis of that work on equity as opposed to efficiency placed it well outside of the central core of economics as a discipline. During that period, research by economists on what they termed "distribution" still concerned the functional components of aggregate income—the relative shares of wages, interest, rent, and profit. Unlike the study of the size distribution of income, which refers to the percentage of the population that falls into certain segments, usually fifths, of the total distribution, and issues of interpersonal equity, research on the functional distribution of income had a direct tie to traditional concerns with efficiency and the allocation of resources.

In addition to lying outside the mainstream, empirical research on well-being and distributional issues prior to 1960 was severely limited by the scarcity of individual household survey data. The primary data sources were the decennial censuses and an occasional survey to which weights were applied to make it nationally representative. Beyond the researchers directly connected with these surveys, such data were available only in tabular form and analysis could focus only on groups, not individuals.

---

5. See the studies by Lydall (1968), Bronfenbrenner (1971), Jencks et al. (1972), Sen (1973), Lampman (1974), Plotnick and Skidmore (1975), Thurow (1975), U.S. Department of Health, Education, and Welfare (1976).

6. See, for example, Musgrave et al. (1951), Lampman (1954, 1959b), and David (1959).

All of these efforts took measured money income as the indicator of economic position—or level of economic well-being—of an individual or a family. Lip service was given to the fact that well-being flowed from sources other than cash income, but little was known regarding the effect of publicly provided services (e.g., education or subsidized transportation) on economic well-being or the impact of in-kind benefits (e.g., health care), leisure time, human capital (e.g., education and training), or age (reflecting life-cycle considerations) on economic position. Moreover, while the distribution of financial wealth had received some study (Lampman, 1959a), the tie between wealth and income and their interaction in defining economic position was little recognized. Although some research on equivalence scales had been undertaken (Friedman, 1952), it was not based on contemporary consumer theory, nor was it used to give recognition to the role of "needs" in defining who was poor. Finally, although the notion of "permanent income" (Friedman, 1957) had an important effect on research into the determinants of aggregate consumption, few economists explicitly recognized the difference between permanent and transitory income in analyzing well-being, inequality, or poverty.

Between 1960 and 1965 a number of studies were devoted to the measurement and distribution of economic well-being. The most significant was conducted by a group of scholars at the Institute for Social Research at the University of Michigan (Morgan et al., 1962). Exploiting a nationally weighted survey of families, these researchers empirically examined a wide range of issues concerning well-being and its distribution, including the measurement and determinants of income inequality and poverty, the level and distribution of public and intrafamily transfers, the relationship of income to family size and structure (an indication of needs), and the effect of wealth holdings on the income distribution. Although the data for undertaking these extensions were less than ideal, this study marked a major step forward in research on inequality and well-being. Robert Lampman had serious reservations about parts of it, but described the work in the following terms: "This book is a major addition to the library on income distribution. It should be widely used by those interested in the specific topics of family income determination, income inequality, disability, philanthropy, and education. It may well turn out to be the basis or intermediate product for new departures in a number of these fields" (1963, p. 317).

Other studies dealt with the structure of income and its distribution among households of various types, the economic status of the aged, and the extent of wealth holding and its concentration within a limited segment of the population.[7]

All of this work was empirical in nature, used microdata, and focused on economic well-being and its distribution among individuals and groups, yet one of its main contributions was to point out how much was not known about aspects of distribution and how limited were existing survey data for answers to these questions. In these early data, the definition of the living unit was insufficient for discussion of the distribution of economic well-being, the sources of income (especially those from assets and from public transfer programs) were poorly distinguished, in-kind and intrafamily transfers were inadequately identified or recorded, and information on asset holdings, fringe benefits, benefits from government programs, and tax liabilities was not available. Moreover, the empirical and theoretical basis for tying family size and structure to income needs and for distinguishing those of temporarily low or high income did not exist. Hence research in this period relied heavily on the census-based definition of income, current cash—and on crude adjustments to it—as the indicator of economic status. From this pespective, it seems that the first official definition and measure of poverty were not far from the state of the art in the academic community.

In the 1965–80 period, poverty research focused on the shortcomings of the early academic and government work. The main areas of interest concerned measurement of the tie between income and wealth, human capital, multiyear low-income status, noncash income, the basic needs of various types of families, the necessity of tracing individual experiences over time so that changes in their living arrangements and wealth positions could be observed, and comprehensive measures of well-being.

This work was motivated by the desire to measure the extent and severity of poverty, but securing an improved measure of economic well-being is an achievement in its own right. Its objective is to obtain an accurate ranking of living units (or individuals) in terms of long-run economic position. Only with this ranking in hand can one proceed to the normative issue of drawing a line that separates poor from nonpoor. In this sense, measuring economic status must precede defining and measuring poverty.

Work on economic status was also motivated by the desire to establish a basis for determining which living units are indeed equal—the desire to establish a firm basis for achieving "horizontal equity." This issue was

7. See the works of Kravis (1962), Lampman (1962), and Steiner and Dorfman (1962).

made more pressing by the post-1965 growth in the level of public expenditures designed to aid the poor. Marilyn Moon and Eugene Smolensky stated: "More comprehensive measures of economic status, which better distinguish poor from nonpoor families, increase the likelihood of policy improvements that will treat those whom society views as equals equally" (1977, p. 2).[8]

The central concern of research designed to measure economic well-being was to identify the access to resources on the part of households (their "resource constraint"), rather than their actual levels of consumption or income, since the latter reflect differences in tastes and choices as well as in opportunities.

Against this background we now turn to individual measurement issues.

Wealth and Economic Well-Being. The first step in identifying the resource constraint was to recognize that financial and physical wealth contributes to economic well-being in much the same way as does cash income. An individual at any point in time can imagine drawing down asset stock so that, upon death, the amount remaining is sufficient to cover desired bequests plus some contingency allowance. This optimal "eating up" of capital adds to the individual's potential consumption in any period.[9]

One way of reflecting the contribution of wealth to economic well-being in a life-cycle context would be to add the annual annuitized value of an individual's net worth to annual cash income. This procedure was followed by Burton Weisbrod and Lee Hansen (1968), who then compared the distribution of families in the U. S. population as ranked by their income–net worth measure with the distribution when families were ranked by current income. They reached two major conclusions: that the degree of inequality was greater under the income–net worth measure; and that older families, because they have relatively larger amounts of net worth and shorter life expectancies, tended to increase their ranking in the distribution of economic position relative to younger families.[10]

8. The concern for establishing measures of horizontal equity has in turn led to an extensive literature on criteria to determine whether transfers do or do not violate horizontal equity standards. See Sen (1973) and Plotnick (1982).

9. An optimal life-cycle consumption-saving pattern was first formalized by Modigliani. See Modigliani and Brumberg (1954).

10. Weisbrod and Hansen also used their expanded measure of economic well-being to explore the implications for evaluating tax progressivity and for estimating consumption behavior. In analyzing the distribution of well-being within the aged population, Moon (1977) found a major change in the ranking of families when the income–net worth measure was used in place of current income. That approach had earlier been criticized by Projector and Weiss (1969) for its failure to distinguish different income expectations from nonwealth sources among families.

Human Capital and Economic Well-Being. While the work of Weisbrod and Hansen recognized the contribution of physical and financial assets to economic well-being, other work attempted to expand the measure to incorporate differences in the capabilities of individuals to generate earnings in the labor market. These capabilities are largely associated with educational attainment, training, or work experience, and are referred to as "human capital." The notion here is that current opportunities should reflect expected earnings as well as current earnings: in principle at least, those with high levels of human capital should be able to borrow against anticipated earnings in order to support current consumption.

One approach was taken by Irwin Garfinkel and Robert Haveman (1977), who developed a measure of economic status that they designated "earnings capacity," defined as the annual income flow a family could attain if all working-age members used their human and physical capital to capacity.[11] It purges the income measure from tastes (by in effect placing a value on the time devoted to leisure when work is deliberately less than full time), reflects the potential rates of return to both physical and human capital, and is close to a permanent-income notion in that transitory, year-to-year fluctuations in actual income are not reflected in the measure. This approach, however, does not go so far as to include the discounted present value of future expected earnings (or earnings capacity) in the measure of economic status.

Like Weisbrod and Hansen, Garfinkel and Haveman explored the implications of their proposed measure on economic inequality and the composition of the lower-status population. They found that measured economic inequality among families was reduced when earnings capacity rather than pretransfer income was used as the status indicator, an expected finding given the more permanent nature of the earnings-capacity measure. The degree of inequality based upon earnings capacity was about equal to that of family income after all transfers were taken into account. And the degree of inequality under both of these measures was about 80 percent of the inequality as judged by pretransfer income. In terms of the composition of the low-status population, Garfinkel and Haveman found a relatively higher incidence of low earnings capacity among blacks, those in large families, and working family heads than if

11. The earnings-capacity concept measures the potential income of an individual on the basis of the individual's socioeconomic characteristics and the observed market returns to these characteristics. Hence age, education, and race, for example, affect the individual's ranking in the distribution of economic position as indicated by earnings capacity. The relevance of life-cycle considerations in measuring economic status and, in particular, economic inequality, was recognized by Paglin (1975), whose work is described later in this chapter.

current income was the measure. The earnings-capacity measure yielded, however, a smaller incidence of low status among farmers, the very young and the very old, and single individuals.

The Accounting Period. A third issue in measuring economic status relates to the role of time. Annual income measures contain both a permanent and a transitory component. Because of transitory effects—those caused by changing macroeconomic conditions, changes in family composition, changes in health status, unusual overtime work, and other "chance" factors—any given year's observed income may produce a misleading estimate of true economic status. Some more permanent (or average) income measure, or at least one that would reflect the uncertainty of future outcomes, would provide a superior indicator. The expectation of income instability may itself be a component of economic well-being if families are "risk averse." Taking into account risk aversion, two families with the same multiyear average income may experience quite different levels of economic well-being, depending on the variability of expected income over the period.

Several studies have attempted to account for this element of uncertainty, and the associated distinction between transitory and permanent well-being implicit in it.[12] A standard approach has been to expand the time period over which the analysis of well-being is measured, thus eliminating some portion of income variability associated with time. Other studies have attempted to secure an estimate of the cost of uncertainty and to adjust measured levels of economic status for these costs.[13] Almost by definition, use of permanent rather than actual income as an indicator of economic position reduces the estimate of aggregate inequality.[14] Moreover, much of the movement into and out of low economic status is eliminated if permanent rather than actual income is used to measure economic position.[15] If, however, the cost of uncertainty

12. See the studies of David (1959), Benus and Morgan (1975), Kohen, Parnes, and Shea (1975), Johnson (1977), and Haveman and Wolfe (1985).

13. In their model for evaluating the social welfare impacts of alternative social policies, Gramlich and Wolkoff (1979) explicitly recognized both the problems of single-year accounting periods in measuring economic status and the well-being costs of uncertainty in future expected income flows.

14. It should be noted that while a more permanent income notion is important for studying the distribution of aggregate well-being in society, it is less relevant for policy. Current-year income is surely a more relevant measure of current need; the aged current-income poor cannot eat from, or borrow against, the income they may have had earlier.

15. The issue of transitory versus permanent components of measured income is closely related to a substantial body of poverty-related research on income mobility and the transitory nature of the poverty population. See Schiller (1976), Smith and Morgan (1980), and Duncan (1984). Research on income mobility is examined in Chapter 6.

for risk-averse individuals is accounted for in estimating the degree of inequality, the impact on the level of true economic inequality is unclear. Thad Mirer concluded that income variability is greater for families with both high and (especially) low permanent incomes: "Measures of the distribution of permanent income are recognized to be useful indicators of the distribution of welfare. But, if income variability leads to a welfare loss . . . , then the distribution of welfare is even more inequitable than one would have determined simply from looking at the distribution of [permanent] income levels" (1974, p. 206).

Accounting for Public In-Kind Transfers. A major development in the measurement of economic status is the incorporation of public noncash transfers into the indicator of economic position. Two issues are of particular relevance: valuation of the transfers, and assignment of the value of in-kind transfers received among various households. Work on the first of these issues has been done by several individuals, perhaps most successfully by Eugene Smolensky and a number of collaborators. Using information on family disposable income and on the various non-cash benefit programs, and applying an economic assumption termed, in the language of the trade, the constant elasticity of substitution (CES) utility function, Smolensky et al. (1977) derived an estimate of the value (in "equivalent cash transfer units") of a variety of noncash benefits.[16] Those benefits that are close substitutes for cash (e.g., food stamps) were found to have higher cash-equivalent values than benefits less likely to be purchased out of cash income (e.g., public housing or medical care). Overall, Smolensky et al. found the benefit weights to be relatively close to unity, suggesting that in-kind transfers do not greatly alter the consumption patterns of recipients. As a result they concluded that using the program cost of these transfers to adjust reported income as a basis for determining family economic status does not yield results which vary greatly from adjustments based on the more appropriate cash-equivalent value of the transfers.

The volume of in-kind benefits in the U. S. transfer system has grown rapidly since 1965, and in 1980 stood at about $80 billion. These in-kind transfers range from welfare benefits (e.g., food stamps and public housing) to social insurance benefits (e.g., Medicare) to human capital investment benefits (e.g., student loans). While in-kind welfare benefits tend to be directed toward families of low economic status, on the whole in-kind transfers rise with family income: more dollars of benefit go to families of high than of low status. The important role of medical care subsidies

16. Earlier contributions to the evaluation of in-kind benefits include Kraft and Olsen (1974), Murray (1974), and Clarkson (1975).

largely explains this pattern. However, because the distribution of in-kind benefits is more equal than the distribution of cash income, adding in-kind benefits to cash income yields a measure of economic well-being that reduces inequality under cash income by about 6 to 8 percent.

If a comprehensive measure of economic status is to be achieved, other forms of in-kind transfers must be considered. Transfers and sharing between and within families are also relevant to identifying economic status, as are other private transfers, especially fringe benefits. Perhaps most important, the value of many publicly produced goods and services—e.g., police protection, loan subsidies, education subsidies—and the burden of taxation must be taken into account. Reliance on measures of well-being that include only cash and in-kind benefits targeted on the poor while neglecting other public benefits and taxes yields a biased view of overall inequality and poverty and an exaggerated picture of government's role in redistributing income. Research to devise a means of measuring these components of comprehensive income, and to estimate the distribution of the resulting values across the population, is in its infancy, and few definitive results have been published.[17]

Income and Needs. Families are not homogeneous and, hence, do not have identical needs. Many factors are likely to determine the effect of an additional dollar of income on the well-being of individuals in a family unit, such as the size of the family and its composition, location, health status, and farm versus nonfarm residence. Research into the development of "equivalence scales," designed to account for economies along various dimensions in providing goods to individuals in different types of households, has a long history in economics.[18] And the use of indices based on such scales is premised on the judgment that economic well-being is better represented by the comprehensive income (or other indicator of economic status) of a living unit (household or family) per unit of need than it is by the absolute level of income or some other well-being indicator.

Since 1965, research on equivalence scales has focused on the development of comparisons of economic well-being among groups distinguished

17. Research efforts to estimate and allocate interfamily and intrafamily transfers include Morgan (1968, 1984), Baerwaldt and Morgan (1971), Smeeding (1975), Moon (1977), and Lampman and Smeeding (1983). The most comprehensive estimates of the tax liabilities of individual families have been made by Pechman and Okner (1974) and Smeeding (1975).

18. See Friedman (1952), Nicholson (1976), Muellbauer (1977), Lazear and Michael (1980), and van der Gaag and Smolensky (1980, 1981). Two works by Muellbauer (1974, 1977) contain references to several other studies of equivalence scales for welfare purposes. Pollak and Wales (1979) emphasize that equivalence scales from demand analysis may not be appropriate for welfare comparisons.

by age, race, and sex. Whereas previous work on equivalence was theoretically ad hoc, this recent work has been based on rigorous consumer demand theory, in which households are viewed as maximizing lifetime utility under a lifetime wealth constraint (see Muellbauer, 1974). In this framework, a full system of demand equations is obtained to construct constant utility equivalence scales. This technique has been used for the purpose of measuring the socioeconomic composition of those who occupy various ranges in the distribution of economic status, in particular the composition of those at the bottom of the distribution (van der Gaag and Smolensky, 1980, 1981). These studies have found that individuals with low economic status are somewhat younger, somewhat "whiter," and substantially less dominated by female family heads than suggested by the official U.S. statistics on poverty.[19]

Equivalence-scale adjustments have also been important in recent analyses of the economic status of the elderly relative to the nonelderly. Although simple income comparisons show the elderly to be far less well off than the nonelderly, the adjustment of the income concept to take account of size and composition (needs) of the household removes about 70 percent of the disparity. When this adjustment is combined with further adjustments regarding the value of durable goods owned, tax liability, and other factors, this research has suggested that, on average, the elderly are just as well off as the nonelderly (even though there are individual cases of very poor old people).[20]

"Comprehensive" Measures of Well-Being. While most studies of comparative well-being have focused on one (or a limited number) of adjustments to the money income measure in the quest for a more comprehensive indicator, Timothy Smeeding (1975) incorporated several adjustments simultaneously in his analysis of the distribution of economic well-being. He included adjustments for (1) underreporting, (2) household federal (but not state or local) tax liability, (3) intrahouse-

19. Van der Gaag and Smolensky (1981) also analyzed a variety of other measures of economic status that recognize family needs, and found the composition of the poverty population to vary widely among them. They concluded: "The more radically a welfare measure departs from simple total household consumption, the younger and larger the family, the more likely the head is to be male, and the more likely it is that the head works, [the more likely is the family to be in poverty]" (p. 26).

20. See Danziger, van der Gaag, Smolensky, and Taussig (1984a, 1984b) for a summary of the findings and the derivation of the equivalence scales. Earlier work on the well-being of the elderly which also relies on needs adjustments is in Moon (1977). More recently, Hurd and Shoven (1982, 1983) have analyzed changes in the economic well-being of the aged, in some cases relying on equivalence-scale adjustments. These adjusted estimates, however, remain based on a one-year income measure, and hence fail to reflect the fact that the elderly who are poor in any single year tend to be permanently poor, while younger single-year poor are only temporarily poor.

hold income transfers, and (4) the cash-equivalent value of a limited set of in-kind benefits of a welfare nature. The resulting indicator of access to resources by the household was then adjusted by the equivalence scale implicit in the official poverty line. For both 1968 and 1972, this comprehensive index of economic status showed from 8 to 12 percent less inequality than did the current-money-income indicator.

The components of economic well-being so far discussed have been analyzed theoretically, estimated empirically by use of microdata (information on individual households obtained in surveys), and consistently incorporated in data bases used to measure the extent of and changes in poverty and inequality over time. Work on other components of economic well-being lags well behind the research cited, but two lines of study should be mentioned: that considering government expenditures in addition to cash and noncash transfers, and that accounting for leisure time and nonmarket production. The most complete analysis of the distributional impact of government expenditures (or, more broadly, the "fisc") was conducted by Morgan Reynolds and Eugene Smolensky (1977). They found the benefits of nontransfer expenditures and the costs of taxes to be, on balance, equalizing—inequality under an indicator of economic status including a value for government spending and taxation is less than under measures that are less comprehensive.[21]

Both Ismail Sirageldin (1969) and Michael Taussig (1973) attempted to allow for leisure time and its value in measures of economic well-being, but the implications of including these values on measured inequality among living units, or on the composition of the lower tail of the distribution, have not been systematically explored.[22] Because the hours of leisure of a family tend to be inversely related to its income, a well-being measure that included leisure would tend to be less unequally distributed than one based on income alone.

Measuring Poverty

Some criticism of the initial measures of the size and composition of the poor population focused on narrow issues; others were more fundamental, going to the very heart of the question of what it means to be poor. Almost all offered alternative means of measurement.

Toward an Absolute Poverty Line. One of the earliest attempts to

---

21. See also Gillespie (1965) and Bishop (1967) for earlier studies of the distributional impact of the fisc.

22. Garfinkel and Haveman (1977) implicitly incorporated a measure of leisure time in their work on the distribution of earnings capacity among households.

develop an alternative to the official definition of poverty as was that of Harold Watts (1969), who emphasized an economic view of poverty that focused on the resources available to an individual (or family) for earning a living or buying goods and services. Following this view of poverty—as opposed to a cultural view that emphasizes attitudes or behaviors—Watts proposed a definition designed to separate tastes (personal preferences) from available resources, emphasizing the latter. "Poverty is, in this view, a property of the individual's situation . . ., poverty is associated solely with severe constriction of the choice set" (p. 371). While acknowledging that the official definition was also premised on this "constraint approach," Watts proposed to move from the crude indicator of the resources constraint embodied in the official measure (current cash income) to a more comprehensive indicator based on Milton Friedman's concept of permanent income, a concept of available resources that abstracts from transitory fluctuations and emphasizes permanent characteristics.[23]

Given this measure of "permanent" command over goods and services, the next ingredient in an economic definition of poverty is a set of lines designating equivalent levels of deprivation for families of different sizes and structures, based on a set of reliable equivalence scales defined in terms of permanent income. With these two components, a ratio of a family's actual permanent income to the level of permanent income required for that family not to be in poverty can be calculated: ratios above one would designate nonpoverty status; those below would fall in the poverty population. Finally, to recognize that poverty becomes more severe at an increasing rate as successive equal decrements of income are experienced, Watts proposed a poverty severity index, calculated as the logarithm of the welfare index. This index reflects the judgment that the rate at which the severity (or pain) of poverty increases as income decreases. While Watts's economic measure incorporates a number of considerations (e.g., reliance on permanent rather than actual income, the increasing severity of poverty as one moves further below the poverty threshold) that make it more attractive than the official measure, it is only useful as a research exercise unless policymakers are willing to specify

23. Watts (1969) defined the comprehensive indicator as "the sum of income flows from property, from sale of labor services, and from transfers (unilateral 'gifts'), from other persons, or from governmental units, whether received in money or in 'real' form. These flows are evaluated at the normal rate they can be expected to maintain over the long run instead of at the current level" (p. 323). He emphasized the inclusion of the directly consumed services of owner-occupied housing in this definition, as well as the annual annuitized value of net worth.

socially accepted relationships among a person's permanent income, his or her needs, and "true" well-being.[24]

In other work, Watts (1967) extended his concern with accurately measuring equivalent levels of real access to resources among families of alternative sizes, structures, and regions of residence. Like the official definition, equivalence among families was based on observed behavior. However, while the official measure relies on the observed "one-third-of-income-for-food" rule to establish poverty thresholds, Watts relied on patterns of expenditures on commodities defined to be "necessities" to measure the threshold. If the fractions of income spent on these "necessities" changes as economic status changes, families with equal expenditures on necessities as a proportion of total spending are viewed as equally well off. The incomes corresponding to these equal proportions are obtained from estimates derived from household expenditure data. This proposed measure, it should be noted, rests on a conceptual basis similar to the equivalence-scale measures based on observed consumption behavior, discussed above. And when the index derived from it is used to measure poverty, the resulting estimates remain in the category of "absolute poverty, access to resources" among poverty measures.

Relative Measures. While the "absolute poverty according to access to resources" approach is reflected in the official measure of poverty and has guided the work of most economists in this area, proposals for a relative measure of poverty have also been put forward. Its advocates point out that an absolute cutoff distinguishing poor from nonpoor is arbitrary and ultimately meaningless; what the U. S. official measure defines as poverty would be considered opulence in many societies. Poverty, they claim, is the condition of people of lowest economic status relative to the rest of the society. And as the status of the nonpoor rises over time, so should the line which divides poor from nonpoor.[25] A relative definition was proposed by Victor Fuchs, who suggested that one-half of median income

---

24. An early attempt to measure the severity of poverty and the effects of policy alternatives in reducing poverty severity is Ribich (1968). Rainwater (1974), using survey responses, attempts to discern the relationship between income and well-being. Watts's proposal is closely related to the literature on distributional weights in benefit-cost analysis. See Haveman (1965), Freeman (1969), Weisbrod (1969), Curtin (1977), and Harberger (1978).

25. John Kenneth Galbraith (1958) made the case for a relative definition of poverty as follows: "People are poverty-stricken when their income, even if adequate for survival, falls markedly behind that of the community. Then they cannot have what the larger community regards as the minimum necessary for decency; and they cannot wholly escape, therefore, the judgment of the larger community that they are indecent. They are degraded for, in a literal sense, they live outside the grades or categories which the community regards as acceptable" (pp. 323–24).

would establish a poverty threshold that would move with the real standard of living of the society as a whole:[26]

Absolute standards of poverty constantly change. It is more reasonable, therefore, to think of poverty in terms of relative incomes. . . . In any given society at any given point in time the "poor" are those in the bottom tail of the income distribution. While there will always be a bottom tail, how far those in it are from those in the middle is probably of critical importance (1965, p. 89).

The case for a measure of poverty related to average levels of income or well-being has appeal, but the argument for an absolute standard is also effective. Recognizing that the very concept of poverty has close ties to inequality in the distribution—an inequality explicitly captured in the relative measures—Robert Lampman has argued that an absolute standard has important characteristics as a policy goal:

While income poverty is a relative matter, I do not think we should engage in frequent changes of the poverty lines, other than to adjust for price change. As I see it, the elimination of income poverty is usefully thought of as a one-time operation in pursuit of a goal unique to this generation. That goal should be achieved before 1980, at which time the next generation will have set new economic and social goals, perhaps including a new distributional goal for themselves (1971a, p. 53).

Lee Rainwater (1974), however, offered evidence that people view poverty as relative—the 50 percent reduction in poverty from 1959 to 1969, as measured by the absolute standard, seems not credible. Other evidence that poverty is indeed perceived as relative was provided by R. W. Kilpatrick (1973). Analyzing responses to survey questionnaires, he found that the level of income that defines what people judge to be "poverty" increases by about 6 percent for every 10 percent increase in the actual average income level.

Subjective Measures. The final approach to an economic measurement of poverty derives from work on the relationship between subjective well-being (based on survey responses designating certain income levels as "good," "sufficient," "bad," etc.) and income. Efforts to scale subjective estimates of well-being to income originated in the research of Bernard van Praag and his associates in the Netherlands (see Goedhart et al., 1971; Hagenaars, 1985), one application of which was establishment of a poverty line. Respondents were first asked what they considered to

26. Fuchs's relative definition was very early, and made no allowance for differential needs associated with differing family sizes, structures, and locations. Extensions of his approach have incorporated equivalence scales similar to those used in the official definition in the analysis of relative poverty (see Plotnick and Skidmore, 1975).

be a minimal level of current, after-tax income for themselves and their families. The answers to these questions were scaled according to an individual welfare function of income of a specified (log-normal) form. These scaled responses were found to depend upon both family size and actual income. For any given family size, there is some level at which people's opinion of what is a minimum income will equal the actual income of the family, conditional on its size. This income level is taken to correspond to the poverty threshold for that family size. It should be noted that this approach, like the official U.S. measure, is based on an economic (i.e., access to resources) concept. Unlike the official U.S. measure, the Dutch line is subjective, resting on the opinions of citizens regarding where the poverty threshold begins. Because the Dutch lines are likely to change over time as the incomes of the respondents change, this measure is in the class of relative measures of poverty.[27]

Other Dimensions of Poverty. The contributions discussed so far have focused on an income-based, or economic, view of poverty. Many think that poverty so defined is a constrained and limited concept, which fails to capture many dimensions of what it means to be poor. In addition to being income poor, one can think of being housing poor, health care poor, education poor, poor in the possession of desirable physical or mental attributes, or being part of a culture which was itself deprived in all these attributes. Anthropologists and sociologists have often referred to the "culture of poverty"—a set of traits that include the social and physical surroundings where the poor reside. These traits generate feelings of lack of esteem by others, lack of self-esteem, antisocial behavior, alienation from the remainder of society, a short time horizon, a lack of participation, and a lack of political power.[28] However, the economic definition of poverty does not deny that such deprivations affect the poor, or suggest that they should not be considered in defining and describing the poor. Lampman wrote of the income definition of poverty:

It has the great advantage over other definitions that income poverty can be measured (or more properly, *indicated*) more readily. Consider the difficulties of measuring the lack of self-esteem, lack of esteem by others, deviant behavior patterns, and lack of political power. Of course, it is true that defining poverty in income terms emphasizes policies that will change income and implies that change in income will cause a change in the psychological, social, and political variables.

27. On the other hand, the implicit poverty lines estimated by any given year's respondents could be taken as normative, to be changed only by the price index. In this form, the Dutch measure would serve as an absolute poverty definition.

28. See Lewis (1965) and Banfield (1968). Spilerman and Elesh (1971) describe the nature of these views and their implications for public policy.

It assumes that the culture or subculture of poverty is more often an adaptation to limited opportunity than it is an independent and causal agent of low income (1971a, p. 54).

Although there has been substantial discussion regarding the desirability of defining poverty in terms of broader deprivation than income alone, there have been relatively few efforts to establish a concrete alternative to an income-based measure. One such effort should be noted. In 1966, the concept of "subemployment" was developed to characterize the labor market problems of disadvantaged workers—youths, minorities, and ghetto residents (Wirtz, 1966). The concept extended the concept of unemployment by including measures of the *adequacy* of employment *and* earnings. It classified as subemployed not only those unemployed but also (1) those who were working part time but wanted full-time work, (2) family heads working full time who did not earn enough to bring their families over the poverty line, and (3) discouraged workers—those no longer seeking work. The number of workers "subemployed" was found to be about three times the number of unemployed workers in ten ghetto areas in eight major cities. When the index was first published by the Department of Labor in 1968, it was criticized widely. A 1970 Census Bureau survey of sixty poverty areas in fifty-one cities permitted development of a more extensive and reliable indicator of subemployment in urban ghetto areas. Again, the subemployment rate was about three times the unemployment rate.

Sar Levitan and Robert Taggart (1974) developed an index of "employment and earnings inadequacy" (EEI), designed to improve on the 1970 Census Bureau measure. They used the same components as that measure, but with a superior measure of unemployment. They also accounted for those whose employment was intermittent and excluded those whose inadequate earnings (or subemployment) did not jeopardize total income adequacy of their household. In their words:

The new index should be based upon an upper and lower bounded adequacy measure, weeding out those in the labor force who are too well off to be considered in need even if they experience employment problems, as well as pulling in those with "hidden" difficulties and frequently ignored needs. The goal is to develop a reasonably workable and broadly accepted concept which, like the employment rate, can be refined and adjusted over the years (p. 33).

The index indicates the proportion of people working, seeking work, or discouraged from seeking work who are unable to provide a minimum income and are also not fortunate enough to have other working family members or other sources of income which ameliorate the consequences of their own labor market problems (p. 35).

The EEI thus incorporates the standard notion of income poverty, but expands it to include those individuals who face particular labor market difficulties. The notion is that the true poor are those of working age who, because of their own characteristics or the structure of the labor markets in which they function, do not earn enough to remove their families from poverty, even though they desire to do so. It is premised on the view that individuals of working age have a right to a job that will remove them and their families from poverty if they have no other source of income. Like the official poverty index, the EEI provides a measure over time of the performance of the economy in providing work to those who need it in order to remove them and their families from poverty. And while it and the official index to which it is related are open to criticism on both statistical and conceptual grounds, they do represent efforts to indicate quantitatively that poverty entails not only inadequate income relative to needs but also deprivation in the access to jobs and earnings sufficient to avoid income inadequacy.[29] Still, even the EEI fails to capture a wide variety of issues relevant to well-being, such as the amount and nature of leisure and the conditions of work.

Measuring Inequality

While poverty concerns the number and status of those in the bottom tail of the distribution of economic well-being, inequality has to do with the general spread of the distribution—the gap between the rich and the poor. Research on inequality, both conceptual and empirical, has a history far longer than that concerned with measuring poverty. Just as the War on Poverty stimulated an outpouring of work on defining and measuring poverty, so did it encourage investigations of the sources of economic disparities among individuals and families. As we have seen, relative measures of poverty are directly tied to the degree of inequality in the income distribution.

Research on inequality has traditionally focused on incomes. As research progressed in the measurement of economic status and well-being, however, studies of inequality began substituting these measures of well-being for the more standard income concepts. The concepts of the welfare ratio, earnings capacity, and comprehensive income were all used after 1965 to ascertain the level of and trends in inequality.[30]

29. I have treated the EEI index as an effort to develop a broader alternative to the official poverty measure, one which considers labor market performance and access to jobs in addition to income attainment. An alternative view is that the EEI is, along with the official poverty index, just another in a long string of indicators of social performance. See U.S. Department of Health, Education, and Welfare (1969).

30. See Morgan et al. (1962), Taussig (1973), Smeeding (1975), Garfinkel and Haveman (1977), and Moon (1977). Cowell (1980) discusses the impact of several measures of

Another development involved formulation of additional indicators of inequality, each with its own conceptual basis and statistical properties. Early work on inequality relied primarily on the share of all income going to equal segments of ranked households (deciles, quintiles), the Lorenz curve displaying this income concentration in segments, and the Gini coefficient measuring the degree of income concentration. More recently, measures have been formulated to incorporate dimensions and characteristics of the distribution not captured in those early measures, including decomposition capabilities, the sensitivity of the measure to changes in the distribution, attributes of the distribution in addition to dispersion, and the capacity of the measure to reflect varying social attitudes regarding inequality ("inequality aversion").[31] Use of these measures in empirical work has given the study of inequality a richness that it did not possess earlier.

One of the measures deserves special note, because of its implications both for interpreting the impact of the War on Poverty on the income distribution and for assessing the seriousness of the degree of inequality (and hence relative poverty). In 1975, Morton Paglin observed that much of the inequality observed in annual measures of economic well-being is due to the pattern of life-cycle earnings. He argued that this pattern (as reflected in age-earnings profiles) is the natural result of the operation of the market system and of human capital decisions in response to market signals—e.g., investing in training for particular types of jobs becoming available, such as computer technology. Being a natural phenomenon, this source of variation in incomes should be removed from the measure of inequality. Empirically, the removal of life-cycle inequality not only reduces the level of measured inequality but also reveals a trend toward reduced inequality in the postwar period (as opposed to little if any change recorded in alternative measures of inequality). Paglin calls his measure the Paglin Gini. His contribution led to substantial debate and comment, and his proposed measure was criticized on several bases, in

---

well-being on the estimate of U.S. inequality, and systematically explores the effect of a variety of income-recipient and accounting-period definitions on measured inequality.

31. See Sen (1973) for a discussion of the various measures and their characteristics. The most prominent and widely used of these indices is that developed by Atkinson (1970), which is strongly tied to the underlying theory of the determinants of inequality, has important decomposition characteristics, and explicitly incorporates tastes toward inequality in the distribution. Following the Sen work, there appeared a long and distinguished set of work on "transfer principles" for choosing among measures of inequality. See Blackorby and Donaldson (1978), Cowell (1980), Shorrocks (1980), Cowell and Kuga (1981), and Plotnick (1982).

particular that it is not clear why life-cycle factors are the only source of inequality that is legitimate and natural.[32]

Poverty Measures and Policy

This chapter emphasizes the stimulus which the War on Poverty provided to economic research designed to improve the measurement of well-being, poverty, and inequality. The previous sections have described some of the major contributions of research to these questions, but that description is only part of the story. Two other points remain: first, the improved measures that were generated by this research entered directly into public debate over antipoverty and social policy during the 1960s and 1970s; second, these advances in empirical research have generated federal government data collection and research activities designed to further improve the measures.

As the antipoverty campaign proceeded, questions other than those involving measurement were raised and debated, three in particular: Who are the truly needy, and are they benefiting from increased social welfare outlays? Given the rapid increase in public spending on the poor, why is the reduction in measured poverty so slow, and so uneven among groups? Why does income inequality seem so resistant to change? The importance of these questions for an overall appraisal of the effectiveness of the War on Poverty is obvious, and a careful reading of the research we have described suggests the nature of the response to these concerns. A few examples may help make this clear.

The first question clearly motivated the work on in-kind transfers and economic well-being which we have described. Much of the increase in social welfare spending was in the form of benefits in kind, and their effect on poor families is reflected in neither the statistics on income distribution nor on measured poverty. Research on in-kind transfers also shed light on the second question, as did the work on equivalence scales, the well-being of the elderly, and earnings capacity. Finally, extensive research on the disparity between posttransfer and pretransfer poverty, and the controversy stimulated by Paglin regarding which components of inequality are socially relevant and which are not, has leavened public discussion of the small effect of policy interventions on measured inequality.

As expected, the findings of this line of research are disparate. Nevertheless, several themes can be discerned. The overall story would run something as follows:

---

32. See Danziger, Haveman, and Smolensky (1977), and other criticisms of the Paglin measure, along with Paglin's (1977) reply.

The rapid growth in public cash and in-kind benefits has been highly targeted on those judged poor by the official measure. However, if the poor are identified by longer-term indicators of well-being—i.e., permanent income, earnings capacity, or full income—more of this government assistance (both cash and in kind) is seen as spilling over to those further up in the distribution. That is, government programs are more effective in helping the current-income poor than those in longer-term poverty. The reduction in officially measured poverty has been slow, however, because these rapidly growing in-kind benefits do not contribute to meeting "needs" as reflected in the cash-income basis of the official measure. A broader indicator of well-being would show a more rapid decrease in poverty attributable to government programs, at least until 1980. Economic inequality was in fact reduced between 1960 and 1980, but only if in-kind transfers are considered and only if those income differences not associated with life-cycle changes are considered. Most analysts, however, are reluctant to base judgments of changes in inequality only on those income components not associated with life-cycle considerations, given that policy measures also influence life-cycle phenomena.

In part because of the importance of this line of economic inquiry to public debate on these questions, the federal government has taken steps to improve the measures of well-being and poverty on which its own analyses of antipoverty and income distribution policy are based. In 1977 the Congressional Budget Office (CBO) published a report, *Poverty Status of Families under Alternative Definitions of Income*, which explicitly addressed the question of the effect of in-kind transfers on the number of individuals living in officially defined poverty. Using 1976 data adjusted for underreporting, the CBO imputed to families the value of in-kind public transfers for food, housing, and medical care. These adjustments resulted in a poverty rate that was only about one-half of the official measure—5.3 percent as compared to 10 percent. The implication was clear: if the enormous growth in in-kind transfers would be properly taken into account through a more comprehensive income definition (neglecting, however, any changes in the needs of low-income groups or other factors), the problem of poverty in the United States would seem to be much less serious than revealed by the official statistics.

Precisely this point was made by a number of influential writers concerned with the direction of national policy. Martin Anderson, who became a principal adviser to President Reagan on social policy issues, wrote in 1978:

According to the Census Bureau, 12.3 percent of all Americans are poor. Revised, more accurate estimates show that if you also take into account the value of the nonmoney income received by poor people, and adjust for the fact that the poor systematically underreport their actual income when asked, the poverty count drops to as low as 3 percent. In effect, the executive branch of the federal government has been telling us that there is four times as much poverty as there really is. . . .

The war on poverty is over for all practical purposes. We should now begin thinking about how to revise our welfare strategies to deal with the problem of preventing poverty, to make programs more effective and efficient, to eliminate those programs that are not needed, and to focus more on the social problems that widespread welfare dependency will bring (pp. 25, 39).

The issue of what effect in-kind transfers exert on the well-being of lower-income families became sufficiently recognized that, in 1980, the Senate Appropriations Committee (and ultimately the Senate) wrote, after referring to the CBO report:

The Committee considers it essential that official poverty statistics reflect, at the earliest possible date, the effect of in-kind benefits. Without such information Congress and the Executive Branch cannot be certain that government transfer programs are properly targeted.

The Secretary of Commerce is . . . directed to continue research and testing of techniques for assigning monetary values to in-kind benefits, and for calculating the impact of such benefits on income and poverty estimates (U. S. Senate, 1980, pp. 33–34).

In response to, and guided by, the congressional request, the Census Bureau issued its own analysis, conducted by Timothy Smeeding, in 1982.[33] In this study, about 40 percent of all food, housing, and medical in-kind benefits (and about 90 percent of all means-tested in-kind government benefits) were analyzed with 1980 data obtained from respondents in the nationally representative Current Population Survey, who were queried regarding their participation in a variety of in-kind benefit programs and the value of the benefits received. While a number of techniques for valuing in-kind benefits were employed, the results were generally consistent with those in the CBO report: "The broadest income definition, which includes food, housing, and medical care with institutional benefits, reduces the poverty rate from 11.1 percent to 6.4 percent based on the market value approach" (U. S. Bureau of the Census, 1982, p. vii).

The report also provided a substantially modified view of the composition of the poor. For the elderly the official poverty rate stood at 14.7 percent in 1979; the inclusion of in-kind benefits in the income concept (at market value) reduced that figure to 4.5 percent. The share of the poverty population represented by black families, by those who resided in central cities, and by female-headed families also fell when in-kind benefits were

33. See U.S. Bureau of the Census (1982). This effort and subsequent research on noncash benefits were reviewed and critiqued by Hill and Morgan (1985).

accounted for, although the poverty rates for these groups remained—and still remain—strikingly high.

Although substantial progress has been made in the post-1965 period, the final word in developing more appropriate measures of economic status and applying them to analyses of poverty and inequality has not been written.

Measurement Issues: How Far and Where Next?

The years after 1965 saw substantial progress in measuring the variables that represent access to resources and needs, which are necessary both to identify the number and composition of the poor and to gauge the level and trends of inequality. From the perspective of the 1980s it is difficult to remember how little was known about these measurement issues, these basic facts, when the War on Poverty began. Major progress has been made on several fronts: (1) the incorporation of in-kind transfers, financial and human capital, the value of leisure time, and intrafamily transfers into a more comprehensive measure of economic well-being; (2) the establishment of long-run indicators of economic position; and (3) the development of theoretically sound measures of equivalence scales. This progress, in turn, depended on the combination of richer, more detailed survey research studies generated with antipoverty financial support,[34] and on the research efforts of economists and other analysts who brought technical expertise to bear on the data.

The progress to date means that any new public effort to reduce poverty would rest upon a far stronger base of data, measurement techniques, and knowledge than was available to social policy planners in 1965, yet a number of issues have barely been touched:

• Employer-provided fringe benefits (especially medical care and paid vacations) form a substantial portion of the economic compensation of some—usually higher-income—workers. The data available for the incorporation of this implicit income flow into measures of individual well-being is sorely deficient, inhibiting progress on this question.

34. The 1960s and 1970s witnessed substantial growth in the development of point-in-time and longitudinal microdata collected in household surveys. Several of these data projects were financed directly by OEO or by programs related to the War on Poverty, including the Surveys of Economic Opportunity, the Michigan Panel Study of Income Dynamics, the National Longitudinal Surveys of Labor Market Experience, the Survey of Income and Education, Project Talent, the Housing Market Practices Survey, and the longitudinal data bases from the several social experiments. References to and discussion of the contents of several of these data bases and their relationship to more recent data collection efforts can be found in David (1985).

- The measurement of the value to individuals of publicly provided benefits other than those in kind is constrained by both theory and data. No generally accepted measurement technique for ascertaining these values exists, and even if it did, the lack of microdata on the consumption of these benefits would preclude their reliable assignment to living units. A similar assessment would apply to taxes other than direct income and payroll taxes.
- Although measures of well-being depend on the variation of price-level differences among living units, individual price and budget constraint data are not available.
- Individual or household well-being is clearly dependent on the variance—or uncertainty—with which income flows or other components of well-being are expected over time. The data and techniques for both measuring and, especially, valuing this uncertainty are primitive. Yet uncertainty regarding future incomes and benefits is an important determinant of perceived well-being (see Haveman and Wolfe, 1985).
- A number of individual characteristics generate needs for which no existing analysis adequately accounts. Present or expected health or disability problems are the primary example. True well-being cannot be reliably assessed until the means for ascertaining the contribution of these characteristics to both needs and to the capability for enjoying resources (including leisure) are developed.
- A wide variety of locational, family-based, or job attributes directly determine economic well-being—children; neighborhood and environmental quality; and the danger, exposure, difficulty, and conditions of jobs come immediately to mind. A full assessment of these factors (some of which are reflected in income flows and prices, others of which are not) is essential if true poverty or inequality is to be assessed accurately. Again, both conceptual developments and data severely constrain progress.

The standard reflected in this catalog of remaining measurement issues is a very high one. Carried to its limit, it implies the need directly to measure individual utility itself—a goal that has eluded, and that will continue to elude, economists and statisticians. Yet this standard, when set against existing knowledge, points to meaningful directions for further research. While the view of observers differ widely on such questions, I regard the following as realistic next steps for progress in this area:

- The collection of longitudinal individual and household data incorporating information on participation in public programs, subjective assessments of both the relationship of income and wealth and the value of nonmarket contributions (e.g., children, environmental quality, work conditions, and uncertainty) to economic well-being, and objective assessments of health status, human capital, and physical wealth.[35]

- Theoretical research on the concepts and techniques for translating (1) subjective appraisals of nonmarket values and (2) the relationship of income and wealth to economic well-being into reliable empirical counterparts.[36]

35. The Survey of Income and Program Participation, now being conducted by the U.S. Bureau of the Census, is a major step in this direction. Extension of the data collected in this survey to subjective evaluations of important components of economic well-being is a logical next step; see David (1985).

36. The current efforts of both economic theorists and econometricians to develop methods of contingent evaluation are a move in this direction, although until now they have focused mainly on the valuing of environmental amenities. These techniques have direct relevance to the measurement of a full concept of economic well-being, and hence poverty and inequality. See Bohm (1972), Bishop and Heberlein (1979), and Brookshire et al. (1982).

5

Analyzing Public Income Support Policy and Its Effects

During the 1965–80 period, welfare assistance and income transfer policy were in a ferment of transition.[1] Charges of various sorts were leveled at the existing system: that it was inadequate to meet current needs, was uneven across the country, discouraged work and family stability, was stigmatizing and demeaning, was fraught with abuse. To correct these problems, a rainbow of proposals was put forward, ranging from modest revisions in administration and in benefit levels to negative and credit income taxes to children's allowances, public employment, and earnings subsidization. In these years every president save Lyndon Johnson was associated with some plan for major reform of the transfer system— Richard Nixon with the Family Assistance Plan (in two forms); Gerald Ford with a program that was drafted but never formally proposed, the Income Security Plan; and Jimmy Carter with the Program for Better Jobs and Income. Each plan caused a political stir and generated a large volume of newsprint. None, however, was enacted.

1. For the purposes of this chapter, the income support system is defined as the set of public programs that provide benefits in the form of cash or close substitutes for cash (e.g., food stamps, medical care, or housing) to individuals or households in order to enhance the level of economic well-being for those with inadequate alternative resources, or to assist in cushioning income losses due to retirement, disability, or the death of a spouse. Both welfare and social insurance programs are included.

The period nevertheless witnessed extensive changes in income transfer policy. The Social Security Amendments of 1967, 1972, and 1978 were incremental but substantial policy changes: Medicare and Medicaid became law; the Supplemental Security Income program unified and made national its predecessor, Aid to the Aged, Blind, and Totally Disabled; the Food Stamp program became a national negative income tax in the form of food vouchers; and the Earned Income Tax Credit provided an earnings supplement to low-income taxpayers with children.

Poverty researchers contributed to each step of this development. It was their description and critique of the system, and their research on its equity and efficiency effects, that fueled calls for reform. Their identification of the objectives to be served by transferring income guided reform proposals. Their analyses of reform objectives informed the designs of proposals offered, and their evaluation of the effects of transfers on economic behavior influenced much of the debate on the proposed reforms. To describe in succinct form the nature of these research contributions is difficult. Their number is large; they stem from many disciplines; they range from the most straightforward of institutional descriptions to the most complex of statistical analyses; they are both analytic and normative.

My discussion of these contributions of social scientists is divided in three parts: (1) a description and critique of the U. S. system of transfers of the mid-1960s; (2) an evaluation of the observed behavioral and distributional effects of income transfers of various types, and (3) the nature of various proposals for reform of the welfare and income support system. Within each of these areas I identify the major questions addressed by researchers and briefly characterize their answers. (Longer discussions of some of the research contributions may be found in Appendixes A and B.) This approach runs the risk of oversimplifying and distorting the conclusions of important and large research efforts, but it has the advantage of conveying in brief form the nature of social science research in this field while citing an extensive bibliography.

The U. S. Income Support System of the 1960s

As we have seen in the previous chapter, at the inception of the antipoverty campaign a sizable body of opinion held that being poor meant lacking money, and hence the cure appeared to be to provide low-income people with additional income. This view easily leads to a focus on income support policy. To those holding this opinion, mainly economists, announcement of a war on behalf of the poor appeared to be a unique opportunity. To reduce poverty, the failures of the existing income support system must be identified, the objectives to be served must be clarified, and changes to achieve these objectives proposed.

An important set of writings in the early 1960s identified the poverty problem as a national issue and established that lack of cash income was its major attribute. John Kenneth Galbraith (1958), Michael Harrington (1962), and Dwight MacDonald (1963), among others, made the nation conscious of substantial segments of the American population living in widely varying situations of economic destitution. These writings presented vivid images of Southern rural, largely black poverty; Appalachian rural, largely white poverty; urban young and heavily black poverty; the poverty of the aged and the disabled. Poverty came to be seen as a national problem, and policymakers responded to it by searching for measures that would be both politically acceptable and effective.

The Welfare System and Antipoverty Policy

Although an economic or income-based definition of poverty came to be accepted, few planning efforts considered the nation's income support system as an important instrument for aiding the poor. The task force established by President Johnson to plan the War on Poverty gave little serious attention to either expansion or reform of that system as a weapon in the arsenal of policy strategies. Instead, macroeconomic policies, education and training, and community action formed the heart of the nation's antipoverty effort. Although an income maintenance scheme was included in the list of policy proposals developed in 1965, it was regarded as peripheral to the main line of attack.[2]

The president's reluctance to employ the transfer system in the antipoverty effort was reflected in his 1965 decision to appoint a special presidential commission, the Heineman Commission, to address the issue of income transfer policy as an instrument in the War on Poverty. Although this appointment was in part designed to delay policy action, the commission stimulated a large set of studies that focused attention on needs-conditioned policies that were, in principle at least, intended to provide relief to the economically destitute. These writings described a "welfare crisis," which they identified with the failure of government income support policies to eliminate poverty or effectively to transfer cash income to the poor. Many of these contributions were written by scholars concerned with public policies and their efficacy; others were

---

2. The full plan of the War on Poverty was not released until several years after the war was initiated—and then only in congressional testimony by the first director of the OEO, Sargent Shriver; see Shriver (1973). See also Patterson (1986) and Brauer (1982) for detailed histories of the early planning and development efforts of the war.

conducted by the presidential commission. Their main purposes were to describe how social security and welfare programs had originated, how they were structured and how they functioned, and to assess whether or not they were effective policy instruments. Most were critical of what they found.

The primary critiques of the welfare system were economics-oriented policy analyses focusing on the incentives, efficiency, and equity of public assistance, together with legal and social analyses of the operation and administration of welfare programs and how they dealt with recipients. Most focused on the AFDC program,[3] the largest and most controversial of the programs operating at that time, though the relationship of it to other welfare and nonwelfare transfer mechanisms was also evaluated. The studies drew attention to several characteristics of the nation's income support system and its potentially serious and adverse economic and social impacts:[4]

1. Inadequate levels of benefit payments.
2. Horizontal inequities in the eligibility criteria applied to (and level of benefits available to) various groups of individuals (e.g., single parents versus two-parent families, working versus nonworking poor) and by geographic region. These inequities were largely attributed to the categorical nature of the system and the fact that states administered it and determined benefit levels.
3. Administrative discretion, resulting in arbitrariness and inequity.
4. High costs of the system, and the extent to which benefit levels nevertheless failed to aid the most needy.
5. Incentives implicit in the programs, especially those that encouraged reductions in work effort, increases in family and marital instability, and geographic mobility.
6. The overlapping nature of the programs and the opportunity for multiple-benefit recipiency.

3. Initiated in 1935 as part of the Depression-era legislation, AFDC provides cash assistance to female-headed families with children. While the operation of the program must conform to federal rules, administrative procedures and benefit levels are established by states. The program was originally viewed as transitional, designed to aid single women (mostly widows) to stay home rather than work while they had small children.

4. Early descriptions of the income support system that focused on these and other problems include U.S. Advisory Council on Public Assistance (1960), Wickenden and Bell (1961), Ten Broek (1964, 1965), Reich (1965), Steiner (1966), U.S. Advisory Council on Public Welfare (1966), *Income Maintenance Programs* (1968), Moynihan (1968), Tobin and Wallis (1968), and President's Commission on Income Maintenance (1969). Later discussions are in U.S. Congress, Joint Economic Committee (1972), and Barth, Carcagno, and Palmer (1973).

7. Inefficiencies due to the presence of in-kind (choice-constraining) rather than cash benefits.
8. Administrative inefficiencies due to multiple agencies and multiple and inconsistent eligibility rules, income definitions, means tests, and work requirements.

It can be seen that these analyses focused on the entire set of interrelated income support programs as of the mid-1960s and also criticized and documented the particular inefficiencies, inequities, and contradictions of the system. They stimulated intense social research into how the welfare system worked and how it affected those served by it.

Two forces combined to stimulate research on the nature and impacts of the income-conditioned transfer system. The first was the set of writings which, viewing this system as a whole, found it ineffective and inadequate. The second was the rapid growth of the costs and caseloads of the AFDC program during the 1960s, in spite of legislation in 1962 designed to encourage recipients to become self-supporting (by providing counseling and training services and permitting certain work expenses to be covered by earnings before welfare grants were reduced), followed by partly punitive legislation in 1967, designed both to mandate and to further encourage work by creating a work-incentive and training program to which recipients could be assigned and by adding a set of financial incentives for work—the so called "30 and one-third rule," which allowed recipients to keep the first $30 earned and one-third of earnings thereafter.

The most detailed research on the welfare system consisted of a study of the Wisconsin AFDC program conducted in 1967–68 by Joel Handler and Ellen Jane Hollingsworth,[5] who investigated the characteristics of AFDC clients, their attitudes toward the program, the relationship of AFDC to work programs, and the role of caseworkers. They found that clients had few skills; the 20 percent who worked at all were in low-paid and difficult jobs. Many incurred high costs of working, and large numbers of nonworkers had sought jobs. About one-half of them wanted work "very much."[6] Over half indicated "embarrassment" at being a

5. The studies of Handler and Hollingsworth were reported in a series of Discussion Papers put out by the Institute for Research on Poverty and in a major research monograph (1971); see References.
6. Handler and Hollingsworth found that Wisconsin welfare recipients did not conform to the popular image of being minority members, recent immigrants to the state, having little marital experience and education, and destined to spend many years on welfare. A comparative analysis revealed, however, that many of the Wisconsin characteristics differed from those of Chicago and New York; see Greenleigh Associates (1960) and Podell (1967).

recipient,[7] though there was little resentment toward aspects of the system commonly thought to be objectionable, such as the means test, unannounced caseworker visits, or other aspects of coercion, nor were there strong feelings of stigma.[8] Caseworkers were found to be strongly oriented toward providing counseling and training to help the client achieve independence and less favorable toward liberalizing earned-income rules or providing a minimum income guarantee. Perceptions differed, however; caseworkers saw themselves as emphasizing employment in dealing with clients, but clients did not agree. Caseworkers had substantial discretion in calculating benefits and, through generous "deductions" from earnings, made it virtually impossible for low-skilled clients to work their way off the welfare rolls.

This research verified many of the more global criticisms of the system—its uneven and discretionary nature, its deleterious and stigmatizing effects on a group of the nation's citizens who were truly poor, generally passive, with little opportunity for working themselves out of their condition.

How Strongly Does the Welfare System Discourage Work?

A recurrent criticism of the transfer system in the 1960s was its discouragement of work through a high "tax rate" on earnings. This charge, and the 1962 and 1967 changes in policy, stimulated research to determine empirically the "true" marginal tax rate in the AFDC program. The earliest work documented what had already been sensed by welfare experts—that substantial administrative discretion was involved in calculating grants, and that the manipulation of work-related expenses was used in some states to reduce work disincentives to very low levels.[9] Empirical studies by Lurie (1974), Bendt (1975), Hutchens (1978), and

---

7. A common criticism of the program was that it "stigmatized" clients, since welfare recipients were viewed as immoral (associated with high rates of illegitimacy, desertion, or parental imprisonment) or undesirable (owing to appearance, low income, or ascribed behavior). Because they were demeaned or embarrassed or uncomfortable or subjected to hostility, recipients, it was hypothesized, came to think of themselves in terms of their labels or their perception of how people view them. Efforts to define stigma can be found in Goffman (1963) and Matza (1966).

8. Weisbrod (1970) found this low level of reported stigma to be consistent with the notion that *marginal* stigma costs are very low, once a person becomes a recipient; stigma represents a fixed cost associated with becoming a recipient; once on the rolls, the net benefits of the program are positive—stigma then becomes irrelevant in subsequent decisions regarding program use.

9. Heffernan (1973) reported that in some states caseworkers took pride in generating enough expenses so that the remaining earned income used to offset benefits fell to zero.

Moffitt (1980) relied upon microdata on AFDC households[10] to estimate the relationship between changes in benefits and changes in earnings—the "true" benefit-reduction rate related to earnings. Their findings verified that, because of the treatment of work-related expenses and the other discretionary elements in calculating benefits, the benefits on average were reduced by far less than 100 or 67 percent in response to earnings. The average estimated benefit-reduction rate was in the 40 to 50 percent range. Moreover, wide variation occurred across states.

The overall result of this research was to blunt strong assertions that work disincentives were implicit in the welfare system and to verify the extent of both administrative discretion and horizontal—largely state-related—inequity in the treatment of recipients.

Should Income Support be Provided in Cash or In Kind?

With implementation of the 1967 Social Security Act amendments, which emphasized integration of social and employment services with public assistance, federal expansion of income support for low-income families began to take the form of in-kind benefits. The Food Stamp program expanded rapidly in the late 1960s, as did Medicare and Medicaid, and the Housing and Urban Development Act of 1968 stimulated rapid growth in public and subsidized housing programs. These policy developments caused researchers to reconsider their traditional opposition to in-kind transfers, and substantial debate on the provision of cash versus in-kind benefits ensued.

The standard case made by economists against in-kind benefits was based on efficiency considerations, stemming directly from neoclassical "indifference curve" analysis, which showed that the beneficiary would achieve at least as much satisfaction, typically more, if given the cash equivalent of the in-kind subsidy. This fundamental proposition was seriously undermined in the late 1960s by analyses that took account of taxpayer preferences, in addition to those of beneficiaries, in discussing efficiency (Aaron and von Furstenberg, 1971; Garfinkel, 1973b). Some level of in-kind provision was found to be efficient, since taxpayers preferred in-kind to cash redistribution in certain cases. Other analysts found even this result to be too limited. Some argued on grounds other than economic efficiency that it was not the role of government to decide how individuals should allocate their consumption (Friedman, 1962);

10. The data used in these studies were from the biennial federal AFDC survey, containing information on benefits, earnings, work-related expenses, and location of a sample of AFDC recipients. See Barr and Hall (1975) for a somewhat different approach and data base.

others emphasized the unintended consequences of government's efforts to influence private consumption patterns (Steiner, 1971); still others argued that the preferences of powerful producer groups could be aided by in-kind provision.

The debate stimulated a number of research efforts to measure the extent to which recipients discounted benefits received in kind as opposed to cash (Browning, 1975; Clarkson, 1976; MacDonald, 1977; Smolensky et al., 1977). These results indicated—again, as consistent with economic theory—that those in-kind benefits that are close substitutes for cash (e.g., Food Stamps) have small recipient discounts, while those less likely to be chosen for purchase out of cash income (e.g., public housing) have larger discounts.

A few studies during this period attempted to estimate the value accruing to taxpayers (as donors) of the provision of in-kind benefits, reflecting the notion that aid to meet specific needs is valued more highly by donors than is unrestricted cash assistance (Aaron and McGuire, 1970; Maital, 1973; Smolensky et al., 1977). The studies suggested that the value of these benefits to donors grew in proportion to donors' income; hence, among high-income taxpayers the cost of in-kind benefits tended to offset their tax cost.

This research supported the standard view that in-kind transfers are less valuable to recipients than equivalent cash transfers, although among most of the existing in-kind transfers (food, housing, medical care), the efficiency loss did not appear to be substantial. Moreover, the recipient loss was partially offset by donor (taxpayer) gains. These results, however, seemed to have little effect on economists' support for cash rather than in-kind transfers (see Barth, Carcagno, and Palmer, 1973).

What Determines Participation in Transfer Programs?

Early criticism of the transfer system regarding horizontal inequities caused by low program participation, plus the rapid expansion in costs and caseloads that occurred after 1965, led to research on the levels and determinants of program participation rates. Why did some eligible individuals choose to participate, others not? Why did participation rates vary widely across particular population groups and programs?

The research findings were diverse. The doubling of the AFDC caseload between 1967 and 1971, for example, was found to result largely from increases in participation of eligible people; by the early 1970s almost all eligibles were enrolled in some states (Boland, 1973; Michel, 1980). Both the Food Stamp and SSI programs, however, were found to have far lower participation rates, ranging from 50 to 60 percent even in the late 1970s.[11] Studies of participation by groups found substantial variation according to region, education, income, and the potential amount of benefits.[12] Lower rates were found in the Midwest; among the more educated, more urban, higher-income eligibles; and especially among those whose participation would yield small benefits.[13] The implication of this last finding is important—namely, low participation rates do not imply that those with substantial need or very low incomes are excluded from the rolls owing either to lack of knowledge or to administrative discretion; in fact, the horizontal-equity criticism of transfer programs in terms of participation rates may be overstated.

A number of studies sought to explain these variations in participation patterns by examining the individual choices made by those who were eligible. Much of this research adopted the utility-maximization framework of economists, in which participation rates were viewed as the outcome of choices between work (and the earnings associated with it) and transfer recipiency (and the income-tested benefits associated with it).[14] The findings strongly indicated that program-benefit parameters affect program participation, as do family labor market opportunities and a variety of other family characteristics taken to reflect tastes. All of the studies, however, encountered difficulty in effectively modeling program administrative characteristics,[15] and all adopted different indicators of program benefit levels. Their findings indicated that nonparticipation was less serious than commonly asserted. They supported the view that outreach and reduction of stigma and administrative discretion are essential if the full benefits of programs are to be made available to those for

11. See MacDonald (1977), Warlick (1981), and Coe (1982). The findings concerning the Food Stamp program were used in litigation against the government, leading in several cases to court-mandated outreach (publicity) efforts.

12. In 1975–76, participation in the AFDC program ranged from 95 percent (District of Columbia) to 56 percent (Arizona), that in the SSI program, from 77 percent (Louisiana) to 20 percent (Nebraska); see Warlick (1981). In 1974, the Food Stamp participation rates ranged from 58 percent (California) to 12 percent (North Dakota); see MacDonald (1977).

13. This finding is consistent with Weisbrod's conjecture that stigma costs are largely fixed, and are associated with the one-time decision of whether or not to participate (Weisbrod, 1970).

14. Examples include Brehm and Saving (1964), Durbin (1973), Barr and Hall (1976), Hall (1981), and Hosek (1982).

15. Subsequent studies have attempted explicitly to understand the contribution of agency or caseworker discretion to program participation. Administrative practices, however, have had to be proxied by acceptance rates, demographic or behavioral restrictions, the treatment of earnings in calculating benefits, and a variety of "process efficiency" variables used to judge agency performance. These analyses point to a substantial and independent role of administrative discretion in determining the program participation rate. See Holmer (1975), Wiseman (1977), and Willis (1977, 1980).

whom they were designed (Warlick, 1981). Interestingly, however, none of these studies attempted to validate the nonparticipation estimates by field research designed to identify those eligible for, but not participating in, transfer programs. All of them are therefore vulnerable to biases in income reports in the standard surveys they used.

What Are the Equity and Efficiency Implications
of a Categorical System?

The categorical nature of the income transfer system (i.e., separate programs for specific groups), in combination with inconsistent benefit-eligibility rules, benefit structures, income definitions, and program administrative arrangements, generated concern over work incentives in the system and over the horizontal inequities it may generate. Lurie (1975) stated: "Because each program was developed without careful regard to the other programs, the programs overlap in coverage, leave gaps in coverage, and often work at cross-purposes with each other" (p. 1). Moreover, when individuals are able to secure benefits from numerous income-tested programs, the benefit-reduction (tax) rates on earned income cumulate, creating the potential for very large work disincentives.

Policy proposals for revision of the transfer system often cited the problems associated with the categorical system as a major rationale for change. The issue of nonintegration occupied a prominent position in the Special Public Welfare Study sponsored by the Subcommittee on Fiscal Policy of the Joint Economic Committee of the Congress (1972–74), and was the focus of a congressionally sponsored conference on transfer program integration, held in 1972 (see U. S. Congress, Joint Economic Committee, 1972, 1974).

Research stemming from the congressional study produced important findings. Consider the issue of multiple program participation: most households who received benefits from one income support program were found to receive benefits from at least one or two more, and up to six or eight in total,[16] resulting in a cumulation of benefit-reduction rates to over 100 percent, so that recipients receive no net gain from increasing earnings in these ranges. More seriously, "notches"—a situation in which $1 of additional earnings leads to a complete cut-off of benefits from a program (in effect, an infinite tax rate)—were found to be widespread in the system.[17] Serious problems of gaps in coverage and horizontal ine-

16. See Storey, Cox, and Townsend (1973). Supplemental evidence on multiple benefits in New York City appeared in Lyon et al. (1976).

17. Hausman (1975). This problem is largely caused by the tie between AFDC and Medicaid benefits; when a recipient's own income increases sufficiently to eliminate AFDC

quities, in addition to the problems of work disincentives and notches, were uncovered in research from the perspective of recipients other than that of the AFDC mother—in particular, the disabled and Food Stamp recipients. While some severely disabled individuals were receiving adequate, if not generous, transfer benefits, others with equally serious impairments remained in poverty (Conley and Noble, 1973; Johnson and Murphy, 1975; Conley, 1979; Muller, 1980). In spite of these levels of multiple recipiency, a study of Food Stamp recipients documented the contribution of cumulated benefits to poverty reduction, and suggested that cumulation rarely pushed otherwise poor families very far above the poverty line.[18]

These research efforts were a direct response to policy concerns with work disincentives and cumulative benefits. They, in turn, contributed to a variety of efforts to devise program changes to reduce both the inequities of the categorical system and the inefficiency resulting from labor-supply disincentives. These program proposals included systematic sequencing of benefits; consolidation or integration of program benefits; uniform definitions of eligibility, income, family size; elimination of notches; offsetting high cumulative tax rates via earnings supplements; and replacement of existing programs with universal negative income tax (or demogrant) programs.[19]

What Should be the Objectives of an Effective Income Transfer System?

Critiques in the mid-1960s led to a search for a statement of objectives that could guide reform of the system. If nearly $30 billion per year was being spent on several dozen programs under a system riddled with gaps, overlaps, inefficiencies and inequities, how could it be redesigned to

---

benefits, the family automatically loses free medical coverage under Medicaid. Aaron (1973) stated: "In concrete terms . . . a mother of three, lucky enough to live in one of the relatively generous states . . . and to receive benefits under all four programs [AFDC, Food Stamps, public housing, Medicaid], can count on a basic guarantee of $5,860. If she can earn $2,000 working part time, her net spendable income will rise $556. But out of the next $5,000 she might earn, her income would rise only $1,307. In fact, her income would be higher if she earned $4,000 than if she earned $8,400, because of the loss of Medicaid and Food Stamps [at the higher earnings level]" (p. 35).

18. MacDonald (1983). Changes in Food Stamp legislation since 1979, the year of Macdonald's data, suggest that fewer families in this range of the income distribution are receiving benefits from multiple programs than reported by MacDonald.

19. These alternatives are extensively discussed in Lurie (1975). See especially the chapters by Hausman (1975), Mirer (1975), Haveman (1975), Aaron (1975), Marmor (1975), and Okner (1975).

achieve its goals at less cost? Would not a single, well-designed program be superior to the large set of categorical programs?

While attention to delineation of goals was not a central part of the social policy literature that accompanied initiation of the War on Poverty, some analyses did attempt to identify objectives. The clearest statement of goals, which did not appear until the early 1970s,[20] outlined eight:

1. Provision of a nominally adequate income level to those who cannot work and, in tandem with social insurance and employment programs, to those who can work.
2. Targeting benefits on those most in need.
3. Coordination and integration of programs to achieve administrative efficiency.
4. Similar treatment of similar individuals (horizontal equity); in particular, reduction of administrative discretion and interstate benefit differentials.
5. Vertically equitable treatment such that those who earn more have more total income.
6. Encouragement of self-sufficiency by providing work incentives.
7. Reduction or elimination of incentives for family breakup.
8. Attention to making the system understandable, coherent, and subject to fiscal control.

Economic Effects of the U. S. Income Transfer System

Dissatisfaction of both policymakers and policy researchers with U. S. transfer programs in the 1960s moved research into two directions. On one hand, scholars wanted to know the quantitative extent of some of the criticism regarding the impacts of income transfer policy: How ineffective was it in reducing poverty or equalizing the income distribution? How large were its potentially adverse labor-supply effects? On the other hand, the research community desired to participate in and contribute to the ongoing public and political debate over how to reform the programs that followed declaration of the War on Poverty. This section describes the first of these research directions; examination of the policy proposals formulated by researchers and analysts follows.

To What Extent Have Transfers Reduced Work Effort?

The question of whether or not welfare programs and income transfer policies cause people to work less has dominated public debate over

20. See Barth, Carcagno, and Palmer (1973). An earlier statement of objectives was offered by Stein (1971).

welfare reform and antipoverty policy. Worries about both the answer to the question and, indeed, the political sensitivity of the question itself, led early planners to exclude income transfer measures from their list of proposed policy instruments. The War on Poverty was to offer, as President Johnson had put it, "a hand up, not a handout." Yet to many social scientists—the economists especially—income transfers seemed the most straightforward and direct way to reduce poverty. The case for an income strategy could not be made, however, until the impacts of transfers on labor supply were actually measured. Hence the development of a minor industry of labor-supply studies of income transfers. (See Appendix B.)

While almost any component of an income transfer program could lead to changes in labor supply, nearly all research on this question focused on the two program characteristics that economic theory suggested would induce a response in work effort—the program's income guarantee level (the payment to a family with no other income) and its benefit-reduction rate (the amount by which benefits are reduced as other income, such as earnings, increases.) A guarantee of income tends to reduce the need to work to achieve some minimal level of living; the higher the guarantee, the greater the disincentive. The benefit-reduction rate reduces the net reward for each hour of work, inducing substitution of leisure for work. Although the estimated wage and income responses varied substantially among the many econometric studies of labor-supply behavior, nearly all indicated that the desired work effort of an individual falls as nonlabor income rises and as the net wage rate falls.[21] The implication for expansion of income transfers was clear, even though the degree of response implicit in the estimates varied. These general results were confirmed by the large-scale experimental studies which were undertaken expressly to measure labor-supply responses to income transfers.[22] Although these studies confirmed the tendency of transfer programs to reduce labor supply, they did not provide any direct estimates of the total effect of the transfer system on work effort.

Two recent studies have addressed this issue of the aggregate labor-supply effect of transfers. Both rely on the large number of empirical labor-supply studies, and both attempt to arrive at an aggregate impact

21. See Cain and Watts (1973) for a sample of these early analyses and a critique of the methods used and the results obtained. Later studies and their results are described and critiqued in Killingsworth (1983).

22. Experimental results are discussed in Watts and Rees (1977), Keeley (1978), and Keeley et al. (1978). The first reference presents the results from the New Jersey Income Maintenance Experiment; the second two report on the labor-supply results in the Seattle-Denver Income Maintenance Experiment. For a review and critique of these studies, see Pechman and Timpane (1975), Rossi and Lyall (1976), and Hausman and Wise (1985). Chapter 9 in this volume also examines this research methodology.

from the estimated results in the individual studies. While large amounts of extrapolation and personal judgment were required in both cases, their results were similar. Danziger, Haveman, and Plotnick (1981), relying on a systematic survey of the studies of actual transfer programs, concluded that aggregate reduction in labor supply attributable to public transfer programs was about 5 percent. Lampman (1978), extrapolating from available estimates of the effects of guarantees (income) and net wage rates (substitution), attributed a 7 percent reduction in labor supply to the growth of income transfer programs and the taxes required to finance them over the period from 1950 to 1975. Because the former study did not include estimates of the disincentive effects of the taxes associated with the transfers, the results from the two studies are consistent.

To What Extent Have Transfers Increased Unemployment?

Several aspects of income support policy, especially the Unemployment Compensation (UC) program (interchangeably termed Unemployment Insurance, UI), would appear to encourage both employers and employees to make decisions that result in higher measured unemployment: the income cushion provided by transfers tends to induce longer job search times; the incomplete experience rating system (by which employer layoff records are translated into their contributions to UC) tends to induce less-than-optimal employer efforts to reduce employment instability; the work-registration requirements of some transfer programs may induce an artificial increase in reported unemployment.

A large number of studies have attempted to measure the various impacts of unemployment benefits.[23] Taken together, the analyses suggest that at high unemployment rates (say 8 to 10 percent), the contribution of income transfers to the measured unemployment rate could be as high as one percentage point. Because a large share of this impact is attributable to the effect of the work-registration requirements in some programs, the true impact of transfers on unemployment is likely to be substantially less, especially at lower rates of unemployment.

To What Extent Have Transfers Reduced Savings?

The link between income transfers—in particular, social security survivor and retirement benefits—and savings is more complex than that between transfers and labor supply, but again the expectation is that increases in

23. The effects of UC on labor supply are assessed in Danziger, Haveman, and Plotnick (1981) and, more recently and fully, in Bosworth (1984). Hamermesh (1977) and Gustman (1980) extensively reviewed primary studies of the relationship between UC and the duration of unemployment. Important contributions on this issue include Feldstein (1976), Clark and Summers (1982), and Moffitt and Nicholson (1982).

public transfers lead to reductions in private savings. Because the system tends to transfer income from higher-income people (with high savings propensities) to lower-income people (who save less, at the margin), total savings are likely to be decreased.[24] In a fully employed economy, the increased consumption would come largely at the expense of investment, and would likely result in some slackening of production and growth.

The potential impact of income transfers on private savings has been extensively researched, especially with respect to the role played by social security. Three possible mechanisms by which these benefits interact with the savings rate have been identified. First, the expectation of social security retirement benefits may lead citizens to save less for their later years. Because the system operates on a pay-as-you-go basis, there is no public saving to offset reduced private saving; and as a result, total saving in the economy will fall. The second mechanism may partly offset this: because of social security, some people may retire earlier and hence require more retirement income than otherwise, causing them to work and save more in their preretirement years, thus increasing total saving in the economy. Finally, again because the social security system works on a pay-as-you-go basis, income is being transferred from young people to older people. If parents wish to leave a specific bequest to children, they may increase its amount so as to offset the increased tax burden on their children caused by the social security system. The result may be an increase in saving, thus reinforcing the second mechanism.

Both time-series and cross-sectional analyses have been undertaken to identify the quantitative impact of social security on savings.[25] The wide variation in the estimates is the source of a major controversy within the economics profession. Feldstein's (1974) assertions of a powerful depressing effect of social security on savings were found to be based on estimates that incorporated a serious computer-programming error. Leimer and Lesnoy (1982) were unable to find a significant savings effect of social security after correcting the error and trying out a variety of alternative models. Acknowledging the error, Feldstein nevertheless continued to find significant negative effects under modified models. A

24. This relationship is implicit in most empirical models designed to simulate the effect of policy changes on the economy. Golladay and Haveman (1977) reported that an increase in the income transfer system of $1 billion through adoption of a negative income tax would increase aggregate consumption spending—at the expense of saving—by $.45 billion. Using a life-cycle framework, however, Blinder (1975) indicated that transfers favoring the poor may, in fact, decrease consumption.

25. Both time-series and cross-sectional studies are reviewed in Danziger, Haveman, and Plotnick (1981) and Aaron (1982). The primary studies are those of Feldstein (1974), Barro (1978), Blinder et al. (1981), Feldstein and Pellechio (1979), Kotlikoff (1979), and Leimer and Lesnoy (1982).

generally consistent story from all of this research—and perhaps the current consensus—is that social security has depressed private savings by a small amount, but that this amount has not yet been measured precisely.

These studies, it should be emphasized, focus on social security survivor and retirement payments alone, not on the effect of the entire income support system, and they do so in the context of full employment. For an economy operating at less than full employment for long periods of time, the effect may be quite different.

Do Income Transfers Affect Other Aspects of Economic Behavior?

A variety of additional economic and behavioral effects have been attributed to transfers—concerning cyclical stability, inflation, human capital investment, demographic decisions (including the choice of living arrangements, childbearing, and marital status), health, locational choices, productivity and attitudes toward work, and labor market efficiency. Although important studies have treated these effects,[26] the research is neither so extensive or intensive as on the impacts of labor supply, unemployment, or savings.

The overall conclusions can be summarized as follows: Income transfers offset about 40 to 50 percent of income losses, and hence serve to buffer the effects of economic setbacks; income transfers have contributed to some extent to price inflation (largely through increased third-party payments for health care, escalating medical care prices); the incentives of income transfers encourage marital separation, larger families, and migration toward high-benefit regions, but the evidence on these effects suggests that the impact has been small; income transfers tend to encourage specialization and job search and hence better job matches, leading to a more efficient labor market, though there is only weak evidence on such effects; income transfers (largely Medicaid and Medicare) have significantly reduced infant and maternal death rates and have improved the other aspects of health status that are affected by additional health care services.

Redistributive Aspects of Transfers

Criticisms regarding the efficiency effects of the income transfer system on labor supply, unemployment, savings, migration, and family structure

26. The primary studies on demographic choices are Bradbury et al. (1977), Hannan, Tuma, and Groeneveld (1978), MacDonald and Sawhill (1978), and Bishop (1980); on cyclical stability, Gramlich (1974) and Hamermesh (1977); on productivity, Abramovitz (1981); on human capital formation, Garfinkel (1973c); and on health status, Davis and Schoen (1978) and Paul Starr (see Danziger and Weinberg, 1986).

carry with them fairly clear indications of the concepts that should be used in gauging impacts. Assertions regarding the equity impacts—those concerning the extent to which transfers alter income inequality—are more difficult to deal with. In the mid-1960s, economists had little experience in measuring the income-distributional effects of policies; no ready-made set of measurement concepts was available, and the questions that one would wish to ask regarding equity had not yet been rigorously posed. When these issues became the focus of policymakers and the topic of public discussion, research economists turned their attention to this issue.

An important line of research attempted to identify the particular equity-based effects of transfer policy that should be measured. A large family of measurement concepts was discussed and proposed for use in quantitative evaluations. A more detailed discussion of these concepts is presented in Appendix A; the following summary briefly identifies the major concepts and the policy questions addressed by each.

A Comprehensive Transfer Account. Public income transfers are of various sorts and interact with a range of other transfers and income-generation mechanisms in the U. S. economy. How can the role of public transfers in transforming "producer incomes" into "user incomes" be observed and measured? A social accounting concept—a unified and comprehensive transfers account—was developed and estimated by Robert Lampman (1957, 1966, 1969c, 1971a, 1984).

Target Efficiency. The establishment of the transfers account framework enabled a variety of other questions to be asked about the impact of transfers. One of the most important was, to what extent does a program benefit those for whom it was designed? Target-efficiency ratios—both vertical and horizontal—were developed and used by Weisbrod (1969) to measure the impact of a program on the target group (relative to other groups) and on individuals within the target group.

Welfare Weights. Target-efficiency ratios suggest that program benefits have value only if they aid those in a particular group. A more sophisticated notion is that the value of a program's benefits depends on the characteristics of the individuals who receive them, higher weights being attached to dollars of benefit going to certain individuals rather than to others. This notion of welfare weights comes out of the "Pareto-optimal redistribution" literature in economics, and was first introduced into the poverty policy area by Ribich (1968) and Watts (1969). A later extension of it was made by Harberger (1983).

The Poverty Gap. One of the most widely used concepts in appraising the effectiveness of poverty policy is that of the poverty income gap—the number of dollars required to lift all poor families to the poverty line. The antipoverty effectiveness of a program can be directly measured by calculating the poverty gap after a program is put in place, minus the gap before the program, divided by total expenditures on the program. The development and use of this concept is closely associated with the work of Lampman.[27]

"Leapfrogging" as an Indicator of Horizontal Inequity. The extent to which an income transfer program benefits some families with particular characteristics and not others has important political consequences. A method of measuring the extent to which programs cause some families to surpass, or leap over, other families in the income ranking was called the leapfrogging ratio. It was first used in an analysis by Plotnick and Skidmore (1975).

Using a variety of these equity measures, a large number of studies have attempted to gauge the redistributive effects of income transfers. While this research has focused on the effect of transfers on the incidence of poverty or the level of inequality, a number of other redistributive impacts have also been analyzed. The general method of these studies is to employ nationally weighted survey data with either reported or imputed information on cash transfers, in-kind benefits, and tax liabilities, and to compare aspects of the income distribution with and without the presence of transfers.[28] More recent studies have, in addition, attempted to adjust reported earned income data to take account of estimated behavioral reponses (e.g., labor supply) in the presence of transfers (see Plotnick, 1980).

This research has produced a number of important results on the equity impacts of income transfers:[29]

- In 1965, public cash income transfers decreased the incidence of poverty by 19 percent (from 21 to 17 percent of the population). By about 1980 transfers reduced poverty by 40 percent (from 22 to 13 percent).
- Income defined to include in-kind transfers caused poverty to decline to about 6 percent in 1980.
- Transfers are concentrated most heavily on the aged and on female-headed households. Over time the reduction in poverty among the aged due to transfers has been substantial. Nonaged women who head

---

27. The poverty gap (or income gap) was first introduced in the 1964 *Economic Report of the President*, to which Lampman contributed. The concept was extensively used by Lampman in his work.

28. See especially Smeeding (1975) and Hoagland (1980).

29. These results are taken primarily from Smeeding (1975), Browning and Johnson (1979), Plotnick and Smeeding (1979), Paglin (1980), Hoagland (1982), and Danziger, Haveman, Plotnick (1986).

households rely heavily on transfers, but transfers have not had an increased effect in reducing poverty for this group over time.

- Public income transfers, including those in kind, increased the income share of individuals in the lowest fifth of the population by about 5 to 6 percentage points (from about 1 percent to about 6 percent) in 1980, up from about 3 percentage points in 1965.
- Public income transfers resulted in a reduction in income inequality (as measured by the Gini coefficient) by about 20 percent in 1980, as compared to about 11 percent in 1965.

Reforming the U. S. Income Support System

The work of social scientists in understanding how the nation's income support system worked and how it affected economic behavior was complemented by a number of attempts to contribute in a more direct way to the public debate on restructuring and extending the transfer system. This debate occurred with regularity during the 1965–80 period, and grew more intense with each new presidential announcement of a plan for reform. The proposals evoked from poverty researchers both analytic critiques and alternative proposals.

The problems posed by this topic seemed ideally suited to economic analysis. The search for policy alternatives was a clear case of "constrained maximization." Benefit coverage should be increased to eliminate inequity, and work disincentives should be reduced; but additional budget costs should be minimized. Administration of the system should entail less discretion and be more uniform, consistent, and integrated; but important distinctions between the deserving and undeserving poor, and those who should and should not be expected to work, should be maintained. The abuses and inefficiencies of multiple-benefit recipiency should be eliminated, but benefit adequacy should be maintained.

In addition to the constraints of costs, work incentives, and adequacy, the search for reform was limited by seriously inconsistent values held by various groups in the population. In-kind benefits were viewed as inefficient by some, but as necessary to achieve taxpapers' objectives by others. Some put high weight on benefit adequacy and full coverage for the population; others considered the maintenance of work effort and the minimization of dependency to have the greatest value. Flexibility and discretion to some was viewed as demeaning interference by others. Horizontal equity requiring coverage of the working poor was valued highly by some, but was thought by others to eliminate the benefits of categorization.

Reforms Proposed by Researchers

Within this setting of multiple constraints and conflicting values, poverty researchers sought options to eliminate the major problems of the existing system while maintaining, and they hoped improving, its contribution to the well-being of the poor. Their reform proposals ranged from small changes in or additions to the system to replacement of the existing system with a fundamentally different structure. The first type envisioned modifications to diminish the problems of incentives, equity, and adequacy. Examples included (1) the "cashing out" of in-kind benefits; (2) the substitution of vouchers for direct in-kind benefit provision; (3) the integration of program benefit structures, eligibility requirements, and income and household definitions; (4) incremental expansion of social insurance transfers (e.g., extended coverage of unemployment benefits); (5) the adoption of earnings supplements, wage-rate subsidies, or payroll tax relief for low-wage or low-earnings workers; (6) the standardization of existing state-run or state-supplemented programs by instituting consistent administrative practices and a national minimum benefit level; and (7) increasing outreach or information efforts to raise program participation rates.[30] The second type of proposal was based on a quite different philosophy and set of objectives than those which underlay the existing system; it is these that we emphasize here.

Most of the proposals to overhaul the system sought to replace the existing mélange of overlapping, categorical transfer programs with a single, uniform system for income support. A prominent proposal was that of Milton Friedman (1962), whose plan predated the War on Poverty. He advocated what he termed a "negative income tax" (NIT), providing support through the national tax system: if an individual's income fell below the sum of allowable exemptions and deductions, he or she would receive a government subsidy of some portion of the difference. In Friedman's view, adoption of an NIT would enable numerous existing categorical transfer programs to be eliminated—including AFDC, Aid to the Aged, Blind and Totally Disabled, and a variety of in-kind assistance programs, such as social services.

This plan paled in comparison with other overhauls proposed at about

30. A sample of the writings containing suggestions or recommendations for modifying or extending the existing system includes Burns (1968), Schorr (1968), U.S. Congress, Joint Economic Committee (1968), Vadakin (1968), Zeckhauser and Schuck (1970), Brazer (1971), Kesselman (1971), Schorr (1971), Levitan, Rein, and Marwick (1972), Barth, Carcagno, and Palmer (1973), Barth (1974), Haveman, Lurie, and Mirer (1974), Lurie (1974); Plotnick and Skidmore (1975), Haveman and Palmer (1982), Lerman (1982).

this time. Robert Theobald (1963) recommended a form of NIT that incorporated a high guaranteed income and a dollar-for-dollar reduction of that subsidy until earned income reached a rather high level—an implicit 100 percent benefit-reduction rate. This plan would have been expensive to install and would have replaced a number of the cash and in-kind transfers which existed at that time. Theobald, however, consistent with his view that the U. S. economy is ever abundant and that people work because they enjoy it, did not address problems of work incentives or economic dislocations.

A third approach lay between that of Friedman and Theobald. The Family Security Program proposed by Edward Schwartz (1964) would have made a "demogrant" (benefit) available to all families, including those without children, at about the poverty line; the benefit would then be taxed at rates which ranged from about 60 percent for the very poorest families to about 90 percent for families with incomes between $3,000 and $4,000. Schwartz considered a major advantage of the plan its elimination of the means test in existing categorical programs, thereby avoiding much of the administrative discretion present in the current system. The plan would also establish uniform national support, eliminating regional differences. His plan encountered a standard difficulty inherent in such comprehensive schemes; by setting the income guarantee at about the poverty line, high marginal benefit-reduction rates were required to avoid major increases in budgetary outlays. The 90 percent benefit-reduction rates in Schwartz's plan would in fact have applied to the "working poor," who were at that time ineligible for income support and who would have experienced substantial work disincentives.

An alternative, and even more comprehensive, program was outlined by Earl Rolph (1967). His "credit income tax" would have provided uniform and universal cash benefits through a refundable tax credit mechanism, with a guarantee at about two-thirds of the poverty line. This portion of the proposal was combined with a totally revamped and streamlined positive income tax, removing all deductions and exemptions and subjecting all income to a constant tax rate of about 25 percent. Rolph made a strong case for this strategy: the problem of "genuine" poverty would be substantially reduced, the incentive problems due to high tax rates would be minimized, the complexity of the existing tax law would be "radically" reduced, the stigma associated with public assistance ("one of the most embarrassing programs in the country") would be eliminated, urban finances would be relieved, the migration of the rural poor to the cities would be ended, and the political forces driving most nonmilitary public spending programs—those designed to provide assistance to some interest group—would be blunted.

These early proposals stimulated efforts to revise and refine the design of NIT and demogrant plans to meet the objections raised to them and to place them into a form in which they could be legislated and implemented. A wide variety of issues surrounded the proposals: the processing and timing of supplement payments, the taxability of the supplements and their integration with the positive income tax, the administration of the plan, the relationship of benefits to family size and composition, the definition of the family unit, and the definition of income. In the process of designing proposals, model statutes were developed which were, implicitly, reform proposals of their own (see Klein, 1966; Green, 1967; Tobin, Pechman, and Miezkowski, 1967; Lampman, 1969).

As these plans were being drafted and refined by scholars and policy analysts, the ideas they contained and the values they reflected were having an impact on an arena more directly tied to policy-making. Both the U. S. Advisory Council on Public Welfare (1966) and the President's Commission on Income Maintenance Programs (1969)—the Heineman Commission—recommended a universal guaranteed income. In the council's view, states would continue to administer public welfare, but a nationwide program of assistance, "based upon a single criterion: need," would be adopted. The recommendations of the Heineman Commission were more far-reaching: "The Commission's main recommendation is for the development of a universal income supplement program to be administered by the Federal government, making payments to all members of the population with income needs" (p. 57). In effect, it set out a full-scale NIT plan with a guarantee at two-thirds of the poverty line and a tax rate of 50 percent. The commission suggested moving the guarantee up toward the poverty line over time, in the process replacing welfare programs. While these proposals were ostensibly those of the appointed commission, they were both influenced by and contributed to the growing body of poverty research during this period.

Presidential Proposals

Pressure for reform of the income support system was sustained by a series of proposals for reform advocated during successive presidential administrations. Nixon's Family Assistance Plan (FAP) appeared in two forms, neither of which passed (Nixon, 1969). Both versions were low-guarantee versions of an NIT for families with children. Too liberal a scheme for conservatives and too conservative for liberals, it ultimately failed because of concerns over labor-supply reduction when its benefit-reduction rate was cumulated with those in other programs.[31]

---

31. The story of FAP's design and final resolution is told in Moynihan (1973) and Burke and Burke (1974). The implicit marginal tax rates in FAP are discussed in Aaron (1973).

As a presidential candidate in 1971, George McGovern proposed a $1,000 demogrant as a welfare replacement scheme. And President Gerald Ford toyed with, but ultimately never proposed, an Income Security Plan structured very much along the lines of FAP. In 1977, Jimmy Carter proposed a Program for Better Jobs and Income (PBJI), which contained an NIT as its centerpiece, but emphasized differential treatment of those expected to work and those from whom work was not expected in return for aid. Lower income-support benefits were granted to the former group, along with a guaranteed public service job in case private-sector employment was unavailable. This proposal, like Nixon's plan, ultimately failed to pass.[32]

Each of these legislative proposals, both formal and informal, engaged activities of poverty researchers, who played an important role in critiquing and analyzing their efficiency and equity effects. In terms of efficiency, analysis focused largely on the labor-supply and savings impacts of income transfer proposals, although studies also sought to identify likely effects on family structure, fertility, and regional output patterns. The equity analyses evaluated the impact of proposed policies on the incidence and composition of poverty, and on inequality in the income distribution. In addition, some considered administrative effects. In the course of this analytical work, new techniques of research were developed and advanced, in particular social experimentation and microdata simulation, discussed in more detail in later chapters.

The earliest contributions of poverty researchers to these reform proposals were evaluations of the basic effects on efficiency and on horizontal and vertical equity to be expected from the more general NIT and demogrant proposals. Their purpose was to examine the proposals analytically, without necessarily undertaking the research necessary for full assessment of efficiency and equity effects.[33] The character of these contributions was thus more that of policy analysis than of basic research.

The second generation of research grew substantially more analytical. These studies attempted quantitatively to assess the impact of proposals on the incidence of poverty and on such behavioral responses as labor supply and savings. They relied largely on survey microdata to gauge quantitative impacts.[34] As this genre of analysis evolved, the data require-

32. See Anderson (1978) for a discussion of the background and contents of PBJI.

33. Examples of such analyses include Tobin, Pechman, and Miezkowski (1967); Diamond (1968); Browning (1973); Garfinkel (1973c); Haveman, Lurie, and Mirer (1974); Haveman (1975).

34. An early example of analysis focusing on distributional effects is Watts and Peck (1975). A number of microdata-based studies analyzed the labor-supply impacts of proposed transfer system reforms, including the papers in Cain and Watts (1973) by Orley

ments became increasingly demanding and the analytical methods increasingly sophisticated.

In evaluating labor-supply effects, two lines of research developed. First, to improve on the estimates of the responsiveness of labor supply to the income and substitution effects in reform proposals, a series of income maintenance experiments were undertaken (discussed in Chapter 9). Actual benefits, calculated from an NIT type of schedule, were given to large samples of randomly chosen families, and their labor-supply patterns were then measured and compared to those of a control group of families. These studies increased the reliability of estimates of the impact of NIT and demogrant proposals of various generosity and designs. In the course of doing so, researchers had to solve the considerable technical and methodological problems described later in this book. The methodology developed in these studies represents a significant advance in social science research and can be directly attributed to the antipoverty effort.

A second task was to incorporate estimates of labor-supply responses (in particular, the estimated income and substitution effects for various groups) available from both the econometric and experimental literature in microdata simulation models which were designed to evaluate the equity and efficiency impacts of reform proposals (see Chapter 11). In this form of modeling, response elasticities are applied to each observation in a nationally weighted survey data base to arrive at national estimates of labor-supply changes resulting from the benefit schedule of a proposed reform of the income transfer system. The expected costs and caseloads of the reform were also estimated. By and large, these studies did not find a large decline in labor supply under proposed reforms, and in a number of cases they recorded increased earnings.[35]

Poverty researchers also undertook studies of specific legislative reform proposals. Some were general studies focusing on incentive patterns, gaps in coverage and adequacy, adverse impacts on particular groups, and antipoverty effects. Others developed and applied new research techniques which have now become a part of the resources on which researchers can draw. And, as was true of studies of more general

---

Ashenfelter and James Heckman; Michael Boskin; Belton Fleisher, Donald Parsons, and Richard Porter; David Greenberg and Marvin Kosters; Robert Hall; and Russell Hill. A more recent analysis is that of Masters and Garfinkel (1977).

35. See Betson, Greenberg, and Kasten (1980, 1982), Haveman, Hollenbeck, et al. (1980), and Robins, West, and Lohrer (1980). These studies employed response coefficients from the experiments. Earlier microdata simulations using response estimates from the econometric studies include Greenberg and Kosters (1973), Rea (1974), and Masters and Garfinkel (1977). The state of the art in microdata simulation modeling was described in Haveman and Hollenbeck (1980) and is the subject of Chapter 11.

reform strategies, these analyses became increasingly sophisticated as analytic techniques advanced and the access to microdata became easier.[36]

Lessons and Future Directions of Poverty Research and Income Support Policy

Without the War on Poverty and the policy initiatives associated with it, the outpouring of research on income transfer policy described in this chapter would not have occurred. There is little question that this research has contributed in a major way to our understanding of the structure and impacts of this area of public policy. It influenced policy debate and brought facts, knowledge, and the scholars themselves closer to the policy process. It also enriched the social sciences.

Several contributions to our understanding of income transfer policy can be identified. First, the early "welfare crisis" literature alerted the nation to the structure of the income transfer system, and the potentially harmful effects associated with programs that were intended to be of help. As described above, ill effects included horizontal and vertical inequities, adverse incentives for work and family structure, and deleterious feelings among individual recipients in the form of stigma and rejection, among others.

This largely descriptive literature had the effect of generating an extensive body of research on the quantitative magnitude of the adverse impacts that were asserted to exist—the second major contribution. By and large, the empirical conclusions deflated the assertions. Causes of the "crisis" were verified, but the magnitude of the untoward results as described in that literature were generally found to be smaller than had been charged. In sum: recipients of welfare benefits do feel stigmatized, but their response to the system is not strongly negative; labor-supply disincentives do exist, but the "true" benefit-reduction rates are substantially less than those asserted; the estimate responses to these rates are sufficiently small that early fears of large-scale withdrawals from the labor force owing to existing or expanded welfare transfers were unfounded.

36. The primary analyses of specific reforms proposals include, for the Family Assistance Plan: Lampman (1969b, 1971b), Handler and Hollingsworth (1970), Zeckhauser and Schuck (1970), Bawden, Cain, and Hausman (1971), Haveman and Lampman (1971), Aaron (1973), Allen (1972), Golladay and Haveman (1977); for Senator Long's Earnings Supplementation Plan: Haveman, Lurie, and Mirer (1974), Haveman (1975); for McGovern's demogrant proposal: Lidman (1973); for the Program for Better Jobs and Income: Danziger, Haveman, and Smolensky (1977), Congressional Budget Office (1977), Betson, Greenberg, and Kasten (1980), Haveman, Hollenbeck, et al. (1980).

Moreover, even though from the recipient's perspective cash transfers are a more effective means of providing support than are in-kind transfers, the cash-equivalent values of the leading in-kind programs are estimated to lie close to the value of cash itself. And when the tastes of nonrecipients are also considered, the contribution of some in-kind benefits to aggregate economic welfare may exceed that of an equal cash contribution.

Concerning participation rates, the studies showed that lack of participation in many cases was the result of voluntary choices of those eligible—the costs of gaining benefits (dealing with social agencies, filling in forms, accommodating periodic audits, as well as the stigma associated with recipiency) were apparently greater than the benefits to be received. Granted that lack of information, administrative barriers, and other impediments to participation played an important role, they do not appear to have been the dominant cause, as ascribed in the early crisis literature. Finally, while a sizable portion of the very lowest income group receives benefits from multiple sources, that pattern is not widespread among those with incomes close to the poverty line. The system is not so unintegrated and inequitable as implied by the early literature.

The third contribution is that the early studies led to a volume of conceptual and empirical work on individual responses to income transfers and their impact on poverty incidence and income inequality. The role of the earlier literature in stimulating this work was, of course, reinforced by (1) substantial research support from government agencies that dealt with the poverty problem, (2) heightened concern with the rapid growth of income transfers during the 1960s and 1970s, and (3) the emergence of an applied field of study with its own approach and methods: program evaluation and policy analysis, the subject of Chapter 8. This field gained major importance in the social science disciplines, especially economics, and led to the development of a wide variety of both conceptual and methodological advances, among them (1) the initiation of social experimentation (Chapter 9) to measure individual responses to policy incentives; (2) the development of longitudinal data bases to permit more accurate measurement of the characteristics of individuals, analysis of the dynamics of changes in their well-being, program participation, and family structure over time, and evaluation of their responses to incentives implicit in public programs; (3) the formulation of statistical techniques to correct for selectivity problems (Chapter 10) and to enable accurate specification of the complex budget constraints implicit in many income transfer programs, especially in the face of multiple program recipiency; and (4) the development of both static and dynamic microsimulation modeling techniques (Chapter 11) for estimating and forecasting cost, caseload, and distributional impacts of proposed policies or policy changes.

Finally, scholars assumed a new role for which they had little prior training, little previous experience, and little understanding of the forces, largely political, at work—the role of policy and program design and evaluation. In the income transfer area, this work centered mainly on NIT and demogrant programs, but they were soon followed by similar endeavors in the areas of labor market policy, housing, health care, and education. These design, analysis, and evaluation efforts formed the core of the evolving subdiscipline of policy analysis or program evaluation. As we will see in Chapter 8, this field grew up within the confines of the traditional disciplines of economics, political science, operations research, and to a lesser extent sociology. Accommodating, absorbing, or contending with this new subdiscipline posed a challenge to each of these standard fields. The ways in which they have dealt with it have had a substantial impact on the structure of, and emphases within, the social science disciplines.

Hence the contributions to social science of researchers who focused on the development and analysis of income transfer policy are substantial. Major conceptual and especially methodological advances can be attributed to research in this area, which would not have been undertaken in the absence of a campaign on behalf of the poor, and the research support that accompanied it. These advances, and the concomitant increase in microdata and data-analysis capabilities, are basic to the academic community.

The future of this genre of poverty research seems unclear. Since 1980 few broad new policy initiatives have been proposed by either policymakers or academics. The critical analysis or design of policy proposals is a languishing art. Studies of the impacts of income support policy continue, but with modest financial support and little enthusiasm. The methodological developments directly traceable to concern with income support policy—social experimentation and microdata simulation modeling—proceed slowly for want of both the substantial research support which they require and interest in their findings. Yet one senses that the retrenchment of the 1980s is not permanent. The increases in poverty and inequality that have taken place in the 1980s may stimulate a renewed commitment in the 1990s to public action for the amelioration of social problems.

If this is true, does this chapter offer any lessons? Two can be suggested. First, it seems important that those policy design and evaluation skills once so much in vogue should not be allowed to atrophy. Their application to items anticipated to be on the social policy agenda in future years would seem to be of high priority. Policies to support successful school-to-work transitions, to encourage the move from transfer rolls to the workplace, to realign public support for the elderly toward young people and children, and to reduce youth unemployment seem prime candidates. Such activities would enhance the required analytic skills and perhaps lead rather than follow policy debate. Presumably, this next generation of program design and evaluation efforts will benefit from the realism gained from the experiences of the 1960s and 1970s.

Second, as the political interest in policy reform again increases, it seems inevitable that the research tools developed in conjunction with the War on Poverty will again be viewed as necessary instruments to gauge the equity and efficiency effects of proposed measures. The maintenance and updating of existing simulation models, the incorporation into them of superior data bases and estimated behavioral relationships, and the search for improved experimental design and evaluation techniques would appear to have high priority. Yet, given the costs of these research activities and the current lack of support for them, it seems unlikely that the social research community will be fully prepared for the next surge of interest in social policy. An opportunity may have been lost.[37]

37. This case is made in Berk et al. (1985).

6

Understanding Social Mobility, Status Attainment, and Income Dynamics

Most poverty research has focused on static issues: demographic structure in a certain period of time, the degree of inequality in observed socioeconomic status, the number and characteristics of people considered to be poor in any year, patterns of social behavior and interaction and their determinants. Less attention has been given to the process by which some people do, and others do not, succeed in attaining economic or social position, or the extent to which people are permanently or only transitionally in high or low status. Yet such questions are of central importance in policy-making designed to remove people from poverty. If most of the poor at any moment in time are in that state only temporarily, a safety-net income support system would seem most appropriate; if permanent poverty is the most common situation, more fundamental and enduring systems of education and training, public employment, and income maintenance would seem to be in order. Similarly, if parental background and race are found to be more important than education in determining economic position, policy approaches will differ accordingly.

Research on the issues of permanent versus transitory poverty and the process of social mobility has been constrained by the need for longitudinal information on individuals. The movement of people up and down the ladder of economic success, either over time or relative to their parents, must be observed if social mobility is to be measured and understood. Rudimentary efforts along this line were made in the 1960s and before, but real progress awaited the development of longitudinal microdata or data allowing the comparison of an individual's current status with his or her earlier status, or with parental status.

Since the late 1960s, increasing information on time-related personal experiences has become available and has promoted progress in understanding the mobility process and resulting social stratification. This chapter examines and critiques the findings produced by the mobility and stratification research effort in sociology—an effort that has been described by one of its central figures as having "made greater progress toward cumulative social science than any other branch of sociological research" (Featherman, 1981, p. 79).[1]

Early Studies of Mobility and Attainment

The study of social stratification and mobility has a long history in sociology. Indeed, "stratification" to sociologists incorporates many of the same issues and concerns that "inequality" encompasses for economists. Speculations, hypotheses, and analysis of perforce fragmentary data on the size and composition of—and the process of entering and leaving—various social classes (strata) has formed the substance of a major field in sociology.

Until about 1960, theoretical and conceptual discussions, supplemented by mobility table analyses, dominated studies in this field, and no unified framework existed for thinking about the process of movement into and out of various social and economic positions. The principal studies were by Sorokin (1927), Burt (1947), Rogoff (1953), Glass (1954), Prais (1955a, 1955b), Lipset and Bendix (1959), Svalastoga (1959), and Matras (1960). They focused on the occupations of individuals at a point in time, and sought to relate later to earlier occupations for an individual, or to relate father's and son's occupations. The extent of these relationships was measured by cross-tabulations producing what were known as occupational mobility tables. Techniques of a simple percentage analy-

---

1. Research on the determinants of poverty status in sociology, psychology, and political science has been far broader than the literature emphasized here. For example, a substantial radical literature attributes poverty and stratification to the structure of the economic system (e.g., Piven and Cloward, 1971). Another line of work emphasizes a "culture of poverty," attributing poverty to the psychological and cultural characteristics of family and community in which people are raised and in which they live. While both provocative and influential, this work is judged not to have led to a major redirection of emphasis within the respective disciplines in either substance or methodology.

sis of origin-by-destination, contingency table analysis using measures of association, and stochastic matrix analysis were applied. The greater the relationship between earlier (or father's) and later (or son's) occupation, the smaller the degree of social mobility that was presumed to exist, and the less permeable the social structure.

There was no formal model of mobility that guided this work, though an informal set of linkages was, at least implicitly, present in some of the discussions. A person's family background (including race), education and training, intelligence and motivation, career or family choices were all viewed as playing some role in determining the status that individuals ultimately attained. These personal variables were usually taken to be the primary determinants of social movement; relatively little attention was paid to the institutional mechanisms by which individual characteristics led to mobility. Nor was there any generally accepted statement concerning how these factors interacted to determine economic position and status. Measurement of the contribution of the various factors was fragmentary, and neglected the structure of the underlying process.

The Socioeconomic Life-Cycle Model

The first systematic sociometric statement of the dynamic process of social mobility appeared in the early 1960s. A paper by Duncan and Hodge (1963) formally presented this process in terms of a socioeconomic life cycle, distinguishing three primary stages: family, schooling, and job. Job (or occupation), conceptualized as "status conferring prestige" and measured on a scale indicating the degree of socioeconomic status (SES), was taken to be the variable to be explained, and family background and education were viewed as determinants of that status (see Figure 6.1). Education, however, was viewed as an intervening variable, determined in part by family background but also making an independent contribution to the status attained. The logic of this causal model indicated that

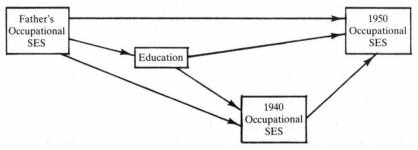

Figure 6.1. Assumed Causal Sequence of Variables (from figure 1 in Duncan and Hodge, 1963, published by The University of Chicago Press © 1963 The University of Chicago).

the following questions were most relevant: (1) What is the gross association between the SES of the occupations of sons and their fathers? (2) How is this association mediated by the intervening factor of educational attainment? (3) What is the net association of educational attainment and SES of sons, apart from the dependence of a son's educational attainment on father's SES? In answering these questions, researchers emphasized the degree to which the process is determinative; that is, the degree to which the data "fit" the hypothesized relationships.

This simple conceptual framework has served as the basis for a large number of empirical investigations of the determinants of socioeconomic status and the pattern of social mobility. The first of the major U.S. studies employing this framework with data on a representative national sample was that of Peter Blau and Otis Duncan (1967), a pathbreaking study resting upon a special sample survey, Occupational Changes in a Generation (OCG), conducted as an adjunct to the March 1962 Current Population Survey (CPS) of the U.S. Bureau of the Census.[2] Their analyses of this data set expanded qualitative knowledge regarding the processes of inter- and intragenerational mobility among men in American society. To do so they employed the causal model outlined by Duncan and Hodge for estimating the relationships of time-ordered events in the life cycle (family background and educational attainment) through a series of recursive regression equations. Their results indicated that son's education (years of formal schooling) was an important determinant of son's status, and that the education variable was the most important channel by which father's education and occupation influenced the son's status. Other important results concerned the quite different impact of family background and education (as transmitter of family background) in affecting the status of sons in farm versus nonfarm groups, and among racial and ethnic groups. They concluded from their evidence that racial discrimination affects occupational allocations of nonwhites, and that such discrimination is not present among whites regardless of ethnic backgrounds.

The same OCG data, supplemented by other data including variables of interest not available in the survey, such as measures of IQ, were used in a subsequent study of the process of status attainment by Otis Duncan, David Featherman, and Beverly Duncan (1972). They described the problem addressed in their study as follows: "Given that occupation is an achieved status, what factors can be identified as influencing this achievement and thus as accounting for the variation in occupational status? . . .

2. The 1962 OCG survey was composed of 20,700 male respondents aged 20–64, and was weighted to represent the 45 million U.S. men in this age range.

What, if anything, about socioeconomic background represents favorable or unfavorable conditions for achievement, and how do these conditions exercise their influence?" (pp. 3–4).

To answer these questions, the authors began with the straightforward causal model of occupational achievement developed by Duncan and Hodge, expressed algebraically as a recursive system of linear equations. Then, incrementally building on this basic model and incorporating data other than those in the OCG survey, they estimated increasingly complex causal structures involving additional family background variables (e.g., family size and race), intervening variables (e.g., intelligence and motivation), and outcome variables (e.g., educational attainment and income). These extensions and replications led the authors to a wide variety of additional conclusions concerning the process by which SES is transmitted over the life cycle, among them: (1) the relatively low SES of black men can be only partly explained by low-status family background—educational, occupational, and wage discrimination play an important role; (2) the differences in intelligence measures between blacks and whites do not account for a large proportion of black-white income differences;[3] and (3) the variety of other background variables in general had the directional effect on SES that would be expected (e.g., positive effects of marital stability, migration, motivation, and intelligence; negative effect of family size).

The contributions to understanding the process of social mobility resulting from analysis of the 1962 data led to plans for a replicate study, accomplished in the 1973 OCG survey (often referred to as OCG II), which, like the first, was a supplement to the March CPS.[4] The purpose of the replication was to monitor the subsequent experiences of the age cohorts distinguished in the 1962 survey over the following decade, thus emphasizing changes in the mobility process over this period.

The primary analysis of the OCG II data was conducted by David Featherman and Robert Hauser (1978), who exploited the replicability of the 1962 survey for the stated purpose of detecting changes in the process of stratification, which changes were taken to indicate the extent to which the American social system was becoming more or less rigid, more or less permeable, providing more or less equality of opportunity.

The authors first obtained regression estimates of the relationships in

---

3. "Substantial occupational and economic [wage] disadvantages occur to black men, [after statistically adjusting to achieve] . . . parity with whites in social origins . . . , education . . . . and IQ scores" (p. 105). The authors also tested the extent to which income (or status) was a determinant of IQ, also a plausible hypothesis. See also Duncan (1968).

4. The sample was composed of 33,600 men, including a special supplement designed to increase the total number of blacks in the survey.

the life-cycle status attainment model of Duncan and Hodge and extensions of this simple model, as well as summary statistics describing the patterns in bivariate mobility tables (estimated from what is known in this literature as "loglinear models"). They then compared these estimates for men of the same age in the two surveys. Through this comparison, which was possible because of the replicate data in OCG I and II, they attempted to measure both the direction and the magnitude of the change in occupational mobility and the processes of stratification from the early 1960s to the early 1970s. These measurements were made over various population subgroups (race, farm origin, ethnic origin, cohort) and concern both intra- and intergenerational patterns of change. In their discussion of status attainment, Featherman and Hauser employed the "human capital" framework of economics in describing the occupation and income "returns" to social background, schooling, and other characteristics. In the process they attempted to test a variety of hypotheses regarding the extent to which industrialization and economic growth have altered social mobility and equality of opportunity, apart from the process of stratification itself.

Featherman and Hauser defined "opportunity" as the degree to which SES is free of dependence on social background; equality of opportunity, hence, implies that the chances that any individual will change social position does not depend on the individual's personal background. Industrialization and economic growth were taken to be equivalent to increases in per capita gross national product, and their effect was assumed to be reflected in changes in the occupational structure and in other determinants of economic status over the 1960–70 decade. The effects of shifts in mobility patterns due to shifts in the aggregate mix of occupations associated with economic growth ("structural mobility") were distinguished from shifts attributable to changes in the endogenous relationship between social background and socioeconomic status ("circulation or exchange mobility").

Their procedures yielded numerous quantitative results. Only a sample of the most important relationships analyzed is described here, in qualitative terms: (1) a time trend of lower correlation between father's occupation and son's occupation, implying increased equality of opportunity;[5] (2) a time trend of increasing mobility from first to current occupations; (3) little change over the period in the substantial relationship between father's and son's SES at the top and the bottom of the occupational distribution, but substantial and increasing mobility in the middle of the

5. Featherman and Hauser attribute this reduced correlation largely to changes in the occupational structure over the period rather than changes in the relationships between social background and SES, or "circulation mobility."

occupational hierarchy; (4) a roughly equal degree of upward and downward mobility over the period; (5) an upward trend in the role of schooling as a vehicle for occupational achievement; (6) a trend toward socioeconomic equality in graded schooling, but little reduction in the degree of inequality in the attainment of college education; (7) a downward trend in the number of years of schooling of a cohort in excess of father's schooling for cohorts since 1922–26; (8) a downward trend in the effect of family background on education and occupational attainment for whites; (9) an increase over time in the strength of the relationship between father's and son's SES among blacks;[6] (10) evidence of a reduction over time in the income returns to education for whites (but not for blacks); (11) strong and increasing effects of educational attainment on the occupation of the first job relative to later jobs; (12) a distinct impact of major historical events (the Great Depression, World War II and its subsequent GI benefits for education, the Vietnam War) and changing school-to-work patterns on the relationship between father's and son's occupations;[7] and (13) a lack of evidence of a class boundary limiting mobility between manual and nonmanual occupational groups.[8]

These findings led the authors to conclude that "opportunity" for men has increased somewhat over time in U.S. society, an important finding that deserves a richer exposition. Figure 6.2 is a graph from Featherman (1979) that summarizes the research results. This information led Featherman to three conclusions. First, the impact of family (social) background on son's status is small and declining over time. Between 1962 and 1973, the percentage of variation in son's SES attainment explained by family background (net of other characteristics) declined from 11 to 7 percent (seen by comparing the bottom rectangles in the two bars). Second, total variation in occupational achievement explained by education increased from 33 to nearly 36 percent.[9] As Featherman stated:

6. This result was interpreted by the authors as reflecting the increasing ability of black families that have achieved some status to assist their children's educational and occupational achievements.

7. Featherman and Hauser employ this evidence to cast doubt on the robustness of the "overeducated American" hypothesis of Freeman (1976), which suggests that the United States has pushed educational levels of its youth beyond the point at which they have a return in excess of the costs. They note that his overeducated cohort is likely to have included a number of people still in school but working part time.

8. That boundary had been suggested earlier by Blau and Duncan (1967).

9. In this framework, education plays two roles in influencing status attainment: a mobility-facilitating role by opening up more occupational opportunities, and a mobility-retarding (or status-retaining) role as families with more education are able to provide additional education, and hence status, to their children. The latter, or status-retaining, effect of education is measured by the "overlapping influence of social background and

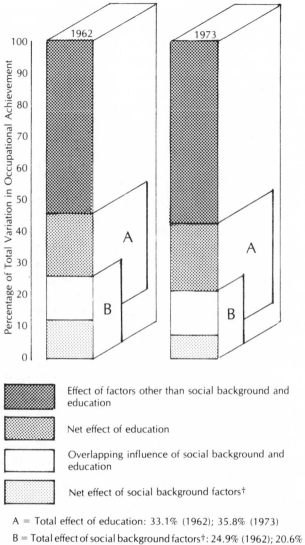

Effect of factors other than social background and education

Net effect of education

Overlapping influence of social background and education

Net effect of social background factors†

A = Total effect of education: 33.1% (1962); 35.8% (1973)

B = Total effect of social background factors†: 24.9% (1962); 20.6% (1973)

Source: March 1962 and March 1973 Current Population Surveys and Occupational Changes in a Generation Surveys.

Figure 6.2. Sources of Variation in Occupational Achievement, Men in the Experienced Civilian Labor Force, Ages 25–64, March 1962 and March 1973 (Featherman, 1979). Published by permission of Transaction, Inc., from *Society*, vol. 16, no. 3, copyright © 1979 by Transaction, Inc.

115

"There is little evidence for a dwindling capacity of education to provide resources for social mobility" (1979, p. 9). Third, between 1962 and 1973 there seems to have been some increase in the degree of achievement explained by factors other than social background and schooling—from 55.9 percent of variation explained to 57.1 percent. While these factors are not identified, they would not seem to have the rigid impacts of home (background) or school, thus indicating that mobility had increased from 1962 to 1973.[10]

While these works form the main line of development in the stratification field, a related set should be mentioned. Both in terms of contribution and number of studies, the body of work referred to as "the Wisconsin study"[11] is significant. This research, conducted under the early leadership of William H. Sewell, later joined by Hauser, focused on a unique body of data—a longitudinal probability sample of 9,000 individuals who were Wisconsin high school seniors in 1957—and resulted in the publication of more than sixty articles and books. The primary volume, by Sewell and Hauser (1975), employed the basic model of status attainment developed by Blau and Duncan (1967), but extended it in several dimensions. More attention was paid to aspiration (educational and occupational) as both outcome and intervening variables, to statistics describing the schools attended (to allow for analysis of individual school effects), and to more disaggregated measures of social background (parental income, mother's status, parental encouragement, and peer and teacher influences). This set of studies focuses far more heavily on the role of social and psychological factors in the attainment process, as

---

education" areas in Figure 6-2, and indicates a slight decrease, from 13.9 percent of the variation in attainment explained in 1962 to 13.5 percent in 1973. The former, or mobility-increasing effect, of education emanates from the individual's social background and is labeled the "net effect of education" in the figure. This net effect in explaining variation in achievement increased from 19.2 to 22.3 percent between 1962 and 1973. On balance, then, the mobility-increasing role of education increased over the 1962 to 1973 period while the status-retaining effect decreased.

10. This optimistic conclusion regarding the large and growing effects of education on attainment and mobility has been questioned on both statistical and analytical grounds. Samuel Bowles, Herbert Gintis, and others have argued that education in fact validates and perpetuates existing status and hence inequality. Their statistical critique of the socioeconomic status attainment literature focuses on the potential biases in estimated impacts due to errors in explanatory variables and the specification of models with omitted explanatory variables. See Bowles (1972), Bowles and Gintis (1972–73, 1976), and Bowles and Nelson (1974). See also the discussion in Chapter 7.

11. In the literature in this field, "the Wisconsin study" refers to the work on the Wisconsin data; the entire quantitative field of status attainment and mobility analysis is often labeled "the Wisconsin school."

opposed to the emphasis on the allocation of sources of variation in attainment, emphasized in the main line of work described above.

The work of Sewell, Hauser, and their colleagues has also led to a wide variety of findings. Many are similar to those already noted, but additional results have also been reported. They can be summarized in qualitative terms as follows: (1) especially parental, but also teacher's, "encouragement" has a significant positive effect on attainment of students, but the "encouragements" themselves are correlated with socioeconomic background (especially those of parents); (2) substantial "talent loss" is due to educational discrimination, which varies by socioeconomic background (see Sewell, 1971); and (3) size of community is, *ceteris paribus*, positively related to the level of educational aspirations. While the Sewell-Hauser group has also pioneered in the development of causal models of the status attainment process, they have given more emphasis than other researchers in this area to the complexity of the status attainment process and the limited ability of the causal models to explain the variation in outcome.[12]

The advances in both methodology and empirical knowledge that this work generated represent a large step forward in research on the processes of status attainment and social mobility. Many sociologists are now likely to acknowledge the "hegemony" (to use Featherman's word) of the socioeconomic life-cycle modeling approach in this important area of sociological inquiry.[13]

12. "Our basic model accounts for no more than 9% of the variance in measured ability, 28% of the variance in educational attainment, 41% of the variance in occupational status, and 8% of the variance in average earnings in the period 1965–1967" (Sewell and Hauser, 1975, p. 184).

13. The complex set of personal and professional relationships that contributed to the success of this major redirection of work in sociology is an important part of the intellectual history of the field. Featherman reported it as follows: "The hegemony of the status attainment approach was sustained by the lineage of intellectual kinship that stemmed from Sewell and Duncan and that found its critical mass at the University of Wisconsin–Madison. Duncan was an undergraduate student of Sewell's at Oklahoma A&M (Duncan's father, Otis Durant Duncan, chaired the Sociology Department). Sewell and Duncan became friends and remained in touch intellectually . . . . Sewell moved to Wisconsin in 1946 and has remained there to the present. Hauser and Featherman were students of Duncan at Michigan and subsequently were hired at Wisconsin. . . . Also at Wisconsin was Archibald O. Haller, a former student of Sewell's, who . . . was instrumental in bringing Featherman to Wisconsin in the Department of Rural Sociology, which Sewell had chaired a decade earlier. These persons, and their students, formed a close network of common intellectual ancestry—a circumstance that encouraged sustained interaction, collaboration, and cumulative effort. Thus, one might say that the dominance of the status attainment approach rested on more than its intellectual base. It drew strength from the informal social

The Determinants of Socioeconomic Status

A number of other studies are related to the Duncan-Sewell research in seeking to identify the factors that contribute to social or economic status, segregating those that relate to such exogenous endowments as family background from those amenable to policy influence. Most prominent has been the work of groups organized and directed by Christopher Jencks. Relying on (and to some extent extending) the basic socioeconomic life-cycle model (as well as a wealth of analyses exploring the determinants of "success"), Jencks and his colleagues (1972) first focused on the empirical roles played by both education and family background in explaining the variation in SES and income. Their emphasis was on understanding the pattern and persistence of economic inequality, and the potential role of family background and education in explaining this persistence.

Although SES was the primary outcome analyzed by Jencks et al., a variety of other outcome variables was analyzed, including scores on standardized tests, educational attainment ("credentials"), and income. The work was both synthetic and integrative; it used estimates and data from a variety of studies, endeavored to place them in a form allowing comparability, and then drew conclusions regarding the contribution of a variety of determinants—family background, schooling, genetic inheritance—on these outcomes. Heavy reliance was placed on differences in outcomes among brothers, based on the judgment that family background is well controlled in such samples. Titled *Inequality*, the study is heroic, piecing together a wide variety of data and information to arrive at basic conclusions, asserted in strong terms. The premise of the volume is the judgment that less inequality in outcome is to be desired, and its objectives are explicitly policy related. Can we determine which factors determine inequality? Can any of the significant factors be manipulated by policy measures? *Inequality* therefore forms an indirect (in some cases direct) appraisal of the potential of the War on Poverty policies that were based on the human capital strategy.

The volume contains a wealth of findings, a few of which are summarized here. Inequality in test scores is largely explained by variation in intellectual inheritance (33–50 percent) and family background (25–40 percent); the remainder is due in varying degrees (but in all cases, with a

---

organization of the discipline and local critical mass—a set of circumstances that may have been unique and implied an idiosyncratic pattern of development for this subdiscipline" (Featherman, 1981, pp. 87–88).

small impact) to economic status, the amount and quality of schooling (i.e., school resources), and racial and economic segregation (e.g., if all elementary schools had the same impact on test scores of sixth graders, the variance in scores would be reduced by only 3 percent). Family background (economic origins, cultural attitudes), cognitive skill, and race are important determinants of educational attainment (and explain over one-half of the observed levels of educational attainment), while quality differences among schools explain very little of the variation in observed attainment. No more than one-half of the variation in occupational status is explained by variation in father's SES, and much of this comes via the educational attainment of the son. Family background alone explains about 32 percent of the variance in SES; years of school attainment is also an important independent determinant of SES, but differences in school quality explain little of the variation. Well over half of the variation in SES is explained by factors other than family background, test scores, or educational attainment (Jencks and colleagues refer to this as "luck"). And finally, less that 25 percent of the variation in income is explained by family background, intelligence and education, taken together. Jencks et al. concluded that in America schooling has failed to reduce inequality in short-term cognitive achievement, long-term educational attainment, and adult income.

Inequality was criticized on a variety of grounds, including the asserted failure of its authors to indicate why schooling should be expected to reduce individual economic inequality (as opposed to increasing aggregate or mean levels of income or well-being, or reducing inequality among important groups), or that citizens and policymakers actually believe that it would or should. While evidence can be adduced on both sides of the issue of whether changes in schools can improve test scores, it has been claimed that Jencks et al. present only the negative side. Moreover, the background and schooling variables that they use are defined so generally that there should be little expectation that major reductions of inequality could be obtained by reducing inequality in them—especially in the face of important supply-side (e.g., age, region, motivation) and demand-side (e.g., differential unemployment patterns, occupational rigidities, effects of trade unions) variables that are neglected in their analysis.

Several methodological criticisms have also been made: inappropriate combinations of data from various sources, inaccuracies in estimating the important relationships, the failure to consider the interdependence of the distribution of individual characteristics and the structure of the labor market, neglect of interactions and nonlinearities, and a single-minded focus on explaining variance as opposed to searching for important policy-related independent variables with sizable and significant co-efficients.[14]

Jencks's second major work, *Who Gets Ahead?*, appeared in 1979 and was in many ways a sequel to the first. Like its predecessor, it attempted statistically to identify the factors apart from heredity that contribute to economic success. Again several data bases were employed, and for each base a common set of questions was asked. Substantial efforts were made to adopt uniform statistical methods and to define comparable samples. Whereas the earlier volume searched for variables that explained variation in outcome, the 1979 volume emphasized the relationships between changes in the determinants of outcome (e.g., family background, education) and changes in the outcomes themselves. The analysis continued, however, to rely on the life-cycle model of Duncan and Sewell, and samples of brothers again were widely used to control for hereditary and family background characteristics.

By and large, the results in the later volume were similar to those in the 1972 study. Family background was found to explain somewhat more of the variation in occupational status than in the earlier volume. The role of education in explaining outcome was somewhat larger in the latter volume than in the earlier one, but remained relatively small. School quality was found to have a very small impact. Controlling for family background and test scores, one additional year of secondary (or college) schooling was estimated to raise income by 4 (or 7) percent. Overall, the role assigned to nonobserved factors ("luck") was somewhat smaller in the 1979 volume than in the 1972 study. Many reservations about the earlier book persisted with regard to this contribution as well, and the contradictions of its findings by results of numerous other studies remains unexplained.[15]

Other Studies of Status Attainment

Two additional approaches to status attainment and mobility should be mentioned. The first is that associated with the work of James Coleman (1964) and Aage Sørensen (1977). Both apply a differential equation methodology to retrospective life-history data in an effort to separate out the effects of structural mobility (those changes in status attainment related to changes in the overall distribution of jobs) and circulation mobility (those changes in status attainment related to changes in the effects of family background and schooling). This procedure has been put

14. See Harvard Educational Review (1973) for a variety of critiques of the work of Jencks. Those by Alice Rivlin, Lester Thurow, and James Coleman are particularly enlightening, as is Jencks's reply.

15. Chapter 7 examines Jencks's studies in the context of the human capital literature.

forward as a superior alternative to the path-analysis, linear-causal models used by Duncan, Sewell, Jencks, and their colleagues. The general findings of the work by Coleman and Sørensen concerning the contributions of family background and education to status attainment do not differ significantly from those in the literature already discussed (based on regression models), but the methodology they developed has special importance.

Finally, starting from a Marxist orientation, Erik Wright and Luca Perrone (1977) and Wright (1980) have attempted to distinguish the effect of class position among occupations (e.g., managers, semi-autonomous employees, the self-employed, workers) on the status attainment process. Their extension of the socioeconomic life-cycle model to reflect the effect of these class-based occupational relationships suggests that class categories help explain both stratification and the structure of the income-determination process within each class.

The Contribution of Status Attainment Research
What has this line of research contributed to knowledge and method in the social sciences? The question can be addressed at several levels. First, without doubt both the work following Blau and Duncan and its related offshoots and extensions have added substantively to knowledge of the processes of status determination and economic mobility in the United States, and changes in these processes over time. The assessment by Glen Cain (1974) of one of the primary works in this field, that by Duncan, Featherman, and Duncan (1972), also applies to its related studies: "This outstanding [work] represents a milestone in the grand research tradition of the development of quantitative models of the processes of achievement and social stratification. . . . it provides 'systematization and synthesis,' 'interpretation and generalization'; in so doing it transcends descriptive fact presentation or, at the other extreme, armchair theorizing" (p. 1508).

Second, the methodological improvements in measurement, estimation, and causal modeling that are embedded in these research efforts are impressive by nearly any standard. This work has played a prominent role within the social sciences, especially sociology, in advancing the application of modern quantitative methods and models to aid our understanding of social problems. Among the subfields of sociology, the area of stratification and mobility has a legitimate, though not undisputed, claim to being "cumulative social science."[16] It has surely made more progress

16. As Featherman (1981) put it: "In the last two decades, the subdiscipline of sociology known as 'social stratification and mobility' has made greater progress toward cumulative

than most of the other branches of this discipline in bringing quantitative methods to bear on measurement of social phenomena and the testing of social scientific hypotheses.

Third, the impact of this research in shaping the national debate on social and antipoverty policy is mixed. The questions asked—What determines economic inequality? Does schooling affect inequality in income and occupational status? What role does inequality of opportunity or racial discrimination play in determining who gets ahead?—are of great policy importance. Yet within this research area two distinct approaches to policy applicability can be observed. The most basic, groundbreaking research efforts—those largely associated with the work of the Duncans, Featherman, Hauser, and Sewell—have been addressed almost exclusively to the scholarly and academic audience. Their objective, it would appear, was to alter the direction of a discipline, rather than affect the level of national debate. It was as if influencing the latter would come only at the cost of achieving the former. The mode of presentation in these works was technical, scholarly, and weighty, making little effort to reach a wider audience. The more derivative efforts, however—those primarily associated with Jencks and his colleagues—were quite the opposite. The emphasis was on using and reformulating the research findings submerged in technical monographs and journals, and presenting the conclusions in an understandable and at times provocative form. Documentation and analysis were confined to footnotes and appendices, and national publicity was attracted. To many, the impact of these works on the climate of opinion was either negative or nugatory. Errors and misinterpretation were emphasized by critics; the polemical style suggested to some that the work was more forensic than social scientific. Nevertheless, nearly a decade after its appearance, a leading stratification researcher applauded Jencks's work for demonstrating the "practical value" of the socioeconomic life-cycle model.[17]

---

social science than any other branch of sociological research. . . . the last 25 years—principally the last decade—have been a historical watershed for American sociology as a social science. Led by statistical applications and technical advances in social stratification research during this period, the day-to-day practice of academic sociology now requires sophistication in middle-range theory specification and estimation—that is, knowledge of mathematics and advanced statistics—that runs far in excess of the typical curriculum of sociologists educated in Europe and America in the 1950s and before" (pp. 79–80).

17. The applause was from Featherman. Aside from the work of Jencks and his colleagues, the socioeconomic life-cycle work has had few other brushes with the world of policy. For a time during the 1960s and 1970s, the social indicators movement attempted statistically to monitor social developments in a variety of dimensions. These efforts recognized, indeed relied upon, the socioeconomic life-cycle model. Duncan himself wrote a chapter recounting OCG I results in the first report of the Panel on Social Indicators

To the question of why this distinguished body of research has had so little impact on other social researchers or the continuing debate over social policy we can offer speculative answers. The first inheres in the very nature of the problem itself: the process of social attainment is extremely complex, and the use of advanced statistical methods to disentangle its elements must, of necessity, generate writings inaccessible to many. Apart from that, however, much of the analysis appears to show lack of concern regarding which variables, either background or intervening, might be subject to alteration through policy, and which might be irrelevant for policy. Without reference to the question of the benefits and costs of intervention, all potential variables tend to carry equal weight. While the content is, or could be made, available for such interpretation, the inclination to do so has been limited. With the exception of Duncan (1968), some discussion by Sewell (1971), and of course Jencks and colleagues (1972, 1979), the remaining authors—and in particular the major monographs in the field—are notably silent on the implications of what they have found. Featherman and Hauser (1978) allude (p. 15) to the potential impact of antipoverty efforts on status (or income), yet they go on to describe in some detail why their study "proffers few if any direct measurements of the many possible causes of change in opportunity" (p. 16). Their purpose it appears is measurement and statistical description of relationships, with little effort to speak to the broader social research community or to draw out the implications of their research findings for the ongoing debate on the nature of social policy.

A second reason lies in the definition of variables and the techniques used for measurement. While educational attainment and income have been employed as outcome variables in later work, occupational status, as measured by the SES indicator developed by Duncan (1961), has received most attention. Although that variable can claim to reflect the perceived status of an attained position, it is not void of statistical inconsistencies and uncertainties (Cain, 1974). For example, the SES indicator has little or no intuitive meaning given that its scale, which spans 0–98, is usually expressed in standard units (a change divided by the standard deviation).[18] And it is not directly obvious that the status of a respon-

---

(Duncan, 1969). Moreover, the plans for the OCG II survey viewed the time-related trends that would become available from the replication of OCG I as themselves social indicators, and federal government support from the National Science Foundation was in part justified on this basis.

18. Cain (1974) addressed the difficulties of the SES scale, as well as its obstacles to interpretation: "After applying the path coefficients to the transformed units, the user will still have to translate the change in occupational scores—two points in the example being

dent's occupation is "the ultimate outcome of the whole process" (Duncan, Featherman, and Duncan, 1972, p. 7).

The difficulty of interpreting the SES indicator of occupational status is compounded by the path-analysis model employed in many of the studies. The path coefficients require translation before their implications have meaning in any metric to which most people can relate—IQ scores, years of education, or incomes. By expressing the variables of the models in standardized values, the natural units of the independent variables of interest—schooling, age, intelligence—become camouflaged, and no easy basis exists for determining how a change in some independent variable of interest affects a change in the outcome variable of interest. Although later works did attempt such translation (Jencks et al., 1972; Sewell and Hauser, 1975; Hauser and Featherman, 1977; Featherman and Hauser, 1978; Jencks et al., 1979), the basic framework continued to inhibit understanding.[19]

Moreover, the great volume and detail of the work has produced a large and unwieldy portfolio of estimated relationships, each with its own sample and specification, so that sorting out what has been learned and appraising its significance is no easy matter. It would seem to be the responsibility of the authors to assist the reader to sort the findings from the nonfindings, the trivial from the important.[20]

---

discussed—into another unit which permits understanding and communication of the result. One can determine that a two-point gain means advancing from brakeman to switchman, bartender to waterworks man, or miner to shoemaker, to take three examples of pairs of occupations separated by two points. . . . In addition, one must calculate the indirect effect—via the direct effect of the father's education on the son's education, and then via the direct effect of the son's education on the son's occupational achievement. Transformations of the path coefficients into raw units and then of the raw units of occupational scores into 'representative' changes in occupations are again required. There is a need for some indicator that would be commonly understood. Indeed, if the authors would provide such translations for the reader, they would no doubt feel compelled to comment on the practical significance of the quantitative relations. This would be beneficial, since they are eminently qualified to do so. As it now stands, much of the significance of the book consists of piecemeal empirical findings, which are difficult to translate into predictions or evaluations of the social processes, and of findings which are mostly of methodological interest" (p. 1500).

19. These concerns are contained in the general methodological criticisms that Cain and Watts (1970), Cain (1975), and others have directed at the work—that the models employed are excessively complex for the purposes at hand, that as a result of the techniques employed the interpretation of findings is difficult, and that the use of the path-coefficient framework rather than more straightforward regression estimates leads the authors to fix upon the issue of variance partitioning rather than the more relevant and interpretable issue of the magnitude of the impact of variables (preferably policy-relevant variables) on outcome.

20. It should be noted that Featherman (1977) has attempted this for the two OCG studies; see the discussion of Figure 6.2, above. See also Jencks et al. (1979).

Finally, the primary outcomes measured in these analyses—stratifica-tion and mobility—bear very little relationship to what most people think of when the terms poverty, inequality, or equal opportunity are used. Judah Matras (1980) has discussed this issue in more detail. His primary point is that in the measurement of "overall level of mobility" the focus has been on those concepts that have been defined above as total, or "circulation," mobility. These refer to estimates of the extent to which respondents report occupations that are different from those of their fathers, or to the magnitude of the statistical interactions between re-spondents' occupations and those of their fathers in various periods, or cohorts. In Matras's view, these measures do not clarify the true meaning of mobility in a society, nor do they correspond to conventional notions of equality. Moreover, the comparisons made have typically been at an aggregate level, designed to describe the openness or permeability of the entire society. Such aggregate measures disguise the reality that some occupations (e.g., an unskilled manual category) may be relatively open, while others (e.g., professional categories) may be relatively closed. "It . . . is only by a considerable stretch of the imagination that most current indicators of 'total' or 'circulation' mobility can be construed as summary measures of the openness of a society's occupational structure." Because these summary measures bear so little relationship to what is currently understood by "openness" or "opportunity," Matras suggests that "we abandon this descriptive and analytical strategy" (p. 413).

My final point regarding the contribution of this area of social research concerns both its theoretical basis and its fundamental conceptual ad-vances. Criticism of this aspect of the work has come largely from within the discipline of sociology itself. Some have challenged the intellectual basis of the research, criticizing its emphasis on individuals rather than on basic elements of the process—elements of social organization—that determine stratification (see Spilerman, 1970). A variant of this theme follows critiques of human capital theory in economics, criticizing the stratification research enterprise for its failure directly to address the systemic problems of poverty, discrimination, or persistent inequality. Other variants have emphasized the neglect of structural aspects of the labor market—segments, classes, firms, industries—relative to back-ground and education in analyzing the determinants of status attainment (see Baron and Bielby, 1980; Wright, 1980). Participants in the main line of this research have acknowledged its limited contributions to the de-velopment of a theory of stratification. Data limitations and the defects of time- and culture-bound studies are cited as the primary culprits, but they have also recognized the need for a "thoroughgoing postulation of dialec-tical relationships that underlie and define the stratification system at any moment" (Featherman, 1981, p. 94); that is, a theory that incorporates explanation of both the structures of the stratification process, and the behaviors and adjustments of individuals who operate within that structure.

In sum, this collective research effort has had a fundamental and pervasive impact on the social sciences, sociology in particular. It has moved research forward in terms of empirical model building and statistical analysis, and has in large measure revolutionized the training and intellectual hierarchy of subfields within the discipline. And it has led to the building of intellectual bridges with other disciplines, evidenced by the adoption by stratification and mobility researchers of human capital concepts from economics and social psychological variables from psychology, and by their contributions to the development of multidisciplinary quantitative techniques in the areas of causal modeling and analysis with latent variables (see, e.g., Goldberger and Duncan, 1973; Jöreskog and Sorbom, 1979). On the other hand, the primary works of scholarship in this area would not rank high on the list of efforts that have contributed most to understanding the nature and causes of inequality and poverty and to providing insights regarding effective strategies for reducing their harmful effects.

Research on Income Dynamics

At the inception of the War on Poverty in 1965, the permanent or transitory nature of poverty—or, in more general terms, the dynamics of family or individual income—was perceived by the poverty research community as an important issue. Until the mid-1970s, however, little could be reliably said about it. Early research on income dynamics was unable to reach definitive conclusions, largely because its studies were forced to rely on matches of individuals over a one- or two-year period rather than on longitudinal data that traced the experiences of the same set of families or individuals over time.[21]

To remedy that deficiency, beginning in 1967, with financial support from the OEO, the Panel Study of Income Dynamics (PSID) was initiated at the Institute for Social Research at the University of Michigan. A sample of five thousand families was selected which, when appropriately weighted, reflected the structure of the U.S. population. These families, and every new household subsequently formed by its members, were surveyed annually to obtain information on a wide variety of economic,

---

21. The earliest studies are President of the United States (1965) and Kelley (1970). Although they indicated that 30 to 40 percent of poor families in one year were not poor in subsequent years, they failed to shake the prevailing view that incomes are generally stable over time and that poverty is largely permanent.

demographic, and especially, labor market characteristics. Because time-related factors were crucial, it was not until the early 1970s that data on income changes over time became available for analysis from the PSID. The early studies using these longitudinal data indicated that poverty (and income) were substantially more transitory than had been previously thought (see Institute for Social Research, 1972; U.S. Department of Health, Education, and Welfare, 1974). A family reported to be in poverty in one year had less than a 50–50 chance of again being recorded poor five years later. About one-third of those poor in a given year were not poor the next; of those who left poverty, nearly half had incomes five years later that were more than 150 percent of the poverty line. However, over 20 percent of the American population fell into poverty at some point during the 1967–72 period.

The picture presented by these data was complex. The poverty population contained a hard-core group of the "permanently poor" of about 5 percent; a larger group of those who moved into and out of poverty with some regularity (for example, the disabled and heads of single-parent families); and a sizable group that experienced poverty for only a short period, in the course of adjusting to such major setbacks as unemployment, sickness, death of or separation from a spouse, or similar personal problems.

Research using the PSID was voluminous after 1972, and its results were published regularly in a series of volumes issued by the Institute for Social Research.[22] These studies of family income fluctuations over time culminated in an important volume (Greg Duncan et al., 1984) that covered a range of topics—the dynamics of poverty, welfare use, and labor market performance; characteristics of the short-term and long-term poor; the intergenerational transmission of welfare recipiency; and trends in black-white and male-female earnings differences. Among its diverse and important research findings, a few deserve to be mentioned here: (1) economic well-being for a typical individual changes markedly over time, with changes in family composition (e.g., divorce, marriage) and movements into and out of the labor force accounting for the largest part of these changes (Staines, 1982); (2) more than half of all persons in the survey lived in families whose real incomes rose over the difficult decade of the 1970s; (3) the large turnover, combined with some stability, that was found to characterize the poverty problem in the first study (in 1974), persisted throughout the 1970s; (4) the long-term poor (i.e., poor in 8 of 10 years) were disproportionately black or living in a female-

---

22. The volumes pulled together the findings from PSID studies undertaken both at the University of Michigan and elsewhere. See Morgan et al. (1974–84).

headed family; (5) like the incidence of poverty, the incidence of welfare recipiency showed substantial movement onto and off of the rolls, leading to the conclusion that "the welfare system does not foster extensive dependency" (p. 91.); (6) the extent of the intergenerational transmission of welfare dependency is very small; (7) prime-aged workers show a surprisingly large degree of volatility in both work hours and wage rates over time, and the pattern of mobility and earnings differences "contradicts rigid theories of dual labor markets . . . [while] supporting the human capital model" (p. 124); (8) although wages of black men have increased as a percentage of wages of white men, there is evidence that the recent growth in white male wages exceeds that of black men; and (9) for both blacks and women, substantial evidence of labor market discrimination exists, after accounting for numerous other factors.

Many of these results challenged conventional wisdom about poverty and discrimination in U.S. society. Poverty is largely a transitory problem and not a permanent state of affairs; long-term welfare dependency is not common, nor is the transmission of dependency from parent to child; a large proportion of Americans need a social safety net at some point in their lives; few workers are trapped in certain types of jobs; the narrowing of racial earnings differences may not continue. These results indicate a greater complexity in the process of income generation than standard cross-sectional studies indicate; the mobility documented in the longitudinal data indicates a rather dynamic and fluid society.[23]

Even more important than these research findings, however, is the opportunity opened by the PSID data for basic research on determinants of income and income changes. This opportunity was well described by Lee Rainwater in his foreword to the volume:

The Panel Study of Income Dynamics is unique in the archives of social science. Its longitudinal perspective on a continuing sample of the American population, accumulating a detailed history over time of people's changing fortunes, permits researchers to analyze the way events and circumstances reported at one point in a person's life are related to the life events and circumstances reported by that person at a later point. Thus it provides social scientists with an unprecedented opportunity to observe the complex patterns of events and developments at individual, family, and societal levels, and study the way these patterns affect the economic well-being of this microcosm of the American population. While its innovative methodology continues to attract growing interest among other social scientists and from government officials in other nations because of the new light

23. These conclusions have themselves been questioned. For example, the research of Mary Jo Bane and David T. Ellwood (1982) indicates that among welfare recipients the duration of recipiency has been found to vary substantially; young unmarried mothers, for example, have far longer welfare durations than do older women who enter the rolls.

it can shed on important social issues, the Panel Study of Income Dynamics remains unparalleled in the world (Greg Duncan et al., 1984, p. vii).

Since the mid-1970s, when data first became available with enough detail to make longitudinal analysis feasible, statistical techniques have been developed and extended for exploiting the rich information contained in the data. These techniques—for analyzing "spells," referring to the duration of such experiences as welfare receipt;[24] intertemporal dependencies and sequences of such events as women's labor force participation or poverty experiences (e.g., Heckman and Willis, 1977; Hill, 1981); duration, hazards, entries, and exits of poverty-related experiences (e.g., Lancaster, 1979; Tuma and Robins, 1980; Hutchens, 1981); and intergenerational transmission (e.g., Corcoran and Datchun, 1981)—as well as the ability to construct more "permanent" indicators of economic status and labor market position[25] represent a major advance in the capability of the social science disciplines to sort out the complex process of social and economic change.

Future Directions

Research on the socioeconomic attainment process and on income dynamics has been methodologically rich and has added substantively to our knowledge of these processes. The story of its evolution characterizes a large part of social science activity in the 1960s and 1970s, when academics, motivated by the controversy surrounding social policy issues and financed by the research support accompanying this controversy, attempted to answer the big questions about social processes and behavior. In doing so they changed prevailing theories, generated new ones, fundamentally altered the practice of their disciplines, and stimulated the collection of improved data. Their findings were controversial, their tie to policy-making indirect and tangential.

These conclusions point to the next steps to be taken. First, this field of study needs to address the charge levied by some that much of the work in it represents data-mining and measurement that are largely unguided by theory and contribute little to the development of new theoretical perspectives. Progress in social theory, it seems, is required if the measure-

---

24. A series of studies by Mary Jo Bane and David T. Ellwood has addressed the issue of spells of welfare receipt and particular types of living arrangements, such as women living alone or heading families. See for example Bane and Ellwood (1983).

25. See for example Garfinkel and Haveman (1977). Reviews of the potential of longitudinal data for labor economics, especially concerning labor supply, are Heckman (1978) and Heckman and MaCurdy (1981).

ments undertaken are to be viewed as more than interesting and, one hopes, unbiased relationships.

Second, the controversies accompanying work in this area will only be resolved if the data available are sufficiently rich to allow explicit testing of the primary hypotheses regarding the roles of background, education, and opportunities in affecting social movement, and the determinants of changes in economic and social status over time. These data needs are substantial and require detailed longitudinal information on a large set of economic and demographic characteristics for a large sample of people over a period of several years. Because the information should be sufficiently detailed to allow tests of a variety of hypotheses regarding social process, it must include information missing in previous data sets (e.g., on the quality and nature of education, sources of income, migration, health and related personal characteristics), and more accurately measure the variables available in prior studies. As described in David (1985), the data collection effort of the Survey of Income and Program Participation is a step in this direction. The modeling and econometric techniques that have been developed since the 1960s owing to the surge of research on social mobility now appear to require for their effective use data far more extensive than what is available.

Both of these points indicate an important and perhaps growing role for ethnographic research—field research involving first-hand and in-depth knowledge of the behaviors, choices, motivations, and constraints of individuals in various family, community, and cultural settings. Such interactive research has potential for both the development of theory about the processes by which people climb and descend the social and economic ladder and the formation of appropriate survey questions which stand some chance of reflecting these motivations and constraints. The case for such research as the next stage of efforts to understand the processes of social mobility was recently argued by Nathan Glazer. In speaking of the highly quantitative nature of poverty research from its beginning, he wrote:

> Why it went this way is clear enough: it was a high-return route. And yet the understandings that are necessary to deal with poverty are elusive. Despite the wealth of quantitative findings, something was missing, and what was missing were intuitively comprehensible models of behavior based on detailed and sustained observation and interaction with the subjects of research, and which, when presented to the searcher after understanding of poverty, leads him to say, "Aha! That's just the way it is." The economist and the quantitative sociologist will enter a proper caveat, pointing out we can't be sure that's just the way it is . . . .
>
> There are elements in human behavior that seem to be based on history, or religion, or a kind of distilled experience, that the economist might sweep

together and sum up under the heading "tastes," that nevertheless explain a good deal of behavior and a good deal of poverty—or escape from poverty. These elements, which ethnographic research makes us alert to, are playing a larger role in our thinking about public policy, and in experimental approaches to dealing with poverty, and will inevitably play a larger role in research. We can call them values, or commitments, or the effects of family upbringing, or inherited beliefs, or character, but they form a hard substratum under the social landscape that we try to manipulate in public policy with a calculated combination of reward and punishment. Sometimes that substratum helps get people out of poverty, and sometimes it keeps them there, despite well-designed policies (1986b, pp. 16, 17).

While these points are well taken, Glazer's own advice should be taken before beginning a full-scale commitment in this area. Standards of replicability, validity, and generalizability all need to be met before such research is likely to lead to a major breakthrough in understanding the processes of social mobility.

7

Disentangling the Processes of Education and Training, Segregation and Discrimination, and Labor Market Operation

To complete the discussion of contributions to social science knowledge attributable to the Great Society initiatives, this chapter covers three additional subject areas: education and training, segregation and discrimination, and labor market interventions. Within each area, I attempt to identify the primary questions that attracted academic interest and to characterize the nature of the contribution provided by poverty research. The questions focus on economic topics.

Education and Training

An explicit goal of the War on Poverty was to offer a hand up, and not a handout, to the poor—to give them the tools to lift themselves out of poverty, as Lyndon Johnson phrased it in his State of the Union address in January 1964. That goal resulted in an emphasis on education and training interventions. A large number of such programs were initiated by the OEO, as exemplified in Head Start, the Performance Contracting and Education Vouchers experiments, the Teacher Corps, Upward Bound, and Job Corps. Legislation also provided federal aid to education, including support for remedial education and the equalization of education resources across jurisdictions and social classes.

The interest of policy planners in this area was shared and supported by social scientists. This was the era of strong—some would say naïve—faith in the efficacy of education. The human capital literature in economics, the status attainment literature in sociology, and "reformist" thought among educationists all reinforced the notion that enlarging educational resources would directly and indirectly (through motivating reforms in school systems) generate improved achievement levels and ultimately increase economic success. Henry Levin (1977; see also Clark, 1966) characterized what he called this "tacit ideology" of the 1960s as follows:

The existence of poverty among families with potential workers is due primarily to the low productivity of such workers; in turn, low productivity is attributable to low skills and initiative that result from the cultural and other disadvantages associated with these groups; finally, government investments in education and in other areas of human capital would increase the opportunities and incomes of workers from such families by raising their productivities and resultant incomes. It was thought that by increasing the job-related skills of the poor, education and training would provide an unusually promising vehicle for raising productivity and alleviating poverty (p. 127).

The public sector's commitment of resources to education and training also stimulated academic research on the economic outcomes of that investment. Looking back on the social science literature in this area, one finds that most of the research appeared to be directed to five basic questions. These questions, and the kinds of research and research answers that were generated, are examined in the following sections.

What Effect Does Incremental Education Have on Earnings?

The economic literature of the early 1960s had already become absorbed with the notion that incremental education yields benefits which can be quantified. Contributions by Houthakker (1959), Miller (1960), Mincer (1962), Weisbrod (1962), Morgan and David (1963), Schultz (1963), Becker (1964), and Bowen (1964) all viewed education as an investment yielding both quantifiable and nonquantifiable returns.[1] The preliminary evidence strongly suggested that the quantifiable returns in the form of earnings increases were substantial and, by themselves, made expenditures on education worthwhile. The specification of this human capital view of education and the crude evidence that was brought to bear on the question were complemented by an important study by Edward Denison (1962), in which, through a growth-accounting approach, as much as one-third of the observed growth rate of real national income per person employed was attributed to education.

These developments, together with the focus of antipoverty policy on

---

1. A review of this early work can be found in Rosen (1977).

education, combined to generate an enormous surge of research, most of it by economists, which refined and elaborated the human capital model and brought increasingly appropriate data and measurement techniques to bear in estimating the true earnings return to education.[2] By 1967 academic interest in this topic had so progressed that a special symposium issue of the *Journal of Human Resources* (Vol. 2, Summer) was devoted to the topic of "Rates of Return to Investment in Education" (see also Hansen, 1970).

These studies found that education did pay off in terms of increased earnings. Rates of return to investment in education beyond the primary school level were in excess of those on alternative investments, such as in physical plant and equipment, and the earnings gains from high school and college degrees appeared to be in excess of their costs. While net returns to education appeared positive for women and minorities, they were lower than those for white men. These results persisted until the late 1970s, when Richard Freeman (1976) documented decreasing economic returns to college attendance, and suggested that perhaps too many resources were being devoted to schooling.[3]

Through What Means Does Education Affect Economic Success?

The literature stemming from the human capital model was, to a large extent, "black box" research—the outcome but not the process was observed. That education increased earnings was not surprising; *how* education increased the chances for economic success was less clear. Complementing human capital research, and stimulated by it, was a more detailed body of work exploring the nature of the educational process and the interaction of it with other influences on and characteristics of children. Somehow, it was believed, these forces combined in a complicated way that resulted in more success for some children than for others. The job of social science research was to ferret out these interactions and thus clarify the process.

Research followed two lines. The first was of a traditional sort: individual scholars working with primary or secondary data of varying quality, sometimes collected as part of a demonstration project and sometimes collected for other purposes, attempted to trace estimates of

2. These studies and their results are reviewed in Mincer (1970), Blaug (1976), and Rosen (1977). They include works by Hansen (1963), Hanoch (1967), Ribich (1968), Weiss (1970), Griliches and Mason (1972), Ribich and Murphy (1975), and Akin and Garfinkel (1977).

3. The "overeducated American" thesis of Freeman was challenged by Haveman and Wolfe (1984), who emphasized the narrow basis of the earnings-based definition of the return to education.

various aspects of schools and teachers on student performance, usually measured by scores on achievement tests, after accounting for other factors. These studies were published in scores of journal articles and government reports, often by scholars affiliated with education schools who had social science background and training.

The second line of research was unique. It involved a large, specially designed national survey, whose objective was to measure the discrepancy in public educational resources available to various racial and income groups. Sponsored by the federal government as part of the Civil Rights Act of 1964, it was undertaken by a select group of highly qualified scholars, and its results were published in a single and much publicized report (Coleman et al., 1966). *Equality of Educational Opportunity*, also known as the Coleman Report, was described by Henry Aaron (1978) as an "intellectual cause célèbre," reaching conclusions concerning the effect of schooling on test scores that were "sensational and devastating" (p. 76). The most remarkable finding from this research was that there were no substantial differences in the level of expenditures on or the volume of educational resources devoted to blacks and whites.

Both lines of research reached much the same conclusion concerning the effects of education: variations in the amount of school resources do not explain much of the differences in achievement levels among students; other factors not adequately measured or not handled well in statistical analyses—specific types of school inputs or environments, family and neighborhood backgrounds—must play the dominant role in explaining success.[4] In part because these conclusions were at variance with findings from the human capital literature, they stimulated considerable controversy. The data in the Coleman Report and in other studies were criticized for their cross-sectional as opposed to "moving picture" nature, for the lack of detailed information on the character of school and home inputs and environments, and for their crude and incomplete information on student achievement. The statistical analyses were flawed, it was charged, on both modeling and interpretational grounds.[5]

This research and the debate it spawned stimulated a variety of other contributions to the question of how education effects success. The social mobility literature in quantitative sociology, discussed in the preceding

4. This general conclusion was reached explicitly by the Coleman Report in a set of analyses which went beyond the basic project mandate regarding "measurement of different resources." It was also the general conclusion reached in a comprehensive review of the numerous other independent studies, conducted by Averch and four colleagues at the Rand Corporation (Averch et al., 1972).

5. See the works of Bowles and Levin (1968), Cain and Watts (1970), Hanushek and Kain (1972), and Smith (1972).

chapter, and the contributions of Samuel Bowles, Christopher Jencks, and their colleagues stand out.[6] Whereas the former found education to be an important determinant of status, reinforcing the conclusions from the human capital literature, the latter concluded that education serves only to convey the advantages of family background, conferring little independent effect. This decade-long controversy had several important impacts on the social sciences. First, it demonstrated how difficult it is to model social processes and to measure policy impacts, even in the case of processes which are apparently well understood. This demonstration was sobering to those who believed that social science research could and should guide policy changes. Second, the studies and their critiques stimulated a search for improved data and statistical methods capable of disentangling the contributions to success of various phenomena, especially education and such background characteristics as parental status and IQ, which operated in a complex and interactive way. These data and methodological gains were important in the development of the disciplines.[7] Third, the character of the empirical results on the relationship of education to economic success called into question the primary theory for understanding this linkage—the human capital model, which became viewed as overly simplistic and naïve. A variety of alternative theories for understanding the connection between education and success were produced: the screening hypothesis, according to which college degrees were simply signals of the basic abilities of those who hold them (see Taubman and Wales, 1974); a radical political-economic view (see Bowles and Gintis, 1976); and the view that "education earlier reduces training costs later" (Stiglitz, 1975; Thurow, 1975). None was by itself totally convincing or immediately accepted, but cumulatively they have added richness to our understanding of the complex ways in which education contributes to economic success.[8]

What Is the Effect of Education on Inequality?

Chapter 6 described the contribution of social research to understanding the processes of mobility and stratification. Implicit in much of this

6. See Bowles and Gintis (1972, 1973, 1976), Jencks et al. (1972, 1979), and Bowles and Nelson (1974).

7. For example, studies by Hanushek (1972) and Summers and Wolfe (1977), using better, more disaggregated data and improved statistical techniques, found that different forms of education provided to different types of students did have large and significant impacts on outcomes. Herrnstein (1973) and others sought to disentangle background characteristics, IQ, and education in determining achievement.

8. Aaron (1978, pp. 94–98) relies on all of these views to piece together an "eclectic view" that reconciles the findings that schooling does generate earnings increases and is a worthwhile investment with the conclusion that the effects of schooling on test scores or of test scores on subsequent income cannot be easily seen or measured.

research is the notion that levels of educational attainment tend to be transmitted through generations, and hence contribute to the maintenance of inequality over time. Scattered through this literature[9] are clues regarding the effect of education on inequality, and the changing nature of this connection over time. When pieced together, they suggest that education plays both a mobility-increasing role and, through its tie to parental socioeconomic position, a mobility-decreasing role, but that former effect exceeds the latter, increasingly so with time.

The first major effort explicitly to address the linkage was undertaken by Christopher Jencks and his associates (1972), who placed education (or schooling) within a variety of other determinants of economic success (e.g., parental background, intelligence) and estimated its role in explaining success. None of these factors were found to explain much of the variation in social outcome, and Jencks concluded that luck, rather than educational attainment and background, has played the major role in determining inequality. As a corollary, schooling was not found to have been an important equalizing force in the United States.

This result was generally viewed as a serious attack on the education strategy of the War on Poverty. As the controversy surrounding publication of the volume (*Inequality*) settled, however, many began to discount the importance of its attack. The question of the effectiveness of education in improving the plight of the poor was viewed as having little to do with the overall effect of education on general inequality in the income distribution.[10]

Economists as well as sociologists investigated the link between education and inequality. Lester Thurow (1972) was one of the earliest to discuss it, and his description of the economic process by which income inequality would be reduced if increased education were provided to the least skilled workers is still apt:

Any increase in the educational level of low-income workers will have three powerful—and beneficial—effects. First, an educational program that transforms a low-skill person into a high-skill person raises his productivity and therefore his earnings. Second, it reduces the total supply of low-skill workers, which leads in turn to an increase in *their* wages. Third, it increases the supply of high-skill workers, and this lowers their wages. The net result is that total output rises . . . , the distribution of earnings becomes more equal, and each individual is still rewarded according to merit (p. 67).

---

9. Primarily in the research by Duncan, Featherman, and Duncan (1972), Sewell and Hauser (1975), Hauser and Featherman (1977), and Featherman and Hauser (1978).

10. As Aaron (1978, p. 91) wrote: "Jencks, in effect, presents evidence that education cannot do something that no informed person claimed it could do, at least since the euphoric early 1960s (i.e., reduce overall inequality)."

Statistical work on the connection has produced mixed findings, however. Jacob Mincer (1974) found that about one-third of the variation in individual earnings is statistically explained by variation in education. More recent work finds results similar to those of Mincer suggesting that schooling, in fact, may contribute to increased inequality.[11]

In hindsight, research on the issue of education and inequality appears to have produced neither findings that have led to consensus nor significant methodological advances. Perhaps its main effect has been to reveal how deeply the educational system is nested in the other institutions of the society (e.g., family structure and status, the labor market, neighborhood), and how complex are its ties to these institutions. Viewed in this way, it is not surprising that research efforts have been unable to justify in clear fashion either the assertion that additional spending on education will reduce overall inequality, or the reverse.

Are Public Education and Training Programs Efficient Investments?

Federal interventions in the education and training area proliferated after 1965, and became an important part of the antipoverty campaign. The list of programs is long, beginning with Head Start in 1965, followed the same year by compensatory programs for low-income children under the Elementary and Secondary Education Act, Upward Bound to prepare poor high school students for college, the Neighborhood Youth Corps and Job Corps to provide work and training, financial aids for poor college students under the Higher Education Act of 1965, and revision of the 1962 Manpower Development and Training Act in 1966 to slant it toward the training of disadvantaged workers.

Accompanying the programs were evaluation studies—efforts to see if there were measurable effects of the programs, and if the value of these effects exceeded the costs. The studies ranged from the most simple comparisons of the achievement, earnings, and employment of program participants before and after participation to very sophisticated econometric or experimental analyses using randomly selected control groups or elaborate statistical controls. They also ranged widely in the extent to which the costs attributed to the project reflected true social opportunity costs and in the length of time individual participants or members of the control group were observed. Because the methods and evaluative

11. Berg (1970), Hansen, Weisbrod, and Scanlon (1970), Chiswick (1974), Dresch (1975), Tinbergen (1975), and Marin and Psacharopoulos (1976). Marin and Psacharopoulos explain the divergence of these findings according to whether or not researchers permit the rate of return on schooling investments to vary with the level of schooling. Those allowing for such dependence generally find that increases in education reduce inequality; those who assume independence find a disequalizing effect of education.

criteria varied so much, and because so many program variations were investigated, no general conclusion seems possible. Some programs, in some settings, for some groups appear to have been successful (see Taggart, 1981; Bassi and Ashenfelter, 1986); others seem to have failed.[12] Stephen Mullin and Anita Summers (1983) reviewed the effectiveness of compensatory education programs and found evidence of a positive, though small, effect on the achievement of disadvantaged students. In a recent review of the effect of education and training programs, Nathan Glazer (1986a) concluded: "We know enough, I would hazard, to suggest that greater resources would be most usefully spent in preschools and elementary schools. There we have evidence that improvement is possible. That improvement, if broadened and sustained, suggests that more poor minority youth will be able to get through high school" (p. 172). Henry Aaron (1978), however, noted the difficulties of evaluating training programs, and stated that "decisions about whether to continue training programs . . . have had to be settled on grounds other than 'scientific evaluation of their effectiveness'" (p. 128).[13]

From the broader view of the social science disciplines, this line of evaluation research has had important impacts. First, the early program evaluations resulted in a set of basic contributions by economists on the appropriate methodology for assessing the value of public activities. These stand as fundamental contributions to the evaluation research literature, and are still referred to in seeking guidance on how to and how not to approach the evaluation of education and training programs (see Weisbrod, 1965; Somers and Wood, 1969; Cain and Hollister, 1970). Second, the substantial research talent that was attracted to this area formed the initial core around which grew the field of policy analysis and evaluation research, discussed in Chapter 8. Third, it was the early efforts systematically to evaluate the impact of federal education and training interventions that encountered what then seemed to be intractable problems of statistical control to obtain reliable assessments. The frustration led directly to econometric work on selectivity bias and to the establishment of the case for explicit social experimentation, discussed in Chapters 9 and 10. Finally, during the years following the start of the War on

12. Earliers reviews of evaluations of the education and training programs are those of Goldstein (1972), Levin (1977), and Stromsdorfer and Farkas (1980). These reviews also examined the methods employed in these studies, which they generally found inconsistent and often at variance with sound program evaluation techniques.

13. Levin (1977) summed up the effects of programs offering training in job skills: "The improvement of job skills strategy does seem to have a slight effect on removing persons from poverty, particularly at the margin, MDTA and perhaps WIN or Work Experience programs seemed to have some impact in this direction, especially for individuals who were very close to the poverty line" (p. 179).

Poverty, a number of the individual evaluation studies became recognized as research efforts which, in themselves, made important contributions to either method or knowledge in the social sciences, especially economics.[14]

How Have the Costs and Benefits of Education Programs Been Distributed?

An important issue in determining the antipoverty impact of educational programs—and in fact the effect of the entire education sector of the economy—is to identify who is gaining access to educational services and who is paying for them. Although education is often justified on grounds of income redistribution, the true distributional effects of education may be quite different from those commonly presumed.

An important early study addressed the distribution of benefits and costs of higher education (Hansen and Weisbrod, 1969). Because of the distribution of college-age children among various income groups, the differences in college attendance rates by income class, the differences in the costs of public institutions that they attend, and the differences in tax incidence for higher education, state-sponsored programs were seen to be distinctly less favorable toward the poor.[15] A number of other studies also indicated the ineffectiveness of the then-existing elementary and secondary education system as an antipoverty endeavor. This conclusion stemmed from demographic and attendance patterns similar to those found in the higher education studies, and from the pattern of state financing of expenditures. One type of research focused on the approach adopted in most states for financing public education via local property taxes and state aids, and found them generally to guarantee educational impoverishment rather than equality (Coons, Clune, and Sugarman, 1970), since the financial mechanisms discriminated in favor of wealthy school districts and against inner-city schools.[16]

These findings generated a variety of policy reform proposals, which once again brought social scientists into direct contact with the policy

14. See for example Garms (1971), Hu, Lee, and Stromsdorfer (1971), Somers and Stromsdorfer (1972), Gramlich and Koshel (1975), Ashenfelter (1978), Kiefer (1979), Willis and Rosen (1979), Farkas, Olsen, and Stromsdorfer (1980), Mallar, Kerachsky, and Thornton (1980), Long, Mallar, and Thornton (1981), and Kemper, Long, and Thornton (1983).

15. The extent of the distribution of subsidies in favor of the rich in the Hansen-Weisbrod study, however, was the subject of debate: a set of exchanges between the authors and several challengers appeared in the *Journal of Human Resources* in 1970–71.

16. The Coons, Clune, and Sugarman study stimulated a number of empirical studies, ultimately resulting in a California State Supreme Court decision in 1976, *Serrano* v. *Priest*, which led to major equalizing reforms in finance in several states.

process. As in other areas, the distinction between social science and policy analysis consequently faded, and the emergence of policy analysis as a distinct area of academic study was accelerated. Many of the proposals were in the area of educational finance and generally sought to alter the disequalizing pattern of benefits and costs by reducing pro-rich subsidies and giving incentives for school attendance to children from disadvantaged families.[17]

Segregation and Discrimination

From the outset of the War on Poverty, the question of economic discrimination on the basis of race was a central, although not always overt, issue. Indeed, some viewed antipoverty measures as a disguised means of aiding racial minorities, intended to move them into the mainstream of U. S. economic life. The problems of racial discrimination had of course occupied social scientists long before declaration of the War on Poverty (see Myrdal, 1944; Becker, 1957), but after 1965 the flow of literature on a variety of aspects of this problem increased rapidly, and the nature of the analysis went far deeper than previous work. Of the various issues raised in this literature, those addressed in the following sections seem the most central. While both theoretical and empirical research has dealt with a wide variety of discrimination patterns—by race, by sex, by age—I focus on black-white differences. The discussion here is brief, in part because far more extensive and critical appraisals of the research in this area have recently appeared. The review by Glen Cain (1986) is particularly notable.

The Economic Basis of Discrimination
The most influential economic contribution to the question of why discrimination of majority groups against minorities exists was undertaken nearly a decade before the War on Poverty began. The basic element in Gary Becker's (1957) analysis was "tastes"; if those in majority groups disliked, say, working with those in minority groups, wage differences would appear, majorities would gain at the expense of minorities, and aggregate economic efficiency would decrease. Similar reasons could explain why minorities would have to pay more for the goods and services they desired, or be denied access to them. The identification of tastes as

17. The primary reform proposals and studies related to them are, on federal school aid, Guthrie and Lawton (1970); on state aid to schools, Coons, Clune, and Sugarman (1970); on fees, grants and loans, Shell et al. (1968), Solmon (1970), Hansen and Weisbrod (1971), Hansen (1972), Hartman (1972), Fuller, Manski, and Wise (1983), and Hansen and Lampman (1983); on vouchers, Jencks (1970) and Center for the Study of Public Policy (1970).

the basis of observed differentials served to justify legislation establishing equal opportunity in housing and employment as a basic right to be enforced by the power of the state.

A quite different theoretical approach to understanding observed differences in economic status among majorities and minorities came to be known as "statistical discrimination" or "market signaling," suggested independently by Edmund Phelps (1972) and Kenneth Arrow (1973). In this view, discrimination exists because of imperfect information and the high costs of obtaining better information. Owing to this informational problem, employers (or sellers) rely on simple methods of evaluating any person's abilities, such as the average perceived performance level of the group to which the person belongs. If minorities (say, blacks or women) are perceived to be less productive on average than are majorities, hiring choices will always favor majorities, even if a particular minority group member is highly qualified. Discrimination will be observed to exist in access to jobs and job ladders, and thereby in earnings and income.[18]

Both of these discrimination theories had important implications. That of Becker reinforced the economist's notion that competition among employers for employees would erode discrimination. The statistical-discrimination approach suggested that competition would not be nearly as effective in reducing discrimination as would measures to alter the statistical perceptions of employers or sellers. Information provision or changes in legislation requiring decisions to be made on the basis of true abilities and not perceived group averages could be the effective means of reducing discrimination. Both of these theoretical approaches gave intellectual basis to support by social scientists of equal opportunity legislation in employment and housing and their involvement in assessing the effectiveness of these measures.[19]

Extent and Causes of the Black-White Income Gap

Becker's work, and a general concern with the relative poverty of blacks in the 1960s, resulted in a large number of studies designed to measure the gap between black and white incomes and changes in the gap over time. A variety of income differentials are relevant (e.g., market income, cash money income, disposable income), as are comparisons among various majority and minority groups (blacks and whites, men and women, aged and youth, white and blue collar workers). Research studies pursued all of these aspects.

18. Other important contributions to this literature include Akerlof (1970), Stiglitz (1973), and Spence (1974).

19. Other theoretical approaches to understanding discrimination and segregation are the dual labor market and radical approaches. These, plus his own bargaining approach, are reviewed and critiqued by Marshall (1974).

One of the earliest "gap studies" was by Batchelder (1964). Concerns with the data and methods used in this early study, in conjunction with evidence that the "decline" reported by Batchelder had turned into an "increase," motivated additional studies in a similar mode. These studies—primary among them are Ashenfelter (1970, 1977), Gwartney (1970); Freeman (1973), and Vroman (1974)—indicated that from the mid-1960s to the early 1970s, black male earnings rose from about two-thirds to three-fourths of those of whites, and that the decline suggested by Batchelder may not have occurred at all. Somewhat later, a set of studies concentrated on disentangling the contribution of discrimination as opposed to worker and job characteristics, to observed racial earnings differences. Those by Blinder (1973), Masters (1975), and Corcoran and Duncan (1979) are important, and are critiqued in Cain (1986). This research on income position was complemented by analysis of statistics on racial differences in poverty incidence (e.g., Plotnick and Skidmore, 1975) and occupational status (e.g., Freeman, 1973; Hall and Kasten, 1973).

The observed gap between black and white income and earnings can be attributed to a number of factors, some of which are manifestations of present or past labor market discrimination against blacks; others involve differences in human capital endowments, differences in demographic structure, and voluntary differences in work effort. With respect to labor market discrimination, evidence of various sorts suggested that employers respond differently to the skills and abilities of black persons than they do to those of white persons in making wage-rate or working-time offers, or in offering a job at all. Largely because discriminatory behavior appeared to be amenable to change through policy intervention, researchers set out to estimate the extent of the observed gap that could be closed if discrimination in the labor market could be reduced or eliminated.

The basic approach used in these studies is called the "residual method." Human-capital-based earnings functions were fit to microdata for blacks and whites. Use of coefficients from the resulting functions for whites together with the socioeconomic characteristics of blacks yields estimates of what blacks would have earned if their characteristics were rewarded in the market as are those of whites. The difference between this amount and what they are actually paid is called labor market discrimination. Several studies employed this method,[20] and their findings on the proportion of the earnings gap accounted for by discrimination in

---

20. See Batchelder (1964), Ashenfelter (1970), Gwartney (1970), Wohlstetter and Coleman (1970), Blinder (1973), Christensen and Bernard (1974), Guthrie (1974), Kiker and Liles (1974), Vroman (1974), Masters (1975), and Garfinkel and Haveman (1978).

the early to mid-1970s were generally consistent: for men, from 35 to 60 percent, depending on whether differences in hours worked are attributed to discrimination or not; about one-half of these percentages for women; and from 30 to 40 percent for family income.

The residual method is faulty to the extent that unmeasured variables not included in earnings functions are correlated with both race and earnings. The method would attribute earnings differences due to these factors to the residual category of labor market discrimination. Even allowing for such biases—and crude tests indicate that they are not large[21]—the results suggest that antidiscrimination policy could play a substantial role in reducing the racial difference in incomes.

These direct estimates of the contribution of labor market discrimination to observed racial earnings and income differences were complemented by another line of research that grew out of the literature on human capital and returns to education. Early studies had already indicated that incremental education provided for blacks had a lower return than that provided whites.[22] Subsequent research gave firm evidence that even though this pattern existed prior to 1960, it had changed substantially since. In an important study Finis Welch found that by the late 1960s, the payoff to education was at least as great for blacks as for whites,[23] and in another study (with James D. Smith) which analyzed 1960 and 1970 census data, he found substantial improvement in black incomes relative to white incomes in the decade of the 1960s, especially among those with more education and those who had entered the labor market more recently (Smith and Welch, 1977). These patterns were taken to support the view that, by the early 1970s, the income payoff of education to blacks relative to whites had increased substantially as compared to its level in the early 1960s. This, combined with the convergence in school-completion levels between the races for younger cohorts, accounts for a good portion of the improvement in relative black earnings.

The combined findings led to the speculation that government affirmative action legislation had resulted in a decline in labor market discrimination. A number of important studies focused on this question, using microdata on specific industries.[24] By and large, the results showed

21. Garfinkel and Haveman (1978). As Aaron (1978) pointed out, it is curious that the analytical method used in these studies has not been subjected to critical evaluation of anything like the extent to "which research on the relation between education and income has been reviewed" (p. 62).

22. Hanoch (1967) was the earliest of these studies. See also Weiss (1970) and Hansen (1972).

23. See Welch (1973, 1975). Other studies did not yield such clear-cut results; see Weiss and Williamson (1972), Haworth, Gwartney, and Haworth (1975), and Carliner (1976).

24. See Smith and Welch (1977), Wallace (1975), Ashenfelter and Heckman (1976), Marshall and Christian (1976).

that little impact could be attributed to direct government action, although in specific sectors and certain occupations, government enforcement efforts seemed to have improved the position of blacks relative to whites. Nevertheless, some researchers were willing to interpret the data as reflecting a substantial decrease in discrimination in the labor market.

This general body of research is difficult to appraise. There is no theoretical or statistical model which can guide efforts to measure reliably the effect of various factors on black-white income differences. Different slices of data at different times tell varying and sometimes conflicting stories. Moreover, it is not clear if the apparently higher return to education for blacks in 1970 relative to 1960 was due to reduced labor market discrimination or to improved schooling provided to blacks, or to other factors (such as interregional migration) correlated with education.

The resulting lacunae in knowledge about the role of economic or demographic factors in determining black-white income gaps has left the field open to other explanations. A highly controversial position was that in some genetically determined way, blacks are inferior to whites. This view, along with research to buttress it, was first espoused by Arthur Jensen (1969). The publication of his study had obvious import concerning the ultimate success to be expected from antipoverty programs; in addition, the findings appeared to other analysts as unsupported by the quantitative evidence. A major body of research and debate ensued, involving charges of inadequate statistical analysis and even the manipulation of data. Although full resolution of the issue is probably beyond the capability of social science research methods, subsequent research on this issue has failed to sustain the initial assertion (Kamin, 1974; Goldberger, 1976a, 1976b, 1978a, 1978b, 1979; Taubman, 1976, 1977).

Housing Segregation

The segregation of blacks and other minorities in isolated communities was apparent well before the start of the War on Poverty, but it was a series of social science research studies which appeared soon after the war was announced that focused attention on its underlying causes. A prominent work by Karl and Alma Taeuber (1965) initiated construction of an indicator of racial segregation that could be applied consistently across urban areas to measure the extent of isolation. The Taeubers also described the social and economic processes by which segregation was maintained and the process of neighborhood evolution as relative population sizes and composition changed over time within the urban area.

The problem of racially segregated housing was generally viewed as a major impediment to improvement in the economic status of blacks, a view that was given substance by a widely quoted study (Kain, 1968). Its argument was that black unemployment was high because of the difficulty faced by blacks in gaining access to employment: new jobs were located in the suburbs and blacks were concentrated in inner cities. This argument buttressed policy efforts in the public housing and fair housing areas and supported the view that public support of urban transportation was essential to reduce black unemployment. Kain's study prompted a number of additional research analyses designed to test the link between ghetto residence and unemployment.[25] By and large these studies failed to sustain the hypothesis, and the causes of both high black unemployment and segregated housing had to be sought elsewhere.

Two explanations—discrimination against blacks, and racial differences in income—were the subject of other research which appeared at about the same time. Richard Muth (1969) concluded that racial differences in incomes, wealth, and tastes were the cause of racially segregated housing. In response it was charged that equalization of incomes would contribute little to reducing the gap in housing differences between blacks and whites so long as discriminatory treatment of blacks by sellers, agents, and financial institutions persisted (Kain and Quigley, 1972; Strazheim, 1974).

Black Political Power

The absence of blacks in the political life of the nation was as vivid an aspect of racial inequalities in the early 1960s as was black poverty and segregation. Yet two decades later blacks were prominently, if not proportionately, represented at most levels of elective office. This rapid and substantial change resulted from a number of factors, all subjected to investigation by political scientists. The role played by OEO's Community Action program, designed to carry out the mandate of the Economic Opportunity Act of 1964 that local projects be "developed, conducted, and administered with the maximum feasible participation of the residents of the areas and the members of groups served," came under detailed and critical review, perhaps because of the unique and controversial nature of this policy. Most of its analysts seem to agree that "community action significantly contributed to black incorporation into the body politic, to the recognition of the political equality of black Americans" (Greenstone and Peterson, 1976, p. 276). Whether this development resulted from the commitment of top-level administrators (Moynihan, 1969; Friedman, 1977), or was a response to agitation and militance at the community level became a matter of disagreement;

25. See for example Mooney (1969), Kain (1974), Masters (1974), and Orr (1975).

evidence was found in support of both views (Piven and Cloward, 1971). Many accounts of the Community Action program were written (e.g., Gilbert, 1970; Brecher, 1973), as were appraisals of the extent to which blacks, who were overrepresented on the boards of local Community Action agencies, influenced the directions in which these programs developed (Hopkins and Clark, 1969; Kramer, 1969; Greenstone and Peterson, 1976). Other work described how these leaders moved from their local positions into the mainstream of U.S. politics (Kotler, 1969; Altschuler, 1970; Greenstone and Peterson, 1976; Eisinger, 1976, 1980).

The Structure and Functioning of the Labor Market

From the inception of the programs of the Great Society, the functioning of the labor market was viewed as a potential culprit in explaining why poverty existed and persisted. Several pieces of evidence lent support to that view: the unemployment rates for unskilled workers and inexperienced youth were far higher than for other groups; research suggested that groups with high poverty rates (usually minorities) were being deliberately excluded from participation; and the potential effects of lack of information, immobility, and structural rigidities (some caused by public policies) had long been documented by labor economists. The declaration of the War on Poverty gave momentum to research on these and related questions.

Labor Markets and Low-Skilled Workers

The notion that labor markets were "Balkanized," in that workers consigned to one compartment had difficulty moving to (and, hence, providing little competition with) other compartments, had previously been discussed in the labor economics literature (e.g., Kerr, 1954). The focus of the War on Poverty on aiding the poor through increasing the earnings of those with low skills raised the question of how this would be accomplished within the existing structure of labor markets. Some researchers in the late 1960s latched onto this issue and argued that antipoverty measures involving training and education were likely to be ineffective because of the dual nature of labor markets and the structure of internal job ladders in some firms.[26] Some evidence was assembled on the segmented nature of labor market operation, and the conclusion reached was that efforts on the supply (workers') side were doomed to fail unless the demand or employers' side of the market could be restructured.

26. Cain (1976) identified the antipoverty effort as a stimulant to this challenge to standard economic theory, citing Rogin's (1956) statement that "new systems of economic doctrines first emerge in the guise of arguments in the context of social reform."

Absent this change, low-skilled and minority workers would be consigned to dead-end, low-paying, unsteady jobs that offered little chance for moving up job ladders and achieving economic success.[27]

These theories concerning labor market operation represented a direct attack on the standard, neoclassical economic theory of labor markets, and were so interpreted. One of the most lively academic debates stimulated by antipoverty concerns centered on the question of whether the new labor market models added anything to properly interpreted standard theory (Wachter, 1974; Cain, 1976). These debates clarified the issues, but additional research was required to better define how labor markets, in fact, operate for low-skilled workers. The evidence suggested that both positions contained some truth: relative wages do appear to change in response to changing demand and supply conditions, but rigidities and barriers at the same time impede that upward mobility required for the rapid reduction of poverty for those with different skin color or other indentifiable characteristics. Immobility across some ill-specified boundaries of the labor market was seen to exist, but not to the extent that advocates of the dual labor market claimed. Substantial evidence, however, was found of "protected" jobs held by various groups or classes in bureaucratic firms and the public sector.[28]

As of the 1980s, while the debate continues, it is clear that the arguments of both those whose anchor is the standard, neoclassical model and those who advocate the dual or segmented market thesis have been leavened by the discussion. Attention to institutional considerations, organizational arrangements, and sociological relationships in the workplace has increased—a legacy of those who attacked the standard model. The need for understanding the role of prices in individual worker and firm decisions and of markets in changing these incentives has dampened the earlier premise that barriers were rigid and impermeable—a legacy of empirical work that was motivated by the standard model.

Minimum-Wage Legislation

The work of both those adopting the neoclassical model of the labor market and those emphasizing the segmented nature of the market was quick to focus on minimum-wage legislation as one impediment to the effective functioning of the market. For the former, the legally imposed minimum wage kept the wage for low-skilled workers from falling even when their unemployment rates grew to very high levels; as a result, the

27. See Doeringer and Piori (1971), Gordon (1972), Edwards, Reich, and Gordon (1975), and Thurow (1975).

28. See Wachtel and Betsey (1972), Wachter (1975), Cotterill (1975), Crandall, MacRae, and Yap (1975), Cain (1976), and Leigh (1976).

potential employer demand for such workers never became effective. The latter group associated the payment of the minimum wage with the lowest of the labor market segments, regarding minimum-wage jobs as largely dead ends.

Economists had long pursued research on the effect of the legal minimum wage on the performance of the labor market, but additional research on this question was stimulated by the War on Poverty (Welch, 1974; Gramlich, 1976; Mincer, 1976). Even so, the conclusions have not proved decisive. The simplest summary is that, although minimum-wage legislation does contribute significantly to high unemployment rates among the unskilled, particularly young workers, it is probably not the primary cause of their lack of employment.[29]

Public Policies to Increase the Employment of Low-Skilled Workers
During the mid-1970s, two forces combined to focus the attention of analysts on the demand side of the labor market. The first was the simultaneous occurrence of high unemployment and rapid price increases. In this context, selective measures to increase the demand for labor were seen as potentially effective instruments for generating increased employment without causing inflationary pressures. Reducing "NAIRU" (the nonaccelerating inflation rate of unemployment) became a key objective. The second force was disillusionment over the potential of employment and training measures for low-skilled workers, in the wake of evaluations that showed only modest impact (Goldstein, 1972). Again, selective employment measures were viewed as a strategy to assure minimally adequate incomes of households that contained able-bodied workers.

The demand-side strategies that were emphasized in the early literature included public employment measures, wage rate subsidies, employment subsidies (both marginal and stock, targeted and general), and public works. Each had its own set of incentives and impacts; distinguishing among them on equity and efficiency grounds absorbed a good deal of research effort during this period. Questions that were analyzed concerned various topics: Do federal funds given to state and local governments for direct job creation (public employment) generate a net increase in jobs, or does "fiscal substitution" occur—i.e., are these funds used to pay for activities that would have been undertaken even if the funds had not been granted?[30] Do employment subsidies (or tax credits) to em-

29. This conclusion is consistent with the results of the Minimum Wage Study Commission (1981).
30. See Wiseman (1976), Johnson and Tomola (1977), and Johnson (1978).

ployers have a greater aggregate employment impact or a smaller inflationary effect than other forms of subsidy or tax cuts?[31] Can direct employment creation policies be effectively used as antipoverty measures?[32] Are selective (or targeted) job creation measures an effective antidote for the distortionary effects of the minimum wage or income-conditioned transfers?[33] Can direct job creation measures meet efficiency standards?[34] How should direct job creation measures be designed in order to enable them to best achieve efficiency and equity goals?[35] Have employment subsidy programs led to an increase in employment, or have they weakened the inflation-unemployment trade-off by securing employment gains without upward pressure on prices?[36]

A wide variety of analytical techniques were employed in these studies, including labor market simulation relying on empirical estimates of relevant supply and demand elasticities,[37] microdata simulation relying on relevant labor-supply response parameters from the negative income tax experiments (discussed in Chapter 9), theoretical analysis relying on both standard equilibrium theory and disequilibrium models, macroeconomic analysis, benefit-cost analysis, and econometric studies of relevant relationships. An overall appraisal of the findings from this research indicated that carefully designed and targeted employment subsidy programs had high potential for yielding net employment increases of low-skilled workers with relatively little inflationary pressure, even in the presence of the minimum wage and other labor market distortions.

Summary

People who are of working age and who can engage in work typically escape poverty on their own, by selling their labor services in markets for

31. See Baily and Tobin (1977), Kesselman, Williamson and Berndt (1977), Hamermesh (1978), Fethke, Policano, and Williamson (1978), Burdett and Hool (1982), Johnson (1982), and Nichols (1982).

32. See Hamermesh (1978) and Betson and Bishop (1982).

33. See Johnson (1978), Haveman (1980), Johnson (1982), and Perloff (1982).

34. See Kesselman (1969, 1978), Greenberg (1978), Haveman (1978), Nathan et al. (1981), and Kemper, Long, and Thornton (1983).

35. See Barth (1974), Bishop and Haveman (1979a), Bishop and Wilson (1982), and Carcagno and Corson (1982).

36. See Bishop and Haveman (1979b), Johnson and Blakemore (1979), and Perloff and Wachter (1979).

37. The effort empirically to analyze the employment and distributional effects of labor market policies generated a complementary line of work in which estimates of the parameters relevant for analyzing market responses were developed and could be embedded in comparative static models for use in the simulation of policy impacts. See Cain and Watts

a wage. Some able-bodied working-age people don't make it, however, and the reasons for their failure are complex. In some cases, the labor services they have to sell are low valued or unsalable; in other cases, sales are hard to make because employers may not like some characteristic of the person (say, color) which is unrelated to his or her skills and productivity; in still other cases, the labor market may be insufficiently flexible to allow sales to be made at market wages because of the minimum wage or other constraints. Each of these possibilities carries with it a variety of implicit policy proposals: improved and additional education and training, equal opportunity legislation, the elimination of union power and minimum-wage laws, the enactment of wage or employment subsidies, the provision of labor market information and job placement services.

When the War on Poverty was announced, these processes were only dimly perceived and distinguished; today, they are central foci in policy discussions about how to reduce poverty or inequality. They have achieved this focal status only because the basic research efforts following 1965 have disentangled them from each other and illuminated the intricate interactions operating within each. While much remains to be learned, much as already been reported.

The research that has been so briefly discussed in this chapter contains theoretical, hypothesis-testing, and empirical or fact-finding components. The theoretical contributions have been rich and diverse. And while they have stimulated substantial hypothesis-testing research efforts, it would be inaccurate to state that any major breakthrough in understanding has resulted, or that scholars have reached a consensus on the theoretical perspective that best explains or characterizes these mechanisms. The standard neoclassical model, now leavened and hedged to accommodate a rich variety of institutional and organization arrangements, still drives most inquiries in these areas. The hypothesis-testing efforts have led to the abandonment of a variety of more extreme views of the determinants of economic success (note the nature-nurture debate, and research on the locational effects of unemployment), but they have failed to generate a clear pattern of evidence and understanding regarding the internal workings of the processes that determine how and why people succeed.

The main contributions have come from fact finding. The fifteen years of research examined here allow us to speak about black-white income gaps and changes in them, about education and training and their contribution to earnings, about the effect of labor market interventions on

---

(1973), Zucker (1973), Cotterill (1975), Crandall, MacCrae, and Yap (1975), Hamermesh (1976), Hamermesh and Grant (1979), and Nichols (1982).

wages and employment with far more assurance than was possible earlier. Relationships that we earlier knew little about, yet acted on as if we did, are now more clearly perceived. It seems unlikely that the next generation of policy-making can proceed as naïvely as did that of the previous generation.

III
Poverty Research and
Social Science Methods

The four chapters in Part III focus on the development of new research methods and approaches in the social sciences that can be traced to the public policy initiatives of the 1960s. The discussion ranges from the broad topic of the impact of the War on Poverty on the formation of a new and distinct approach to social research (policy analysis and evaluation, Chapter 8) to its impact on a narrow but important statistical issue (selectivity bias, Chapter 10).

Chapter 8 examines the emerging area of policy analysis and evaluation research in the 1960s. Interest in this applied research approach extended farther than the poverty issue, accompanying all issues with public policy content. The focus of federal policy on the poverty problem, however, gave social researchers concerned with topics related to this issue both a forum and support, and moved poverty research into the center of the policy analysis and evaluation field. During the late 1960s, research on social and antipoverty policy issues dominated this new approach to social science research, and provided this nascent subdiscipline with some of its basic research methods and important case studies. Conversely, those researchers committed to making social science relevant to public policy contributed to an effort that emphasized the application of research and knowledge to the making of policy. The parallel and symbiotic relationship of the War on Poverty and the planning-programming-budgeting system was a major factor in stimulating both the supply of and the demand for policy analysis and evaluation research.

Social experimentation, discussed in Chapter 9, represented both a major new social science research method and an important emphasis in the policy analysis and evaluation research field. Nearly all of the large and costly social experiments concerned aspects of antipoverty policy, and all were supported by the poverty program or the federal agencies involved in poverty-related issues. Without the explicit declaration of a war to eliminate poverty, this advance in methods would have been long delayed and would not have had the emphasis and content that it does.

The concern of Chapter 10 is far narrower than that of the preceding two chapters. Problems of selectivity bias plague many areas of socioeconomic research, but especially those relying on survey-based microdata. Reliable comparisons among groups affected by social policies, reliable evaluations of the impacts of policy on those affected, and reliable extrapolation to the entire population of research done on a limited group require that the processes by which those on whom the analysis focuses be identified and considered in the course of analysis. The required evaluation of antipoverty programs brought this issue to the fore, stimulating an important line of econometric work designed to account for selectivity processes in empirical work. Selection adjustments are now an important and accepted technique used in empirical work throughout the social science disciplines.

The final chapter in Part III discusses an applied research method used both in the most practical forms of policy analysis and in academic research. Microdata simulation models trace the impacts of exogenous changes, including policy measures, on individuals according to the characteristics of both the individuals and the measures. Such simulations are an important tool of policy analysts and have also been used to provide cost and caseload estimates of proposed policies. This research method, developed with the support of funds from antipoverty programs, was applied in the design of, and used to answer questions raised in the debate over, many social program proposals. As with the other research methods discussed in this section, the rapid progress in the development of microdata simulation techniques in the 1960s and 1970s is directly attributable to concern with the problem of poverty in America.

8

Policy Analysis and Evaluation Research

The year 1965 was important in the evolution of policy analysis and evaluation research as an independent branch of study. Two developments within the federal government in that year, the Great Society program initiatives and the executive order establishing the planning-programming-budgeting system (PPBS), were crucial in this regard. Both offered standing, legitimacy, and financial support to scholars who would turn their skills and interests to consideration of the efficiency with which public measures allocate resources, their impacts on individual behavior, their effectiveness in attaining the objectives for which they were designed, and their effects on the comparative well-being of rich and poor, minority and majority, and residents of particular regions.

The policy developments initiated in 1965 represented a set of social interventions on an unprecedented scale. All who were involved with them wanted to know if they were working, who was affected by them, and how. Those with the skills for and interest in answering such questions found both funding support and an attentive audience. The social science community responded. The same year saw the governmentwide adoption of the formal evaluation and analysis methods that had earlier been applied in Robert McNamara's Defense Department through the PPBS. The president's Executive Order requiring adoption of that system gave employment and financial support to thousands who wished to

155

apply their analytical skills to issues of efficiency, effectiveness, and equity.

Although social scientists had performed policy-relevant research before the 1960s, nothing could be identified as a unique approach or a particular set of questions that such studies should address. Nor was there a distinct program to train individuals for this type of research, or an identifiable association of scholars to promote such studies and to facilitate communication among those engaged in it. The development of a new branch of work after 1965, policy analysis and evaluation research, altered that situation.

This chapter will argue that the War on Poverty and Great Society interventions and the federal government's adoption of PPBS played major roles in this development; that without these policy measures the practice of policy analysis and evaluation research as we know it today would be substantially different.

Definitions

Social research, whatever its form, involves attempts to understand and explain human behavior. Viewed in this broad way, any attempt to draw a boundary between traditional, objective social science research and more normative policy analysis and evaluation research is bound to be arbitrary. Some basic social science research also provides analysis and evaluation of the impacts of public policies, and some of the efforts of policy analysts and evaluation researchers have resulted in basic research contributions in the social science disciplines. Nevertheless, a few distinctions seem in order.

Traditionally, research in the social science disciplines has been "positive" in its orientation. That is, basic social science research has sought to understand the world of human and social behavior. The question posed is, What is the nature of social behavior, and can those factors which influence and determine it be identified and their impact measured? This approach emphasizes the positive issue of understanding what is; little attention is given to establishing norms for what should be, or how to attain these norms if they are accepted. The process of social research thus involves model building, hypothesis formulation and testing, and general application of the scientific method. These traditional methods are well known and widely discussed. Policy analysis and evaluation research are akin to them, yet quite different.

The key characteristic of policy analysis and evaluation research is a focus on the activities of the public sector and their impact on the larger society. Governments, at any level, are viewed as endogenous to the social system; hence their activities are extensions of the society from which they derive. These public activities in turn affect the behavior of citizens and their well-being. As determinants of behavior and well-being, the characteristics of government interventions and the processes by which they affect the human condition are topics as important to study as any other causal phenomena. Consequently, the analysis and evaluation of the impact of public policies on individual well-being and behavior has as much claim to be a central component of social scientific research activity as any other form of study. Policy analysis and evaluation research can therefore be defined as the effort to understand the effects of the activities of government on its citizens—and, in particular, to evaluate the effects of particular programs on those aspects of behavior designated as the objectives of the intervention.

An example will clarify this distinction between traditional social science and policy analysis and evaluation research. A traditional study might deal with the phenomenon of illegal behavior, inquiring as to its extent, its nature, its causes, and its consequences. A policy analytic study, on the other hand, might focus on available measures for reducing illegal behavior; it would examine the success rates of each compared with their costs, the difficulties of administering and implementing each of the alternatives, and the distribution of the benefits and costs of each among citizens with various characteristics. The goal of such a study would be to identify the alternative that seems most effective in achieving the objective, relative to its costs. The potential political feasibility of the options might also be explored. In a similar vein, an evaluation research study would seek to appraise the performance of actual programs in reducing illegal behavior, and inquire into the characteristics of program, administration, or environment that make some options more effective than others. While the traditional study is positive in that simple understanding is sought, policy analysis and evaluation research are normative. In the latter, the goal of reducing illegal behavior is accepted; a variety of means of achieving this goal exist; the task is to identify those strategies that most effectively achieve the objective.

In addition to this positive-normative difference, it is possible further to distinguish "policy analysis" from "evaluation research." Policy analysis is generally viewed as the more normative, being concerned with the structure and operation of government programs and the extent to which they are or are not effective in attaining their goals. Policy analysis is interpreted somewhat differently by economists and political scientists, but to both the term covers studies of the character, implementation, and impacts of particular public interventions. For political scientists, the emphasis is on the process by which policies come to be adopted and constructed; the focus is on the functioning of political and administrative processes. For economists, policy analysis is taken to mean the application of standard tools of economic analysis to estimate the resource allocation (or efficiency) and the equity (or distributional) impacts of policies. In this perspective, the efficiency criterion of microeconomics is incorporated into the techniques of benefit-cost analysis to produce the practice of "policy analysis." Citizens' tastes and preferences are taken to be exogenous (not determined by the policy change) and social objectives are well defined; the task is to employ analysis to identify those strategies that are most effective in attaining these objectives.

"Evaluation research" is more akin to what is generally known as applied social research. Its emphasis is on identifying and measuring the relationship between government interventions and their impacts on people's behavior or performance. For evaluation research, as opposed to applied social research more generally, the causal variables of interest are those that are directly manipulated by government programs. What, for example, is the causal effect of a government training program on a variety of human behaviors and performances, such as labor market success? In this sense, evaluation research could be thought of as a subset of applied social research (see Behn, 1981).

In practice, policy analysis and evaluation research are distinguishable from standard social science research, which tends to be undertaken in response to and in the context of evolving knowledge, fads, outside demands, and the perceived "needs" of an academic discipline. Its goal is to add to the stock of knowledge regarding that aspect of human behavior of concern to a discipline, and the success of such research is determined by the members of the discipline and their use of the findings of the research. Policy analysis and evaluation research, on the other hand, respond to a conscious effort by government to change behavior or performance by means of public policy; they involve the examination and measurement of the impact of that policy on human well-being, behavior, and performance. While the goal of standard social science research is to advance the discipline, the primary goal of policy analysis and evaluation research is to provide information to policymakers on the impact of public measures designed to change behavior or outcomes. The hypotheses to be tested in standard social science research evolve from the researcher's own insights and interests; the hypotheses relevant to policy analysis and evaluation research are automatically provided by the very form of the intervention at which research is directed, and its objective and goals. Does a particular education and training program increase the cognitive achievement or employment and earnings of those affected; if so, by how much? Hence the emphasis of the more narrowly focused and directed policy analysis and evaluation research is on direct utilization of findings by those concerned with planning policy. It is the purpose of such research directly to assist policymakers in formulating and designing policy changes to encourage specific behaviors.

It should also be emphasized that the research methods applied in both types of study are similar. For quantitative work in both standard social science and in policy analysis and evaluation research, careful identification of the causal factors at issue is required, as is the ability to measure the contribution of a particular stimulus to some response, holding constant all other stimuli. Hence the need for experimental designs, reliable data, and statistical techniques to yield accurate measures of effect of stimulus x on result y are essential in both forms of activity.

Origins

The notion that analysts should be concerned with understanding how social policy interventions affect human behavior and well-being has early roots in all of the social science disciplines. Not all scientists, however, support the inclusion of this objective in the mission of their disciplines, and many fear that close ties to policy concerns will erode basic progress in the disciplines themselves. Acceptance of the policy analysis role of social science was given impetus by the Progressive movement at the turn of the century, which held that application of the scientific method to political problems could lead to more effective governmental performance. Lester Ward in 1906 referred to "scientific legislation"—that which he hoped would be practiced by policymakers who recognize that it is "their duty to devise ways and means for scientifically controlling [the] forces" of human nature. And an actual evaluative research study concerning the effect of drill time on spelling achievement, using cross-sectional variation in drill times among schools, was reported in 1906.

Starting in about 1920, a variety of social interventions were undertaken, with provision for the systematic evaluation of their results. Some of these studies concerned changes in industrial plant organization and their impact on worker morale; a second set concerned the effects on public health programs and health education on health status and medical practices. Policies peculiar to the Great Depression of the 1930s—work relief, direct relief, public housing, juvenile delinquency programs— were subjected to quasi-rigorous analysis to determine their effects on participants. Until World War II, what little policy research and evaluation existed was the domain of the disciplines of sociology, psychology, and public health; economists and education researches made few contributions.

In the postwar period, until 1965 policy analysis and evaluation research was largely conducted by social psychologists, who scientifically examined and reported the effects of leadership styles on children's behavior and performance, of community organization on resident morale, of antidiscrimination efforts on attitudes toward blacks, of a voluntary work camp on productivity and morale, and of public housing on health and social adjustment. In most of these studies, appropriate questions regarding cause and effect were asked. The data collection and analysis techniques used to answer the questions, however, were typically inadequate, and robust conclusions were impeded. The statistical techniques were crude; raw comparisons of typically inadequate proxies for the effects of concern were often used. The use of experimental designs, baseline interviews, and control for attrition and other forms of selectivity were basically nonexistent. Conclusions rested on impressions as much as on data and analysis, and little attention was given to identifying the objectives addressed by interventions. Because of these characteristics, policy analysis and evaluation research in the social science research community was not highly regarded at the outset of the 1960s. Edward Suchman (1967) wrote that social science researchers had been reluctant to undertake evaluation studies because of the general inadequacy of such studies as judged by "scientific standards."

New Demands in the 1960s

The announcement of an all-out effort against poverty in 1964 and the ensuing plans for a Great Society, as well as the private-sector efforts that had already begun, played a leading role in the surge of policy analysis and evaluation research activity after 1965. Two precursors of the federal effort were the urban Gray Areas projects funded by the Ford Foundation and the youth crime prevention projects funded by the President's Council on Juvenile Delinquency. Both interventions were designed with the aid of social scientists, both had social scientists on their staffs, and both included substantial evaluation efforts as part of the program. And as mentioned in Chapter 2, the OEO, the administrative arm of the War on Poverty, was staffed by individuals trained to perform the policy analysis that characterized McNamara's Defense Department. Many of the early participants in designing and implementing antipoverty policies were social scientists, convinced that their research methods could help government analyze program activities so as to expand the successful and weed out those that did not work. The presidential order establishing PPBS in 1965 formalized the role of policy analysis and evaluation research within government.

The story of the introduction of the rational decision-making paradigm into collective choices has been told before.[1] Henry Aaron (1978) characterized the role of policy analysts during these years as follows:

A . . . central aspect of the War on Poverty derives from the fact that it began just when program evaluation with the tools of economics gained currency. The year after the War on Poverty was declared, the planning, programming, and budgeting system (PPBS) was introduced. . . . Under this procedure planners sought ways to achieve objectives, taken as given, by the least costly means.

In fact, the most vigorous civilian evaluation programs grew up where the programs of the War on Poverty were concentrated . . . . Because of prodding by the Administration, the new legislation setting up OEO and other programs required large-scale efforts to evaluate and to measure the eagerly anticipated benefits from the new programs. In the spirit of the times, the new agencies attracted many young economists and other professionals who could simultaneously work on behalf of goals and principles they cherished and apply their newly acquired professional skills (p. 30).

The confluence of the role of social scientists in the planning and design of Great Society programs, the establishment of the new budgeting system in 1965, and the requirement for program evaluation written into virtually all new social legislation passed in the 1960s and 1970s led to a vigorous demand of government agencies for the services of policy analysts and evaluation researchers. This growth in demand, it should be emphasized, originated in the executive branch of government, a development that was viewed as a threat by Congress. It reinforced a growing view in the late 1960s that presidential power had eclipsed that of the legislature, that the system of checks and balances was being undermined.[2] The Congress responded by increasing staff budgets, im-

1. See the accounts of Moynihan (1969), Sundquist (1969), Kershaw (1970), Levine (1970), Rivlin (1971), and Levitan and Taggart (1976).

2. This concern was reflected in congressional hearings as early as 1968, when Senator Henry Jackson and the Committee on Foreign Relations which he chaired voiced strong concern over the use of specialist-analysts as opposed to "generalists," and its implications for Congress's ability to govern in the face of the control over information and analysis by the executive branch. In 1968, the Joint Economic Committee of the Congress undertook a major study of PPBS (U.S. Congress, Joint Economic Committee, 1969) and its policy implications. In his Foreword to that study, Senator William Proxmire (1969) reflected the more general concern with the effect of PPBS on the executive-legislative balance: "The most basic and elementary step which the Congress needs to take in improving the appropriation process is to develop a capability to ask the right questions. . . . The right basic questions are those having to do with the outputs of a program and its inputs and the

posing analysis and evaluation mandates on internal staffs and congressional agencies (e.g., the General Accounting Office), and establishing new offices with analytical capabilities (e.g., the Congressional Budget Office). It is not possible in these pages to trace the full dimensions of the resulting growth in the demand for policy analysis and evaluation research, but a few indicators can be noted:

- In 1967, the General Accounting Office (GAO) was required by amendments to the Economic Opportunity Act to evaluate the antipoverty programs. In 1970 the Legislative Reorganization Act required the GAO to evaluate the results of programs and to develop the staff capability to undertake benefit-cost analysis.
- By 1969 nearly all federal agencies had established evaluation research and policy analysis programs, often at the Assistant Secretary level, and had staffed them with social scientists committed to program evaluation. In 1969 about 2,500 staff positions existed in the federal government in support of program budget and analysis activities.
- The Legislative Reorganization Act of 1970 changed the name of the Legislative Reference Service to the Congressional Research Service (CRS) and authorized expansion of its budget, staff, and research and evaluation capabilities. By the early 1980s, CRS was providing in-depth analytical assistance under more than four hundred assignments a year; its budget grew from $213,000 in 1945 to nearly $10 million by the early 1980s.
- The Office of Technology Assessment was created in 1972 to provide to the Congress analysis and evaluation of policy decisions likely to have major and long-term environmental and technological consequences.
- In 1974 the Budget Control and Impoundment Act established the Congressional Budget Office (CBO) to provide nonpartisan analysis of the federal budget and other issues of interest to Congress. Today the CBO employs over two hundred analysts. The same act authorized the GAO to establish an office for program evaluation and review, which ultimately became the Institute for Program Evaluation.[3]
- Contracting for policy research and evaluation activities by the federal agencies grew enormously after 1965, and was estimated to be nearly $200 million in 1980.

---

economic values of each. They are questions concerning the total costs of program decisions, and not just the given year costs. They are questions having to do with the distribution of a program's costs and benefits among the people. We must, for example, determine the economic losses which will be sustained (or gains which will be forgone) if program X is reduced by 10 or 50 percent, or increased by 10 or 50 percent" (pp. viii–ix).

3. In 1972, .2 percent of the GAO's work force was composed of social scientists; by 1978, 6 percent were social scientists and only half of newly hired professional staff were auditors or accountants.

- A survey undertaken by the National Association of Budget Offices indicated that in 1970 "effectiveness analysis" was done in eight state budget offices, "productivity analysis" in fourteen. By 1975 these numbers had increased to thirty-two and thirty-one, respectively.
- A 1973 report by the GAO cited forty legislative acts which mandated program evaluation efforts. Six specified the percentage of funds to be set aside; eight others specified the form of data collection efforts.
- Compendia of federal government program evaluation studies by the GAO identified 1,700 reports completed in the fiscal years 1973–75, and another 1,700 completed in the fiscal years 1975–77. Most of the citations listed were for agencies concerned primarily with social policy and programs, and most of the policy analysis and evaluation research reports were prepared by contractors or consultants to the federal government (U.S. Comptroller General, 1978).

Even though the volume of resources devoted to policy analysis and evaluation research activities cannot be precisely quantified, there is little doubt that the post-1965 growth in this area has been enormous. Following the PPBS mandate, the executive branch of the federal government established offices for policy analysis and evaluation research throughout its major agencies.[4] The staffs in these offices consisted largely of social science analysts, and the size of the staffs grew rapidly until the mid-1970s. The response of the Congress was described above. Thus a series of interlocking developments—the influence of social scientists and policy analysts in the Kennedy and Johnson administrations, the legislative success of the War on Poverty and Great Society proposals, the role of social scientists in the implementation and design of the new social programs, the PPBS order, and the early examples set by OEO and the Department of Health, Education, and Welfare in establishing policy analysis and evaluation research offices—contributed to the burgeoning demand for analysis and evaluation and for the providers of these services during the 1960s and 1970s.

Since the mid-1970s, the course of policy analysis and evaluation has taken several turns, and the priority afforded the offices established to perform these tasks has decreased, increasingly so after 1980. Although the second Nixon administration abolished both OEO and much of the formal structure of the PPBS, the position of the offices was not downgraded, and in several prominent departments—Health, Education and Welfare; Labor; Housing and Urban Development; Agriculture—these offices expanded their resources and influence. To a limited extent, the Carter administration endeavored to elevate such functions, and at one

4. An examination of the progress made by 1969 in implementing these offices in each of the major federal agencies is given in Achinstein (1969).

point attempted a regeneration of the decision-making role of policy analysis and evaluation research through the concept of zero-based budgeting. This initiative did not have sustained presidential backing, however, and subsequently faltered. The nadir of the institutionalized policy and evaluation research effort came with the first Reagan administration. Cuts in social spending and antagonism to social science research in particular resulted in large reductions in the budgets, staff, and morale in policy and evaluation research offices throughout government.

Despite these shifting signals, a substantial number of analytical and evaluation offices in both the legislative and executive branches of the federal government—GAO, CBO, CRS—remain vital, active, and staffed with competent policy researchers. The growth in the attention given by the national government to policy analysis and evaluation research in the post-1965 period also carried over to the state and local governments, after a lag in time.

New Resources for Research

A main theme of this volume is that social science, social scientists, and their institutions—universities, research centers, and research firms—are reactive beings and institutions. Fields of study and even entire disciplines wax and wane in response to changes in the interests of the society at large, changes in the demand for the students and services which they produce, and changes in the financial support provided for the activities in which they engage. The growing interest in, demand for, and financial support of policy analysis and evaluation researchers during the 1960s and 1970s was not ignored by academia.

Course Offerings and Graduate Training

Among the earliest responses of the academic community was the development of courses in applied policy analysis and evaluation research. They emphasized the "science" of policy evaluation: microeconomics, experimental design and implementation, survey instruments and data collection, statistical analyses, causal modeling, decision models, and benefit-cost analysis. Some courses already existed, or were established, within the standard social science departments of economics, sociology, political science, and psychology. More often such training-oriented courses grew up in special policy analysis or evaluation research programs or in disciplines closely related to direct service provision—schools of social work, public administration, urban and regional planning, public health, and education. In several cases individual courses, programs of study, or training programs were initiated and supported by private foundations and government agencies which wished both to increase the analytical capabilities of existing staff and provide a pool of new researchers from which to recruit. The offer of funds was readily accepted by universities and the social scientists involved: existing courses were modified, new courses added, training programs developed.

Schools of Public Policy

A conspicuous change within the university community was the formation and development of separate programs providing undergraduate, but especially graduate, training in policy analysis and research. In his discussion of the origin of these schools of public policy, Aaron Wildavsky (1985) described their motive and purposes:

The immediate impetus [to the formation of] graduate schools of public policy was undoubtedly the Great Society . . . . What were the schools for? One thing they had in mind was a vague analogy to schools of business. These had status on campus. They were tied to external constituencies. They received support. Their graduates were employed. . . . In general, schools of policy were designed to be organizations that would do for the public sector what business schools had done for the private sector (pp. 25–26).

Principal among the several schools and programs that emphasize training in policy analysis and evaluation research are the Graduate School of Public Policy at the University of California, Berkeley; the Hubert H. Humphrey Institute of Public Affairs at the University of Minnesota; the Institute for Public Policy Studies at the University of Michigan; the John F. Kennedy School of Government at Harvard University; the Lyndon Baines Johnson School of Public Affairs at the University of Texas at Austin; the Maxwell School of Citizenship and Public Affairs at Syracuse University; the School of Urban and Public Affairs at Carnegie-Mellon University; and the Woodrow Wilson School of Public and International Affairs at Princeton University. Appendix C describes the origins, objectives, size, and structure of each of these programs.

Most of the public policy programs were created in the 1960s and early 1970s, often with the financial support of major private foundations (especially the Ford Foundation). During the 1970s, all were centers of growth within their universities (see Wildavsky, 1985). These programs typically offer both master's and doctoral training in policy analysis and evaluation research. Their programs differ, but each has at its core a firm emphasis on applied social science research. With few exceptions, even students interested in traditional public administration cannot avoid courses stressing microeconomics, benefit-cost analysis, decision models, evaluation design, and the statistical methods essential for doing rigorous program evaluation.

Research Centers, Think Tanks, and the Private Research Industry

Increased federal financing of research and evaluation also promoted the growth or reorientation of private research centers and the birth of the private research industry. This sector completed the triangle: private institutions hired and employed the new cadre of social scientists trained in policy analysis and evaluation research methods, and supplied the government with the studies that were mandated by legislation or desired for purposes of policy planning.

Perhaps the most prominent example of a research center established in response to the new era of evaluation studies is the Institute for Research on Poverty at the University of Wisconsin–Madison. The OEO planners concluded that their efforts would benefit from a basic research organization, much as the Pentagon relied upon the Rand Corporation. The University of Wisconsin was selected as the site for a university-based yet independent institution, mandated to undertake basic and applied social science research on "the nature, causes, and cures of poverty." Established in 1966, it received an annual core grant from the OEO that grew to over $1 million by 1970 and, together with other private and public grants, supported a staff that during the decade of the 1970s consisted of about forty economists, sociologists, and other social scientists, most of whom also had academic appointments at the university. When the OEO was dismantled in 1973, its research function was transferred to the Department of Health, Education, and Welfare (reorganized as the Department of Health and Human Services in 1979), which continued to fund the national research center at Wisconsin. By 1980, Institute publications included six hundred fifty discussion papers, thirty-five books, and eighteen special reports, and the Institute had sponsored ten research conferences. It also had primary responsibility for the design and analysis of the first two negative income tax experiments (see Chapter 9).

A variety of other research institutions were either formed or re-oriented in response to the federal demand and funding support for policy and evaluation research. With the support and encouragement of the Johnson administration, in particular the Department of Housing and Urban Development, the Urban Institute was established in Washington,

D.C., in 1968.[5] In contrast with the Institute for Research on Poverty, it had no tie to a university. In part because of its location, its research staff maintained close links with federal policy planners in a variety of domestic policy areas, and its activities were financed primarily by government contracts and grants. By the mid-1970s, its research staff had grown to over one hundred fifty and its annual budget to over $10 million. In 1979 it formed its own publishing house, which by 1983 had one hundred fifty titles in print.

More distinctly policy analytic centers also thrived during this period and, following the supply of dollars, directed their work toward poverty and social policy issues. The Brookings Institution increased its emphasis on social policy and social experimentation in place of its traditional concern with public finance and macroeconomic policy. The American Enterprise Institute for Public Policy Research (AEI), established in 1943, also Washington-based, expanded after the mid-1960s and published a steady stream of critiques and evaluations of federal policy initiatives, largely in the economic and social policy areas. By the early 1980s it employed over one hundred twenty-five scholars and other professional employees. Both Brookings and AEI were financed more heavily by private sources than was the Urban Institute. Other examples of the privately financed response to the "rational government" emphasis on public policy are the Hoover Institution at Stanford University and the Manhattan Institute for Policy Research in New York City (both associated with a more conservative outlook) and the Institute for Socio-Economic Studies in White Plains, New York.

These research centers illustrate one type of response to social policy efforts. Another was the growth of a major evaluation research industry, composed of private research firms, both profit and nonprofit. In terms of resources, output, and training, they were perhaps more important in the development of the field of evaluation than either the universities or the research centers. Among the more prominent are Mathematica Policy Research, Inc., the Rand Corporation, Abt Associates, and SRI (formerly affiliated with Stanford University and known as the Stanford Research Institute). Unlike the organizations described above, these

---

5. Johnson's remarks at the first meeting of the Urban Institute's board of trustees characterize the tenor of the times: "Its research must be of the highest quality but also of the greatest practicality. Its work must be to distinguish the long range from the temporary, the real from the illusory. Above all, the Institute must operate in a climate of intellectual freedom and organizational independence. The search for truth must be uncompromising, unhindered by partisan coloration or blocked by conventional wisdom." (Quoted in the Institute's *Annual Report*, 1980.)

firms have no research agendas of their own; they respond to the priorities of the federal government and other organizations as reflected in the funds made available through competitive grant awards. Their success varies directly with the government's interest in policy analysis and evaluation studies. Since 1965 they have employed a large number of the graduates of schools of public policy and other university programs that emphasize applied social research. Their involvement in the practice of policy analysis and evaluation research contributed greatly to the training of economists, sociologists, psychologists, and statisticians in the applied techniques of this field. Most of these analysts now identify their work more closely with the field of policy analysis and research than they do with the discipline in which they received their primary training.

Publications

In addition to training practitioners of the trade and selling the products of their efforts, members of guilds seek ways of more generally displaying their wares and communicating with each other. Among scientific guilds, this takes the form of new journals, magazines and other publication outlets. This new field of policy analysis and evaluation research was no exception.

In 1965, at the beginning of the growth in interest in this area, there already existed a journal, *Public Policy*, published annually by Harvard University since 1940. Before 1969, when it was taken under the wing of the Kennedy School, it had a small audience and emphasized largely descriptive, public administration issues. The two disciplines primarily represented in it were political science and public administration. When Harvard reorganized its public administration program as the Kennedy School of Government, the journal fell into its domain. The quality of the publication was upgraded, and its contents reflected the new social science research emphasis of the analysis and evaluation field.[6]

In 1975, a few years after the establishment of its Graduate School of Public Policy, the University of California at Berkeley announced the publication of a new journal, *Policy Analysis*. Standard sections within the journal were titled "Analysis and Issues," "Clients and Analysts," "Methods and Practices," and "Teaching."[7] Although not explicitly stated, the purpose of the publication was to provide a more analytical, if

6. In 1969, *Public Policy* changed from an annual review to a quarterly journal with the purpose of "using the scientific method to explain, predict, or prescribe public policy."

7. The uncertainty about the nature of the field was reflected in an "Editor's Query" in the first issue of *Policy Analysis*: "I have heard conflicting reports about the origins, both intellectual and governmental, of the term 'policy analysis.' I would like to hear from any of our readers who might clear up this confusion."

not more technical, forum for presenting research and results in the field of policy analysis.

In 1981, following the formation of a professional association of practitioners of policy analysis, the Association for Public Policy Analysis and Management, the two publications were merged into the *Journal of Policy Analysis and Management.*[8] The new periodicial was designed to continue the traditions of both journals, but soon took on its own character. Articles tended to be shorter, less academic in presentation, less technical and more catholic in the range of issues addressed than its predecessors. By 1984 the journal had a subscription list of over fourteen hundred.

Similar developments occurred in evaluation research. In 1972 the first issue of *Evaluation*, a quarterly, appeared. Billed as "a forum for human service decision-makers," the journal was supported by funds from the National Institute of Mental Health. Its articles are nontechnical, presenting new applications of evaluation techniques, discussions of problems and successes of evaluation efforts, of effects on policy of evaluation studies, and the procedures undertaken in designing evaluation studies.[9] Its circulation list grew rapidly, reaching thirty thousand in 1980. In the same year the public subsidy terminated, however, and the magazine published its last issue.

Evaluation was aimed at the community of practitioners. A more technical journal, *Evaluation Quarterly* (later renamed *Evaluation Review*), appeared in 1977. Its purpose was to publish "papers reporting the findings of evaluation studies in such fields as child development, health, education, income security, manpower, mental health, criminal justice, and the physical and social environments" and "methodological developments, discussions of the state of the art, and commentaries related to the application of research results." Its intent was to serve as a "forum for researchers, planners and policymakers." *Evaluation Review* has never achieved the circulation levels of *Evaluation*, largely because of its specific focus on "applied social research." Its circulation in 1983 was about eighteen hundred.

A range of other publications reflected the intellectual development of

---

8. Another journal, *Policy Sciences*, is in the tradition of *Policy Analysis* and *Public Policy*, but emphasizes political science rather than economics.

9. The publication's stated purpose was as follows: "*Evaluation* is designed to draw together information on evaluation activities from all the relevant human service fields, to enable those involved in such activities to communicate with each other, and to inform various publics of the presence and vitality of these activities. . . . It is oriented toward those who wish to understand better how to proceed with evaluation efforts and also how to deal with the consequences of such efforts."

the field. In the late 1960s a variety of texts and manuals emerged, emphasizing such particular topics as methodology, field experiments, or evaluation principles.[10] Together with a sizable number of volumes of readings concerning both methodological and applied studies, they were used as text material in courses, mostly at the graduate level, on evaluation in social science departments and professional schools. Many of these texts and manuals emphasized social program evaluation and research (applied research); others focused on methods and techniques of analysis that were applicable to public investments in physical resources, such as transportation and water supplies (benefit-cost analysis), or military decisions (cost-effectiveness analysis). A major congressional study in 1969 (U.S. Congress, Joint Economic Committee, 1969), a three-volume compendium of fifty papers written by prominent theorists and practitioners of policy analysis and evaluation research, was the earliest of several publications that collected and dispersed the best writings in the field. Reflecting the economic efficiency and equity concerns of applied welfare economics, the congressional study contained sections on the theoretical bases for public sector interventions, the institutional constraints on achieving efficient public policies, analytical and methodological problems in evaluating public programs, the status and accomplishments of PPBS in the federal government, and the next steps for analysis and evaluation in federal policy-making.

A number of commercial publishers began annual series of publications on the topics identified in the congressional study. The first was a 1971 volume, *Benefit Cost Analysis*, which in its second year changed the title to *Benefit-Cost and Policy Analysis*. It continued through 1974. The Sage Publishing Company initiated two series, each directed toward a particular set of concerns in the policy analysis and evaluation research fields: *Evaluation Studies Review Annual*, first published 1976, and *Policy Studies Review Annual*, which began in 1977. Sage has also developed other materials—manuals, handbooks, methodological texts, and descriptions of analysis and evaluation practice—addressed to the growing community of evaluation researchers and policy analysts.

Professional Associations

In addition to new programs of instruction and training and publication outlets, the development of new fields or disciplines is usually accompanied by the establishment of professional associations. Such groups

10. A number of these volumes are cited and discussed in Caro (1971). A leading example is Suchman (1967).

promote communication among individuals in the field, facilitate presentation of research findings, and offer a forum for discussion of mutual concerns. The field of policy analysis and evaluation research has followed this pattern.

The first organization, the Evaluation Research Society, was formed in the mid-1970s. A leader in its founding was Marcia Guttentag, whose writings influenced the early development of this research area. The organization's stated purpose is "to improve the theory and practice of evaluation" by providing "a forum . . . to exchange ideas and experiences on the planning, conduct, and use of evaluation." Attendance at its annual meetings is about one thousand. Most of the members of the society are psychologists and sociologists; few are economists.

The policy analysis wing of the field was somewhat slower in organizing a professional association. After a prolonged period of consultation with research organizations and universities with strong interests in policy studies and analysis, the Association for Public Policy Analysis and Management was created in 1980 "for the purpose of encouraging excellence in research, teaching, and practice in the field of public policy analysis and management, including decision-making and policy-making theory, quantitative and other methods for analyzing public policies and their implementation and management, as well as the application of policy analytic theory and methods to substantive policy problems." The association sponsors an annual conference, publishes (as noted above) the *Journal of Policy Analysis and Management*, and supports other activities to foster interaction among those in the several disciplines that practice policy analysis. The annual meeting is attended by about three hundred people. Most of its members are economists, academics associated with public policy institutes and schools, and researchers employed by private research and consulting organizations.

The Policy Studies Organization is concerned with public policy analysis from an institutional or political science viewpoint. It publishes two journals, *Policy Studies Journal* and *Policy Studies Review*, and has a membership of about twenty-three hundred.

Policy Analysis, Evaluation Research, and Social Science: An Assessment

Much has been written about the effect of policy analysis and program evaluation on the making of public policy, and much of that writing has emphasized the difficulty of altering a political process which moves in accord with its own power relationships and is governed by objectives whose overlap with the goals of efficiency, effectiveness and equity—the major concerns of the analysis and research community—is slim at best.[11] Another aspect of the policy analysis and evaluation research effort has been largely ignored, however: its influence on the community of social scientists and applied social researchers in universities, government, and research centers and firms. As a consequence of the policy developments that led to a formation of the new field of policy analysis and evaluation research, all universities of note have been forced to address the issue of whether or not to establish or expand a program of public policy studies. If established, should it be primarily a teaching or a research organization? Should it emphasize doctoral training, or be a professional program? Should it be a component of an existing department or school, or stand alone? What should be its ties to departments or programs of public administration, economics, political science, sociology, and the other social science disciplines? Should it be regarded as a professional school or program or as a scientific discipline in its own right? Questions of size and administrative structure followed.

Many universities—nearly all of the major national institutions—responded affirmatively, and policy analysis and evaluation research stands as an identifiable program, department, or school within them. The creation of these organizations directly affected the standard disciplines, in particular economics, political science, and sociology. Research and instructional staff are typically drawn from these departments, and new appointments made to these programs often involve tenure in one of the disciplines.

As is natural, an expanding component in an organization that is otherwise fairly constrained in size is able to exert substantial leverage on both the objectives and operation of the entire organization. Perhaps more fundamentally, the growing relative demand for the services of those academics trained in and performing policy analysis and evaluation research activities—the demand for trained staff from private research firms, government agencies, and think tanks, and the demand for consultant services from these same organizations—has led to a reorientation of curricula, faculty composition, and program emphasis within the traditional social science disciplines as well.

Although difficult to document, one senses that in the mid-1980s the disciplines of economics and political science, and to a lesser extent sociology and psychology, are far more oriented to understanding and appraising what it is that government is and "should be" doing than they

---

11. These studies include Haveman (1976), Weiss (1977), Aaron (1978), Lynn (1978), Stromsdorfer (1979), Covello (1980), and Behn (1981).

were in the mid-1960s. This concern for the practice of policy analysis and evaluation research has also spread to many disciplines and quasi-professional fields that are derivative from (and in some sense satellite to) the traditional fields. It is the rare program, school, or department of urban and regional planning, education, public administration, business administration, health services, social work, and law that does not have courses or areas of concentration devoted to the subject of policy analysis and program evaluation. There is little doubt that the confluence of the antipoverty effort and the movement to rationalize government, reflected in PPBS, has played a major role in this evolution.

This discussion, however, leaves untouched fundamental questions concerning the field of policy analysis and evaluation research. Has it yielded important intellectual contributions which have carried over into the social science disciplines? Has it been responsible for major theoretical or methodological breakthroughs which have influenced science generally? Does it deserve to be regarded as a distinct discipline in its own right? If so, how does it relate to the traditional social science disciplines? Is it complementary to existing fields, or is it perceived as failing to meet the highest standards of the social sciences, and thus poses a threat? These questions cannot be answered definitively; each observer has his or her own view of the larger contributions of this post-1965 development. The following propositions, drawn from a variety of assessments of the accomplishments, status, and standing of this applied, policy-oriented development in the social sciences, offer a balanced appraisal.[12]

- Policy analysis and evaluation research have progressed to the point that some studies have attained levels of reliability sufficient to have a major impact on the policy-making process, especially in the area of social policy.
- While some striking examples of breakthrough studies are in evidence, much of what passes as policy analysis and evaluation research does not meet the standards of quality and reliability of the standard social science disciplines.
- The highest quality of talent in the social sciences has not gravitated toward the policy analysis and evaluation research field; this, together with the political and funding context in which policy research occurs, has contributed to the perception of many social scientists that much of what passes as applied social research fails to meet acceptable scientific standards.

12. The assessments include Rossi and Wright (1977), Rossi, Wright, and Wright (1978), Stromsdorfer (1979), Behn (1981), Mundel (1985), and Wildavsky (1985).

- Universities, because of a wide variety of constraints, have not been at the forefront in the performance of large-scale applied social research projects. Responsibility for these projects rests primarily with private research firms and think tanks; the universities have emphasized the training of policy analysts and evaluation researchers.
- The shortcomings in quality of work and talent in policy analysis and evaluation research are in large part due to the exceedingly rapid growth of demand for such applied social research; there are now strong signs that the average quality of evaluation research studies is improving significantly.
- The post-1965 growth in the demand for policy analysis and evaluation research sparked a number of methodological and data collection advances in the social sciences. Corrections for selectivity bias in econometrics and the development of social experimentation and microdata simulation modeling are methodological developments attributable in part to this demand. The rapid increase in readily available, large-scale, cross-sectional and longitudinal survey data is also a by-product of this emphasis.
- The focus on social problems that is the hallmark of the policy analysis and evaluation research area has generated an ongoing set of important and interesting issues that have been and will continue to be grist for the practice of social science. Because of the development of this policy emphasis, social science is now more relevant and more interesting than it would otherwise be.

9

Social Policy Experimentation

The designs for a Great Society involved a wide variety of policy interventions that were intended to alter social positions, change the nature of social interactions, and modify the behavior and performance of low-income people. Because U.S. policymakers had little experience in such matters and were uncertain about how to proceed, many of the interventions were called "demonstration projects." Relative to previous efforts, they represented a strong attempt directly to change individual behavior and economic status.

In this environment social experimentation was born. At the time that the OEO was initiating demonstration projects through its Community Action program, it was also considering a major income support proposal—a negative income tax (NIT) that would replace much of the nations's welfare system with a uniform income guarantee, conditioned on family size, which would gradually diminish as earnings rose above zero. Through the NIT, income support would be provided to male-headed as well as female-headed families, large state differences in benefit levels would be reduced, and work disincentives would be minimized because dollars earned would not result in equivalent benefits lost. Relative to the existing income support system, the NIT was a major innovation; its adoption would have been better termed an overhaul than reform.

In discussions of the NIT within OEO, the work-incentive issue was viewed as crucial in determining its political feasibility (Levine, 1970; Lampman, 1976). The notion of a guaranteed income was considered by many as inviting large reductions in work effort, primarily by men who were family heads. To those involved in the debates, it was clear that the labor-supply effects of an NIT could not be adequately evaluated from existing studies, which were based on cross-sectional data, or from a simple field test. It required an evaluation of the work-effort behavior of those covered by an NIT as compared to those who were not covered—in short, a controlled experiment.

Such experimentation had long been practiced in the biological sciences and psychology, but for a variety of reasons involving ethics, cost, and complexity the use of this research technique by economists and other social scientists had been minimal. It had, however, been discussed by some social scientists,[1] and it appeared ideally suited for reliably estimating the labor-supply effects of an NIT. The decision to launch an experimental undertaking of this nature marked the beginning of social experimentation as a social science research tool and as an essential instrument of policy analysis and program evaluation. That development is the subject of this chapter.

The Nature of Social Policy Experimentation

Soon after the War on Poverty began, social researchers and policy analysts became discouraged regarding their ability to assess the effects of the new interventions on recipients, to measure the benefits of programs and compare them with the costs, and to make cross-program comparisons of effectiveness. In 1971 Alice Rivlin, who had been intimately involved in these efforts, wrote: "Systematic analysis has improved our knowledge of the distribution of the initial costs and benefits of social programs. . . . [but] little progress has been made in comparing the benefits of different social action programs. . . . Little is known about how to produce more effective health, education, and other social services" (p. 7; see also Rees, 1974). And, regarding the analysis of behavioral responses to social programs, Harold Watts argued in an internal OEO memorandum in 1965 that standard cross-sectional analysis would never be able accurately to estimate the labor-supply and other behavioral responses to, say, income support policy reforms.[2]

---

1. See the discussion in Orcutt and Orcutt (1968), Campbell (1969), and Rivlin (1971).

2. See also Campbell (1969). An even stronger statement of this view was expressed in a paper by Orcutt and Orcutt that circulated widely in 1967 (published in 1968): "It would appear that possibly several million dollars per year are needed for a moderately comprehensive and highly attractive program of systematic incentive experimentation in the United

At about this same time, a growing number of economists became interested in a research technique that appeared to hold promise for providing reliable answers to questions regarding the behavioral impacts of social policy interventions. The technique involved the application of the experimental method of the biological sciences to human subjects.

The idea behind a social experiment to test an NIT was simple: design a basic plan and establish a set of income guarantees and benefit-reduction rates (also termed tax rates, referring to the rate at which earnings above the guarantee are taxed away through reduced benefits) judged to be in the relevant range; choose a sample of households for whom an NIT is a viable policy option; randomly assign these households to an NIT group (the experimental group), the remainder forming a control group; administer the NIT plan to households in the experimental group for some period of time; measure the work-effort patterns of those in the experimental group relative to the labor-supply patterns of those in the control group; adjust for any other factors not taken into account in the experimental design; and attribute the remaining difference in labor supply to the NIT.

Behind this simple idea lies a wide variety of technical, empirical, and implementation issues, of which the following are the most important:

- What variables should be emphasized in the experimental design? How many combinations of income guarantees and tax rates should be tested?
- What experimental units should be included? Individuals? Couples? Two-parent families? Single-parent families? In what environment should the experiment be placed in order to secure the desired level of relevance and generality of results? Urban or rural areas? Large towns or small? Suburbs or inner cities?
- How large a sample is required in order to achieve acceptable levels of statistical reliability for each plan tested? How should those in the experimental group be allocated across the plans tested so as to maximize the statistically reliable information obtained, given the cost?

States. Relative to the billions being spent on research in the physical and biological sciences, a few million per year seems paltry. Yet is this much feasible? To us it is obvious that [social experimentation] research is of greater social importance than an accelerator costing an initial two hundred and fifty million [dollars] and requiring an annual research budget of perhaps an additional sixty million. What do policy makers controlling the availability of research funds think though? No doubt we are now rich enough to afford both kinds of research, but will we? Time will tell if our society is mature enough to use that most basic and powerful of all scientific tools, experimentation, in learning to master critical social problems" (p. 759).

- What behavioral variables should be measured for units in both the experimental and control groups? Should only labor-supply responses (hours worked, weeks worked, earnings) be measured, or should a variety of other variables of interest (e.g., consumption patterns, family structure) also be measured?
- For how long should the experimental treatment be administered in order to secure a reliable measure of long-run response? One year? Three? Five?
- How is the experiment to be "fielded"; how are observation units to be chosen, enrolled, and have the treatment administered? How can its administration be structured so as to minimize Hawthorne effects (i.e., a behavioral response simply to being in an experiment, rather than to the specific treatment)?
- What statistical techniques are to be employed in analyzing the results of the experiment? Simple control-experimental comparisons? Or complex models to reflect design characteristics of the experiment or to adjust for the self-selection of units of observation into the experiment or for their attrition over the course of the experiment?
- To what extent can the observed responses of a sample of randomly selected and isolated individuals be taken as evidence of the impact of a national program?

Although the difficulty of these issues was, at some level, perceived by economists and other social scientists at this time, by the late 1960s a number of leading social science investigators had become enthusiastic supporters of this mode of research, concluding that the gains available from social experimentation exceeded the disadvantages, which included its large financial costs. Alice Rivlin stated what many social scientists and policy analysts believed at this time:

On balance, I believe the advantages of social experimentation far outweigh the disadvantages, and that the federal government should follow a systematic experimentation strategy in seeking to improve the effectiveness of social action programs. The process will not be easy or quick or cheap. . . . But unless we begin searching for improvements and experimenting with them in a systematic way, it is hard to see how we will make much progress in increasing the effectiveness of our social services (1971, pp. 118–19).

The New Jersey Experiment: First of Its Kind

The favorable attitude of social scientists toward the potential of social experimentation was linked with the nation's first social experiment, the

New Jersey Income Maintenance Experiment.[3] Early in 1967, OEO granted funds to the Institute for Research on Poverty at the University of Wisconsin–Madison, which subcontracted to Mathematica Policy Research, Inc., a for-profit research firm in Princeton, New Jersey, for an experiment to test the labor-supply effects of an NIT. The coalescence of the interests of academic social scientists and the policymakers at OEO in a social experiment of this nature was described by Robert Lampman:

OEO was looking for new ways to establish the cost-effectiveness of alternative negative-income-taxation patterns, and academic econometricians were eager to take social science over the threshold into the realm of controlled experimentation. It was a rare combination of willing parties meeting at the right time, and it generated extraordinary enthusiasm to go ahead with an experiment. This enthusiasm was sufficient to prevail even in the face of serious questions about how well this experiment would serve the interests of policymakers or social scientists (1976, pp. xvi–xvii).

The history of the decision to undertake the New Jersey experiment has been told several times, and will not be repeated here (see Levine, 1970; Lampman, 1976; Rossi and Lyall, 1976). Several points in that history are relevant. First, many economists and other social scientists believed that an NIT had merit for reducing poverty that far exceeded its disadvantages (as perceived at that time). It was widely regarded as an idea whose time had come. Second, the potentially adverse labor-supply responses of adult men to an income guarantee plan were seen as the crucial policy question concerning the ultimate merit of an NIT. It represented the efficiency cost that would be associated with the equity gain in the form of poverty reduction. Third, experimentation with human subjects was viewed as a last resort; no other means of securing

3. The acknowledgements in an early paper advocating this method of policy evaluation, that of Orcutt and Orcutt (1968, cited in the previous note) illustrate this linkage: "A December 1966 draft of an exciting proposal by the United Planning Organization of Washington, D.C. provided the original stimulus for this paper. Entitled, 'A Proposal for a Demonstration of New Techniques in Income Maintenance,' the draft was written by Miss Heather Ross, a Brookings Research Fellow in 1966–67. William Baumol, Martin David, James Duesenberry, Robert Ferber, Robert Lampman, Robert Solow, Henri Theil, James Tobin, Harold Watts, and William H. White were of great help developing the substance of our current paper. We hope it has and will continue to contribute to the undertaking and execution of planned experimentation in this important area" (p. 754). The Ross proposal, submitted to OEO in 1966, was the subject of considerable discussion within the agency and among academics. The scholars acknowledged by Orcutt and Orcutt form a stellar cast of prominent social scientists, most of them economists. The experimental idea in the proposal did affect thinking in OEO, and was developed further by its research staff and others in the academic community.

reliable estimates on labor-supply responses appeared possible. Fourth, the experiment was a feasible undertaking of the federal government, largely because it could be justified as a demonstration project, and hence funded by OEO's Community Action program. It took on the rationale and aura which protected this program. Finally, while its status as a demonstration project was important in securing agency funding, the experiment gained support at the congressional level because it had the backing of the social science research community.

The New Jersey undertaking was the nation's first full-scale social experiment. From the award of the original grant to submission of the final report late in 1973, the experiment absorbed a total of six and one-half years. The four years of the operating phase were sandwiched between 44 months of planning and design and 16 months of data analysis. The experiment cost about $8 million, one-third of which went for payments to participating families.

To ensure that reliable estimates of relevant labor-supply responses could be secured, 1,375 intact "permanently poor" families containing a prime-aged man (between 18 and 58 years old) were selected for participation, 725 of whom were randomly assigned to one of eight NIT plans. The allocation of families to the various plans (including the control group) was guided by the Conlisk-Watts model, which is itself a major methodological contribution to the social sciences (see Conlisk and Watts, 1969).

The results of the experiment indicated that the response of the husbands of the families was small and not statistically significant. Wives, however, showed large and statistically significant reductions in labor supply owing to the experiment. Family labor-supply reductions fell into the 5 to 10 percent range. Contrary to the other groups, blacks showed very little response to the NIT incentives.[4]

Although diverse and sometimes inconsistent with theoretical expectations, the results shed considerable light on a policy question of prime concern in all welfare-reform discussions: To what extent will income-conditioned cash transfer programs affect the labor supply of male family heads? To the extent that the results of the experiment could be generalized to the nation's low-income population, they indicated that a national program of income-conditioned transfers, providing benefits at the level of those in the program, would have relatively small effects on the labor supply of men who headed families.

If one calculates the cost of an NIT program on the assumption of no

4. The most comprehensive description of the experiment and evaluation of its labor-supply results are in Watts and Rees (1977).

labor-supply response, then these results strongly suggest that the cost so calculated will be too low. However, the added cost produced by the work response is a rather small portion of the total cost—not over 20 percent, and probably closer to 10 percent. The estimates suggest that a substantial part of this added cost is, in effect, compensation for mothers whose withdrawal from paid employment is likely to be offset by increased child care and "home employment." There is a further suggestion that tax (benefit-reduction) rates higher than 50 percent may lead to a more pronounced reduction in work effort and consequently a larger addition to total cost. Whatever the percentage change in income, a higher tax rate requires that more of the change will be made up in benefits.

As the first controlled social experiment, the New Jersey project was subjected to detailed scrutiny from the research community. Within six months of the presentation of the final report on the experiment, the Brookings Institution sponsored a conference of nearly fifty social scientist and policy analysts to review the results of the experiment (Pechman and Timpane, 1975). Five papers were commissioned from researchers not associated with the experiment who reviewed and evaluated the design, the analyses of effects, and the policy implications of the experiment. At about the same time, an in-depth review of the history and conduct of the experiment and an evaluation of its results were sponsored by the Russell Sage Foundation (Rossi and Lyall, 1976).

The reviews produced a wide-ranging critique. The focus of the experiment on the labor-supply issue was seen by some as too restrictive, making the project an empirical test of microeconomic theory, rather than an effort designed to yield policy-relevant information. The choice of the experimental units was criticized as being too limited; e.g., little could be said about the work response of female family heads to an NIT or to the national costs of such a program. Further, the treatments chosen were sufficiently similar to preclude evaluation of the relative effects of tax rates and guarantees, and the choice of sites so restrictive as to eliminate the possibility of generalizing the results to larger population groups. There were four basic criticisms:

1. Limiting the eligible population in the experiment to families with incomes of less than 150 percent of the poverty line resulted in a truncated sample that inhibited achievement of unbiased estimates of response.
2. The experiment was plagued with problems of attrition, in part caused by a decision of the state of New Jersey to institute a welfare plan for male-headed families after the start of the experiment. This also

created substantial difficulty in achieving unbiased estimates of response.

3. The preexperimental values of important variables related to labor supply (e.g., wage rates, hours worked, and earnings of all household members) were measured in far less than ideal fashion.

4. The duration of the experiment may be too short to permit reliable estimates of the effects of a permanent program.

The Second Generation of Experiments

The New Jersey project represented the general acceptance of large-scale social experimentation as a valid research tool for estimating important behavioral responses to proposed policy interventions. The fact that it was successfully designed and fielded, and that it yielded estimated responses that passed the scrutiny of the research community,[5] led to a wide variety of additional, publicly funded social experiments.

Table 9.1 lists the most significant of these experiments and presents basic facts regarding them.[6] The table proceeds chronologically, although the income maintenance (1–4), labor market (8–9), and electricity pricing experiments (10) are grouped together.

The tabular progression shows the evolution of the experiments. The early ones were primarily in the income maintenance or welfare area, followed by efforts to test alterations in the provision of education,

5. Rossi and Lyall (1976) concluded: "First, the NIT Experiment is a remarkable achievement in design, data collection, and analysis. Second, it is difficult to imagine a set of social scientists doing much better in those respects given the state of prior knowledge concerning the substantive area and the state of the art concerning field experiments. Third, ranked in relation to other larger scale researches of contemporary period, the NIT must be considered, if not first, at least among the best two or three" (pp. 6–7). They also found "much to admire in the boldness of the experimenters in venturing upon what history will undoubtedly regard as one of the major 'firsts' in policy related empirical social research, in their unflagging devotion to carrying out a long-term research endeavor, and in the technical skills with which the resulting data were handled. Nothing we can say can detract from the considerable accomplishment that this experiment represents for social science research" (p. 175).

Pechman and Timpane (1975), while more cautious in their appraisal, summed up the consensus of the Brookings conference participants: "It was generally agreed that the New Jersey experiment was conducted with diligence and intelligence, that the insights gained in program design have improved subsequent experiments, and that the administrative feasibility of a negative income tax has been demonstrated. In addition, the experiment corroborates and improves on other contemporary findings about labor-supply response of workers to a negative income tax" (p. 13).

6. The contents of Table 9.1 are drawn from Greenberg and Robins (1985), who identify 29 social experiments in the post-1965 period. Their total costs amount to about $150 million more than those in Table 9.1.

health, and housing subsidies to low-income families. The latest experiments, beginning in the mid-1970s, emphasized the work effort and productivity effects of employment and training interventions and the electricity usage response under altered utility-pricing arrangements. The experiments grew more complex through time. Whereas the initial projects involved relatively simple treatments with relatively straightforward hypotheses to be tested, the subsequent labor market experiments involved more complicated treatments, often involving several interventions designed to be mutually supportive (e.g., income support plus counseling plus training). Because these treatments were not independently assigned, the findings of these more complex experiments are difficult to interpret.[7]

Stated in constant (1983) dollars, the ten social experiments listed in the table involved a total cost of about $1.1 billion, of which about $450 million can be attributed to research and administrative costs. Relative to the total volume of annual poverty research and poverty-related research expenditures identified in Chapter 3—about $75 million and $300 million, respectively, in 1980 (current dollars)[8]—this support for social experimentation research is large indeed. A brief examination of the most important of these projects is in order.

The Seattle-Denver Experiment

The Seattle-Denver Income Maintenance Experiment, often referred to as SIME-DIME, was the largest and most comprehensive of the NIT experiments. It was formally launched in Seattle in 1970 and in Denver in 1971 under contracts between the states of Washington and Colorado and the Department of Health, Education, and Welfare. The experiment was administered by Mathematica Policy Research, Inc.; SRI (formerly the Stanford Research Institute) designed the experiment and was given major responsibility for evaluating it.

Approximately 4,800 families were enrolled. Most of those assigned to experimental NIT plans were potentially eligible for payments for a period of either three or five years. A very small number of families were enrolled into experimental plans lasting up to twenty years. To be eligible for enrollment, families had to contain at least one able-bodied, nonaged adult. If only a single adult was present, the family was also required to have one or more dependent children. The sample consisted of lower-income black, white, and Hispanic families with either one or two parents

---

7. Greenberg and Robins (1985) suggest three "eras" in social policy experimentation, making still other distinctions between earlier and later experiments.

8. The $75 million and $300 million estimates exclude expenditures on social experimentation. These are classified as demonstrations. See Chapter 3.

Table 9.1. The Major Social Experiments

	Date of Field Work	Final Report Date	Nature of Treatment
1. New Jersey Income Maintenance	1968–72	1974	NIT
2. Rural Income Maintenance	1969–72	1976	NIT
3. Gary Income Maintenance	1971–74	None	NIT plus day care
4. Seattle-Denver Income Maintenance	1970–78	1983	NIT plus employment counseling and educational vouchers
5. Education Performance Contracting	1970–71	1972	Cash payment as incentive for academic performance
6. National Health Insurance	1974–81	Forthcoming	Different fee for service health insurance plans with alternative coinsurance rates and deductibles, plus a pre-paid group plan.
7. Housing Allowances[b]	1973–77	1980	Cash housing allowance
8. National Supported Work Demonstration	1975–79	1981	Temporary employment with group support and behavioral reinforcement
9. Employment Opportunity Pilot Project[e]	1979–81	1983	Employment preceded by required job search and training (if necessary)
10. Electricity Time-of-Use Pricing (15 experiments)	1975–	1979–	Time-of-use electricity price schedules

Source: Greenberg and Robins (1985), plus author's data.

Note: n.a. = not available or not applicable.

[a]Number of students remaining in the program the entire school year. The initial sample comprised 24,000 students split evenly between control and experimental groups.

[b]There were three different housing allowance experiments during the 1970s. They have been folded together here for brevity.

Table 9.1. (*continued*)

Response Measured	Number of Participants	Research and Administrative Costs (1983 dollars, in millions)	Total Costs (1983 dollars, in millions)
Labor supply of head, spouse, family	1,216 families	$15.4	$22.2
Labor supply of head, spouse, family	809 families	$9.5	$15.6
Labor supply of head, spouse, family and use of day care	1,780 families	$33.0	$45.2
Labor supply, marital stability, earnings capacity of head, spouse, family	4,784 families	$97.8	$132.7
Educational improvement of junior high students	19,399 students[a]	n.a.	$14.3
Demand for health care and change in health status	2,823 families	$94.4	$115.0
Use of allowance; effect on quality, supply, and costs of housing; administrative feasibility	—[c]	$160.4	$352.2
Administrative costs, effects on antisocial behavior, changes in earnings	6,606 individuals	$16.9[d]	$126.8
Effect on welfare caseload, private sector labor market, use of program, administrative costs and feasibility	Open to all heads of households on public assistance	n.a.	$246.0
Alterations in electricity use levels and patterns among residential consumers	n.a.	n.a.	≈$50.0

[c] One of the housing allowance experiments was based on open enrollment; the other two involved random selection of participants.

[d] Research only.

[e] Terminated before completion.

185

present. Many of the families might be considered middle class, however, since those enrolled were required to have incomes below the *median* national income. Participation was restricted to residents of Seattle and Denver, but families could continue in the experiment if they moved out of those cities.

The experiment had two main goals within its rather elaborate design. The first was to determine the effect of alternative NIT plans on the work behavior of the poor, a goal similar to that of the New Jersey experiment. The second was to test the feasibility and effectiveness of educational vouchers provided to low-income workers. SIME-DIME tested eleven NIT plans with income guarantees ranging from slightly below to about 40 percent above the poverty threshold and tax rates ranging from about 50 to 70 percent. With this range of tested guarantees and tax rates, the designers hoped to detect the impact of a meaningful array of plans. Families were randomly assigned to one out of the eleven NIT plans or to control status.

The work-effort findings from the experiment were released in 1983 (U.S. Department of Health and Human Services, 1983). The results showed that the NIT plans caused substantial reductions in labor market activity, particularly among persons enrolled in the plans of longer duration (five years) and among women.[9] Prime-aged men reduced their annual hours of work by 9 or 10 percent in response to the plans; their spouses reduced annual work hours by 17 to 20 percent; and women heading single-parent families reduced annual work hours by more than 20 percent—some by as much as 30 percent. These work reductions are larger than those reported in the New Jersey experiment, and were enough to cause alarm not only among conservatives already opposed to an NIT but also among centrists with no strong opinions about the desirability of such income support. Taken by themselves, the estimated work reductions have little to tell us about the overall desirability or feasibility of enacting an NIT;[10] such a program has impacts far beyond

9. The estimate of the impact on women heading single-parent families is based on the responses of women in the five-year group during the fourth and fifth experimental years. Remaining estimates are based on reported responses of enrollees in both the three- and five-year groups during the second and third experimental years.

10. The work reductions appear to be fairly substantial, but the work disincentive (i.e., the size of the guarantee) was also quite substantial, larger in fact than that which would be provided under most proposed NIT plans. The Seattle-Denver plans tested an average income guarantee of 115 percent of the poverty threshold and a marginal tax averaging only about 50 percent. The experiment also provided rebates for state, federal, and FICA taxes on earned income. About 80 percent of enrolled families faced a break-even level (the point at which no public supplement was needed) that was more than one-and-a-half times the poverty threshold, and 50 percent faced a break-even more than twice the poverty level. By

labor-supply effects. Nevertheless, they did affect the welfare reform proposals submitted by the Carter administration.[11]

The second objective of the experiment was to test the effectiveness of issuing education and training vouchers to low-income breadwinners. Families in the experiment were randomly assigned to one of three employment and training programs or to control status.[12] Participation in the program was reasonably high.[13] Not surprisingly, much of the subsidy went to pay for schooling that probably would have been obtained in the

---

contrast, the combined income guarantee provided by AFDC and food stamps was, in 1984, below the poverty level in most states, and the break-even level for AFDC is below the poverty level in all but 15 states (Department of Health and Human Services, 1983, p. 6).

11. The results showed convincingly that the work incentive provided by an NIT's low marginal tax rate was more than offset by the work disincentive effects caused by higher overall transfers. For example, simulations based upon the Seattle-Denver results demonstrated that replacement of the current welfare and food stamp programs with a national NIT that has a guarantee equal to three-quarters of the poverty line and a marginal tax rate of 50 percent would reduce aggregate labor supply in two-parent families by about 1 percent. Labor supply in two-parent families with annual incomes below $5,000 would be reduced by more than 8 percent. Although it is difficult to find these estimates, by themselves, to be discouraging, they contain an implication that is dispiriting to policymakers who wish simultaneously to support incomes and increase the self-reliance of needy families. According to the Seattle-Denver estimates, under the NIT plan just described it would cost the government $1.79 in transfer outlays to raise the net income of poor two-parent families by $1.00. In other words, 44 percent of the net program costs of the NIT would be "consumed" by breadwinners in the form of leisure. (The net program cost of the NIT is the amount by which NIT transfers exceed those now paid under the welfare and food stamp programs.) See Aaron and Todd (1979), and U.S. Department of Health and Human Services (1983).

12. Assignments to the employment and training programs were conducted in such a way that analysts were able reliably to distinguish the separate impacts of those program and the tested NIT plans. All three of the labor market programs provided a structured course of manpower counseling to help participants decide on an appropriate strategy of employment, education, and training. This course was voluntary, informational in content, and nondirectional (that is, participants were not encouraged to pursue any particular course of action). One of the tested programs offered no service beyond this counseling. The other two offered subsidies to pay for some or all of the direct costs of schooling or training. Two levels of voucher subsidy were tested. In the more generous plan, 100 percent of direct training costs were reimbursed by the experiment. In the other plan, only 50 percent of costs were reimbursed. Participants could use their vouchers to pay for any education or training they chose, so long as it was at least tangentially related to improving their future job prospects. The purpose of the vouchers was to encourage eligible breadwinners to invest in worthwhile training and education, which according to human capital theory should have improved participants' employability and future earnings.

13. About one-fifth of family heads in two-parent families used the 50 percent vouchers, and over one-third used the 100 percent vouchers. About one-third of single mothers eligible for the 50 percent vouchers used them, as did nearly one-half of those eligible for the 100 percent vouchers.

absence of the program. The more generous subsidy program succeeded in encouraging extra investment in formal schooling (as opposed to technical training), the increase averaged about one-half an academic quarter among men eligible for the subsidies and about one to one and one-half extra quarters among eligible women.[14] Even though the experiment apparently led to increased investment in schooling by participants, there was no observed payoff in the job market.[15]

The National Supported Work Demonstration

Public commitment in the 1970s to assist hard-to-employ workers in finding jobs is well illustrated by the Supported Work program, which was a research and demonstration effort rather than a comprehensive employment program. It began in 1975 and was scheduled to last five years. Its basic objective was to determine if providing work experience lasting about one year to individuals with severe employment problems would increase their subsequent earnings and labor market performance. The work experience was provided under conditions of gradually increasing demands, close supervision, and work in association with a crew of peers. The guiding principle of the demonstration was that "by participating in the program, a significant number of people who are severely handicapped for employment may be able to join the labor force and do productive work, cease engaging in socially destructive or dependent behavior, and become self-supporting members of society."[16]

14. Note that this was the impact on program *eligibles*; the impact on program *participants* was of course much greater. The 50 percent subsidy also encouraged some extra schooling, but the increases were smaller. See Bureau of Social Science Research (1982).

15. On the contrary, persons eligible for vouchers—in comparison to control-group members—suffered short-term reductions in wage rates, earnings, and employment during the initial phase of their eligibility. This is as expected, since some individuals reduced work effort while participating in training. However, participants never showed consistent earnings gains over the entire six-year span for which information is available, a period which includes a fairly lengthy spell after participants had completed their schooling. One explanation is that the vouchers induced significant short-term reductions in work effort and work intensity by subsidizing an alternative use of time—enrollment in formal schooling. After the training was completed, participants' earnings failed to rise above the level observed in the control group because of the amount and character of extra schooling obtained—the amount was on average very small, and it was apparently not particularly relevant to the participants' labor market situation. A second explanation concerns the effect of a rather poor and generally deteriorating labor market on the earnings potential of those who reduce (or cease) their work in order to obtain additional schooling. In such a labor market, the returns to work experience and job-keeping may be in excess of those to increased schooling. It is difficult to make training pay off if there are few jobs available.

16. This quote (from p. 1) as well as some of the material for this section is drawn from Manpower Demonstration Research Corporation (1980). See Hollister, Kemper, and Maynard (1984).

Four groups of employment-handicapped workers were eligible for the program: women who were long-term recipients of AFDC, convicts recently released from prison, former drug addicts, and young school dropouts who often had a delinquency record.[17] Administrators at each of the fifteen sites chosen for the program were given responsibility for defining the type of work on which they would focus[18] and the source of local funds on which they would draw, but the entire program had a common research and evaluation component. Over its five-year life, the demonstration provided services to over 10,000 persons, although at any one time the number of participants at any site was limited to 300. The evaluation of the demonstrations was based on interviews with 3,214 participants and 3,402 controls.[19]

The performance of the four enrolled groups varied considerably. Supported Work proved most effective in moving the welfare women who had recent work experience into gainful employment. It also had a significant impact on the ex-addict group. Among ex-offenders the results were marginal and not statistically significant, and no long-term positive results were found for the group of young dropouts. Overall, participants remained in the program an average of 6.7 months, even though the goal of the demonstration was about twelve months of participation.[20] The average cost to the public per recipient was $5,740, but because most participants stayed in the program less than one year, the average cost per service year was over $10,000. This cost declined steadily over the five years of the demonstration and is about the same as the service-year cost in other targeted training programs.

The Manpower Demonstration Research Corporation and Mathematica Policy Research conducted a very careful benefit-cost evaluation of the demonstration.[21] Their results showed that the demonstration had

17. The participants suffered severe employment handicaps. Fewer than one-third had graduated from high school, most were black or Hispanic, fewer than one-quarter were married, the number of weeks worked in the year prior to enrollment averaged six or seven, and (except for the female welfare group) arrest rates ranged from 54 to 100 percent.

18. The type of jobs provided varied across sites. They included home rehabilitation, recapping tires, building furniture, and operating day care centers. Some of the products made by participants were sold in the market in order to raise revenues for the program.

19. Each person in the research sample was interviewed before participation and had up to four additional interviews at nine-month intervals.

20. Thirty percent of the participants were fired because of poor performance; and equivalent number, however, moved on to full-time regular jobs. (The successful transition rate improved steadily over the course of the program.) About 10 percent (25 percent of the long-term welfare women) had to be released, whether they wanted to leave or not, after twelve months of participation, which was the maximum time they could stay in the program.

21. The benefits and costs of the program were computed from three different perspec-

considerable net social payoff for the AFDC women, primarily owing to the long-term earnings gains that were indicated and the value of the output from the demonstration jobs. Benefits also exceeded costs for the ex-addicts, in large part because of the reduction in socially destructive behavior (i.e., crime) and their gains in employment and earnings. For ex-convicts the results were less conclusive: the net benefit of the program may have been positive or negative, depending on the assumptions used to value the benefits of the program. Not surprisingly, in view of the apparent ineffectiveness of the demonstration among the young dropouts, the program's cost was found to outweigh its benefits for that group.

Other Social Experiments

The Rural Income Maintenance Experiment was administered by the Institute for Research on Poverty. Rural, mostly farm, families in selected low-income counties in Iowa and North Carolina were assigned to experimental and control statuses. The treatment administered to the experimental families was an NIT, and work-effort responses were the central issue of concern. A major empirical and analytical issue in the rural experiment concerned the difficulties in reliably measuring work effort and income flows related to work effort for individuals whose major occupation was farming.

Although the primary interest of the Gary Income Maintenance Experiment was also work responses to a negative income tax, this experiment was distinguished by its treatment, which combined income support with manpower training. In this sense, its design was a precursor of SIME-DIME. The findings from the rural and Gary experiments are generally consistent with those from New Jersey and SIME-DIME, although the response elasticities vary substantially.

The Performance Contracting Experiment was initiated in response to a policy proposal that received substantial attention during the late 1960s (see Gramlich and Koshel, 1975). It addressed the question, Can private firms with their special educational approaches yield gains in student achievement beyond those provided by the public schools, when the

---

tives: that of program participants, that of taxpayers, and that of society as a whole (participants and taxpayers). The social benefits include the output produced by workers in the program, increases in their postprogram earnings, reductions in criminal activities, and savings from reduced participation in other public employment, training, or drug treatment programs. The social costs include all program operating costs (excluding transfer payments, however, because these are simply a redistribution of income). The benefit-cost tabulations were based on extrapolations over the typical working life of the participants, with benefits assumed to decay at a rate of 50 percent every five years, except among AFDC mothers, where no decay rate in benefits was assumed.

remuneration of the firms is based upon the gains in achievement that they are able to record? Although problems of design and implementation plagued the experiment, its results did not point to major gains in student achievement or innovation in the nature of educational services provided.

In terms of size and cost, the Housing Allowance Demand (see Friedman and Weinberg, 1980) and Health Insurance (see Newhouse et al., 1982) experiments were among the largest. In both cases, the goal was to test the response of families to differentially subsidized prices—for rental housing in the first, health care services in the second. At issue was the efficiency of improving the economic status of low-income families through permitting choice among the services provided at subsidized prices relative to outright public provision. The instrument was rent subsidization in the housing case, and coinsurance in the health insurance experiment. Both experiments were complex in design, and attended mainly to the nature of demand-side responses to alternative subsidization arrangements. The housing experiment was hindered by a low acceptance rate for the subsidies, and consequent difficulties in reliably observing responses. The health experiment also experienced design problems, but did reveal that families economize in their demand for health services when confronted with the need to pay for some fraction of the cost of the services provided.

The Employment Opportunity Pilot Project (EOPP) was perhaps the most tumultuous of the experiments, marked by shifting objectives and premature cancellation (see Mathematica Policy Research, Inc., 1983). The purpose of the experiment was to estimate participation rates and potential effects of a guaranteed jobs program similar to that proposed in Carter's welfare reform package. In addition to simply providing a test of the guaranteed jobs concept, which was expected to be very expensive, the architects of EOPP also hoped to test new approaches to job finding among the hard-core unemployed. The program was subjected to changing aims and designs as administrations changed, and was terminated before any benefit-cost evaluation could be done. The results did indicate, however, that participation by disadvantaged workers in public job creation programs would be rather meager, that job assistance efforts do seem to result in higher employment rates, and that short-term, low-subsidy employment vouchers have little impact on employment.

Finally, there are the fifteen time-of-use residential electricity pricing experiments which have been completed or are ongoing (see Aigner, 1985). Their purpose is to test the elasticity of demand of residential electricity users to price variation by time of day or season. These experiments have established that usage at peak periods is responsive to prices, and that usage reductions at the peak are not fully offset by increases in off-peak usage. While they support the conclusion that total electricity usage and capacity requirements can be reduced by time-specific pricing arrangements, there is little consistency in the demand elasticity estimates that they have produced.

Assessment of Social Policy Experimentation

The social policy experiments stand as the clearest example of a break-through in the methodology of social science research attributable to the War on Poverty. Such an approach to understanding human behavior and responses had long been contemplated by social scientists (and had in fact been used by psychologists in small-group situations), but it was the combination of the Great Society initiatives and the drive for more rational public decisions that propelled this type of research into the field in the late 1960s.

My assessment of this development focuses on five sets of questions: (1) Is social policy experimentation a cost-effective research strategy? (2) Are there lessons in the past experiments for improving the design and increasing the reliability of the results of a next generation of experiments? What is the value of the findings of the experiments in comparison to what could have been learned from existing data, and relative to the cost? (3) Are there net benefits attributable to the experiments, over and above their contributions to knowledge regarding behavioral responses to policy interventions? (4) Have the findings from the experiments had an influence on public policy decisions? Should policymakers be influenced by their findings? (5) Have the experiments had an impact on the social sciences, and on social science research methods?

Each of the major experiments has been subjected to the detailed scrutiny of the research community, both during its course and after termination.[22] The Brookings Institution, the Russell Sage Foundation, the Rand Corporation, the National Bureau of Economic Research, and scholars from many universities and research organizations have been involved in these assessments. Most have found the research efforts devoted to the experiments to be impressive, and several important developments in both the design of the experiments and the analysis of their results have been noted. The Conlisk-Watts design model (Conlisk and Watts, 1969) and the methods for evaluating impacts in the face of selectivity and nonrandom assignment problems (see Hausman and

---

22. Several literature reviews on social policy experimentation exist. See Rieken and Boruch (1974); Ferber and Hirsch (1982); Rossi and Freeman (1982).

Wise, 1985, and Chapter 10, below) are among the most significant of these methodological advances.

The results and findings of the experiments, however, have not been appraised as favorably as has their contribution to methods of design and evaluation. From experiment to experiment, the same set of technical problems is cited as contributing to a lack of reliability in the resulting estimates of behavioral response. The litany of problems and their impacts on the reliability of the empirical findings found in the assessments of the latest experiments reads like a recital of those primary analytical criticisms of the New Jersey experiment made more than a decade earlier:

- Insufficient sample sizes, insufficient variation in the treatment variables, and inadequate definition of the treatment variables.
- Selectivity problems involving restrictions imposed on the participating population, or self-selection possibilities for participation.
- Sensitivity of results to the specification of the estimating model, with no basis for testing the accuracy of the assumed statistical properties.
- Short duration of the experiments, precluding the estimation of long-run impacts.
- Self-selected attrition of participants from the experiment.
- Estimation of behavior which responds to nonconvex budget constraints and which is intermittent, with simple linear constraint models assuming continuous demands or supplies.
- The difficulty of estimating market effects from the individual response estimates available from microexperiments.
- The presence of Hawthorne-type effects.
- Inadequate data both on important "shift" variables and preexperimental data on the primary response variables.

There are several explanations for this apparently unchanging catalog of problems. In some cases, the state of the theoretical and empirical art was and is simply too crude to permit them to be avoided, even with substantial additional research resources. These problems include nonrandom attrition from or selection into the sample, estimation of behavior given complex and ultimately unknown budget constraints, inadequate data on the backgrounds of respondents or their previous behavior, and the difficulty of estimating market effects from individual responses. Some of these impediments affect both social experimental research and standard microdata analysis. Advances in modeling and data collection have been made with respect to all of them, but progress is painfully slow.

A second explanation is that avoiding the problems or reducing them

to more tolerable levels is prohibitively costly; budget constraints imposed on each experiment resulted in the occurrence of the same set of
problems, but of various intensities. The problems in this category concern deviations from the pure random-assignment experimental model,
and include the restrictions imposed on participating populations, inadequate sample sizes, insufficient variation in treatment variables, ad
hoc specification of response models, and the short-run nature of the
experiments. Presumably, these problems will exist at some level so long
as restrictions on social experimental research budgets exist.

Finally, the problems may have persisted because the later designers of
experiments learned little from the experience of the earlier experimenters. This explanation appears to have some basis, especially across
the substantive areas over which experimentation was done.[23]

In the face of these limitations, an important question involves the
value of the findings of the experiments relative to existing estimates and
to the costs of obtaining them. By and large, assessments of experimental
findings have not found them to be notably more reliable than estimates
based on cross-sectional data. In assessing the findings of the housing
allowance experiments, Rosen (1985) concluded that "if the goal was to
obtain new and improved estimates of the behavioral responses to housing allowances, . . . the money would have been better spent on augment-
ing conventional data sources" (p. 72). In discussing the findings of the
health insurance experiments, Harris (1985) stated that "economists and
other social scientists have spent disproportionately too much effort on
the design and interpretation of microexperiments" (p. 145). Finally,
Stafford (1985) wrote of the income maintenance experiments that "at a
minimum, the experiments have reduced the variance of labor supply
parameters, even if they have not shifted the means very much" (p.
121).[24]

These generally pessimistic assessments rest upon the weaknesses
enumerated above. When set against estimates from some ideally de-

23. For example, in discussing the reasons for the poor designs of the electricity pricing
experiments, the first of which started in 1975, Joskow (1985) wrote: "When the earliest
experiments were structured, those involved had simply not thought very deeply about
what the data generated might be used for. [They] were motivated more by narrow
adversarial and litigation concerns than by interest in sound economic analysis. . . . There
was no *inherent* reason for these early experiments to have been so poorly designed" (pp,
43–44).

24. This claim, it should be noted , amounts to little praise, since the ten conventional
male labor-supply analyses that Stafford reviewed have a range of uncompensated wage
elasticities of + .11 to − .55, a range of compensated wage elasticities of + .86 to − .04, and
a range of income elasticities of − .06 to − .51. It would be surprising if estimates from any
new study added to this set failed to reduce the variance.

signed and flawless experiment, negative appraisals are probably appropriate. However, when set against the reliability of existing estimates from nonexperimental research, such conclusions seem exaggerated. Most of the problems affecting the experiments also plague nonexperimental empirical studies of behavioral responses, and appear in even more virulent form there. Moreover, nonexperimental analyses are burdened by additional problems that were at least partly avoided by the experiments. The absence of preobservation measures of the variables of interest and the weakness of the variables available for control come immediately to mind. The fact is that the parameter estimates from the social experiments are, in general, more reliable than those previously available. They set the standard in the various areas that have been subjected to experimentation. They are the best game in town. Any new estimates are, and should be, judged by comparison to them. This does not mean, of course, that the value of the increment to knowledge provided by the experiments is worth the cost.

Given this mixed appraisal of the reliability of the experimental findings, we need to draw the lessons of the experiments for the design of future research on behavioral responses to policy incentives. If, on the basis of past experience, there was agreement on the characteristics of the optimal research design for response estimation, one could anticipate that a second generation of experiments would yield more reliable results. Unfortunately, little such agreement exists.

Hausman and Wise (1985) have presented the most concrete proposal for an experimental research design which would avoid or minimize many of the deficiencies that have flawed past experiments. They advocate a simple microexperiment with few treatments, large sample sizes, and full randomization so as to avoid the need for complicated structural models based on strong and nontestable specification assumptions. This suggestion is not, however, widely supported by those most heavily involved in experimental research. In the face of constrained research budgets, trading off knowledge acquisition against research costs seems inevitable.[25] Moreover, even in the pure experimental model proposed by Hausman and Wise, unavoidable problems of selection into and attrition from the experiment will exist. And while they advocate a variety of sophisticated statistical techniques to correct for these problems, there is little assurance that estimates derived from them will be similar, and if not, which is to be preferred.

25. Conlisk (1985) finds the justification for this proposal "incomplete," and "sees no reason to suppose that a good design will be the sort of simple design Hausman and Wise have in mind. Nor [do I] see a useful way to substitute simple rules of thumb . . . for a full-blown, optimal design analysis specific to the context at hand" (p. 212).

A second proposal designed to reorient the direction of experimentation has been offered by Harris (1985), who finds the shortfalls in the health insurance experiment overwhelming. His proposal is to substitute macroexperimentation—the assignment of treatments to randomly selected groups, communities, or markets with others, also randomly selected, serving as controls—for microexperimentation. As with the Hausman and Wise proposal, the claims made for macroexperiments appear to be seriously overdrawn, and a variety of difficulties with such an approach—cost, political feasibility (and hence self-selection), control and admimistration, and the lack of a true control group—to be understated (see Orr, 1985).

Even though neither the critiques of the results of the experiments nor the proposals for altered experimental strategies are very satisfying, they do make clear that the early experimental efforts contain lessons of value for future social policy experimentation, should pursuit of such a research strategy again seem feasible or desirable.

If we were seriously contemplating a new form of social experimental research today, we would clearly do things differently and probably better than we did them before.[26] We would be more discerning regarding the particular issues on which social experimentation would be justified, more sensitive to the interaction between the nature and design of the experiment (e.g., micro- versus macroexperimentation) and the policy question of interest, more careful in designing the experiment to avoid problems of selectivity and attrition bias and inadequate specification of treatments and response, and more thorough in administering and monitoring the implementation phase of the experiment. In terms of the design of microexperiments, we would opt for simpler, less complicated treatments, and invest more in collecting preexperimental data on the relevant aspects of behavior. While remaining aware of the consequences of truncating the population eligible for participation, we would not necessarily proceed to full randomization in sample selection and treatment assignment as proposed by Hausman and Wise.

If, then, it is accepted that the behavioral response estimates from the experiments—their primary purpose, output, and benefit—have fallen short of the high expectations that motivated them, are there other benefits attributable to the experiments that can be used to justify their high costs? A large number of additional effects have been cited in critiques of the experiments, almost all of which are secondary or side effects, most of them unanticipated when the earliest experiments were

---

26. Planning for another generation of social policy experimentation is reflected in Berk et al. (1985).

fielded. These include (1) the initiation and fostering of more thoughtful and comprehensive discussions of the policy measures under consideration; (2) the development of economic concepts and statistical techniques that will be useful in subsequent scientific work; (3) increased knowledge regarding the efficient administration and monitoring of programs; (4) estimates of (or at least insights into) take-up rates under new or altered policies, and hence improved cost estimates; (5) the generation of valuable longitudinal microdata sets enabling subsequent analyses of economic behavior; (6) use of the mantle of experimentation to present results regarding economic behavior that are also available from other studies in a more persuasive, convincing way; and (7) contributions to scientific progress by pointing out behaviors inconsistent with standard theory, hence stimulating the development of new or extended theories.

While many of these benefits may have accrued from the experiments, there exists little more than sketchy evidence as a basis for assessing their value. Discussion of them can consist of little more than a set of catalog entries. Moreover, while such side benefits of social experimentation can be noted, the associated costs of experimentation must also be weighed. The substantial research resources and brainpower devoted to experimentation would have been employed in some other enterprise in the absence of this new research endeavor. The secondary or side benefits forgone from these activities are surely as real as those attributed to the experiments. These forgone benefits are secondary costs attributable to experimentation; they fit into many of the same categories as the side benefits cited, and are also as unmeasured and unseen.

A fourth question in assessing the value of the experiments concerns their impacts on policymakers and their decisions. This question has also been addressed by several commentators, and from several perspectives (see, for example, Pechman and Timpane, 1975; Aaron, 1978; Aaron and Todd, 1979; Stromsdorfer, 1979; Burtless and Haveman, 1984; and Greenberg and Robins, 1985). As with the discussion of the secondary benefits of social experimentation, the evaluations provided are anecdotal, impressionistic, and contradictory. In some cases, positive effects of experimental evidence on policy-making have been cited; in other cases the evidence has been ignored; in still other cases unanticipated findings from the experiments on issues quite separate from the main behavioral responses being studied have set policy debates off in directions that few would have predicted. Henry Aaron (1985), somewhat optimistically, has reached the conclusion that the "serendipitous findings of the income-maintenance and housing-allowance experiments will more than repay the U.S. Treasury the cost of the experiments in short order" (p. 276). Nevertheless, both he and others have suggested that the social experiments have been a force for slowing the adoption of new policies (see Burtless and Haveman, 1984; Greenberg and Robins, 1985).

Unfortunately, the discussion in this area again seems to ignore the need for a comprehensive framework within which all effects can be considered. No meaningful conclusion is possible by tracing the policy impacts of a single activity (e.g., social experimentation) in the absence of a similar tracing of the policy impacts of the forgone activities—both research and nonresearch—which would have occurred but never did.

The final question in assessing social policy experimentation concerns its impacts on social science and social scientists. This effect is, of course, one of the several byproducts of experimentation that have been already noted, but it is the central focus of this volume. The social experiments affected the community of social researchers and social scientists in important ways. They represented a high point in the experience of that community: research methodology that came out of the academy was put to use by government, and the services of social scientists were demanded by those responsible for the formulation of public policy. These developments were invigorating, and the resources and enthusiasm devoted by social scientists to the venture were unprecedented. It is too early to reach definitive conclusions regarding the impact of the social experimentation movement on the nature and practice of social science, but a few comments at this point seem appropriate.

The commitment of resources to experimentation has, to some degree at least, changed both the general perception of the social sciences and the perception that social scientists have of their own disciplines. Social science gained access to the experimental technique whose absence had always caused it to appear "less scientific" than the natural sciences. In terms of perceived self-esteem, this impact of social experimentation should not be overlooked.

Second, the procedures for and requirements of scientific experimentation involving human subjects and social policy treatments involved a new set of design and evaluation methods that were relatively unknown and rarely practiced in the social sciences. These research methods and design techniques have become a part of the curricula in many standard social science departments and the focus of courses in schools of public policy. Social experimentation research became a part of advanced training for many applied social scientists in the years after 1970.

A third point concerns the impact of the research experience of the experiments on those involved in them and the subsequent activities of these scholars. The researchers involved in the experiments—and their students—gained a form of knowledge, training, and experience which subsequently became highly valued by both government agencies and academic social science departments. Those people now occupy positions throughout government and universities. Within social science departments, these individuals contribute to the maintenance of a commitment to applied research in an environment in which increasing emphasis is directed to theoretical concerns (Berk, 1981). Others moved toward the private sector, contributing to the development of profit and nonprofit research firms which specialize in providing research and evaluation studies to government, often under contract. These organizations continue to thrive, providing a demand for social science researchers and a supply of services which sustain an emphasis on rational study and experimentation as a basis for social policy.

10

Methods for Correcting Selectivity Bias

The 1970s saw major advances in statistical techniques that enabled social science researchers to deal with an endemic problem in the analysis of social behavior—that of selectivity bias. The problem became an issue and a major focus of attention among econometricians in the 1970s largely because of its pervasive presence in the efforts to evaluate the behavioral effects of the social experiments and of federal education and training programs for the poor. The tie between poverty research and the development of statistical techniques for correcting selectivity bias, "perhaps the most important development for social science statistical methods during the 1970s," is the focus of this chapter.[1]

The Occurrence of Selectivity Bias

A bias in estimated relationships is likely to occur when the analysis is based on a sample of observations (data points) that is not representative

1. "Perhaps the most important development for social science statistical methods during the 1970s was the [formulation of techniques to deal with] self-selection, censored samples (where some variables are unmeasured for certain individuals who should be in the sample), truncated samples (where all variables are unmeasured for certain individuals who should be in the sample), and limited dependent variables (variables restricted to some subset of values)" (Stromsdorfer and Farkas, 1980, p. 14).

of the larger population for which inferences are desired. This situation will arise when the sample on which estimates are based is composed of individuals who have self-selected themselves into the sample (because, say, they were highly motivated), or who have been selected to be in the sample by some unknown set of criteria, or, in the case of social science experimentation, who have been assigned nonrandomly to various treatment categories or have left the experiment through attrition.[2]

The earliest discussion of the problem of selectivity bias in the economics literature occurred in the late 1950s, in the work of H. Gregg Lewis on the effect of union membership on wages (Lewis, 1959). Although Lewis did not identify the problem as one of selection, he described how employers and employees selected either union or nonunion agreements because of personal preferences for one or the other arrangements, and noted that estimates of the extent of union status on wages must control for such preferences insofar as they are correlated with wages. If such correlation exists and is not controlled for, selectivity bias occurs.

Since the early 1970s, concern with bias due to selection has been reflected in labor market studies. In 1973, for example, when Glen Cain and Harold Watts reviewed a large number of studies analyzing the effect of income-support policies on labor supply, they confronted numerous instances of samples that were composed of low-income families. The result was that selection into the sample was endogenous to the dependent variable—labor supply or earnings—being studied.[3] A similar problem was encountered in the New Jersey Negative Income Tax Experiment, in that the normal income of families selected for participation in the experiment was required to be below 150 percent of the poverty line. Because analysis of the labor-supply effect of various wage and income incentives focused on family earnings, the distribution of this dependent variable would be truncated because selection of the sample was based on this variable.

A related problem arose in the evaluation of public education and training programs when the process by which those selected to participate and those selected not to participate in the program was not random. In studying the effects of such training programs, Orley Ashenfelter (1978)

2. See the volume edited by Hausman and Wise (1985) for a discussion of the sample selection problems encountered in designing and evaluating social experiments.

3. The particular case of selection on the dependent variable, illustrated in the Cain and Watts (1973) example, has a history dating back to 1903 in the work of Karl Pearson. Pearson's statement of the problem, and one in 1950 concerning the selection of low-production cows out of the sample used for estimating relationships of age and milk production, are cited in Goldberger (1981).

confronted the situation where those participating in the training program were both a select group and were experiencing low earnings, absolutely and relative to the comparison groups, at the time the program was initiated. For some workers, earnings just prior to the start of the program may be correlated with earnings after the program is completed; for others, low current income may reflect only a temporary decline in earnings. Moreover, the process of selection into the program was clearly not random—program administrators were instructed to enroll unemployed workers. Again, the selectivity bias problem existed because some of the factors that determined the presence of the person in the sample on which the estimation was to be done were also determinants of the outcome variable—postprogram earnings, in this case.

Other examples of the problem arose after 1965 in efforts to evaluate compensatory education programs (Campbell and Erlebacher, 1970; Garfinkel and Gramlich, 1973), to estimate the determinants of the length of time on welfare (Amemiya and Boskin, 1974), and to evaluate responses to incentives established in the income maintenance, housing, and health insurance experiments (Hausman and Wise, 1985). A large number of econometric developments were stimulated as a result.[4]

A Simple Statement of the Problem

Considered most generally, the selectivity bias problem is one of a family of specification error problems in econometric estimation; in this case, it is the problem of missing variables. The variables lacking are those which are related to *both* the presence of an observation in the sample being analyzed *and* the behavior or performance of the observation. If the nature of the missing variables and their relationship to being in the sample and to behavior is known, the direction of the bias in the estimate of interest can be determined, though its magnitude is unknown. In many cases, however, neither the nature of these unobserved variables nor their relationship to presence in the sample or to outcome is known. All that is known is that bias in some direction exists.

This problem can be stated as follows:[5] Assume that an outcome variable y (say, individual earnings) is linearly related to a treatment z (say, participation in a training program), an unobserved variable w (say, individual true ability), and a random term ε:

---

4. See Goldberger (1972, 1981, 1983), Amemiya (1973, 1974, 1978), McFadden (1973), Heckman (1974, 1978a, 1978b, 1979, 1980), Hausman and Wise (1977, 1979), Crawford (1979), Kiefer (1979), Olsen (1980), Lee and Maddala (1983).

5. This discussion relies heavily on Barnow, Cain, and Goldberger (1980).

(1) $y = \alpha z + w + \varepsilon.$

The analyst desires an accurate measure of α, reflecting the impact of differences in z on differences in y. The problem of empirical estimation turns on the fact that w is unobservable and very likely correlated with z. In this case, it can be shown that a measured α does not capture the true effect of z on y. In principle, pure random assignment of individuals to z status would guarantee that the measured α estimates the true effect. Similarly, if all of the variables that determine assignment to z status were included in the equation, the estimated value of α would be unbiased. However, without *full* knowledge of the variables that would allow such modeling of the selection process, estimates of α will be biased owing to "selection" into the sample. If a partial set of variables correlated with w are entered into equation (1), the estimated value of α will still be biased. The bias will be either positive or negative depending on the covariance of z status and unobserved w, conditional on the variables included. Hence, the conditional covariance of z and w is the key to estimating an unbiased value of α, the coefficient of interest.

Consider, for example, a situation in which an education program is provided a sample of students, chosen to be in the program by administrators who desire participants with a high level of motivation but from low-income families. The control group is, say, the set of students interviewed by administrators, but not chosen. The objective of the program is to increase cognitive test scores, and preprogram and postprogram scores are available for all students. The evaluation of the program is to be done using information for all of the students—both those in the program and the control group—and the dependent variable in a regression modeled after (1) is the difference in preprogram and postprogram test scores. Thus, z is a 0–1 variable reflecting participation or nonparticipation in the program; w is a set of control variables such as age, sex, race, and so on.

Because the participating students have been selected into the program on the basis of motivation and family income, these background variables, either observed or unobserved, are correlated with z, presence in the program. If unobserved, the estimate of α will be biased because of selectivity—the treatment, variable z, will be standing for motivation and family background, as well as the treatment provided by the program. If family income is known and is introduced into the regression, the selectivity problem will be less serious, but it may still exist: z will now be standing for program participation, as well as the unobserved level of motivation, with which it is correlated. Only if both family income and student motivation are accurately measured and included in the regression will the estimated α reflect the impact of the program, unbiased by the selected sample of students who were participants. In effect, by including in the estimation model those variables which both affect the outcome, y, and determine selection into the sample, the measured effect of the treatment on the outcome, α, reflects only the treatment, unbiased by the selection process, which is now fully controlled for in the regression.

Correcting for Selectivity Bias

Statistical work on truncated distributions and limited dependent variables has been of long standing in the mathematical statistics and econometrics literature. Although closely related to the sample selectivity problem, this work was not directly connected to it. Takeshi Amemiya (1973) cites work on truncated normal distributions going back to the 1940s, and attributes to James Tobin (1958) the first effort to deal with the existence in regression analysis of dependent variables with a truncated normal distribution. Such truncation may well result from sample selection, as the labor-supply example cited above (Cain and Watts, 1973) illustrates. In his own work, which extends Tobin's approach to the truncated normal dependent variable problem, Amemiya gives no indication of the relationship of this problem to the problem of selectivity bias (or censored examples) (Amemiya, 1973, 1974, 1978). Similarly, the early econometric work on limited dependent (or dummy) variables (McFadden, 1973; Heckman, 1978) gave little if any indication of a familial relationship of this problem to that of selectivity as it arose in the evaluation and behavioral research that accompanied the War on Poverty. This, in spite of the fact that all these problems share many statistical characteristics and pose many of the same difficulties for empirical estimation.

Several approaches have been taken in the social science literature to correct for bias in those cases in which the selection variables, w, are unobserved. The following paragraphs briefly describe a few of these approaches.

The earliest encounters with the selectivity problem adopted rather crude and ad hoc adjustment techniques. One of the earliest was Reuben Gronau's effort to establish the value of married women's time (Gronau, 1973). For married women who are engaged in market work, the observed wage rate serves as a reliable indicator of how they value their time. However, at any point in time, about 50 percent of wives do not engage in market work. The value of their time depends on their productivity in producing nonmarket goods and the value that they attach to leisure hours, i.e., the value of time in the absence of market opportunities. This value is the wife's "reservation wage" for supplying labor services to the market.

Working from a model of the intrafamily allocation of time, and assuming that the value of time of nonworking wives in leisure and nonmarket work activities depends on the husband's wage rate and family income, this value can, under certain assumptions, be ascertained from observed data on wives' labor force participation decisions.[6] In particular, because working wives are a self-selected group from the frequency distribution of the value of time of all wives, both knowledge of the observed wage offer distribution (which is truncated by the self-selection process) plus a set of assumptions is required.[7] Then the nature of the joint distribution (density function) of the potential market wage and the value of time in the absence of market observations (and hence, the full distribution of the value of time) can be estimated, along with the "true" value of wives' time.

While Gronau's was an innovative first step in developing a technique for estimating an unobserved value—the "price" of wives' time—when the observed measures of this value are from a self-selected (truncated) sample, his procedure has major limitations.[8] Recognizing these limitations, Gronau warned the reader that his estimates were "fragile," and that they should be handled with care.

Shortly after his work was published, techniques for coping with selectivity bias were extended in a number of directions. Major contributions were made by James Heckman (1974, 1976, 1979). In his early work, a utility-maximization framework was adopted and a shadow (nonmarket) wage and market wage framework, analogous to that of Gronau, was developed. A shadow wage function was established, and it was shown that this function can be derived if the ordinary labor-supply function is a positive function of wage rates. In Heckman's formulation, a likelihood function is specified and maximized over a sample of married women to yield unbiased estimates of the parameters of functions that determine

6. This is so because the observed labor force participation decision depends on the joint distribution of the potential market wage and the value of the wife's time in the absence of market opportunities.

7. Gronau assumes that the potential market wage and the value of time in the absence of market opportunities are distributed independently and with a normal bivariate joint distribution.

8. For example, he was forced to assume that the determinants of the observed market wage do not affect the price of time for wives who do not work, and that neither market work nor work in the home convey direct utilities. Moreover, the age, education, and family-income variables used to determine market and nonmarket values are limited and arbitrary. They were used because available, and not for theoretical reasons.

labor force participation, hours worked, the observed wage rate, and the shadow price of time.

The statistical procedure employed by Heckman was an extension of the tobit model (named for Tobin) to a simultaneous equations system, and is substantially more advanced than the technique used by Gronau. Information on the extent of work (in addition to simply labor force participation) is used in the analysis, and correlation across the disturbance terms of the relevant equations (reflecting omitted variables, such as ability) is permitted. In effect, Heckman's procedure allows information on women who do not work to affect estimates of many parameters of the market and the shadow wage, and these more fundamental parameters underlying the decisions concerning whether to work, and how much, are utilized in deriving the unobserved nonmarket wage function. In this framework, the self-selection of some women into labor force participation is modeled directly in the maximum likelihood formulation, and an estimate of the value of their time is thereby obtained. This estimate will be unbiased if the assumed underlying distributions and error-term specifications are correct.

Heckman's later work focuses on another source of the selectivity bias problem. In this case, the researcher may create the bias by discarding observations with incomplete information. For example, a longitudinal study of manpower training may use a rule that drops all observations on participants or controls who fail to be reinterviewed. In this case, it is not so much the presence of "attritors," but the decision by the analyst to ignore the attritor's observation that produces selectivity bias. A fitted regression using only the included observations will confuse α with the probability of dropping an observation, and the estimate of α will be biased. In other words, the estimated value of α will simultaneously reflect the effect both of z on y and the decision rule used to drop incomplete observations.

Viewed in this way, selectivity bias is a form of specification error, and Heckman's approach is to develop a procedure for purging the estimates of this error. Beginning with a framework similar to that of Barnow, Cain, and Goldberger (1980), Heckman specifies the selectivity bias problem as the following model in which the decision rule to exclude some observations is correlated with variables that determine the outcome:

(2) $\quad y_1 = x_1\alpha_1 + \varepsilon_1,$

(3) $\quad y_2 = x_2\alpha_2 + \varepsilon_2,$

where y_1 is the outcome, x_1 is a variable(s) that determines outcome, y_2 is an index of the exclusion of observations, x_2 is the decision rule for excluding observation, and ε_1 and ε_2 are error terms. Heckman assumes the ε_1 and ε_2 have a bivariate normal distribution and from this constructs the inverse Mills ratio—a function that declines as the probability of an observation being retained in the sample increases.[9] The parameters needed to construct the inverse Mills function can be found by applying probit analysis to equation (3).[10]

A further contribution in the development of selectivity correction techniques is that of Ashenfelter (1978, mentioned earlier), who focused on evaluating the effects of training and education programs on the earnings of participants when selection to the program was not random. His technique relies on longitudinal data for both participants and nonparticipants, and seeks to capture the effects of permanent characteristics on earnings by observing the true effect of past earnings on current earnings. By using this relationship, fitted to data on nonparticipants in the model explaining the effect of the program on trainees, the desired effect of the program can be measured without bias.[11]

Finally, a number of contributions were made to correcting for selectivity bias in its various guises in the social experiments (Goldberger, 1972; Cain, 1973; Barnow, Cain, and Goldberger, 1980). Among the techniques developed are a number that involve the explicit modeling of the

9. The inverse Mills ratio is a transformation of the probability of being in the sample, a transformation that depends on assumptions concerning the distribution of errors.

10. In the polar case, where all the observations are included, the inverse Mills ratio approaches zero, equation (2) can be estimated with least squares techniques, and α_1 will be unbiased. The essence of Heckman's procedure is captured in four steps. First, equation (3) is estimated using probit analysis on the entire sample. In effect, this estimation describes the determinants of the inclusion-exclusion (selection) process, and allows for consistent estimation of the inverse Mills ratio. Second, the estimated inverse Mills ratio is constructed for each observation. This ratio is treated as an observed variable that proxies for the omitted (and unobserved) variables that ideally should be included in equation (2). Next the estimated inverse Mills ratio is added to equation (2), and this specification is estimated with least squares over the subsample of included observations. This produces consistent coefficient estimates of the treatment effect, α_1. Finally, a consistent estimate of the regression variance is calculated in order to find correct standard errors of the estimated coefficients for constructing confidence intervals. As with the maximum likelihood procedure, this technique yields unbiased estimates of the α_1 coefficient, which describes the causal relationship of interest. Because of the simplicity of this four-step approach, it has been employed in numerous applied studies to correct for selectivity bias (or data exclusion) problems.

11. In the Ashenfelter procedure, selectivity bias is avoided only if past earnings patterns reflect the impact of all relevant characteristics on earnings, including those that explain selection into the trainee group. Again, a variety of assumptions regarding error terms and specification are required.

joint selectivity-response behavior and their estimation, using joint maximum likelihood techniques based on explicit assumptions regarding the underlying distributions (Hausman and Wise, 1977, 1979).

In nearly all of the approaches taken, information on the selection process itself is used to obtain unbiased estimates of α. In effect, the presence or absence of an individual in the treatment group (the "z status" of the individual) is modeled in an equation in which z is the dependent variable. With restrictions placed on this equation, proxies for the unobserved variables that determine selection are obtained from it, and entered into the equation explaining outcome. Through this procedure, an attempt is made to purge the estimate of α of any preexisting differences among individuals of different z statuses. In one form of restriction, variables which determine the allocation to z status, but that do not affect outcome y, are included in the selection equation but not in the outcome equation. In a second procedure, a functional form for the relation between the partial set of variables available and the true set of variables determining selection (w in [1]) is specified, as well as a nonlinear relationship between z status and the partial set of variables. The resulting nonlinear effect of the partial set of variables on outcome y is used to control for any remaining relationship between z status and true ability. With this procedure the relationship of the partial set of available variables and z status can be distinguished from the relationship of the partial set of available variables and outcome, y.

Finally, there is a still more general case in which a nonlinear functional form for the partial set of available variables emerges through full maximum likelihood estimation, assuming that the distribution of the w variable and that determining selection is bivariate normal, and that the functional relationship of the partial set of variables to w and the selection variable is linear.

While this discussion has been limited to the selectivity bias issue, it should be emphasized that a wide range of other statistical and empirical developments of substantial importance in social research have been fostered by efforts to evaluate the effects of social policy interventions. Some of these developments are closely related to the work on selectivity bias, including the emphasis on the use of panel data to separate fixed effects from population heterogeneity in correcting for selectivity (e.g., Ashenfelter, 1978; Chamberlain, 1978; Kiefer, 1979), the formulation of generalized models and estimation techniques for analyzing relationships where the dependent variable is truncated in some way (Amemiya, 1984, surveys these developments), the development of discrete-choice modeling techniques and their extension to multiple-choice formulations (Amemiya, 1981), the development of models for handling the presence of multiple sources of selectivity (Catsiapis and Robinson, 1982; Ham, 1982; Lee and Maddala, 1983), procedures for obtaining unbiased estimates from choice-based samples constructed to secure generalizable results (Manski and Lerman, 1977), and the delineation of the conditions under which the widely used techniques for adjusting for selection bias are effective (e.g., Goldberger, 1981, 1983; Arabmazar and Schmidt, 1982).

A related development also grew out of the objective of estimating program impacts, especially in the face of selectivity caused by program attrition. In an evaluation of the effect of a negative income tax plan on marital dissolution, Tuma, Hannan, and Groeneveld (1979) developed a continuous-time, event-history model which directly handled the attrition problem. This approach uses event-history data describing each individual's status at each of several points in time. Relying on the Markov property—that the probability of a person occupying a given state in the future is completely determined by the nature of the state that he or she currently occupies—the model evaluates the effects of the experimental treatment on marital dissolution. In this dynamic, continuous-time framework, attrition is treated as a separate "absorbing state," and its effects on the evaluation of impacts on marital dissolution are thereby accounted for. The models of change in continuous time that have been developed by these sociologists are in their own right a major advance in social science method. One review of the technique stated: "From both methodological and substantive points of view, this . . . statistical technique is likely to affect common practice for years to come. . . . with their model of event histories in continuous time, Tuma et al. have provided what may be the most attractive analysis strategy yet devised for [understanding individual change over time]" (Stromsdorfer and Farkas, 1980, p. 18).

Application of the Statistical Techniques

The econometric approaches to adjust for selectivity bias employed by Gronau, Heckman, Ashenfelter, Goldberger, and Hausman and Wise are among the primary techniques that have been developed to deal with this problem. The extensive use of these techniques in the poverty research literature indicates both the pervasiveness of the problem and the extent of their contributions. Nearly all evaluations of income maintenance experiments, education programs, housing subsidies, health and occupational safety programs, as well as labor market interventions, are required to deal with some variant of selectivity bias. The statistical technique used to handle the problem in each case will be determined to some extent by the nature of the program being evaluated, insofar as program design characteristics determine the form in which selectivity bias appears.[12]

Table 10.1 describes a few poverty research and evaluation studies that have relied on econometric techniques to correct for the selectivity bias problems that were confronted. The purpose of the table is to illustrate the range of these problems in poverty research and the nature of the statistical methods that have been used to adjust for them. In the compensatory education experiment (1), students were selected into the program by a process which was not well understood, and which could not be explicitly modeled. The problem was recognized, and a crude and somewhat arbitrary adjustment was made to correct for selectivity. This was one of the earliest confrontations of the selectivity problem in the social experimentation research.[13] In the income maintenance experiments (2), selectivity-related problems can stem from several sources: sample selection based on an endogenous variable, treatment assignment based on an endogenous variable, self-determination of participation, and self-selection out of the experiment through attrition. A variety of maximum likelihood models have been developed to reflect the joint determination of the response to the policy treatment and the participation or assignment process. These methods build on and extend the basic Heckman approach. All of the income maintenance experiments confronted these selectivity problems with various intensities, and the corrections made ranged from ad hoc adjustment techniques to complex and state-of-the-art estimation methods (as reflected in the references cited in 1 and 2).

A primary difficulty of the manpower training program evaluations (3) stems from their nonexperimental character and the concern that some unobserved variable (e.g., motivation) may both influence participation in the program and observed earnings. The correction techniques in this area rely on longitudinal data to purge the estimated results from selectivity problems. Items 4 and 5 both deal with a selectivity problem con-

12. For example, in evaluating an NIT experiment, the source of the selectivity bias is likely to be the result of participant attrition from the program. Conversely, the source of selectivity bias in a manpower training program could be the result of correlation between some unobserved variable and program participation.

13. An even earlier evaluation study, that of the Head Start program (Cicarelli et al., 1969) had been criticized on grounds that potential selective problems had biased the estimated results (Campbell and Erlebacher, 1970). A series of papers by Goldberger, Barnow, Cain and others formalizing the selectivity problem and correction techniques for dealing with selectivity bias can be traced to their confrontation of the issues of selectivity in the Head Start Performance Contracting evaluations. See Goldberger (1972), Barnow (1973), and Cain (1973).

fronted in the housing allowance experiments, in which households selected to participate had first to meet some minimum housing constraint. They are listed separately to indicate the wide range of correction techniques used in recent studies, from rough adjustment procedures to full-scale, joint-participation-response maximum likelihood methods.

Summary and Critique

Although concern with the problem of selectivity bias had existed since the late 1950s, it was not until the early 1970s that researchers began seriously to consider its empirical consequences and to search for corrections to the problem. Early efforts to correct for selectivity were in the labor economics area. It was, however, the legislative mandate to evaluate the plethora of social programs of the War on Poverty, including the social experiments, that placed the bias issue high on the agenda of statisticians and quantitative social researchers.

The work of econometricians and other applied researchers in developing techniques to correct for selectivity bias has had a major and pervasive impact on empirical economic and sociological research on the determinants of human behavior and on the evaluation of social and antipoverty programs. The sensitivity of researchers to the potential of selectivity bias in empirical research is now widespread, and the studies that incorporate statistical corrections for the selectivity problem number in the hundreds. Seldom does an empirical study of the determinants of human behavior (earnings, labor supply, mobility, fertility, schooling, consumption) based on microdata fail explicitly to confront this issue. These econometric developments have occurred both within the tradition of quantitative research unrelated to the War on Poverty—for example, in traditional labor economics—and in the research explicitly stimulated and supported by this policy effort.

While the methods developed to correct for selectivity bias represent a large step forward in social science research techniques, the impression should not be left that no problems remain. Most of the techniques that have been developed are both difficult and costly to implement. There are few researchers with sufficient training to make use of them, and the estimation procedures are not available in standard software packages. More serious, at their core all of the techniques rely on some set of assumptions about the shape of the distribution of the underlying data. These assumptions typically involve normality or symmetry and are both strong and arbitrary; if they do in fact not hold, the estimated results may be at least as biased as making no correction for selectivity (see Stromsdorfer and Farkas, 1980; Little, 1982). The "fit" of some of the more

Table 10.1. Selected Poverty Research Studies and Adjustments for Selectivity Bias

Authors	Nature of Study	Relationship to Be Estimated	Nature of the Problem
1. Garfinkel and Gramlich (1973)	Evaluation of OEO Performance Contracting Experiment	Impact of program on student test scores	Selection process for participation not random
2. Burtless and Hausman (1978); Hausman and Wise (1979)	Evaluation of Gary Negative Income Tax Experiment	Income and wage effects from a negative income tax on labor supply	Differential attrition from experiment by effect of treatment; sample selection and treatment assignment on endogenous variables
3. Kiefer (1979)	Evaluation of manpower training program	Impact of manpower training on productivity and earnings	A static (fixed) effect of, say, ability, which is unobserved, correlated with participant status and outcome (earnings) effect
4. Friedman and Weinberg (1980)	Evaluation of Housing Allowance Demand Experiment	Effect of housing allowances on housing expenditures	Design of experiment nonrandom; those not meeting a minimum housing requirement dropped from treatment status (or placed in control group)
5. Hausman and Wise (1980)	Evaluation of Housing Allowance Demand Experiment	Effect of housing allowances on housing expenditures	Design of experiment required a minimum housing requirement be met for participation, and hence not random in determination of treatment-control group

Table 10.1. (*continued*)

Correction Procedure	Character of Correction Procedure
A crude variant of Ashenfelter method, using observed pretest-posttest relationship for all students to adjust estimated treatment effect on participants	Ad hoc, resting on numerous assumptions regarding true relationships and underlying distributions
Extension of maximum likelihood approach of Heckman (1974, 1976, 1979) and Barnow, Cain, and Goldberger (1980) to joint determination of participation and response	Consistent, state-of-the-art estimation methods
A first-difference version of the Ashenfelter technique, to purge treatment status of unobservable and time-persistent individual effects	A modification and further development of the Ashenfelter method
Direct estimation of observed housing expenditures of control group used to adjust estimated effect of treatment on housing expenditures for experimentals	Ad hoc, resting on numerous assumptions regarding true relationships and underlying distributions
Analyzed jointly the participation decision (selection) and the housing consumption decision in a maximum likelihood model incorporating a piecewise continuous budget constraint to estimate the shape of utility functions	Consistent, state-of-the-art estimation method

213

advanced models is also difficult to assess, since the diagnostics required for such assessment are not easily obtained. Even the more straightforward aproaches (e.g., Heckman's two-stage estimation) confront difficult problems of implementation: the specification of the selection equation must often be arbitrary, the assumed joint disturbance distribution may be violated, insufficient variance may exist in the estimated equation, and the estimated standard errors required for diagnosis may be biased.

Although these problems inhibit the more widespread application of the techniques, their development nevertheless stands as a major methodological advance. As with other such methodological developments, the knowledge frontier for this generation of researchers will be a standard part of the research toolkits of the next generation. These methods exist in large part because of the important role played by antipoverty policy in both highlighting the problem and supporting the research from which this advance in technique emanated.

11

Microdata Simulation Models for Evaluating Public Policy

Since the early 1960s, major advances in the development of survey information obtained from representative samples of the population have been made in the United States and other countries. These surveys contain detailed demographic information (e.g., age, race, sex, marital status, region), economic data (e.g., earnings, income, labor supply, occupation), and personal characteristics (e.g., education, health, ethnic origin) on population samples ranging from a few hundred to over 100,000 individuals and/or families. Some of the U.S. surveys are aimed at special problems or issues (such as the National Health Interview Survey), while others are more general, designed to yield more comprehensive estimates of population characteristics (examples are the Census Bureau's annual Current Population Survey, CPS; or its Survey of Income and Education of 1976). Some of them are one-time, cross-sectional surveys (the two Surveys of Economic Opportunity, 1966–67); others are periodic, often annual, surveys that ask questions of similarly chosen samples composed of different individuals, as is true of the CPS; still others are longitudinal, in that the same individuals are followed over time, information on them being collected periodically (e.g., the Michigan Panel Study of Income Dynamics or the National Longitudinal Surveys). These data bases containing detailed information on microeconomic decision makers—individuals, families, or firms—are the raw material on which microdata simulation builds.

Given the information on a large number of microeconomic units available from any one of these surveys, together with the sampling weight attached to each unit (indicating the number of units in the nation for which that observation stands), one obtains a picture of the demographic and economic structure of the population. When placed on computer tape, this wealth of information is available to be tabulated, organized, manipulated, and analyzed in any way a researcher or analyst may choose to use it. Because the information available on each observation is similar to that required to determine tax liability or the level of income transfer benefits (e.g., family size and structure, income of various types, extent of work, marital status), such data bases can be used to evaluate the effect on each sampled observation (and hence on various population groups or the entire population) of actual or proposed governmental tax or transfer policies. In particular, by programming the procedures and rules followed by the administrators of transfer programs or stated on tax forms, the computer can calculate the transfer benefits or tax liability of each observation, any group of observations, or the population as a whole. With empirical estimates of how observations (individuals or firms) respond in terms of labor supply, savings, consumption expenditures, or migration to the incentives implicit in policy changes, these behavioral reaction patterns can also be incorporated into the computer model.

This computer-based process of estimating the effects on each observation of actual or proposed policy measures is microdata simulation modeling. By aggregating the simulated individual impacts over the population, the total costs of policies (especially, proposed policies) can be estimated, as well as the number of households or individuals or firms in the population that are affected by the policy, and the impact of the policy on poverty or inequality in the income distribution, or on profit levels. Moreover, if the nature of behavioral responses in some dimension is incorporated into the model, the aggregate effect of the policy change on the response in question (e.g., labor supply, savings, investment, employment) can be evaluated.

Since the mind-1960s, microdata simulation modeling has increasingly replaced a variety of other procedures used by analysts to estimate the costs and caseloads of policy changes proposed or under consideration. As Robert Harris (1978) described them, these earlier tools "consisted of a few scraps of data, the back of an envelope, a sharp pencil, and an imaginative or foolhardy analyst." The substitution of microdata simulation techniques for such tools has substantially increased the reliability and replicability of the estimates, reduced the possibility of manipulating analyses to serve particular needs, and allowed a far wider range of policy alternatives to be analyzed and assessed. Moreover, microdata simulation techniques have served as an important research instrument for scholars and analysts interested in tracing the impact of public spending and taxing policies on the level and incidence of poverty, income inequality, the impacts of government policies on various groups, sectors, and regions and, most recently, the trade-off of efficiency and equity implicit in alternative taxing or spending policies.

The following discussion is limited to the uses of microdata in simulation modeling. In fact, the availability of computer-accessible survey data has dramatically increased the potential for standard econometric analyses of cross-sectional and longitudinal data in estimating a wide variety of behavioral relationships of interest to economists and other social scientists. One of the most extensive uses of microdata has been in estimating the labor-supply, savings, migration, and family structure responses of households to a variety of public interventions, primarily public tax and transfer policies. Several of these studies were reviewed in Danziger, Haveman, and Plotnick (1981). Investigators have also endeavored to identify the research and other analytical uses of the survey information in a number of the major microdata collection projects, in particular the Michigan Panel Study of Income Dynamics (see Morgan et al., 1974–84) and the National Longitudinal Surveys of Labor Market Experience (Parnes et al., 1970–81).

A Brief History

One can identify several factors that stimulated the rapid growth of microdata simulation modeling techniques after the mid-1960s. First, the growth of the nation's income support system began in earnest in the 1960s, spurred by the advent of new social programs, whose growth prompted demands from policymakers for closer scrutiny of their effects. Evaluations of how they meshed with the earlier welfare programs instituted in the 1930s were sought, and analysts were asked to determine how these interventions served the objectives for which they were undertaken. Second, as the programs increased in size and impact, not only policymakers but also parties directly affected—states, which administered many of the programs; recipients; and taxpayers—sought reliable data on the impacts of the policies on various groups and sectors, and an assessment of who was winning and who was losing. Third, during the 1960s, computer capability for handling and manipulating these large data sets became available at increasingly reasonable cost. Combined with this was, fourth, the growing number of social researchers who were trained in computer technology and applied microeconomic analysis, and were sensitive to the potentials for meshing the two. Fifth, the late 1960s saw a substantial relaxation of the constraint on reliable microdata useful for comprehensive and systematic analysis. During this period, a number of self-weighting national sample surveys with significant numbers of observations became available on computer tape: the Consumer Expenditure Survey (13,000 households, 1961–62), the Surveys of Economic Opportunity (65,000 households, 1966–67), the CPS (50,000 households, now available for each year since 1965); and the Panel Study of Income Dynamics (5,000 households longitudinally observed annually since 1968). Finally, Congress was becoming increasingly impatient with poor data and cost estimates on program proposals forthcoming from the administration. Much of this information appeared to be designed more to secure program passage than to enable objective appraisal.

Harris (1978) cites the case of Medicaid, enacted in 1965, which was touted as adding $.25 billion to the existing medical aid programs for public assistance recipients, costing $1.3 billion. Instead, program costs grew to $3.2 billion by 1968, and $12 billion by 1979, even though benefits and eligibility were pared in the interim. Shortly after the Medicaid experience, Senator William Proxmire (1969), in his Foreword to a three-volume congressional study concerning the analysis and evaluation of public expenditures, wrote: "Congress cannot respond to the demands of the people, cannot establish proper national priorities, cannot improve the quality of its decisions, cannot properly scrutinize the executive budget unless it equips itself to ask the right questions . . . having to do with the outputs of a program and its inputs and the economic values of each . . . [and] the distribution of a program's costs and benefits among the people" (pp. viii–ix; see also footnote 2, Chapter 8, above).

In this context, the potential for using computer models for simulating socioeconomic changes seemed enormous. Pioneering work in the development of such models had been under way for some time, at Yale University and at the University of Wisconsin–Madison, led by Guy Orcutt and his colleagues. Orcutt's early work demonstrated the potential for simulating policy changes at a low level of aggregation—say, the household—and then aggregating the simulated results up to any level that would be of help and interest to policymakers.

Although Orcutt's work had been available in the scholarly literature since the early 1960s (Orcutt et al., 1961), the first known application of the technique was the development of a model for analyzing the impacts of changes in federal tax policy on public revenue and on various categories of taxpayers (Pechman, 1965). Shortly after this, a model designed to evaluate the effects of income transfer and welfare programs was developed at the University of Michigan by Harvey Brazer (1968), and was used to analyze the costs and impacts of alternative tax and children's allowance programs.

The First Generation: Static Models

The first quasi-official use of microdata simulation for policy analysis began in 1968, under the sponsorship of the President's Commission on Income Maintenance Programs, and was used by the commission's staff in evaluating a number of alternative negative income tax and other welfare reform plans. Gail Wilensky (who had worked with Brazer) and Nelson McClung (who had been employed at the U.S. Treasury) were primarily responsible for the development and application of the commission's model (see McClung, 1970; Wilensky, 1970). The model, which came to be known as RIM (Reforms in Income Maintenance), was based on the first Survey of Economic Opportunity, a supplement to the Current Population Survey that oversampled the (especially nonwhite) poor, containing detailed information on 30,000 households. Upon termination of the commission's work, the model was taken over by both the Department of Health, Education, and Welfare and the Urban Institute.

Shortly after the commission's task was completed President Nixon, newly elected, authorized design work on a welfare reform which eventually became his Family Assistance Plan (FAP). During this work and the subsequent debate on the proposal, the RIM model—modified, revised, and extended—was extensively used to provide interested parties (including the Congress and the administration) data on the costs and caseloads of the plan and various alternatives to it.

The use of the model in the FAP debate was described by Daniel Patrick Moynihan (1973), then on the White House staff and centrally involved in welfare reform design:

By early 1969 a simulation model had been developed which permitted various versions of FAP to be "tested" and costs to be estimated. Most of this work was done by The Urban Institute, which made its information available to all who requested it. Thus, in time the Congress was to have before it the same data as the executive branch has worked from. So did persons outside government, persons for the program and persons against it. This was a situation probably without precedent in the development of major social legislation; it disciplined and informed the debate for those in any degree disposed to restraint in the discussion of public issues. Once the President had made the proposal, and congressional hearings were beginning, the Administration could in good conscience make statements about the effects it would have which never previously could have been made with any pretense to accuracy (p. 190).

This use of estimated impacts and costs raised the technique of microdata simulation modeling to a level of recognition and acceptance which it had never before attained.

Employment of RIM for policy analysis uncovered a number of major problems and defects with the model, and a major redesign effort was undertaken at the Urban Institute (Moeller, 1973). The result was a larger and more elaborate microdata simulation model called TRIM (Transfer Income Model). TRIM is essentially a computer program, the core of which contains detailed statements of the rules and regulations of many federal and state taxation and income transfer programs. Through this program, the computer scans the detailed characteristics of each observation and calculates a benefit or a tax liability, much as would a program administrator in a Social Security Administration or Internal Revenue Service office. The data base to which TRIM was most often applied was the CPS. In addition to being edited and corrected for missing information, the CPS data were adjusted for program changes made after the survey and "aged" so as to bring the structure of the sample up to that believed to exist in periods after the survey period. (The "aging" of the population can best be thought of as the transmigration of individuals through time by application of sets of demographic and economic adjustment factors.) To estimate the effects of proposed new programs or revisions of existing programs on individual households, the parameters of the computer program are adjusted so as to reflect the changes being proposed, including the interdependence of the benefits and tax liabilities. By comparing the status of households with and without the policy change in effect, and by aggregation across households in various ways, the impacts of an alteration in policy can be estimated along many dimensions.

TRIM was used in a large number of policy simulations: to count the number of households that would be eligible for program benefits and to estimate the total benefits (program costs) if all who were eligible for them took them; to estimate the incidence of poverty under different income definitions and program structures; to estimate the extent of program inefficiency due to the nonintegration of benefits; to project the costs and caseloads of existing programs; and to estimate the impacts of a wide variety of potential transfer system reforms, some of which ultimately became policy proposals, as did President Carter's Program for Better Jobs and Income (for examples see Blechman, Gramlich, and Hartman, 1974; Lerman, 1974; U.S. Congress, Joint Economic Committee, Subcommittee on Fiscal Policy, 1974; Sepanik, Hendricks, and Heinberg, 1975; U.S. Department of Health, Education, and Welfare, 1976; U.S. Congress, Congressional Budget Office, 1977).

Simultaneously a number of other microdata simulation models were being designed, implemented, and used for policy analysis. At the Brookings Institution, Joseph Pechman, Benjamin Okner, and Joseph Minarik constructed a model to be used in simulating the incidence of the existing tax system (under various incidence assumptions) and that of various proposals to alter the tax-transfer system (Okner, 1972). The estimates which the MERGE model yields reflect the various assumptions on incidence patterns for the policy changes which are analyzed, and in most publications concerning this work, a wide variety of incidence assumptions, ranging from very progressive to very regressive, have been employed. Through use of this file the aggregate incidence of the entire U.S. tax system—federal, state, and local—on income classes has been simulated, as well as the tax burden implications of proposed changes in the tax system.

The original MERGE file was based on the combination of two microdata bases and included information on 72,000 family units for the year 1966. More recent files portray the structure of U.S. families in 1970 and 1975, and the 1975 file has been projected to 1980 and 1985. The two component data bases in this model are the U.S. Internal Revenue Service File, containing information from about 90,000 federal income tax returns, and general household or family surveys such as the 1967 Survey of Economic Opportunity (used for the 1966 file), the 1971 CPS (used for the 1970 file), and the 1976 Survey of Income and Education (used for the 1975 file).

A number of analyses not before possible were made with the MERGE files. These include simulations of the first-round impact of the entire U.S. tax system on the size distribution of income (and on various demographic groups and income sources) under a variety of incidence assumptions, a variety of tax credit plans for aiding low-income families, a number of other income maintenance proposals, and a series of proposals for "reforming" the federal income tax (Pechman and Okner, 1974; Break and Pechman, 1975; Okner, 1975; Watts and Peck, 1975; and Pechman, 1985).

Dynamic Microsimulation

The most ambitious of the microsimulation models developed during the period after 1965 was the DYNASIM model of the Urban Institute. As its title suggests, the objective of this model is to forecast through time the implications of major demographic and economic trends. This distinguishes it from both the TRIM and MERGE models, which are static, one-period models.

The DYNASIM model[1] begins with a representation of the U.S. population: the 1–in–10,000 sample from the 1970 Census. This sample of families is then "aged" to years after 1969 by incorporating relationships based on the observed pattern of behavior of members of the U.S. population. This aging is done on a year-to-year basis and accounts for annual changes in the composition of the population due to death, marriage, divorce, education, and geographic migration. In effect, the model looks at each individual in the original sample and, on the basis of that individual's characteristics, calculates a probability that he or she will give birth, marry, die, become divorced, obtain more education, or move. These probabilities are then employed actually to attribute such changes to individuals in the sample through a type of simulation exercise (the Monte Carlo technique). As a consequence, the original sample is transformed into a new, second-year population, which has a different size, a different family structure, a different distribution of income and education, and a different pattern of geographical location. This simulated second-year population then becomes the basis for simulating the third-year population, and so on.

In addition to the dynamic demographic simulation, the DYNASIM model also has a labor sector. In it, an individual's wage income is generated from year to year by imputing labor force participation, hours worked, and a wage rate—again based on exogenous characteristics such as age, sex, and race. The model also contains a component that enables the imputation of income from a number of government and private transfer programs—social security, private pension funds, Unemployment Compensation, and several welfare programs. As with the TRIM model this component assigns benefits on the basis of program eligibility and payment rules and the relevant characteristics of families.

Although the DYNASIM model has a large number of potential uses and policy applications, its implementation has been quite limited. Some explorations have been made into the effect of expected changes in the work behavior of women and divorce patterns on the distribution of

1. The model is most fully described in Orcutt, Caldwell, and Wertheimer (1976) and Haveman and Lacker (1984). The latter also describes a related dynamic model developed in the late 1970s by ICF Inc., a private research firm. That model, called PRISM, has been used along with DYNASIM to estimate the costs and distributional effects of a variety of social security and private pension reform proposals. The DYNASIM model has also led to data collection and modeling efforts to construct a dynamic and recursive model of the West German economy; see Merz (1982).

earned income and transfer income. In addition, the model has been used to forecast the future costs and caseloads of a limited number of public transfer programs, and of the costs and distributional consequences, through time, of a number of proposed reforms in retirement income policy (see for example Wertheimer and Zedlewski, 1978; Schieber and George, 1981).

Microsimulation Incorporating Behavioral Responses

For purposes of policy simulation, none of the models discussed to this point evaluates the effects of policies beyond the first round—that is, beyond the direct allocation of transfer payments and taxes among households. No behavioral responses to taxes and transfers in the form of work effort, consumption, migration, or family structure are incorporated into these models. A later stage of microdata simulation efforts has attempted to incorporate such second-round effects into the models.

The most comprehensive of these later models was developed at the Department of Health, Education, and Welfare for the purpose of analyzing welfare reform proposals during the Carter administration, and became known as the KGB model (after the constructors of the model, Richard Kasten, David Greenberg, and David Betson). The model can be used to simulate proposed changes in income transfer programs and in the positive tax system, and explicitly analyzes both the various interactions among income transfer programs, taxes, public employment programs, and labor-supply adjustments to changes in taxes and transfers.[2]

As compared to first-generation static models or the dynamic models, there are two important advances incorporated into the KGB model. The first is the addition of a simulation submodel for determining which individuals on a microdata file would be eligible for a public service job and, of those eligible, which would actually take such a job. Second, and more significantly, the model simulates the probable work-effort responses of individuals resulting from changes in tax and transfer policies, on the basis of estimated labor-supply response parameters. As is well known, changes in net wage rates and income levels affect the incentives of individuals to work, and changes in tax and transfer policy alter both net wage rates and income levels. Earlier models had been, appropriately, criticized for neglecting these responses. In the KGB effort, estimated parameters of the response of individuals to changes in net wage rates and incomes, using data from the large-scale Seattle-Denver income

---

2. An earlier effort to incorporate experimental labor-supply responses into a microdata simulation model is that of Myles Maxfield (see Maxfield, 1980).

maintenance experiments, were incorporated into the model.[3] As a result of these extensions, the estimates of program costs and the number of recipients, as well as the estimated impacts of policy changes on various subgroups of the population, reflect both the earnings and public service employment responses of individuals to the policy change estimated. Because these behavioral response estimates are large in magnitude, the resulting estimates from the KGB model are likely to be substantially more reliable than those in earlier estimates in which labor-supply effects are ignored. Moreover, the results available from the model implicitly yield estimates of the equity and efficiency trade-off implicit in any proposed change in taxation or income transfer policy. The KGB model was used to analyze a number of welfare-reform variants in the planning process that led to the final version of the Program for Better Jobs and Income. In addition, a variety of more extensive negative income tax, credit income tax, and wage subsidy plans have been evaluated using the model (see Betson, Greenberg, and Kasten, 1980, 1982; Betson and Bishop, 1982).

While the KGB model was the most ambitious effort to incorporate behavioral responses into estimation, other models have also addressed this issue. One developed at the Institute for Research on Poverty (known as the RESIND model, an acronym standing for the Regional, Employment, and Sectoral Income Distribution model) incorporates estimates of the consumption expenditure response of individuals to the income changes caused by alterations in tax and transfer policy. The RESIND model also yields estimates of the induced industry, occupation, and regional impacts of the policy change. The logic of the model is straightforward: Changes in disposable income from income transfer programs (and the taxes required to finance them) lead to changes in the level and composition of consumption expenditures for those affected by the policy measures. These expenditure changes will affect the demands experienced by (and hence the output of) the various industries which supply consumers. Such changed output patterns will, in turn, alter the demands placed on supplying industries, because of the interdependence of the industries in the economy; all sectors, located in various regions of the economy, will experience such changes in gross outputs. In response to increased or decreased output levels, production sectors will alter the demand for labor of various occupational groups. These changes in occupational demands, in turn, imply changes in the distribution of

---

3. For discussion of the labor-supply parameter estimates from SIME-DIME, see Keeley et al. (1978).

earnings and income—to the extent that the relative change in demand for high-skilled workers differs from that for low-skilled workers.

The RESIND model has been used to analyze the regional and distributional impacts of FAP, a variety of negative and credit income tax proposals, and the Program for Better Jobs and Income (see Danziger and Haveman, 1977; Golladay and Haveman, 1977; and Haveman et al., 1980).

A model that also incorporates interindustry relationships and yields estimates of regional output impacts is the IDIOM model developed by Stephen Dresch and his associates (Dresch and Updegrove, 1980). IDIOM was primarily designed to evaluate the sectoral impacts of exhaustive public spending programs, but could also be modified to evaluate the effects of change in transfer and tax policy.

Two special-purpose models also incorporating behavioral responses were the CHRD (Comprehensive Human Resource Data) system developed by the Department of Energy (King, 1980) and the HRRC (Human Resources Research Center) Health Care Sector Simulation Model, developed by Donald Yett and his associates (Yett, 1979; Yett et al., 1980). The former was a very detailed household and sectoral model developed to evaluate the impact of various energy policies—rationing, taxes, price controls, and conservation. It reflected consumer responsiveness to income and price changes by incorporating income and price elasticities of demand for energy into the model. The other model, HRRC, analyzes the impact of policy proposals—for example, national health insurance—on the output and price performance of most health care service sectors and on consumers. Behavioral responses to demand and supply changes are incorporated into the submodels for each of the sectors, and the models are linked by a series of demand-supply market interrelationships, hence incorporating a number of important feedback mechanisms.

Applied General Equilibrium Analyses

The most recent extension of the microeconomic simulation methodology is the development of large-scale computable general equilibrium systems. The earliest, and ultimately one of the most advanced, of these numerical general equilibrium models was that of the U.S. economy developed by John Shoven and his associates (Shoven, 1972; Fullerton et al., 1980; Ballard, Shoven, and Whalley, 1985; and Ballard et al., 1985). The model integrates the U.S. tax system with consumer demand behavior (by household), producer behavior (by industry) with savings and investment activity, and in addition incorporates foreign trade activity and government purchase policy. Markets are simulated and the changes in equilibrium prices and quantities due to the change in tax (or transfer) policy that is modeled are calculated. Although the model is basically static, extensions involving the effects of saving and investment behavior are being developed. The model contains nineteen producer goods industries, sixteen consumer goods, and twelve types of consumers, classified by income category. Capital and labor are supplied by households to industry, and are mobile among industries. The demands of consumers are consistent with utility theory, and markets are taken to be perfectly competitive. Industry production is characterized by specific forms of production functions, and intermediate use of outputs is governed by standard input-output relationships. Taxes affect the cost structures of industries, the prices of goods demanded by consumers, and their incomes. As indicated, the model is not dynamic; labor supply is exogenous and not affected by changes in tax policy. By means of this model, the effects of changes in tax policy (in particular, the integration of corporate and personal income taxes) on prices and outputs by industry, after-tax real income by consumer group, and real national income have been estimated.[4]

An Assessment of Microdata Simulation Modeling

The existing models reflect a wide range of approaches to microeconomic simulation. Some are designed to estimate the impact of policy measures on households or individuals in a static context. In some of the static models, behavioral responses to price and income changes caused by the policy are imputed to microdata observations (e.g., households). Others are dynamic, using time-specific microdata as the basis for simulating dynamic demographic changes and their interaction with policy variables through time. Some of them employ actual observations taken from longitudinal surveys of households or businesses as data points, while others construct households or other data points with a few identifying characteristics that are designed to represent actual households or businesses.[5] A number of the models are national in scope; others focus on portions of the national economy (e.g., the business sector, urban areas, the health care sector, or specific regions). Still others seek to estimate disaggregated impacts in which regions, industries, occupations,

---

4. A comprehensive review of this model and others of its genre is given in Shoven and Whalley (1984).

5. A transaction model of the U.S. economy described in Bennett and Bergmann (1980) falls into the latter category.

and income classes are distinguished, in addition to national totals. These models involve a number of sequential behavioral responses as the simulated effects of a policy change spread through the economy. Finally, some of the models rely on complex algorithms for their solutions, while others are "solved" simply by imposing the rules or schedules of a postulated public program on the characteristics of the microdata observations.

Through microdata-based models, richer analyses than were previously possible—involving simulated impacts of actual and proposed public policies on detailed demographic and income groups, industries, regions, and occupations—can be undertaken. In many of the models, these impact estimates can reflect behavioral responses to a program, the effect of the program and its induced responses through time, and the linkages and interdependences that are inherent in the economic system. And because the models are based upon microdata, estimates can be made of the impact of a policy change on narrowly defined sectors of the economy (regions, industries, occupations) and specific demographic and economic groups.

The benefits of such analyses are important for both research and policy. To the extent that program costs depend upon the response of individuals to the income and incentive effects of the program, the cost estimates obtained are likely to be more accurate than those based on techniques that ignore behavioral responses. Similarly, if it matters who benefits and who is hurt by a proposed policy change, and the extent of gains and losses, such detailed sectoral analyses are important in the design of programs and policies.

These advantages stem from the ability of microdata simulation techniques to use available detailed information on the initial state of microunits, to give literal representation to the nature of policy changes, to use estimated empirical relationships in incorporating behavioral responses into simulated impacts, to generate univariate and multivariate distributions from simulated microunit outputs, and to aggregate these microunit outputs as relevant or desired. The microunit-based nature of the estimation procedure has significant advantages over more aggregative, or macroeconometric, approaches in terms of both the reliability of results and the estimation and testing of the models. Orcutt et al. (1980) emphasized the likely improvement in the reliability of estimates:

While much of social science theory, theorizing, and research relates to the behavior of individuals, families, and firms, we do not know how to aggregate nonlinear microrelations into macrorelations. For example, if family saving depends on family income, wealth, and life-cycle variables, then aggregate saving will depend on the joint distribution of family incomes, family wealths, and family life-cycle attributes. Not only would such a macro saving function be difficult or impossible to specify and estimate directly, but it would not be used appropriately in a macro-model without the availability of a joint distribution of all of these microvariables. With microanalytic models, relations for microunits are used without aggregation. Instead, outputs of microrelations are aggregated as desired and without difficulty (p. 86).

These analytic gains do not come without cost, however. The construction, estimation, operation, and updating of the models require very large research, computer, and survey costs. Because of their complexity, size, and especially their reliance on microdata, the operational cost of a number of these models is likely to exceed that of some of the major national macroeconometric models. The complexity of microdata and the computer-intensive technology inherent in simulation analysis make the research process in this area both time-consuming and frustrating. The potential for calculation and programming errors is very large, and because of the cumulative and linked nature of such models, errors discovered in an early stage require the recalculation of estimates developed in later stages. Similarly, minor restructuring of earlier parts of models (the potential for which is enormous) requires recalculation and often reprogramming of later stages in the analysis. And efforts to expand the complexity of such models (for example, to include dynamic relationships and intertemporal changes in family or enterprise structure) run the risk of introducing debilitating computational difficulties.

The problem of appropriately modeling behavioral responses to program, price, or income incentives is the primary difficulty confronted by microdata simulation efforts. For most of the standard behavioral responses (e.g., labor supply, savings) the range of elasticity estimates available in the literature is substantial (see for example Cain and Watts, 1973; Hamermesh and Grant, 1979; Killingsworth, 1983; Shoven and Whalley, 1984). Moreover, the procedures required in order accurately to model labor-supply and other behavioral responses to taxes and transfers in the face of nonconvex and kinked budget constraints (e.g., the need to locate the specific budget constraint for each observation) are demanding ones and have not yet been incorporated into the standard simulation models. Under these circumstances, the choice of response coefficients and elasticities to be included in any microsimulation model is somewhat arbitrary, and sensitivity analysis using coefficient estimates from other studies is necessary to establish reasonable bounds around the estimates. Because this problem is so pervasive—involving not only individual response functions to program structures, but also relationships of input and output, regional trade investments, marginal output and labor requirements, and labor demand and earned income—the reliance on sensitivity analyses becomes unmanageable as the range of upper- and lower-bound estimates of the final variables of interest expands significantly. While there are means of controlling this growth, the ultimate interpretation of results is problematic.[6]

The final problem concerns the reliability of the underlying microdata. Most of the models rely on survey data, the weaknesses of which— misreporting, missing data, inadequate sample design—are well known. These problems may undermine the reliability of more aggregate analyses as well as microdata studies. However, because microdata simulation requires the manipulation of each of numerous observations, the difficulty is heightened. Related to this is the fact that no substantial effort to define the statistical properties of microsimulation estimates has been undertaken. Furthermore, virtually all of the extant models involve some amount of ad hoc manipulation of the data in order to achieve results, which increases the difficulty of establishing model validity. This problem is especially severe in the dynamic models, where behavior may change over time and where the impact of data errors on the results increases the farther out in time one moves.

A final note on this research methodology concerns its impact on the role of the social researcher and policy analyst. In the conference paper quoted above, Orcutt et al. (1980) found the future role of the social scientist to be importantly affected by the advent of microdata simulation modeling:

> He will increasingly play a role as a contributor to a larger joint effort, rather than operating as a solo practitioner. . . . The development of macroeconomic policy analysis since World War II is instructive. . . . [It] has led to the decline of the single scholar constructing macroeconomic models in his office with a desk calculator in favor of the institutionalized team capable of constructing, applying, modifying, and maintaining extremely large and complex models embodying hundreds of equations (p. 101).

Some view this development less favorably than do Orcutt and his colleagues, believing that the potential for critical thinking, theorizing, and conceptual analysis which is a traditional and central function of social science will be undermined. Michael Taussig (1980), for example, a discussant of the Orcutt et al. paper, responded to its characterization as follows:

6. A paper by Browning (1985) illustrates this problem. Using a range of empirical parameter estimates in the published literature for but four values relevant to estimating changes in the welfare cost associated with taxation changes (marginal tax rate, compensated supply elasticity, change in the average tax rate, earnings effect of a balanced budget change in taxes), he concludes that the marginal welfare cost of an increase in tax revenue of $1 varies from 10 cents to $3.00.

Why not work instead on a factory assembly line? . . . If the main role [of researchers] is to think critically about current policy or to work on improving the conceptual framework for predicting behavioral responses to changes in program parameters or to estimate the quantitative dimensions of such behavioral responses or to devise radical innovations in the basic policy framework, then the author's view just does not fit (p. 113).

Microdata simulation modeling developed rapidly in the United States in the late 1960s and 1970s, but interest in and support of this research technique has decreased substantially in the 1980s. The primary sources of financial support for the development and use of these models were the federal agencies in the social and human resources fields that were responsible for designing policy changes and program reforms. When the demands on these agencies for policy proposals and analyses of the impacts of these proposals were strong, the need for modeling efforts and the resources available to support them were substantial. Since 1980, however, the federal government has emphasized program retrenchment in the interests of a smaller government sector, and not reform designed to improve the effectiveness and equity impacts of programs. Moreover, the motivation and justification for policy change has become based more on the hope that desirable effects will follow from the changes implemented than on social research regarding how policy changes are likely to affect individual behavior and well-being. As a result, funding for the continued development and use of the models has been dramatically reduced, researchers trained and experienced in microdata simulation techniques have tended to turn to other activities, and a large number of the existing models lie dormant, unmaintained, and unused. Until policymakers once again decide to utilize the insights and findings of social research in the development of social and economic policy, the prospects for major advances in this field of scientific endeavor are not high.

Microdata Simulation and Social Science Research

It was clearly the combined impact of the War on Poverty, the desire to construct a Great Society, and the drive for more rational government policies that provided the primary stimulus for the development of microdata simulation modeling. The demand for more sophisticated, reliable, and detailed estimates of the social and economic effects of proposed social policies accompanied these events, as did the supply of resources required for the design and construction of this empirical tool.

The extensive use made of the models and the estimates that they yielded in policy debates on poverty and social policy reforms both within the administration and in the Congress stimulated their development and the interest in and resources devoted to them. The commitment of the academic research community to their development was considerable, in part because of the resources available for this work and because of the interest of policymakers in the results. Individual scholars and research groups at several of the major universities and research centers were all actively involved in either developing their own models or in contributing to model development.

In several ways, the developments in microeconomic simulation modeling have had a significant impact on the social science disciplines, economics in particular. First, as described above, they represent important advances in the frontier of predictive model building. The reliance on microunits and the need to model their behavior adds an important dimension to models designed to evaluate the impact of public policy measures and other exogenous changes on the economy—a dimension that is not reflected in the existing macroeconomic models. The challenges that these models posed for data handling and computer processing, model execution and solution, and the complex sequencing of simultaneous and recursive socioeconomic relationships stretched the capability of quantitative social scientists.

Second, the ability of these models to incorporate econometrically estimated relationships—for example, income and net wage on labor supply, socioeconomic characteristics on consumption, migration, marriage, childbearing—increased the priority given to the reliable estimation of these relationships. Estimation of the determinants of these behaviors had been a long-standing focus of both quantitative economics and sociology. The same increased availability of survey data in the 1960s that enabled the construction of microdata simulation models also increased the capability of social scientists to model and estimate these relationships. And, since the constructors of the large models provided a demand and a home for such estimations, the effort given to this form of research grew substantially. The increased quantitative estimation of behavioral determinants in both economics and sociology after the mid-1960s, and the development of microdata simulation modeling during the same period, were complementary phenomena.

Finally, as described, the ability of microdata models to provide detailed estimates of policy impacts on highly disaggregated groups met an important need during the days of the War on Poverty and Great Society, in the late 1960s and early 1970s. It was then that all policy initiatives, both those in the antipoverty and social action area and those with more general objectives, were forced to answer the question, "What does it do for the poor?" With the success of programs and program proposals contingent in part on the answer to this question, microdata simulation became viewed as the primary research tool capable of providing the desired information.

As a corollary, those researchers and analysts involved in developing and using microdata simulation models in the policy process were highly visible and in high demand. To many, this represented what it was that social scientists could and should be doing, and the composition of activities within the disciplines reflected this judgment. Work on model development, modeling techniques, solution algorithms, microdata collection and processing, and the estimation of behavioral relationships and the responses of individuals to the incentives contained in policy measures all burgeoned during this period. Given the nature of the policy issues to which these modeling efforts were primarily addressed—programs of welfare reform, food stamps, employment subsidies, public employment, income transfer policy, tax reform—it can be hardly doubted that the War on Poverty and the policy emphases to which it gave rise had an important role in stimulating these developments in the social sciences.

Epilogue

This volume was initiated in 1981, at a time when the War on Poverty appeared to be concluded, and a large and deliberate retrenchment in the policies that constituted that effort began. The purpose of its writing was to appraise the research accomplishments of the preceding fifteen years that could be said to have exerted a lasting effect on the social science community. To what extent had this burst of social policy interventions altered what it is that social scientists study, and how they study it?

Now, reviewing the volume five years later, it is clear that 1981 was not the end of an era, but only the beginning of a period of moderate curtailment. Programs to reduce poverty were scaled back and their objectives and approaches were modified. They were not, however dismantled, the early rhetoric notwithstanding. Public concern with the problem of poverty has increased in part because of the increase of poverty due to the recessions of 1979–80 and 1981–82. Federal policy seems to be once again edging toward directly addressing the social ills that accompany poverty, with attention to the distinction between those able and not able to work. A sizable group of members of Congress seems unwilling to allow the issue of poverty to disappear from the nation's agenda of important concerns. Indeed, the tax reform of 1986 had the reduction of federal income taxes for the poor as one of its explicit objectives.

The social science research community has not ceased to make progress in understanding the nature and causes of, and cures for, the problem of poverty, although it has proceeded at a slower pace. Demonstration projects concerning workfare, adolescent pregnancy, and child support assurance have been undertaken, but there have been few new social experiments that have built on the lessons of the earlier efforts. The Survey of Income and Program Participation, for which planning began in the 1970s, is the only major new federally sponsored data-collection effort. Yet research using the experimental data has continued. The natural incentives that drive academic and research life have sustained a continuing flow of research studies, the support for which has been secured from a variety of private and state sources in response to the reduction in federal government support. The impacts that were reported and behaviors that were revealed in the first round of studies some years ago have been subjected to deeper and more probing investigations. Most have been sustained; some modified.

In terms of methodology, progress has also been made in the 1980s. Even though encouragement from the government has been reduced, scholars have continued to study and refine the procedures for undertaking reliable social experiments. Models for estimating the behavioral responses to interventions have been extended and their properties examined. The continuous-time, event-history analyses and the procedures for dealing with problems of selectivity and attrition, discussed in Chapter 10, are important examples.

Research efforts designed to establish and to measure economic well-being and to track the degree of inequality in the distribution of well-being regularly produce new estimates. Although largely hidden from the view of the media, the Bureau of the Census has made notable advances in developing an extended measure of well-being which incorporates the value to recipients of in-kind transfers. Using this measure, the distribution of well-being over time has been studied, as has the incidence of poverty under various measures of economic well-being. The need for a revised and extended official measure of poverty is widely recognized, and it seems only a matter of time before a formal new government-sponsored research and study effort is undertaken to establish such a measure. As Harold Watts recently wrote: "Now is an especially good time to consider how the measures might be changed. It appears that most of the weaknesses can be corrected and our poverty measures enriched without doing major violence to the intuitive and vernacular notion of what it means to be poor" (1986, p. 22).

After the several abortive attempts to reform the welfare system in the 1970s, one would have guessed that it would be a long wait before another such effort would be mounted by a presidential administration. Yet in 1986, at this writing, the federal government is again involved in a study project designed to propose legislation or changes in regulations reforming the welfare system. The motivation for this effort is quite different from those of the 1970s, yet the desire to make the system more supportive of family stability and recipient independence are goals shared by all of the plans. And while concern for adequacy has been replaced by the desire to minimize the government's commitment, the basic questions being addressed are not dissimilar from those studied by the reform projects of the 1970s: How can we best encourage individual work effort and initiative? How can we most effectively integrate training and work programs with cash assistance? How can we encourage absent parents to maintain concern and financial support for the children with whom they no longer live? Interestingly, these questions and the approaches taken to answer them inevitably rely on the data, insights, and knowledge generated during the 1965–80 period. It is as if this knowledge now both defines the questions and sets bounds around the answers which can be offered while still remaining responsible and credible.

Even the strong views of Charles Murray and George Gilder concerning the poor and the welfare system both rest on and are constrained by the data, evidence, and knowledge generated and published as an outgrowth of War on Poverty research. Their interpretation of that evidence, while quite different from that of some other members of the social science research community, has in fact enlivened the discussion among social researchers—it has forced them to scrutinize just what it was that their research had found, what it all added up to, and what issues they did not but should have addressed. The resulting debate has required poverty researchers to identify which among the many and sometimes contradictory research findings are robust and reliable, and what in fact is the bottom line of these hundreds of research studies, each of which claimed to add something to our understanding regarding the causes and cures of poverty. This debate and the challenge that it represents have generated a spurt of research that has still better defined the questions of import and brought evidence to bear on them.

The challenge of these critics, while widely and not always inappropriately viewed as irresponsible and as a direct misrepresentation of some research findings, has in fact stimulated the social sciences. It represents an effort to subject research findings to a rather different ideological perspective and interpretation. This challenge has been a healthy one for the social research community. It has reminded us that policy research does not derive primarily from the rationalistic view that drove so much of the War on Poverty enterprise. It has driven home the basic point that in the social policy area research findings will not be speedily transformed into policy changes. Values and ideologies ultimately govern the formulation of policy, and research findings and knowledge play the role that rules and referees play in athletic contests. They have forced many advocates to consider and to address the research literature in making their policy pronouncements, and to critique research findings before proceeding to advocacy. This body of research has, in effect, forced reason on to what might otherwise have stood as only the writings of ideologues.

What lies ahead for social science as it relates to the issue of poverty? While the future of an enterprise as diverse as social research cannot be forecast with any reasonable degree of accuracy, a few thoughts may be offered. First, the 1965–80 period was unique. Social scientists living now are not likely to again witness a burst of policy interest and support matching that which came with the Great Society initiatives. Concerns with minority youth unemployment, with the failures of the public schools, with crime rates, with family dissolution and births out of wedlock, with the apparently growing disparity between the elderly and children, and with the nature and apparent growth of an underclass in the urban black community have and will continue to strike both the conscience and the interest of policymakers. But only the naïve would anticipate new and large-scale government support for research on any of these problems in the near future.

Second, it seems inevitable that a good deal of the next generation of research on the nature and causes of poverty and on the behavior of the poor will be more narrow and more focused than that of the earlier period. That body of research from 1965 to 1980 was often more broad than deep. New problem areas were opened up; theorizing and empirical testing were both of the first-generation sort. The next stage is likely to consist of a deeper and more careful sifting out of the issues and of the application of more reliable and sophisticated methods to the estimation of the relationships of interest. While not as exciting as the previous period of research, it is rather more in line with the traditional way that science has proceeded.

Finally, the next generation of social research on the poverty problem is also likely to contain an increased emphasis on directly understanding the condition of poverty and the attitudes and motivations of the poor. This research will be less narrow and measurement-oriented than much past poverty research—less dominated by economists and the estimation of formal causal models. For a growing number of social researchers, the problems have come to be seen as more complex than they were earlier thought to be. Cultures, outlooks, perceptions, roles, expectations, horizons, opportunities, social constraints, and neighborhood ethos have increasingly become more accepted as playing a pivotal role in determining both the nature and the causes of poverty. Gaining understanding of these processes will require a research approach which relies more heavily on the interactions of social scientists with those whose behavior and condition they wish to understand.

While the argument for ethnographic research—such as that of Nathan Glazer, quoted at the end of Chapter 6—is more optimistic than I feel comfortable with, the general point regarding the inadequacy of conventional social research—"the economic analysis and large-scale correlations and regressions," as Glazer put it—stands. Clearly, the challenges to standard poverty research from both those within the disciplines and those who have attacked it from a more ideological and polemical stance have forced the social science research community to rethink what it does, how it is to be done, and most important, the role that research findings should play in the larger and value-laden social policy process.

The research gains attributable to the War on Poverty are large and impressive. They should be extended and pressed; they are worthy. But they do not answer all of the questions. Future poverty research should build on these past advances, but do so recognizing both the ultimate limits of social research and its competition with ideology and politics in the making of poverty policy.

Appendices
References
Index

Appendix A: Concepts for Measuring the Equity Effects of Transfers

Policy actions in the 1960s—the announcement of the War on Poverty, the Great Society policy initiatives, and the very rapid growth of budgetary costs for income transfers—focused attention on the role of such transfers in reducing poverty and equalizing incomes. Policymakers began asking questions to which social science researchers had previously paid scant attention: How do public income transfers fit with the wide range of other transfer mechanisms that are employed, such as private transfers among individuals and family members? How can the growth of these programs be explained? What is the value of transfers to recipients, and how can this value be measured? What should be the criteria for evaluating the worth of transfer programs—efficiency, or equity? Once the programs are in place, how can the effects of income transfers be measured and assessed?

Among the most basic of the conceptual contributions for placing the role of income transfers into its proper setting is the framework developed by Robert Lampman.[1] Social transfers, in his view, are far broader than simply public welfare or public income transfers. The American system of transfers encompasses all public and private means for providing both money incomes and goods and services to persons on a basis other than their current money income. His framework incorporates many public expenditures not involving cash flows (e.g., education, health, and other social services), certain taxes (those required to pay for personally received transfers), private inter- and intrafamily flows, certain subsidies and employer benefits, and private foundation and charitable giving. Lampman's major contribution was in establishing a unified and comprehensive *transfers account* by which all transfer flows, both public and private, could be assembled and observed in their role of transforming "producer incomes" into "user incomes."

1. This approach evolved over a substantial period (see Lampman, 1957, 1966, 1969c, 1970, 1971a), and was highlighted in his book *Social Welfare Spending: Accounting for Changes from 1950 to 1978* (1984).

241

Using this transfers account framework, Lampman (1971a) estimated that public income transfers constituted only about 40 percent of the $132 billion of total American transfers in 1966, and that these public programs often served many of the same purposes as other, nonpublic transfers. These transfer programs, he found, made a major contribution to the total income available to poor people—in 1966, three-fourths of the 16.1 million pretransfer poor families received transfers, the mean amount of which was over $1,800, and over one third of these families were taken out of officially defined poverty by transfers. Public income transfers, Lampman concluded, contributed heavily to the antipoverty impact of transfers. While the entire transfer system raised the income share of pretransfer-poor families from 3 percent to 9 percent, public transfers accounted for 5 of the 6 percentage points of gain.

This comprehensive approach to viewing the American system of transfers[2] brought to the surface a wide range of questions about the impacts of the system that had not before been raised in a coherent fashion. What groups in the population were net recipients of transfers? How did their transfer benefits compare with their other sources of income? What groups were effectively excluded from the transfer system? How do the various components of the system differentially affect the poor and other sizable socioeconomic groups? What is the effect of the transfer system on inequality in the distribution of income? To what extent do programs designed to aid the poor provide benefits to nonpoor citizens? How should one evaluate the benefits of cash and in-kind programs designed to aid low-income families?

Lampman, and others working in the "social accounting" subdiscipline of economics, developed a variety of concepts and analytical techniques for answering questions regarding the performance of the income transfer system. Complementing the transfer system account introduced by Lampman was the concept of "target efficiency," first introduced by Burton Weisbrod (1969). Focusing on the collective objective of income redistribution (and, especially, on the benefit side of the redistributional process, namely, "helping the needy"), Weisbrod attempted to define criteria for choosing among alternative redistributive policies. Six were identified: (1) administrative cost, (2) allocative efficiency (or incentive effects), (3) stigma effects, (4) balancing of consumer (recipient) and taxpayer sovereignty, (5) flexibility over time, and (6) target efficiency. In

---

2. In his research, Lampman relied heavily on basic information on public transfer and social welfare programs published by the Social Security Administration. See Merriam and Skolnick (1968).

simplest terms, target efficiency concerns the extent to which a program distributes its benefits to the group(s) for whom the program was designed. The simple concept, however, had two distinct aspects: To what extent does the program benefit *only* the target group (vertical target efficiency) and to what extent does the program reach all of the members of the target group (horizontal target efficiency)? Attainment of the first aspect is measured by the ratio of benefits received by members of the target group to total benefits; attainment of the second aspect is measured by the ratio of beneficiaries in (or benefits to) the target group to the total number of persons in (benefits "needed" by) the target group. Only in the limiting case, in which (1) a program's benefits went *only* to members of the target group and (2) those benefits met the "needs" of *all* members of the target group, would both the vertical and the horizontal aspects of target efficiency be attained.

The target efficiency concept in its pure form is, essentially, dichotomous. A unit of benefits either goes to a member of the target group, or it does not. And if a unit of benefit accrues to someone not in the target group, how is it to be valued? Weisbrod posed this question in the following terms:

The question is whether a program such as compensatory education for the disadvantaged or retraining for the hard-core unemployed—which are aimed at particular kinds of people—should count any benefits (outputs) that accrue to persons not in the target group, and if so, whether these benefits should be given the same weight per dollar as benefits to the intended beneficiaries (1969, p. 185).

Stated in this form, the target-efficiency ratios are indices of cost effectiveness (or program performance) and hence raise all of the standard evaluation questions that grow out of this benefit-cost framework. For one thing, benefits which accrue to non-target-group members may have real efficiency gains (or costs) even though they convey no redistributive gains. These efficiency effects should be counted in evaluating the program. Moreover, target groups are typically not thought of in such an absolute manner. Individuals are not viewed as either needy or not needy; rather they are more or less needy. If "deservingness" is, in fact, a continuum, it is necessary that benefits going to individuals along the continuum receive different weights.

The conceptual basis for developing a set of welfare weights for individuals of different economic statuses (or other characteristics) is well established in two rather distinct lines in the welfare economics literature: that associated with the Bergsonian social welfare function approach and that developed more recently in the "Pareto optimal redistribution" literature.[3]

The first explicit application of the welfare weighting procedure to antipoverty programs was by Ribich (1968). Recognizing the merit of a poverty line to distinguish recipients in the target group from other recipients, yet also recognizing that benefits to some who are a small distance above the poverty line but still in need also have redistributive value, Ribich adopted a second poverty line, somewhat above the first. Then, a unit of benefits going to a person below the low poverty line would be weighted more highly than benefits going to people between the two lines, and benefits to people above the top line would be given a zero redistribution value.[4] As he stated:

The required inference . . . is that the bottom poverty line describes the point where taxpayers are willing to give up one dollar—no more, no less—to see poor people in this particular income range benefit by one dollar. Thus, gains near the bottom poverty line should be weighted by approximately full value. Gains between the bottom and top poverty lines can be graduated between one and zero, and gains below the bottom line weighted at greater than one. With these weights established, comparisons between competing anti-poverty programs can proceed in a more reasonable and equitable fashion (p. 30).

More recently, an extension of the target-efficiency concept and its implied need for weighting benefits going to target group members was made by Harberger (1983). His procedure, which he calls the "basic needs" approach, seeks to reflect in the evaluation of programs the external benefits associated with improvement in the circumstances of members of the target group. "Most people genuinely feel that it is 'good' for the sick to be healed, the hungry fed, the illiterate taught, [and] the homeless sheltered" (p. 105). It is the consumption by target group members of particular goods and services (e.g., food, health care, housing) up to an "adequate" level of consumption that creates an external benefit,[5] and the trick is to integrate the value of this basic needs external benefit into the evaluation.

Operationally, Harberger proposes that an elected authority establish

3. See Eckstein (1961) for a clear presentation of the first approach. Early experiments employing this approach are found in Haveman (1965) and Weisbrod (1968). The second approach is found in Hochman and Rodgers (1969), where utility interdependence is relied upon to integrate both efficiency and redistributive objectives. A critique of the welfare weighting procedure is found in Harberger (1978).

4. Watts (1969) adopted a similar weighting approach in his proposal for a revised poverty index.

5. Hence, this approach has its intellectual roots in the Pareto optimal redistribution (and in-kind transfer) tradition rather than the social welfare function tradition.

a linear relationship between the maximum efficiency cost it would be willing to bear for the first units of consumption pertinent to some basic need (e.g., food) and the level of consumption "beyond which society simply does not recognize a basic needs externality" (p. 124; that is, where the externality benefit is zero) and employ the weights from this relationship in valuing the benefits of a program aiding the target group.[6] Harberger argues that this approach is conceptually superior to the distributional-weights approach (in that it does not violate the postulates for achieving allocative efficiency), and that it places the weight on the consumption of particular basic goods by the target group (an outcome on which non-target-group members place value), and not simply on the level of their income.

Other concepts and measurement techniques have also become part of the contemporary lexicon of poverty researchers. Most of these are measurement techniques, and all relate in some fashion to the horizontal and vertical equity impacts implicit in Weisbrod's target-efficiency notion. Similarly, all complement Lampman's comprehensive "transfers account" framework.

A basic concept in measuring the target or antipoverty effect of either individual transfers or the transfer system is the "poverty income gap"— the total number of dollars of income required to provide all pretransfer-poor families sufficient income to move them above the poverty line. The relationship of this measure to the concept of target efficiency is direct. Defining the poor to be the target group of a transfer program, the total level of program expenditures if the program were to be both horizontally and vertically target efficient would equal the poverty income gap. The income gap measure has been used extensively in measuring the anti-poverty effectiveness of individual transfer programs. In this use, the ratio of the change in the poverty income gap attributable to a program to total expenditures of the program is taken to be an index of antipoverty effectiveness.[7]

Another important evaluation and measurement concept following from the target-efficiency notion is closely tied to the vertical equity of the transfer system. "Leapfrogging" occurs if the welfare ratio of some

6. In this framework, any individual whose basic needs in some dimension are not met is a member of the target group.

7. A corollary of this effectiveness ratio is what Plotnick and Skidmore (1975) have called the "leakage ratio" (1 minus the change in the poverty income gap attributed to transfers divided by the transfers received by the pretransfer poor). This ratio is designed to measure the extent to which pretransfer-poor families receive sufficient transfers to move them well above the poverty line. For example, a ratio .25 implies that three-fourths of the poor's transfer income reduced the gap, while one-fourth was "leaked," since it provided more money than necessary to escape poverty.

family after all transfers is greater than that of another family, whereas before transfers the first family's welfare ratio was lower. Transfers, in effect, caused one family to leap over another in terms of total income.[8]

All of these equity-based concepts are now standard research tools. All were developed by poverty researchers in their efforts to evaluate the effectiveness of transfer programs.

8. This transfer evaluation concept was also developed in Plotnick and Skidmore (1975), who estimated that in the mid-1970s about 30 percent of the pretransfer poor leaped over pretransfer nonpoor households, and that this percentage was increasing.

Appendix B: Estimating the Labor-Supply Effects of Income Transfers

Economists responded to concern over the labor-supply effects of income transfers with an outpouring of empirical research. These studies, employing a variety of data and methods, were all designed to evaluate the impact of transfer programs on the work effort of recipients and potential recipients. They found that transfer benefits can, and generally do, induce recipients to work less than they would otherwise. In response to transfer benefits, some recipients reduce the number of hours they work; others withdraw from the labor force completely. Less labor supply leads to less production for the market. Less work or labor force participation by recipients could, of course, provide more work for others, but output would not decline only if there were 100 percent replacement. Because both theory and empirical work on this "replacement effect" is minimal, this appendix concentrates on analyzing the work response of individual recipients to transfer income.

Understanding this work response is difficult, for several reasons. One relates to the pattern of work incentives that these programs, and changes in them, create. For example, if the program is income tested so that benefits fall as earnings increase, the realized wage rate from working will be reduced by the program. Moreover, the existence of a transfer program, and even more so of the entire transfer system, cushions any loss of income experienced by a person, whether that loss is voluntary or not. While both the realized wage-rate effect and the cushioning effect of income transfer programs imply an adverse effect on work effort (or labor supply), something more fundamental may occur. When an entire system of transfers is put into place, people's evaluation of the benefits and costs of working (or working hard), the benefits and costs of entering the labor force early when young or leaving later when old, the benefits and costs of avoiding layoffs or terminations, the benefits and costs of hurrying back to work when laid off, and the benefits and costs of seeking advancement and promotions may all be altered. These changes involve not only alterations in the reward for or costs of working, but also long-run changes in attitudes toward work and toward various kinds of work.

To evaluate the labor-supply effect of income transfer programs or the transfer system itself, then, one must establish a "counterfactual"—an estimate of the quantity of labor supply if the transfer program or the transfer system did not exist. For example, in evaluating the effect of public retirement benefits on labor supply, one must determine both how much more younger people would work if they knew there would be no public provision for their support after retirement, and how much longer older people would continue working (and how much work they would do) if they knew there was no public retirement benefit program, or a smaller program. While it is possible to define such counterfactuals, it is substantially more difficult to measure reliably how the world would be if the transfer system were not in place.

Because of the intractability of this counterfactual problem, researchers have, by and large, focused on a more manageable question. Instead of asking how much the existence of a particular program has reduced labor supply in the economy, they have inquired into the effect on work effort of small expansions (or other changes) in the system.

While changes in almost any provision of a transfer program might affect work incentives of beneficiaries, two key financial characteristics of transfers—the guarantee and the benefit-reduction rate—are probably most important. The guarantee, which often varies with family size, is the payment to a person who, or family that, has no other income. The benefit-reduction rate is the percentage by which payments are reduced as earnings (or other income) increase. For example, if benefit payments are reduced by 60 cents for each dollar of earnings, the benefit-reduction rate is 60 percent. In most income transfer programs in the United States, benefit-reduction rates are positive and rather high: benefits are highest when a family has a small amount of pretransfer income, and they fall markedly as income rises. This is true of Aid to Families with Dependent Children (AFDC), food stamps, Supplemental Security Income (SSI), Unemployment Compensation (UC), and Old Age and Survivors Insurance (OASI) for those younger than age 72. In some transfer programs, however, benefit-reduction rates equal zero; neither OASI benefits for those aged 72 or more nor veterans' disability payments are reduced as earnings rise.

Standard economic theory leads to predictions about the way changes in the income guarantee and the benefit-reduction rate of a program will affect labor supply. These predictions may be summarized as follows. The income guarantee in a transfer program increases the beneficiary's income opportunities. If the individual prefers to engage in activities other than market work (and his or her tastes and the wage rate do not change), it follows that increases in transfer income will lead to decreases in market work. Thus, the income guarantees in income transfer programs have an income effect that reduces labor supply. Moreover, the larger the income guarantee, the more the individual can afford to engage in activities other than work, and hence the greater the reduction in market work.

An increase in the benefit-reduction rate in an income transfer program reduces the reward for working an extra hour. Other things being equal, a decrease in this reward would lead to reductions in market work. This effect of higher benefit-reduction rates is called the substitution effect. The rate, however, not only reduces the benefits of working a marginal (one extra) hour, but also reduces the beneficiary's total income (by reducing his or her transfer benefits). It thus puts the recipient in a position where he or she can less easily afford to work less. Therefore changes in program benefit-reduction rates have an income effect as well as substitution effect, and the two effects work in opposite directions. Theoretically, it is not known whether the income effect or the substitution effect associated with a change in the benefit-reduction rate is more important.

If the guarantee and the benefit-reduction rate in a transfer program were to increase, the beneficiaries would experience an increase in income opportunities and a reduction in the costs of not working. The combination of the substitution effect (related to the benefit-reduction rate) and the total income effect (related to both the benefit-reduction rate and the income guarantee) would tend to induce reductions in labor supply. An increase in only the guarantee of a transfer program would also reduce labor supply. Although the effective wage rate would be unaffected by the change, the individual could afford to work less because of the increase in his or her income from the larger guarantee. Thus, static economic theory predicts that transfer programs with income guarantees and either zero or positive benefit-reduction rates will lead to reductions in labor supply by their beneficiaries.

Considerations other than those reflected in static economic theory may also effect the labor supply of recipients. For example, a number of programs (e.g., UC, AFDC, and food stamps) have work tests or work-registration requirements which may offset the effects of the guarantee and the tax rate.[1] Or again, while static economic theory addresses the

---

1. UC, for example, has a work test. If recipients refuse to search for a job or reject "suitable" employment, they are denied benefits. Application of this test surely raises the work effort of some UC beneficiaries above what it would be if their labor-supply responses were not so "regulated." Similarly, required work registration for food stamps and AFDC

question of contemporaneous work effort, income transfer programs may influence how individuals allocate their working time across the life cycle. Consider, for example, removing social security from an economy in which it is present. If individuals viewed the program as an income guarantee in retirement years, the program may have caused some people to reduce their labor supply and savings (including the purchase of private retirement pensions) in the years before retirement—an intertemporal shift in work patterns attributable to social security. Hence, if social security is eliminated, people would tend to work and save more before retirement.[2]

Substantial research efforts have been devoted to measuring the effects of the various determinants of labor-supply decisions, including the incentives implicit in income transfer programs. These studies have tended to confirm the expectation that, other things being equal, work effort falls as nonlabor income rises and as the effective (or net) wage rate falls.

By holding constant all variables that might affect labor supply except, say, nonlabor income, these studies have attempted to measure the impact of changes in this variable (which can be interpreted as being equivalent to an income effect) on labor supply. Similarly, if only wage rates (as a proxy for the effect of transfer program benefit-reduction rates on wages) are allowed to vary, we can evaluate the substitution effect of transfer programs. A typical study (Masters and Garfinkel, 1977) estimated that, for prime-aged males, a $1,000 increase in nonlabor income is associated with a 1 percent reduction in labor supply. Percentage reductions are greater for aged persons (10 percent) and women and youths (4 percent). For a 10 percent increase in the tax rate of transfer programs, this study finds a 2 percent reduction in the labor supply of female family heads and a 4 percent reduction in the work effort of wives. The labor supply of men does not appear to be greatly affected by marginal changes in the wage rate.

These general results were, by and large, confirmed by the two large-scale experimental studies designed to test the labor-supply effects of proposed negative income tax plans, as described in Chapter 9. As with

---

probably prevents some recipients from reducing their work effort as fully as they would in the absence of such a provision.

2. A second example of the intertemporal shift in labor supply caused by income transfers is also provided by the social security system. Because of the high benefit-reduction rate on earnings after age 65 that is incorporated into the social security program, work effort in that age range is discouraged relative to work effort during younger years. In effect, the wage rate before retirement rises relative to that in retirement years. There is evidence to suggest that just such an intertemporal labor supply reallocation has occurred because of the program. See Burkhauser and Turner (1978).

the cross-sectional studies, the responsiveness of female family heads and wives was substantially greater than that of husbands.

In sum, these experimental and econometric studies have relied on an incremental approach to understanding the effects of transfer policies on labor supply. The question is: What effect do changes in transfer programs—an increase in income guarantees or a reduction in benefit-reduction rates—have on labor supply? While their results measure the magnitude of changes in labor supply that are attributable to changes in guarantees or benefit-reduction rates, they do not lead to any direct conclusions regarding the total effect of the public transfer system on work effort.

Two recent studies have drawn on these incremental behavior estimates in an attempt to answer this question. Both rely on the large number of empirical studies of the determinants of labor supply, in particular income transfer programs. In the first study (Danziger, Haveman, and Plotnick, 1981), the authors systematically surveyed all of the empirical studies of the labor-supply effects of income transfer programs available in 1981 in an attempt to estimate how the entire income transfer system altered labor supply. The income transfer programs on which substantive labor-supply studies were available included OASI, Disability Insurance (DI), UC, and AFDC. The studies yielded program-specific estimates of work-effort reductions. In addition, the authors extrapolated from the results of these studies to estimate in approximate fashion the work-effort effects of the Workers' Compensation and Black Lung programs, Veterans' disability compensation, SSI, Veterans' pensions, food stamps, and housing assistance.

The estimates based on this survey are reproduced in Table B.1.[3] In the authors' words, their direct estimates from the four programs on which research exists

suggests that because of labor supply reductions by transfer recipients, total work effort in the economy was 3.3 percent less than it would have been. Adding the reductions due to the other programs . . . gives a total reduction of 4.8 percent. . . . In an economy with involuntary unemployment, however, not all of this supply would be employed. If the unemployment rate were 7.0 percent, and if the increased labor supply of transfer recipients would find employment at a rate equal to that of other workers, the net loss of employment time would be about 4.5 percent. Because those receiving transfer benefits tend to have below average wage rates, the loss of total earnings is probably about 3.5 percent (pp. 998–99).

---

3. These estimates are based primarily on the following studies: for OASI, Clark and Johnson (1980), Gordon and Blinder (1980); for UC, Hamermesh (1977); for DI, Leonard (1979), Parsons (1980a, 1980b); for AFDC, Hausman (1981), Moffitt (1983).

Table B.1. Reduction in the Labor Supply of Recipients of Major Income Transfer
Programs as a Percentage of Total Labor Supply of all Workers

Program	Reduction of Work Hours by Transfer Recipients as a Percentage of Total Work Hours of All Workers
Social Insurance	
Old Age and Survivors Insurance	1.2
Disability Insurance	1.2
Unemployment Compensation	0.3
Workers' Compensation and Black Lung	0.7
Railroad Retirement	*
Veterans' disability compensation	0.4
Medicare	*
Public Assistance	
AFDC	0.6
SSI and Veterans' Pensions	0.1
Food stamps and housing assistance	0.3
Medicaid	*
Total	4.8

Source: Danziger, Haveman, and Plotnick (1981, p. 996).
*Denotes under .05 percent.

Using an alternative approach focusing on particular demographic
groups rather than programs, Lampman (1978) also attempted to provide
an estimate of the aggregate labor-supply impact of income transfers. The
counterfactual to the existing system of programs and required taxes was
assumed to be the system that existed in 1950. Hence the estimate
provided relates to the aggregate labor-supply reduction caused by the
expansion of social welfare benefits during the twenty-five years after
1950. This estimate was also based on the empirical studies referred to
above and on the allocation of benefit and tax growth among various
demographic groups in the population. Lampman concluded that the
increase in social welfare benefits from 9 percent of GNP to 21 percent in
the 1950–76 period caused the quantity of labor supplied to the economy
to be 7 percent less than it would otherwise have been. The percentage
breakdown in this aggregate reduction is as follows:

Demographic Group	(%) Reduction
Age 62 and over	27
Disabled under age 62	10
Female household heads with children	10
Age 18 to 24	14
Other women	34
Other men	5
Total	100

This result is consistent with the 4.8 percent figure of the first study. The programs in Table B.1 exclude some major components of the social welfare expenditure system (e.g., education). Moreover, that study did not include the disincentive effect of the taxes required to finance the growth in outlays.

The labor-supply issue has been central in the public debate over income transfer policy—indeed, antipoverty policy more generally— since the mid-1960s. The progress made in quantifying the magnitudes involved has contributed to more rational discussion about the impact of policy changes on work effort and has shifted the discussion toward other important but less well-recognized impacts of these policies (e.g., family structure and dependence). These gains are due to the surge of research on the labor-supply question attributable to the War on Poverty.

Appendix C: Major Institutions Offering Programs in Public Policy Analysis and Evaluation Research

Graduate School of Public Policy, University of California, Berkeley

Established in 1969 by a grant from the Regents of the University of California, the school admits about seventy-five students per year and has ten full-time faculty members tenured within it. Its aim is to train policy "practitioners" who are concerned with "bureaucratic efficiency, program effectiveness, and the equity with which government resources are distributed." Courses are designed to train students to frame correctly public policy problems, policy analysis, and evaluation research methodologies and to teach techniques for implementation of public policies. Training in the first year emphasizes policy analysis rather than economics or quantitative methods. During the second year a thesis-equivalent study of a policy problem is required as the end result of a required summer internship. The second year involves primarily elective courses in applied areas (e.g., social welfare) or one of the social science disciplines.

The school offers a small doctoral program, admitting less than five students per year.

The Hubert H. Humphrey Institute of Public Affairs, University of Minnesota

Founded in 1977 as a descendant of the university's School of Public Affairs, the Humphrey Institute offers master's programs in public affairs and planning. Its objective is to give "an understanding of the social and political circumstances in which the design and implementation of public policy occur and a capacity for rigorous analysis of public policy issues." The institute has about one hundred and ten students, twenty faculty, ten senior fellows, and thirty adjunct faculty. Its goal is to fuse policy analysis

254

with the education of graduate students and public-sector administrators. A seminar program is offered for mid-career professionals. Policy analysis skills are taught by a series of research and analysis projects arranged in four clusters around such subjects as the effect of science and technology on society and strategies to encourage international cooperation. The general goal of the policy projects is to provide students with practical and research experience and to focus on newly emerging policy problems.

Institute for Public Policy Studies, University of Michigan, Ann Arbor

The present institute grew out of the Institute for Public Affairs, which was established in 1914 for the purpose of training city managers. By the 1960s the original purpose was viewed as too narrow, and the objectives of the institute were broadened. With the help of a Ford Foundation grant, in 1968 it was reorganized as the Institute for Public Policy Studies, offering the degree of Master in Public Policy (MPP). The faculty and curriculum were expanded to include mathematics, micro- and macroeconomic theory, statistics, econometrics, and political science. The stress in the curriculum is on the interdisciplinary nature of policy analysis and the problems confronted by policy analysts. Students typically do about half of their class work outside of the institute in other departments and schools, such as economics, urban and regional planning, the law school, and the Graduate School of Business. The institute also offers dual degrees and certificates in areas ranging from gerontology to history to natural resources. Every MPP student is required between the first and second year to intern at least ten weeks in an agency or firm performing work related to public policy.

During the late 1970s the institute established a separate program in international studies, emphasizing the area of international relations and economics.

A Ph.D. program was inaugurated in the early 1970s and admits about five students a year, all of whom already possess the equivalent of an MPP. Each doctoral student develops his or her own program, but the stress on the application of policy analysis and evaluation research is reflected in the nine-month internship required in public policy–related work.

John F. Kennedy School of Government, Harvard University

In 1966 Harvard's Graduate School of Public Administration was renamed the John F. Kennedy School of Government. The Kennedy

School is the largest of the public policy academic institutions. Its purpose is to "create a deeper understanding of the major substantive issues of public choice," "train leaders for government," and "serve as a focal point convening leaders . . . to work on major issues of national policy." The school offers a variety of programs and degrees, including a Master of Public Policy (MPP) that stresses analytic and managerial skills, a Master of Public Administration for students with special backgrounds, and a series of annual summer programs for public-sector administrators.

The curriculum for MPP students follows a set of core courses divided among economics, quantitative methods, and the environment of public policy. The degree requires a thesis on an applied problem concerning some aspect of public policy. Students have the option of taking classes outside of the school; they must, however, focus their course work within a specific area such as energy, health, human resources, or international development. The school also offers joint degrees in law and business.

The student body numbers over six hundred, but only one hundred fifty are admitted each fall to the MPP program. There are over seventy faculty members, and a larger number of faculty from other schools and departments who are affiliated with the school.

The Lyndon Baines Johnson School of Public Affairs, University of Texas at Austin

The LBJ School was founded in 1970. Five programs lead to a Master of Public Affairs degree; about eighty students each year receive the degree. The school's program is interdisciplinary and focuses on "research related to concrete policy problems." Thirty faculty members are associated with the school.

The school attempts to teach in an intensive manner through a combination of academic coursework, applied research, and internships, and to prepare its students for a public-sector career. Over time the course work has changed, but the school remains dedicated to training future policy analysts. A Master of Public Affairs (MPA) requires core course work, two group research projects, and an internship between the first and second year. The school offers joint degrees in law, engineering, business, and a program designed for people wishing to reorient or retool in mid-career.

The Maxwell School of Citizenship and Public Affairs, Syracuse University

The Maxwell School has twenty full-time faculty members and another eight to ten faculty associated with the school. It offers the degree of

Master in Public Affairs (MPA) and a Ph.D., along with joint MPA-Law degrees and MPS-Social Work degrees. Its goal is to produce graduates who have a sound grasp of a policy area and the generalist's tools required to be an effective public manager. Its policy areas include state and local government finance, health policy, public management, technology and information, and development administration. Training at the school focuses more on preparing administrators with policy analysis backgrounds for state and local government than on preparing analysts for the federal government. Most students receive practical training through an internship during the regular school year.

School of Urban and Public Affairs, Carnegie-Mellon University

The school was founded in 1968 with a grant from the Mellon family. It offers the degree of Master of Science in Public Management and Policy, and a Ph.D. in Urban and Public Affairs. The master's program places weight on the "skills of analysis and synthesis." Analysis applies such quantitative and qualitative skills as accounting, microeconomics, and organizational management. Synthesis is defined as the ability to draw together the analytic skills to solve particular problems related to public policy programs. Master's students may spend as much as a quarter of their classwork in synthesis course work.

Master's students have three options after fulfilling core requirements. The public management option aims at developing analysts who are able to direct program "change constructively and ethically." The public policy program trains analysts who can handle sophisticated methodology as well as having evaluation research experience in several different areas. The final option is public financial management and analysis, which stresses statistical methods (econometrics and forecasting) and financial analysis (investment strategies and budgeting) in order to train analysts who are technically proficient and creative in solving public finance questions.

The doctoral program is designed to educate public policy researchers and teachers. The emphasis is on quantitative methods.

The school admits approximately sixty master's students each fall and has thirty doctoral students and a full-time faculty of about forty.

Woodrow Wilson School of Public and International Affairs, Princeton University

The School of Public and International Affairs, which had existed at Princeton since 1930, was renamed the Woodrow Wilson School of Public and International Affairs in 1948. The school received a large private gift in the early 1960s, which permitted substantial growth. It offers a bachelor's degree in Public Affairs, a Master of Public Affairs (MPA) degree, and a doctoral program. For the MPA there is a core curriculm emphasizing economic analysis and quantitative skills. Students may choose from among four fields of study, including international relations and development studies. The MPA program admits sixty students a year; the doctoral program admits six to eight students, who usually already possess and MPA or its equivalent. There are about fifty faculty members associated with the school, most of whom hold joint appointments with another department.

The school emphasizes an interdisciplinary approach, although much of the weight of a student's education is placed on economics. The school's intent is to train students "who . . . are able to simplify complex public problems into manageable components, who are informed consumers of materials based on sophisticated analytic techniques, who are adept at administration and incisive in analysis and evaluation, and who can recognize and deal effectively with the wide range of values inherent in public affairs problems."

References

Aaron, Henry J. 1967. "The Foundations of the 'War on Poverty' Reexamined." *American Economic Review* 5:1229–1240.

Aaron, Henry J. 1973. *Why Is Welfare So Hard to Reform?* Washington, D. C.: Brookings Institution.

Aaron, Henry J. 1975. "Alternative Ways to Increase Work Effort under Income Maintenance Systems." In Irene Lurie, ed., *Integrating Income Maintenance Programs*. New York: Academic Press.

Aaron, Henry J. 1978. *Politics and the Professors: The Great Society in Perspective*. Washington, D.C.: Brookings Institution.

Aaron, Henry J. 1982. *Economic Effects of Social Security*. Washington, D.C.: Brookings Institution.

Aaron, Henry J. 1985. "Discussion." In Jerry A. Hausman and David A. Wise, eds., *Social Experimentation*. Chicago: University of Chicago Press.

Aaron, Henry J., and Burtless, Gary, eds. 1984. *Retirement and Economic Behavior*. Washington, D.C.: Brookings Institution.

Aaron, Henry J., and McGuire, Martin. 1970. "Public Goods and Income Distribution."*Econometrica* 38:907–1220.

Aaron, Henry J., and Todd, John. 1979. "The Use of Income Maintenance Experiment Findings in Public Policy, 1977–78." *Industrial Relations Research Association Proceedings, 1979*. Madison, Wis.: IRRA.

Aaron, Henry J., and von Furstenberg, George M. 1971. "The Inefficiency of Transfers In-Kind: The Case of Housing Assistance." *Western Economic Journal* 9:184–191.

Abramovitz, Moses. 1981. "Welfare Quandaries and Productivity Concerns." *American Economic Review* 71:1–17.

Abramson, Mark A. 1978. *The Funding of Social Knowledge Production and Application: A Survey of Federal Agencies*. Washington, D.C.: National Academy of Sciences.

Achinstein, Asher. 1969. "Constraints on Policy Analysis and Policy Implementation in the Federal Agencies." In U. S. Congress, Joint Economic Committee, *The Analysis and Evaluation of Public Expenditures: The PPB System*. Washington, D.C.: GPO.

Aigner, Dennis J. 1985. "The Residential Electricity Time-of-Use Pricing Experiments: What Have We Learned?" In Jerry A. Hausman and David A. Wise, eds., *Social Experimentation*. Chicago: University of Chicago Press.

259

Akerlof, G. A. 1970. "The Market for Lemons: Quality Uncertainty and the Market Mechanism." *Quarterly Journal of Economics* 84:488–500.

Akin, John, and Garfinkel, Irwin. 1977. "School Expenditures and the Economic Returns to Schooling." *Journal of Human Resources* 12:460–480.

Allen, Jodie T. 1972. "A Funny Thing Happened on the Way to Welfare Reform." Working Paper, Urban Institute, Washington, D.C., January.

Altschuler, Alan. 1970. *Community Control*. New York: Pegasus.

Amemiya, Takeshi. 1973. "Regression Analysis When the Dependent Variable Is Truncated Normal." *Econometrica* 41:997–1016.

Amemiya, Takeshi. 1974. "Multivariate Regression and Simultaneous Equation Models When the Dependent Variables Are Truncated Normal." *Econometrica* 42:999–1012.

Amemiya, Takeshi. 1978. "The Estimation of a Simultaneous Equation Generalized Probit Model." *Econometrica* 46:1193–1205.

Amemiya, Takeshi. 1981. "Qualitative Response Models: A Survey." *Journal of Economic Literature* 19:1483–1536.

Amemiya, Takeshi. 1984. "Tobit Models: A Survey." *Journal of Econometrics* 24:3–61.

Amemiya, Takeshi, and Boskin, Michael. 1974. "Regression Analysis When the Dependent Variable Is Truncated Lognormal, with an Application to the Determinants of the Duration of Welfare Dependency." *International Economic Review* 15:485–496.

Anderson, Martin. 1978. *Welfare: The Political Economy of Welfare Reform in the United States*. Stanford: Hoover Institution Press.

Appel, Gary L. 1972. "Effects of a Financial Incentive on AFDC Employment: Michigan's Experience between July 1969 and July 1970." Institute for Interdisciplinary Studies, Minneapolis, Minn., March.

Arabmazar, Abbas, and Schmidt, Peter. 1982. "An Investigation of the Robustness of the Tobit Estimator to Non-Normality." *Econometrica* 50:1055–1063.

Arrow, Kenneth. 1973. "The Theory of Discrimination." In Orley Ashenfelter and Albert Rees, eds., *Discrimination in Labor Markets*. Princeton: Princeton University Press.

Ashenfelter, Orley. 1970. "Changes in Labor Market Discrimination over Time." *Journal of Human Resources* 5:403–430.

Ashenfelter, Orley. 1977. "Comment on Black/White Male Earnings and Employment, 1960–1970." In F. Thomas Juster, ed., *The Distribution of Economic Well-Being*. Cambridge, Mass.: Ballinger, for the National Bureau of Economic Research.

Ashenfelter, Orley. 1978. "Estimating the Effect of Training Programs on Earnings." *Review of Economics and Statistics* 60:47–57.

Ashenfelter, Orley, and Heckman, James. 1973. "Estimating Labor-Supply Functions." In Glen G. Cain and Harold W. Watts, ed., *Income Maintenance and Labor Supply: Econometric Studies*. New York: Academic Press.

Ashenfelter, Orley, and Heckman, James. 1976. "Measuring the Effect of an Anti-Discrimination Program." In Orley Ashenfelter and James Blum, ed.,

Evaluating the Labor Market Effects of Social Programs. Princeton: Industrial Relations Section, Princeton University.

Atkinson, Anthony B. 1970. "On the Measurement of Inequality." *Journal of Economic Theory* 2:244–263.

Averch, H. A., et al. 1972. *How Effective Is Schooling? A Critical Review and Synthesis of Research Findings*. Santa Monica, Calif.: Rand Corporation.

Baerwaldt, Nancy, and Morgan, James. 1971. "Trends in Inter-Family Transfers." Working Paper, Survey Research Center, University of Michigan, Ann Arbor.

Baily, M. N., and Tobin, James. 1977. "Macro-Economic Effects of Selective Public Employment and Wage Subsidies." *Brookings Papers on Economic Activity*, no. 2, pp. 511–541.

Ballard, C. L.; Shoven, John B.; and Whalley, John. 1985. "General Equilibrium Computations of the Marginal Welfare Costs of Taxes in the U.S." *American Economic Review* 75:128–138.

Bane, Mary Jo, and Ellwood, David T. 1982. "Slipping Into and Out of Poverty: The Dynamics of Spells." John F. Kennedy School of Government, Harvard University, Cambridge, Mass. Mimeo.

Bane, Mary Jo, and Ellwood, David T. 1983. "The Dynamics of Dependence: The Routes to Self-Sufficiency." John F. Kennedy School of Government, Harvard University, Cambridge, Mass. Mimeo.

Banfield, Edward C. 1968. *The Unheavenly City: The Nature and Future of Our Urban Crisis*. New York: Little, Brown.

Barnow, Burt S. 1973. "Evaluating Project Head Start." Discussion Paper no. 189–73, Institute for Research on Poverty, University of Wisconsin–Madison.

Barnow, Burt S.; Cain, Glen G.; and Goldberger, Arthur S. 1980. "Issues in the Analysis of Selectivity Bias." In Ernst W. Stromsdorfer and George Farkas, ed., *Evaluation Studies Review Annual*. Vol. 5. Beverly Hills, Calif.: Sage Publications.

Baron, James, and Bielby, William T. 1980. "Bringing the Firms Back In: Stratification, Segmentation, and the Organization of Work." *American Sociological Review* 45:737–765.

Barr, Nicholas A., and Hall, Robert E. 1975. "The Taxation of Earnings under Public Assistance." *Economica* 42:373–384.

Barr, Nicholas A., and Hall, Robert E. 1981. "The Probability of Dependence on Public Assistance." *Economica* 48:109–123.

Barro, Robert J. 1978. *The Impact of Social Security on Private Saving: Evidence from the U. S. Time Series*. Washington, D.C.: American Enterprise Institute for Public Policy Research.

Barth, Michael. 1974. "Market Effects of a Wage Subsidy." *Industrial and Labor Relations Review* 45:737–765.

Barth, Michael C.; Carcagno, George J.; and Palmer, John L. 1973. *Toward an Effective Income Support System: Problems, Prospects, and Choices*. Madison, Wis.: Institute for Research on Poverty, University of Wisconsin–Madison.

Batchelder, Alan B. 1964. "Decline in the Relative Income of Negro Men." *Quarterly Journal of Economics* 78:525–548.

Bawden, D. Lee, ed. 1984. *The Social Contract Revisited*. Washington, D.C.: Urban Institute Press.

Bawden, D. Lee; Cain, Glen G.; and Hausman, Leonard. 1971. "The Family Assistance Plan: An Analysis and Evaluation." *Public Policy* 19:345–353.

Bawden, D. Lee, et al. 1976. "Rural Income Maintenance Experiment: Summary Report." Special Report no. 10, Institute for Research on Poverty, University of Wisconsin–Madison.

Becker, Gary S. 1957. *The Economics of Discrimination*. Chicago: University of Chicago Press.

Becker, Gary S. 1964. *Human Capital: A Theoretical and Empirical Analysis, with Special Reference to Education*. New York: Columbia University Press, for the National Bureau of Economic Research.

Becker, Gary S. 1965. "A Theory of the Allocation of Time." *Economic Journal* 75:483–517.

Behn, Robert. 1981. "Policy Analysis and Policy Politics." *Policy Analysis* 7:199–226.

Bendt, Douglas. 1975. *The Effects of Changes in the AFDC Program on Effective Benefit Reduction Rates and the Probability of Working*. Princeton, N.J.: Mathematica Policy Research.

Bennett, Robert L., and Bergmann, Barbara R. 1980. "Policy Explorations with the Transactions Model of the U. S. Economy." In Robert H. Haveman and Kevin Hollenbeck, eds., *Microeconomic Simulation Models for Public Policy Analysis*. Vol. 2. New York: Academic Press.

Benus, Jacob. 1974. "Income Instability." In James Morgan, ed., *Five Thousand American Families—Patterns of Economic Progress*. Vol. 1. Ann Arbor: Institute for Social Research, University of Michigan.

Benus, Jacob, and Morgan, James. 1975. "Time Period, Unit of Analysis, and Income Concept in the Analysis of Income Distribution." In James D. Smith, ed., *The Personal Distribution of Wealth*. New York: National Bureau of Economic Research.

Berg, Ivar. 1970. *Education and Jobs: The Great Training Robbery*. New York: Praeger.

Berger, Suzanne. 1980. "Introduction." In Organisation for Economic Co-operation and Development, *The Utilization of the Social Sciences in Policy Making in the United States*. Paris: OECD.

Berk, Richard. 1981. "On the Compatibility of Applied and Basic Research: An Effort in Marriage Counseling." *American Sociologist* 4:204–15.

Berk, Richard A.; Boruch, Robert; Chambers, David; Rossi, Peter; and Witte, Anne. 1985. "Social Policy Experimentation: A Position Paper." *Evaluation Review* 9:387–429.

Betson, David, and Bishop, John. 1982. "Work Incentive and Distributional Effects." In Robert H. Haveman and John L. Palmer, eds., *Jobs for Disadvantaged Workers: The Economics of Employment Subsidies*. Washington, D.C.: Brookings Institution.

Betson, David; Greenberg, David; and Kasten, Richard. 1980. "A Microsimulation Model for Analyzing Alternative Welfare Reform Proposals: An Application to the Program for Better Jobs and Income." In Robert H. Haveman and Kevin Hollenbeck, eds., *Microeconomic Simulation Models for Public Policy Analysis*. Vol. 1. New York: Academic Press.

Betson, David; Greenberg, David; and Kasten, Richard. 1982. "A Simulation Analysis of the Economic Efficiency and Distributional Effects of Alternative Program Structures: The Negative Income Tax Versus the Credit Income Tax." In Irwin Garfinkel, ed., *Income-Tested Transfer Programs: The Case For and Against*. New York: Academic Press.

Bishop, George A. 1967. "Tax Burdens and Benefits of Government Expenditures by Income Class, 1961 and 1965." Research Publication No. 9, Tax Foundation, New York.

Bishop, John. 1980. "Jobs, Cash Transfers, and Marital Instability: A Review and Synthesis of the Evidence." *Journal of Human Resources* 15:301–334.

Bishop, John, and Haveman, Robert. 1979a. "Targeted Employment Subsidies: Issues of Structure and Design." In *Increasing Job Opportunities in the Private Sector*. Special Report no. 29. Washington, D.C.: National Commission on Manpower Policy.

Bishop, John, and Haveman, Robert. 1979b. "Selective Employment Subsidies: Can Okun's Law Be Repealed?" *American Economic Review* 69:124–130.

Bishop, John, and Wilson, Charles. 1982. "Effects on Firm Behavior." In Robert H. Haveman and John L. Palmer, eds., *Jobs for Disadvantaged Workers: The Economics of Employment Subsidies*. Washington, D.C.: Brookings Institution.

Bishop, Richard C., and Heberlein, Thomas A. 1979. "Measuring Values of Extra-Market Goods: Are Indirect Measures Biased?" *American Journal of Agricultural Economics* 61:926–930.

Blackorby, Charles, and Donaldson, Donald. 1978. "Measures of Relative Inequality and Their Meaning in Terms of Social Welfare." *Journal of Economic Theory* 18:59–80.

Blau, Peter, and Duncan, Otis D. 1967. *The American Occupational Structure*. New York: John Wiley.

Blaug, Mark. 1976. "The Empirical Status of Human Capital Theory: A Slightly Jaundiced Survey." *Journal of Economic Literature* 14:827–855.

Blechman, Barry M.; Gramlich, Edward M.; and Hartman, Robert W. 1974. *Setting National Priorities: The 1975 Budget*. Washington, D.C.: Brookings Institution.

Blinder, Alan S. 1973. "Wage Discrimination: Reduced Form and Structural Estimates." *Journal of Human Resources* 8:436–455.

Blinder, Alan S. 1975. "Distribution Effects and the Aggregate Consumption Function." *Journal of Political Economy* 83:447–475.

Blinder, Alan S.; Gordon, Roger; and Wise, Donald. 1981. "Rhetoric and Reality in Social Security Analysis: A Rejoinder." *National Tax Journal* 34:473–478.

Bohm, Peter. 1972. "Estimating Demand for Public Goods: An Experiment." *European Economic Review* 3:111–130.

Boland, Barbara. 1973. "Participation in the Aid to Families with Dependent Children Program (AFDC)." In U. S. Congress, Joint Economic Committee, Subcommittee on Fiscal Policy, *Studies in Public Welfare: The Family, Poverty, and Welfare Programs: Factors Influencing Family Instability*. Paper no. 12, Part I. Washington, D.C.: GPO.

Boskin, Michael J. 1973. "The Economics of Labor Supply." In Glen G. Cain and Harold W. Watts, eds., *Income Maintenance and Labor Supply: Econometric Studies*. New York: Academic Press.

Bosworth, Barry. 1984. *Tax Incentives and Economic Growth*. Washington, D.C.: Brookings Institution.

Bowen, William G. 1964. *Economic Aspects of Education*. Princeton: Industrial Relations Section, Princeton University.

Bowles, Samuel. 1972. "Schooling and Inequality from Generation to Generation." *Journal of Political Economy* 80:5219–5251.

Bowles, Samuel, and Gintis, Herbert. 1972–73. "I.Q. in the U.S. Class Structure." *Social Policy* 3 (double issue):65–96.

Bowles, Samuel, and Gintis, Herbert. 1976. *Schooling in Capitalist America: Educational Reform and Contradictions of Economic Life*. New York: Basic Books.

Bowles, Samuel, and Levin, Henry. 1968. "The Determinants of Scholastic Achievement: An Appraisal of Some Recent Evidence." *Journal of Human Resources* 3:3–24.

Bowles, Samuel, and Nelson, Valerie. 1974. "The 'Inheritance of I.Q.' and the Intergenerational Reproduction of Economic Inequality." *Review of Economics and Statistics* 56:39–51.

Bradbury, Katharine, et al. 1977. "The Effects of Welfare Reform Alternatives on the Family." Special Report no. 13, Institute for Research on Poverty, University of Wisconsin–Madison.

Brady, Dorothy S. 1951. "Research on the Size Distribution of Income." In *Studies in Income and Wealth*. Vol. 13. New York: National Bureau of Economic Research.

Brauer, Carl M. 1982. "Kennedy, Johnson, and the War on Poverty." *Journal of American History* 69:98–119.

Brazer, Harvey. 1968. "Tax Policy and Children's Allowances." In Eveline Burns, ed., *Children's Allowances and the Economic Welfare of Children*. New York: Citizens Committee for the Children of New York.

Brazer, Harvey. 1971. "Tax Policy and Children's Allowances." In Theodore Marmor, ed., *Poverty Policy*. Chicago: Aldine.

Break, George, and Pechman, Joseph A. 1975. *Federal Tax Reform: The Impossible Dream*. Washington, D.C.: Brookings Institution.

Brecher, Charles. 1973. *The Impact of Federal Antipoverty Policies*. New York: Praeger.

Brehm, Carl T., and Saving, Thomas R. 1964. "The Demand for General Assistance Payments." *American Economic Review* 54:1002–1018.

Bronfenbrenner, Martin. 1971. *Income Distribution Theory*. Chicago: Aldine.

Brookshire, David S.; Thayer, M. A.; Schulze, W. D.; and d'Arge, R. C. 1982. "Valuing Public Goods: A Comparison of Hedonic and Survey Approaches." *American Economic Review* 72:165–177.

Browning, Edgar K. 1973. "Alternative Programs for Income Redistribution: The NIT and the NWT." *American Economic Review* 63:38–49.

Browning, Edgar K. 1975. *Redistribution and the Welfare System.* Washington, D.C.: American Enterprise Institute for Public Policy Research.

Browning, Edgar K. 1985. "On the Marginal Welfare Cost of Taxation." Department of Economics, Texas A.&M. University. Mimeo.

Browning, Edgar K., and Johnson, William R. 1979. "Taxes, Transfers, and Income Inequality." In Gary M. Walton, ed., *Regulatory Change in an Atmosphere of Crisis: Current-Day Implications of the Roosevelt Years.* New York: Academic Press.

Burdett, Kenneth, and Hool, Bryce. 1982. "Effects on the Inflation-Unemployment Trade-off." In Robert H. Haveman and John L. Palmer, eds., *Jobs for Disadvantaged Workers: The Economics of Employment Subsidies.* Washington, D.C.: Brookings Institution.

Bureau of Social Science Research. 1982. *Vouchering Manpower Services: Past Experiences and Their Implications for Future Programs.* Report to the National Commission on Employment Policy. Washington, D.C.: Bureau of Social Science Research.

Burke, Vincent J., and Burke, Lee. 1974. *Nixon's Good Deed: Welfare Reform.* New York: Columbia University Press.

Burkhauser, Richard, and Turner, John. 1978. "A Time-Series Analysis of Social Security and Its Effect on the Market Work of Men at Younger Ages." *Journal of Political Economy* 86:701–715.

Burns, Eveline, ed. 1968. *Children's Allowances and the Economic Welfare of Children: The Report of a Conference.* New York: Citizens Committee for the Children of New York.

Burt, Cyril. 1947. "Family Size, Intelligence, and Social Class." *Population Studies* 1:177–186.

Burtless, Gary, and Hausman, Jerry. 1978. "The Effect of Taxation on Labor Supply: Evaluating the Gary Negative Income Tax Experiment." *Journal of Political Economy* 86:1103–1130.

Burtless, Gary, and Haveman, Robert H. 1984. "Policy Lessons from Three Labor Market Experiments." In R. Thayne Robson, ed., *Employment and Training R&D.* Kalamazoo, Mich.: Upjohn Institute for Employment Research.

Cain, Glen G. 1973. "Regression and Selection Models to Improve Nonexperimental Comparisons." In C. A. Bennett and A. A. Lumsdaine, eds., *Evaluation and Experiments: Some Critical Issues in Assessing Social Programs.* New York: Academic Press.

Cain, Glen G. 1974. "Review of 'Socioeconomic Background and Achievement,' by Duncan, Featherman, and Duncan." *American Journal of Sociology* 79:1497–1509.

Cain, Glen C. 1976. "The Challenge of Segmented Labor Market Theories to Orthodox Theory." *Journal of Economic Literature* 14:1215–1257.

Cain, Glen G. 1986. "The Economic Analysis of Labor Market Discrimination: A Survey." In *Handbook of Labor Economics*, ed. Orley Ashenfelter and Richard Layard. Amsterdam: Elsevier Science Publishers (North-Holland).

Cain, Glen G., and Hollister, Robinson. 1970 (3d ed. 1983). "Evaluating Social Action Programs." In Robert H. Haveman and Julius Margolis, eds., *Public Expenditure and Policy Analysis*. Boston: Houghton Mifflin.

Cain, Glen G., and Watts, Harold W. 1970. "Problems in Making Policy Inferences from the Coleman Report." *American Sociological Review* 35:228–242.

Cain, Glen G., and Watts, Harold W. 1973. "Toward a Summary and Synthesis of the Evidence." In Cain and Watts, eds., *Income Maintenance and Labor Supply: Econometric Studies*. New York: Academic Press.

Campbell, Donald T. 1969. "Reforms as Experiments." *American Psychologist* 24:409–420.

Campbell, Donald T., and Erlebacher, Albert. 1970. "How Regression Artifacts in Quasi-Experimental Evaluation Can Mistakenly Make Compensatory Education Look Harmful." In Jerome Hellmuth, ed., *Compensatory Education: A National Debate*. Vol. 3, *Disadvantaged Child*. New York: Brunner-Mazel.

Carcagno, George J., and Corson, Walter. 1982. "Administrative Issues." In Robert H. Haveman and John L. Palmer, eds., *Jobs for Disadvantaged Workers: The Economics of Employment Subsidies*. Washington, D.C.: Brookings Institution.

Carliner, Geoffrey. 1976. "Returns to Education for Blacks, Anglos, and Five Spanish Groups." *Journal of Human Resources* 11:172–184.

Caro, Francis G. 1971. "Evaluation Research: An Overview." In Caro, ed., *Readings in Evaluation Research*. New York: Russell Sage Foundation.

Catsiapis, George, and Robinson, Chris. 1982. "Sample Selection Bias with Multiple Selection Rules: An Application to Student Aid Grants." *Journal of Econometrics* 18:351–368.

Center for the Study of Public Policy. 1970. "Financing Education by Grants to Parents: A Preliminary Report." Submitted to the Office of Economic Opportunity, Washington, D.C. Mimeo.

Chamberlain, Gary S. 1978. "Omitted Variable Bias in Panel Data: Estimating the Returns to Schooling." In *The Econometrics of Panel Data*. Paris: Colloque International du CRNS, Annales de l'INSEE.

Chiswick, Barry R. 1974. *Income Inequality*. New York: Columbia University Press, for the National Bureau of Economic Research.

Christensen, Sandra, and Bernard, Keith. 1974. "The Black-White Earnings Gap." *Journal of Human Resources* 9:376–389.

Cicarelli, Victor, et al. 1969. "The Impact of Head Start: An Evaluation of the Effects of Head Start on Children's Cognitive and Affective Development." Report presented to the Office of Economic Opportunity. Westinghouse Learning Corporation, Ohio University.

Clark, K. B. 1966. "Education of the Minority Poor: The Key to the War on Poverty." In *The Disadvantaged Poor: Education and Employment*. Third Report of the Task Force on Economic Growth and Opportunity. Washington, D.C.: Chamber of Commerce of the United States.

Clark, Kim, and Summers, Lawrence. 1982. "Unemployment Insurance and Labor Market Transitions." In Martin Neil Baily, ed., *Workers, Jobs, and Inflation*. Washington, D.C.: Brookings Institution.

Clark, Robert, and Johnson, Thomas. 1980. *Retirement in the Dual Career Family*. Final Report for the U.S. Social Security Administration. Raleigh, N.C.: North Carolina State University.

Clarkson, Kenneth. 1975. *Food Stamps and Nutrition*. Washington, D.C.: American Enterprise Institute for Public Policy Research.

Clarkson, Kenneth. 1976. "Welfare Benefits of the Food Stamp Program." *Southern Economic Journal* 43:864–878.

Coe, Richard. 1982. "Participation in the Food Stamp Program, 1979." Working Paper C–13, Department of Economics, University of Notre Dame.

Cohen, Wilbur J. 1968. "A Ten-Point Program to Abolish Poverty." *Social Security Bulletin* 31 (December): 3–13.

Coleman, James S. 1964. *Mathematic Sociology*. Glencoe, Ill.: Free Press.

Coleman, James S., et al. 1966. *Equality of Educational Opportunity*. Washington, D.C.: GPO.

Congressional Budget Office. 1977. *Poverty Status of Families under Alternative Definitions of Income*. Washington, D.C.: GPO.

Congressional Budget Office. 1979. "An Analysis of the Administration's Social Welfare Reform Amendments of 1979." Washington, D.C.: GPO. November.

Conley, Ronald W. 1979. "Should We Break up Workers' Compensation?" In Edward Berkowitz, ed., *Disability Policies and Government Programs*. New York: Praeger.

Conley, Ronald W., and Noble, John, Jr. 1973. "Workmen's Compensation Reform Changes for the 1980's." *American Rehabilitation* January/February.

Conlisk, John. 1985. "Discussion." In Jerry A. Hausman and David A. Wise, eds., *Social Experimentation*. Chicago: University of Chicago Press.

Conlisk, John, and Watts, Harold W. 1969. "A Model for Optimizing Experimental Designs for Estimating Response Surfaces." *Proceedings of the American Statistical Association*, pp. 150–156.

Coons, John; Clune, William H.; and Sugarman, Stephan. 1970. *Private Wealth and Public Education*. Cambridge, Mass.: Belknap Press, Harvard University Press.

Corcoran, Mary, and Datcher, Linda. 1981. "Intergenerational Status Transmission and the Process of Individual Attainment." In James Morgan et al., *Five Thousand American Families—Patterns of Economic Progress*. Vol. 9. Ann Arbor: Institute for Social Research, University of Michigan.

Cotterill, Philip. 1975. "The Elasticity of Demand for Low-Wage Labor." *Southern Economic Journal* 41:520–525.

Covello, Vincent T. 1979. "Poverty Research in the United States: A Review of

Federal Programs and Research Organizations." In *Evaluating Federal Support for Poverty Research*. Washington, D.C.: National Academy of Sciences.

Covello, Vincent T., ed. 1980. *Poverty and Public Policy: An Evaluation of Social Science Research*. Boston: G. K. Hall.

Cowell, Frank A. 1980. "On the Structure of Additive Inequality Measures." *Review of Economic Studies* 47:521–531.

Cowell, Frank A. 1984. "The Structure of American Income Inequality." *Review of Income and Wealth* 30:351–375.

Cowell, Frank A., and Kuga, Kiyoshi. 1981. "Inequality Measurement: An Axiomatic Approach." *European Economic Review* 15:287–305.

Crandall, Robert; MacRae, C. Duncan; and Yap, Lorene. 1975. "An Econometric Model of the Low-Skill Labor Market." *Journal of Human Resources* 10:3–24.

Crawford, David L. 1979. "Estimating Models of Earnings from Truncated Samples." Ph.D. diss., Department of Economics, University of Wisconsin–Madison.

Curtin, Richard. 1977. *Income Equity among U.S. Workers*. New York: Praeger.

Danziger, Sheldon, and Haveman, Robert H. 1977. "Tax and Welfare Simplification: An Analysis of Distributional and Regional Impacts." *National Tax Journal* 30:269–284.

Danziger, Sheldon; Haveman, Robert; and Plotnick, Robert. 1981. "How Income Transfer Programs Affect Work, Savings, and the Income Distribution: A Critical Review." *Journal of Economic Literature* 19:975–1028.

Danziger, Sheldon; Haveman, Robert; and Plotnick, Robert. 1986. "Antipoverty Policy: Effects on the Poor and Nonpoor." In Sheldon H. Danziger and Daniel H. Weinberg, eds., *Fighting Poverty: What Works and What Doesn't*. Cambridge, Mass.: Harvard University Press.

Danziger, Sheldon; Haveman, Robert; and Smolensky, Eugene. 1977. "The Measurement and Trend of Inequality: A Basic Revision: Comment." *American Economic Review* 67:505–512.

Danziger, Sheldon, and Plotnick, Robert. 1977. "Demographic Change, Government Transfers, and Income Distribution." *Monthly Labor Review* 100 (April):7–11.

Danziger, Sheldon; van der Gaag, Jacques; Smolensky, Eugene; and Taussig, Michael. 1984a. "Implications of the Relative Economic Status of the Elderly for Transfer Policy." In Henry J. Aaron and Gary Burtless, eds., *Retirement and Economic Behavior*. Washington, D.C.: Brookings Institution.

Danziger, Sheldon; van der Gaag, Jacques; Smolensky, Eugene; and Taussig, Michael. 1984b. "Income Transfers and the Economic Status of the Elderly." In Marilyn Moon, ed., *Economic Transfers in the United States*. Chicago: University of Chicago Press, for the National Bureau of Economic Research.

Danziger, Sheldon H., and Weinberg, Daniel H., eds. 1986. *Fighting Poverty: What Works and What Doesn't*. Cambridge, Mass.: Harvard University Press.

David, Martin. 1959. "Welfare Income and Budget Needs." *Review of Economics and Statistics* 41:393–399.

David, Martin. 1985. "Introduction: The Design and Development of SIPP." *Journal of Economic and Social Measurement* (special issue on the Survey of Income and Program Participation) 13:215–224.

David, Martin, and Leuthold, Jane. 1968. "Formulas for Income Maintenance: Their Distributional Impact." *National Tax Journal* 21:70–93.

Davis, Karen, and Schoen, Cathy. 1978. *Health and the War on Poverty*. Washington, D.C.: Brookings Institution.

Denison, Edward F. 1962. *The Sources of Economic Growth in the United States and the Alternatives before Us*. New York: Committee for Economic Development.

Diamond, Peter A. 1968. "Negative Taxes and the Poverty Problem—A Review Article." *National Tax Journal* 21:288–303.

Doeringer, Peter, and Piore, Michael. 1971. *Internal Labor Markets and Manpower Analysis*. Lexington, Mass.: Heath.

Dresch, Stephen. 1975. "Demography, Technology, and Higher Education: Toward a Formal Model of Educational Adaptation." *Journal of Political Economy* 83:535–569.

Dresch, Stephen, and Updegrove, Daniel. 1980. "IDIOM: A Disaggregated Policy-Impact Model of the U.S. Economy." In Robert H. Haveman and Kevin Hollenbeck, eds., *Microeconomic Simulation Models for Public Policy Analysis*. Vol. 2. New York: Academic Press.

Duncan, Greg, with Richard D. Coe, Mary E. Corcoran, Martha S. Hill, Saul D. Hoffman, and James M. Morgan. 1984. *Years of Poverty, Years of Plenty: The Changing Economic Fortunes of American Workers and Families*. Ann Arbor: Institute for Social Research, University of Michigan.

Duncan, Otis Dudley. 1961. "A Socioeconomic Index for All Occupations." In A. J. Reiss et al., *Occupations and Social Status*. New York: Free Press.

Duncan, Otis Dudley. 1968. "Inheritance of Poverty or Inheritance of Race?" In Daniel Patrick Moynihan, ed., *On Understanding Poverty*. New York: Basic Books.

Duncan, Otis Dudley. 1969. "How Much Opportunity Is There?" In Panel on Social Indicators, *Toward a Social Report*. Washington, D.C.: U.S. Department of Health, Education, and Welfare.

Duncan, Otis Dudley; Featherman, David L.; and Duncan, Beverly. 1972. *Socioeconomic Background and Achievement*. New York: Seminar Press.

Duncan, Otis Dudley, and Hodge, R. W. 1963. "Education and Occupational Mobility." *American Journal of Sociology* 68:629–644.

Durbin, Elizabeth. 1973. "Work and Welfare: The Case of Aid to Families with Dependent Children." *Journal of Human Resources* 8:103–125.

Eckstein, Otto. 1961. "A Survey of the Theory of Public Expenditure Criteria." In *Public Finances: Needs, Sources, and Utilization*. Princeton, N.J.: Princeton University Press.

Edwards, Richard; Reich, Michael; and Gordon, David, eds. 1975. *Labor Market Segmentation*. Lexington, Mass.: Heath.

Eisinger, Peter. 1976. *Patterns of Interracial Politics: Conflict and Cooperation in the City*. New York: Academic Press.

Eisinger, Peter. 1980. *The Politics of Displacement: Racial and Ethnic Transition in Three American Cities*. New York: Academic Press.

Farkas, George; Olsen, Randall; and Stromsdorfer, Ernst. 1980. "Reduced Form and Structural Models in the Evaluation of the Youth Entitlement Demonstration." In Stromsdorfer and Farkas, eds., *Evaluation Studies Review Annual*. Vol. 5. Beverly Hills, Calif.: Sage Publications.

Featherman, David L. 1977. "Has Opportunity Declined in America?" Discussion Paper no. 437–77, Institute for Research on Poverty, University of Wisconsin–Madison.

Featherman, David L. 1979. "Opportunities are Expanding." *Society* 16:4–11.

Featherman, David L. 1981. "Stratification and Social Mobility: Two Decades of Cumulative Social Science." In James F. Short, Jr., ed., *The State of Sociology: Problems and Prospects*. San Francisco: Sage Publications.

Featherman, David L., and Hauser, Robert M. 1978. *Opportunity and Change*. New York: Academic Press.

Feldstein, Martin S. 1974. "Social Security, Induced Retirement and Aggregate Capital Accumulation." *Journal of Political Economy* 82:905–926.

Feldstein, Martin S. 1976. "Temporary Layoffs in the Theory of Unemployment." *Journal of Political Economy* 84:937–957.

Feldstein, Martin S., and Pellechio, Anthony. 1979. "Social Security and Household Wealth Accumlation: New Micro Econometric Evidence." *Review of Economics and Statistics* 61:361–368.

Ferber, Robert, and Hirsch, Werner. 1982. *Social Experiments and Social Policy*. Cambridge: Cambridge University Press.

Fethke, Gary; Policano, Andrew; and Williamson, Samuel. 1978. *An Investigation of the Conceptual and Qualitative Impact of Employment Tax Credits*. Kalamazoo, Mich.: Upjohn Institute for Employment Research.

Fleisher, Belton M.; Parsons, Donald O.; and Porter, Richard D. 1973. "Asset Adjustments and Labor Supply of Older Workers." In Glen G. Cain and Harold W. Watts, eds., *Income Maintenance and Labor Supply: Econometric Studies*. New York: Academic Press.

Freeman, A. M. 1969. "Project Design and Evaluation with Multiple Objectives." In U. S. Congress, Joint Economic Committee, *The Analysis and Evaluation of Public Expenditures: The PPB System*. Washington, D.C.: GPO.

Freeman, Richard. 1973. "Changes in the Labor Market for Black Americans, 1948–72." *Brookings Papers on Economic Activities*, no. 1, pp. 67–120.

Freeman, Richard. 1976. *The Overeducated American*. New York: Academic Press.

Friedman, Joseph, and Weinberg, Daniel. 1980. "Consumption in an Experimental Housing Allowance Program: Issues of Self-Selection and Housing Requirements." In Ernst W. Stromsdorfer and George Farkas, eds., *Evaluation Studies Review Annual*. Vol. 5. Beverly Hills, Calif.: Sage Publications.

Friedman, Lawrence M. 1977. "The Social and Political Context of the War on Poverty: An Overview." In Robert H. Haveman, ed., *A Decade of Federal Antipoverty Programs: Achievements, Failures, Lessons*. New York: Academic Press.

Friedman, Milton. 1952. "A Method of Comparing Incomes Differing in Composition." In *Studies in Income and Wealth*. Vol. 15. New York: National Bureau of Economic Research.

Friedman, Milton. 1957. *A Theory of the Consumption Function*. Princeton, N.J.: Princeton University Press, for the National Bureau of Economic Research.

Friedman, Milton. 1962. *Capitalism and Freedom*. Chicago: University of Chicago Press.

Fuchs, Victor. 1965. "Towards a Theory of Poverty." In *The Concept of Poverty*. Washington, D.C.: Chamber of Commerce of the United States.

Fuller, W. C.; Manski, C. F.; and Wise, D. A. 1983. "The Impact of the Basic Educational Opportunity Grant Program on College Enrollments." In Elhanan Helpman, Asaff Razin, and Ephraim Sadka, eds., *Social Policy Evaluation*. New York: Academic Press.

Fullerton, Don; King, A. Thomas; Shoven, John B.; and Whalley, John. 1980. "Corporate and Personal Tax Integration in the United States: Some Preliminary Findings." In Robert H. Haveman and Kevin Hollenbeck, eds., *Microeconomic Simulation Models for Public Policy Analysis*. Vol. 2. New York: Academic Press.

Galbraith, John Kenneth. 1958. *The Affluent Society*. Boston: Houghton Mifflin.

Gallaway, Lowell E. 1965. "The Foundations of the 'War on Poverty.'" *American Economic Review* 55:122–130.

Garfinkel, Irwin. 1973a. "On Estimating the Labor Supply Effects of a Negative Income Tax." In Glen G. Cain and Harold W. Watts, eds., *Income Maintenance and Labor Supply: Econometric Studies*. New York: Academic Press.

Garfinkel, Irwin. 1973b. "Is In-Kind Redistribution Efficient?" In *Quarterly Journal of Economics* 87:320–330.

Garfinkel, Irwin. 1973c. "A Skeptical Comment on the Optimality of Wage Subsidy Programs." *American Economic Review* 63:447–453.

Garfinkel, Irwin, ed. 1982. *Income-Tested Transfer Programs: The Case For and Against*. New York: Academic Press.

Garfinkel, Irwin, and Gramlich, Edward M. 1973. "A Statistical Analysis of the OEO Experiment in Educational Performance Contracting." *Journal of Human Resources* 8:275–305.

Garfinkel, Irwin, and Haveman, Robert H. 1977. *Earnings Capacity, Poverty, and Inequality*. New York: Academic Press.

Garfinkel, Irwin, and Orr, Larry L. 1974. "Welfare Policy and the Employment Rate of AFDC Mothers." *National Tax Journal* 27:275–284.

Garms, Walter. 1971. "A Benefit-Cost Analysis of the Upward Bound Program." *Journal of Human Resources* 4:206–220.

Gilbert, Neil. 1970. *Clients or Constituents: Community Action in the War on Poverty*. San Francisco: Jossey-Bass.

Gillespie, W. I. 1965. "Effect of Public Expenditures on the Distribution of Income." In Richard Musgrave, ed., *Essays in Fiscal Federalism*. Washington, D.C.: Brookings Institution.

Glass, D. V., ed. 1954. *Social Mobility in Britain*. London: Routledge and Kegan Paul.

Glazer, Nathan. 1986a. "Education and Training Programs and Poverty." In Sheldon H. Danziger and Daniel H. Weinberg, eds., *Fighting Poverty: What Works and What Doesn't.* Cambridge, Mass.: Harvard University Press.

Glazer, Nathan. 1986b. "Poverty and Poverty Research, Then and Now." *Focus* (newsletter of the Institute for Research on Poverty) 9 (Summer):16–17.

Goedhart, Theo; Halberstadt, Victor; Kapteyn, Arie; and van Praag, Bernard M. S. 1977. "The Poverty Line: Concept and Measurement." *Journal of Human Resources* 12:503–520.

Goffman, Erving. 1963. *Stigma.* Englewood Cliffs, N.J.: Prentice-Hall.

Goldberger, Arthur S. 1972. "Selection Bias in Evaluating Treatment Effects: Some Formal Illustrations." Discussion Paper no. 123–72, Institute for Research on Poverty, University of Wisconsin–Madison.

Goldberger, Arthur S. 1976a. "Mysteries of the Meritocracy." In N. Block and G. Dworkin, eds., *The IQ Controversy: Critical Readings.* New York: Random House.

Goldberger, Arthur S. 1976b. "On Jensen's Method for Twins." *Educational Psychologist* 12:79–82.

Goldberger, Arthur S. 1978a. "Pitfalls in the Resolution of IQ Inheritance." In N. E. Morton and C. S. Chung, eds., *Genetic Epidemiology.* New York: Academic Press.

Goldberger, Arthur S. 1978b. "The Non-Resolution of IQ Inheritance by Path Analysis." *American Journal of Human Genetics* 30:442–445.

Goldberger, Arthur S. 1979. "Heritability." *Economica* 46:327–347.

Goldberger, Arthur S. 1981. "Linear Regression after Selection."*Journal of Econometrics* 15:357–366.

Goldberger, Arthur S. 1983. "Abnormal Selection Bias." In *Studies in Econometrics, Time Series, and Multivariate Statistics.* New York: Academic Press.

Goldberger, Arthur S., and Duncan, Otis Dudley. 1973. *Structural Equation Models in the Social Sciences.* New York: Academic Press.

Goldstein, Jon. 1972. "The Effectiveness of Manpower Training Programs: A Review of Research on the Impact on the Poor." In U. S. Congress, Joint Economic Committee, Subcommittee on Fiscal Policy, *Studies in Public Welfare.* Paper no. 3. Washington, D.C.: GPO.

Goldstein, Morris, and Smith, Robert. 1976. "The Estimated Impact of Antidiscrimination Programs Aimed at Federal Contractors." *Industrial and Labor Relations Review* 29:523–543.

Golladay, Frederick, and Haveman, Robert. 1977. *The Economic Impacts of Tax-Transfer Policy: Regional and Distributional Effects.* New York: Academic Press.

Gordon, David M. 1972. *Theories of Poverty and Underemployment.* Lexington, Mass.: Lexington Books.

Gordon, Roger H., and Blinder, Alan S. 1980. "Market Wages, Reservation Wages, and Retirement Decisions." *Journal of Public Economics* 14:277–308.

Gramlich, Edward M. 1974. "The Distributional Effects of Higher Unemployment." *Brookings Papers on Economic Activity*, no. 2, pp. 293–336.

Gramlich, Edward M. 1976. "The Impact of Minimum Wages on Other Wages,

Employment and Family Incomes." *Brookings Papers on Economic Activity*, no. 2, pp. 409–451.

Gramlich, Edward M., and Koshel, Patricia. 1975. *Educational Performance Contracting*. Washington, D.C.: Brookings Institution.

Gramlich, Edward M., and Wolkoff, Michael J. 1979. "A Procedure for Evaluating Income Distribution Policies." *Journal of Human Resources* 14:319–350.

Green, Christopher. 1967. *Negative Taxes and the Poverty Problem*. Washington, D.C.: Brookings Institution.

Greenberg, David. 1978. "Participation in Public Employment Programs." In John L. Palmer, ed., *Creating Jobs: Public Employment Programs and Wage Subsidies*. Washington, D.C.: Brookings Institution.

Greenberg, David, and Kosters, Marvin. 1973. "Income Guarantees and the Working Poor: The Effect of Income-Maintenance Programs on the Hours of Work of Male Family Heads." In Glen G. Cain and Harold W. Watts, eds., *Income Maintenance and Labor Supply: Econometric Studies*. New York: Academic Press.

Greenberg, David, and Robins, Philip. 1985. "The Changing Role of Social Experiments in Policy Analysis.' In Linda Aiken and Barbara Kehrer, eds., *Evaluation Studies Review Annual*. Vol. 10. Beverly Hills, Calif.: Sage Publications.

Greenleigh Associates Inc. 1960. *Facts, Fallacies, and Future: A Study of the Aid to Dependent Children Program of Cook County, Illinois*. New York: Greenleigh Associates.

Greenstone, J. D., and Peterson, P. E. 1976. *Race and Authority in Urban Politics*. Chicago: University of Chicago Press.

Griliches, Zvi, and Mason, William. 1972. "Education, Income, and Ability." *Journal of Political Economy* 80:S74–S103.

Gronau, Reuben. 1973. "The Intrafamily Allocation of Time: The Value of the Housewives' Time." *American Economic Review* 63:634–651.

Gustman, Alan. 1980. "Analyzing the Relation of Unemployment Insurance to Unemployment." Working Paper no. 512, National Bureau of Economic Research, Cambridge, Mass.

Guthrie, Harold W. 1974. "The Prospect of Equality between White and Black Families under Varying Rates of Unemployment." *Journal of Human Resources* 9:342–360.

Guthrie, J., and Lawton, S. 1970. "The Distribution of Federal School Aid Funds." *Educational Administration Quarterly* 6:47–61.

Gwartney, James. 1970. "Changes in the Nonwhite/White Income Ratio, 1939–67." *American Economic Review* 60:872–883.

Hagenaars, Aldi J. M. 1985. *The Perception of Poverty*. Amsterdam: North-Holland.

Hall, Arden. 1976. "The Determinants of Participation of Single-Headed Families in the AFDC Program." Research Memorandum no. 32, Stanford Research Institute, Menlo Park, Calif.

Hall, Robert E. 1973. "Wages, Income, and Hours of Work in the U.S. Labor Force." In Glen G. Cain and Harold W. Watts, eds., *Income Maintenance and Labor Supply: Econometric Studies*. New York: Academic Press.

Hall, Robert, and Kasten, Richard. 1973. "The Relative Occupational Success of Black and Whites." *Brookings Papers on Economic Activity*, no. 3, pp. 781–795.

Ham, John. 1982. "Estimation of a Labor Supply Model with Censoring Due to Unemployment and Underemployment." *Review of Economic Studies* 49:335–354.

Hamermesh, Daniel. 1976. "Econometric Studies of Labor Demand and Their Application to Policy Analysis." *Journal of Human Resources* 11:507–525.

Hamermesh, Daniel. 1977. *Jobless Pay and the Economy*. Baltimore: Johns Hopkins University Press.

Hamermesh, Daniel. 1978. "Subsidies for Jobs in the Private Sector." In John L. Palmer, ed., *Creating Jobs: Public Employment Programs and Wage Subsidies*. Washington, D.C.: Brookings Institution.

Hamermesh, Daniel. 1981. "Taxes, Transfers, and the NAIRU." In Lawrence Meyer, ed., *The Supply-Side Effects of Economic Policy*. Boston: Kluwer-Nijhoff.

Hamermesh, Daniel, and Grant, James H. 1979. "Econometric Studies of Labor-Labor Substitution and Their Implications for Policy." *Journal of Human Resources* 14:518–542.

Handler, Joel F., and Hollingsworth, Ellen Jane. 1968. "How Obnoxious is the 'Obnoxious Test'? The Views of AFDC Recipients." Discussion Paper no. 31–68, Institute for Research on Poverty, University of Wisconsin–Madison.

Handler, Joel F., and Hollingsworth, Ellen Jane. 1969a. "The Administration of Social Services in AFDC: The Views of Welfare Recipients." Discussion Paper no. 37–69, Institute for Research on Poverty, University of Wisconsin–Madison.

Handler, Joel F., and Hollingsworth, Ellen Jane. 1969b. "The Administration of Welfare Budgets: The Views of AFDC Recipients." Discussion Paper no. 39–69, Institute for Research on Poverty, University of Wisconsin–Madison.

Handler, Joel F., and Hollingsworth, Ellen Jane. 1969c. "The Characteristics of AFDC Recipients: A Comparative View." Discussion Paper no. 41–69, Institute for Research on Poverty, University of Wisconsin–Madison.

Handler, Joel F., and Hollingsworth, Ellen Jane. 1969d. "Stigma, Privacy, and Other Attitudes of Welfare Recipients." Discussion Paper no. 49–69, Institute for Research on Poverty, University of Wisconsin–Madison.

Handler, Joel F., and Hollingsworth, Ellen Jane. 1969e. "Work and the Aid to Families with Dependent Children." Discussion Paper no. 45–69, Institute for Research on Poverty, University of Wisconsin–Madison.

Handler, Joel F., and Hollingsworth, Ellen Jane. 1970. "Work, Welfare, and the Nixon Reform Proposals." Reprint no. 60, Institute for Research on Poverty, University of Wisconsin–Madison.

Handler, Joel F., and Hollingsworth, Ellen Jane. 1971. *The "Deserving Poor": A Study of Welfare Administration*. Chicago: Markham.

Hannan, Michael T.; Tuma, Nancy B.; and Groeneveld, Lyle P. 1978. "Income and Independence Effects on Marital Dissolution: Results from the Seattle-

Denver Income Maintenance Experiments." *American Journal of Sociology* 84:611–633.

Hanoch, Giora. 1967. "An Economic Analysis of Earnings and Schooling." *Journal of Human Resources* 2:310–329.

Hansen, W. Lee. 1963. "Total and Private Rates of Return to Investment in Schooling." *Journal of Political Economy* 71:128–141.

Hansen, W. Lee. 1972. "Equity in the Finance of Higher Education." *Journal of Political Economy* 80:S260–S273.

Hansen, W. Lee, ed. 1970. *Education, Income, and Human Capital.* New York: Columbia University Press, for the National Bureau of Economic Research.

Hansen, W. Lee, and Lampman, Robert. 1983. "Basic Opportunity Grants for Higher Education: Good Intentions and Mixed Results." In Robert H. Haveman and Julius Margolis, eds., *Public Expenditure and Policy Analysis.* 3d ed. Boston: Houghton Mifflin.

Hansen, W. Lee, and Weisbrod, Burton A. 1969. *Benefits, Costs, and Finance of Public Higher Education.* Chicago: Markham.

Hansen, W. Lee, and Weisbrod, Burton A. 1971. "A New Approach to Higher Education Finance." In Mel Orwig, ed., *Financing Higher Education.* Iowa City: American College Testing Program.

Hansen, W. Lee; Weisbrod, Burton A.; and Scanlon, William J. 1970. "Schooling and Earnings of Low Achievers." *American Economic Review* 60:409–418.

Hanushek, Eric. 1971. "Teacher Characteristics and Gains in Student Achievement: Estimation Using Micro-Data." *American Economic Review* 61:280–288.

Hanushek, Eric, and Kain, John. 1972. "On the Value of Equality of Educational Opportunity as a Guide to Public Policy." In Frederick Mosteller and Daniel Patrick Moynihan, eds., *On Equality of Educational Opportunity.* New York: Random House.

Harberger, Arnold C. 1978. "On the Use of Distributional Weights in Social Cost-Benefit Analysis." *Journal of Political Economy* 86:S87–S120.

Harberger, Arnold C. 1983. "Basic Needs versus Distributional Weights in Social Cost-Benefit Analysis." In Robert H. Haveman and Julius Margolis, eds., *Public Expenditure and Policy Analysis.* 3d ed. Boston: Houghton Mifflin.

Harrington, Michael. 1962. *The Other America: Poverty in the United States.* New York: Macmillan.

Harris, Jeffrey. 1985. "Macroexperiments versus Microexperiments for Health Policy." In Jerry A. Hausman and David A. Wise, eds., *Social Experimentation.* Chicago: University of Chicago Press.

Harris, Robert. 1978. "Microanalysis Simulation Models for Analysis of Public Welfare Policies." Working Paper no. 819–1, Urban Institute, Washington, D.C.

Harrison, Bennett. 1972. "Education and Underemployment in the Urban Ghetto." *American Economic Review* 62:796–812.

Hartman, Robert W. 1972. "Equity Implications of State Tuition Policy and Student Loans." *Journal of Political Economy* 80:S142–S177.

Harvard Educational Review. 1973. *Perspectives on Inequality*. Harvard Educational Review Reprint Series no. 8, Cambridge, Mass.

Hauser, Robert M., and Featherman, David L. 1977. *The Process of Stratification: Trends and Analyses*. New York: Academic Press.

Hausman, Jerry A. 1981. "Labor Supply." In Henry J. Aaron and Joseph A. Pechman, eds., *How Taxes Affect Economic Behavior*. Washington, D.C.: Brookings Institution.

Hausman, Jerry A., and Wise, David A. 1977. "Social Experimentation, Truncated Distributions, and Efficient Estimation." *Econometrica* 45:919–928.

Hausman, Jerry A., and Wise, David A. 1979. "Attrition Bias in Experimental and Panel Data: The Gary Income Maintenance Experiment." *Econometrica* 47:455–473.

Hausman, Jerry A., and Wise, David. 1980. "Discontinuous Budget Constraints and Estimation: The Demand for Housing."*Review of Economic Studies* 67:75–96.

Hausman, Jerry A., and Wise, David A. 1985. "Technical Problems in Social Experimentation: Cost versus Ease of Analysis." In Hausman and Wise, eds., *Social Experimentation*. Chicago: University of Chicago Press.

Hausman, Leonard J. 1968. "The AFDC Amendments of 1967: Their Impact on the Capacity for Self-Support and the Employability of AFDC Family Heads." *Labor Law Journal* 19:496–508.

Hausman, Leonard J. 1975. "Cumulative Tax Returns in Alternative Income Maintenance Systems." In Irene Lurie, ed., *Integrating Income Maintenance Programs*. New York: Academic Press.

Haveman, Robert H. 1965. *Water Resource Investment and the Public Interest*. Nashville: Vanderbilt University Press.

Haveman, Robert H. 1975. "Earnings Supplementation as an Income Maintenance Strategy: Issues of Program Structure and Integration." In Irene Lurie, ed., *Integrating Income Maintenance Programs*. New York: Academic Press.

Haveman, Robert H. 1976. "Policy Analysis and the Congress: An Economist's View." *Policy Analysis* 2:235–250.

Haveman, Robert H. 1978. "The Dutch Social Employment Program." In John L. Palmer, ed., *Creating Jobs: Public Employment Programs and Wage Subsidies*. Washington, D.C.: Brookings Institution.

Haveman, Robert H. 1980. "Direct Job Creation." In Eli Ginzberg, ed., *Employing the Unemployed*. New York: Basic Books.

Haveman, Robert H., ed. 1977. *A Decade of Federal Antipoverty Programs: Achievements, Failures, and Lessons*. New York: Academic Press.

Haveman, Robert H., and Hollenbeck, Kevin, eds. 1980. *Microeconomic Simulation Models for Public Policy Analysis*. 2 vols. New York: Academic Press.

Haveman, Robert H.; Hollenbeck, Kevin; Betson, David; and Holmer, Martin. 1980. "A Microeconomic Simulation Model for Analyzing the Regional and Distributional Effects of Tax-Transfer Policy: An Analysis of the Program for Better Jobs and Incomes." In Robert H. Haveman and Kevin Hollenbeck, eds., *Microeconomic Simulation Models for Public Policy Analysis*. Vol. 2. New York: Academic Press.

Haveman, Robert H., and Lacker, Jeffrey. 1984. "Discrepancies of Projecting Future Public and Private Pension Benefits: A Comparison and Critique of Two Microdata Simulation Models." Special Report no. 36, Institute for Research on Poverty, University of Wisconsin–Madison.

Haveman, Robert H., and Lampman, Robert. 1971. "Two Alternatives to FAP's Treatment of the Working Poor." Discussion Paper no. 94–71, Institute for Research on Poverty, University of Wisconsin–Madison.

Haveman, Robert H.; Lurie, Irene; and Mirer, Thad. 1974. "Earnings Supplementation Plans for 'Working Poor' Families: An Evaluation of Alternatives." In Arnold C. Harberger et al., eds., *Benefit-Cost and Policy Analysis—1973*. Chicago: Aldine.

Haveman, Robert H., and Palmer, John L., eds. 1982. *Jobs for Disadvantaged Workers: The Economics of Employment Subsidies*. Washington, D.C.: Brookings Institution.

Haveman, Robert H., and Wolfe, Barbara. 1984. "Schooling and Economic Well-Being:The Role of Non-Market Effects." *Journal of Human Resources* 19:377–408.

Haveman, Robert H., and Wolfe, Barbara. 1985. "Income, Inequality, and Uncertainty: Differences between the Disabled and Nondisabled." In Martin David and Timothy Smeeding, eds., *Horizontal Equity, Uncertainty, and Economic Well-Being*. Chicago: University of Chicago Press, for the National Bureau of Economic Research.

Haworth, Joan; Gwartney, James; and Haworth,Charles. 1975. "Earnings, Productivity, and Changes in Employment Discrimination in the 1960s." *American Economic Review* 65:158–168.

Heckman, James. 1974. "Shadow Prices, Market Wages and Labor Supply." *Econometrica* 42:679–694.

Heckman, James. 1976. "The Common Structure of Statistical Models of Truncation, Sample Selection and Limited Dependent Variables and a Simple Estimator for Such Models." *Annals of Economic and Social Measurement* 5:475–492.

Heckman, James. 1978a. "Dummy Endogenous Variables in a Simultaneous Equation System." *Econometrica* 46:931–959.

Heckman, James. 1978b. "Longitudinal Studies in Labor Economics: A Methodological Review." Department of Economics, University of Chicago. Mimeo.

Heckman, James. 1979. "Sample Selection Bias as a Specification Error." *Econometrica* 147:153–161.

Heckman, James. 1980. "Addendum to Sample Selection Bias as a Specification Error." In Ernst W. Stromsdorfer and George Farkas, eds., *Evaluation Studies Review Annual*. Vol. 5. Beverly Hills, Calif.: Sage Publications.

Heckman, James, and MaCurdy, Thomas. 1981. "New Methods for Estimating Labor Supply Functions: A Survey." In Robert Ehrenberg, ed., *Research in Labor Economics*. Vol. 4. Greenwich, Conn.: JAI Press.

Heckman, James, and Willis, Richard. 1977. "A Beta-Logistic Model for the Analysis of Sequential Labor Force Participation by Married Women." *Journal of Political Economy* 85:27–58.

Heffernan, W. Joseph. 1973. "Variations in Negative Tax Rates in Current Public Assistance Programs." *Journal of Human Resources* 8 (Supplement): 56–68.

Heller, Walter. 1966. *New Dimensions in Political Economy*. Cambridge, Mass.: Harvard University Press.

Herrnstein, Richard. 1973. *IQ in the Meritocracy*. Boston: Atlantic Monthly Press.

Hill, Martha. 1981. "Some Dynamic Aspects of Poverty." In James Morgan et al., eds., *Five Thousand American Families—Patterns of Economic Progress*. Vol. 6. Ann Arbor: Institute for Social Research, University of Michigan.

Hill, Russell. 1973. "The Determinants of Labor Supply for the Working Poor." In Glen G. Cain and Harold W. Watts, eds., *Income Maintenance and Labor Supply: Econometric Studies*. New York: Academic Press.

Hoagland, G. William. 1982. "The Effectiveness of Current Transfer Programs in Reducing Poverty." In Paul Sommers, ed., *Welfare Reform in America: Perspectives and Prospects*. Boston: Kluwer-Nijhoff.

Hochman, Harold M., and Rodgers, James D. 1969. "Pareto Optimal Redistribution." *American Economic Review* 59:542–557.

Hollister, Robinson G., Jr.; Kemper, Peter; and Maynard, Rebecca A. 1984. *The National Supported Work Demonstration*. Madison, Wis.: University of Wisconsin Press.

Holmer, Martin R. 1975. "The Economic and Political Causes of the 'Welfare Crisis.'" Ph.D. diss., Department of Economics, Massachusetts Institute of Technology.

Hopkins, Jeanette, and Clark, Kenneth. 1969. *A Relevant War against Poverty: A Study of Community Action Programs and Observable Social Change*. New York: Harper.

Hosek, James. 1982. "The AFDC-Unemployed Fathers Program: Determinants of Participation and Implications for Welfare Reform." In Paul Sommers, ed., *Welfare Reform in America: Perspectives and Prospects*. Boston: Kluwer-Nijoff.

Houthakker, Hendrick S. 1959. "Education and Income." *Review of Economics and Statistics* 41:24–28.

Hu, Teh-Wei; Lee, Maw Lin; and Stromsdorfer, Ernst W. 1971. "Economic Returns to Vocational and Comprehensive High School Graduates." *Journal of Human Resources* 6:25–47.

Hurd, Michael, and Shoven, John. 1982. "Real Income and Wealth of the Elderly." *American Economic Review* 72 (May):314–318.

Hurd, Michael, and Shoven, John. 1983. "The Economic Status of the Elderly." In Avi Bodie and John Shoven, eds., *Financial Aspects of the U.S. Pension System*.Chicago: University of Chicago Press.

Hutchens, Robert M. 1978. "Changes in AFDC Tax Rates, 1967–1971." *Journal of Human Resources* 13:60–74.

Hutchens, Robert M. 1981. "Entry and Exit Transitions in a Government Transfer Program: The Case of Aid to Families with Dependent Children." *Journal of Human Resources* 16:217–237.

Income Maintenance Programs. 1968. Hearings before the Subcommittee on Fiscal Policy of the Joint Economic Committee, U.S. Congress. 2 vols. Washington, D.C.: GPO.

Institute for Social Research, Survey Research Center. 1972. *A Panel Study of Income Dynamics.* Ann Arbor: Institute for Social Research, University of Michigan.

Jencks, Christopher. 1970. "Giving Parents Money for Schooling: Education Vouchers." *Phi Delta Kappan*, Vol. 51.

Jencks, Christopher, et al. 1972. *Inequality: A Reassessment of the Effect of Family and Schooling in America.* New York: Basic Books.

Jencks, Christopher, et al. 1979. *Who Gets Ahead? The Determinants of Economic Success in America.* New York: Basic Books.

Jensen, Arthur. 1969. "How Much Can We Boost IQ and Scholastic Achievement?" *Harvard Educational Review* 39:1–123.

Johnson, George. 1978. "Structural Unemployment Consequences of Job Creation Policies." In John L. Palmer, ed., *Creating Jobs: Public Employment Programs and Wage Subsidies.* Washington, D.C.: Brookings Institution.

Johnson, George. 1982. "Allocative and Distributional Effects." In Robert H. Haveman and John L. Palmer, eds., *Jobs for Disadvantaged Workers: The Economics of Employment Subsidies.* Washington, D.C.: Brookings Institution.

Johnson, George, and Blakemore, Arthur. 1979. "The Potential Impact of Employment Policy on the Unemployment Rate Consistent with Nonaccelerating Inflation." *American Economic Review* 69:119–123.

Johnson, George, and Tomola, James. 1977. "The Fiscal Substitution Effect of Alternative Approaches to Public Service Employment Policy." *Journal of Human Resources* 12:3–26.

Johnson, William. 1977. "Uncertainty and the Distribution of Earnings." In F. Thomas Juster, ed., *The Distribution of Economic Well-Being.* Cambridge, Mass.: Ballinger, for the National Bureau of Economic Research.

Johnson, William G. 1979. "Disability, Income Support, and Social Insurance." In Edward Berkowitz, ed., *Disability Policies and Government Programs.* New York: Praeger.

Johnson, William G., and Murphy, Edward H., Jr. 1975. "The Response of Low-Income Households to Income Losses from Disability." *Industrial and Labor Relations Review* 29:85–96.

Jöreskog, Karl J., and Sorbom, Dag. 1979. *Advances in Factor Analysis and Structural Equation Models.* Cambridge, Mass.: ABT Books.

Joskow, Paul. 1985. "Discussion." In Jerry A. Hausman and David A. Wise, eds., *Social Experimentation.* Chicago: University of Chicago Press.

Kain, John F. 1968. "Housing Segregation, Negro Employment, and Metropolitan Decentralization." *Quarterly Journal of Economics* 82:175–197.

Kain, John F. 1974. "Housing Segregation, Black Employment, and Metropolitan Decentralization: A Retrospective View." In G. von Furstenberg, B. Harrison, and W. Horowitz, eds., *Patterns of Racial Discrimination*. Vol. 2: *Employment and Income*. Boston: Heath.

Kain, John F., and Quigley, John M. 1972. "Housing Market Discrimination, Home Ownership, and Savings Behavior." *American Economic Review* 62:263–277.

Kamin, Leo. 1974. *The Science and Politics of IQ*. New York: John Wiley.

Kapteyn, Arie, and van Praag, Bernard. 1976. "A New Approach to the Construction of Family Equivalence Scales." *European Economic Review* 7:313–335.

Keeley, M. C. 1978. "The Labor Supply Effects and Costs of Alternative Negative Income Tax Programs." *Journal of Human Resources* 13:3–36.

Keeley, M. C.; Robins, Philip; Spiegelman, Robert; and West, Richard. 1978. "The Estimation of Labor Supply Models Using Experimental Data." *American Economic Review* 68:873–887.

Kehrer, Kenneth. 1977. "The Gary Income Maintenance Experiment: Summary of Initial Findings." Report to the U.S. Department of Health, Education, and Welfare, Washington, D.C. March.

Kelley, Terrence. 1970. "Factors Affecting Poverty: A Gross Flow Analysis." In *The President's Commission on Income Maintenance Programs: Technical Studies*. Washington, D.C.: GPO.

Kemper, Peter; Long, David; and Thornton, Charles. 1983. "A Benefit-Cost Analysis of the Supported Work Program." In Robert H. Haveman and Julius Margolis, eds., *Public Expenditure and Policy Analysis*. 3d ed. Boston: Houghton Mifflin.

Kerr, Clark. 1954. "The Balkanization of Labor Markets." In E. W. Bakke et al., eds. *Labor Mobility and Economic Opportunity*. New York: John Wiley.

Kershaw, Joseph. 1970. *Government against Poverty*. Washington, D.C.: Brookings Institution.

Kesselman, Jonathan. 1969. "Labor Supply Effects of Income, Income-Work, and Wage Subsidies." *Journal of Human Resources* 4:275–292.

Kesselman, Jonathan. 1971. "Conditional Subsidies in Income Maintenance." *Western Economic Journal* 9:1–20.

Kesselman, Jonathan. 1978. "Work Relief Programs in the Great Depression." In John L. Palmer, ed., *Creating Jobs; Public Employment Programs and Wage Subsidies*. Washington, D.C.: Brookings Institution.

Kesselman, Jonathan; Williamson, Samuel; and Berndt, Ernst. 1977. Tax Credits for Employment rather than Investment." *American Economic Review* 67:339–349.

Kiefer, Nicholas M. 1979. "Population Heterogeneity and Inference from Panel Data on the Effects of Vocational Education." *Journal of Political Economy* 87:S213–S226.

Kiker, B. F., and Liles, W. P. 1974. "Earnings, Employment, and Racial Discrimination: Additional Evidence." *American Economic Review* 64:492–501.

Killingsworth, Mark R. 1983. *Labor Supply*. Cambridge: Cambridge University Press.

Kilpatrick, R. W. 1973. "The Income Elasticity of the Poverty Line." *Review of Economics and Statistics* 55:327–332.

King, J. A. 1980. "The Comprehensive Human Resources Data System: A Model for Estimating the Distributional Impacts of Energy Policies." In Robert H. Haveman and Kevin Hollenbeck, eds., *Microeconomic Simulation Models for Public Policy Analysis*. Vol. 1. New York: Academic Press.

Klein, William. 1966. "Some Basic Problems of Negative Income Taxation." *Wisconsin Law Review* 46:776–785.

Kohen, Andrew I.; Parnes, Herbert S.; and Shea, John R. 1975."Income Instability among Young and Middle-Aged Men." In James D. Smith, ed., *The Personal Distribution of Income and Wealth*. New York: National Bureau of Economic Research.

Kotler, Milton. 1969. *Neighborhood Government*. Indianapolis: Bobbs-Merrill.

Kotlikoff, Laurence J. 1979. "Testing the Theory of Social Security and Life Cycle Accumulation." *American Economic Review* 69:396–410.

Kraft, John, and Olsen, Edgar. 1977. "The Distribution of Benefits from Public Housing." In F. Thomas Juster, ed., *The Distribution of Economic Well-Being*. Cambridge, Mass.: Ballinger, for the National Bureau of Economic Research.

Kramer, Ralph. 1969. *Participation of the Poor: Comparative Case Studies in the War on Poverty*. Englewood Cliffs, N.J.: Prentice-Hall.

Kravis, I. B. 1962. *The Structure of Income: Some Quantitative Essays*. Philadelphia: University of Pennsylvania Press.

Lampman, Robert J. 1954. "Recent Change in Income Inequality Reconsidered." *American Economic Review* 44:251–268.

Lampman, Robert J. 1957. "The Effectiveness of Some Institutions in Changing the Distribution of Income." *American Economic Review* 47 (May):519–535.

Lampman, Robert J. 1959a. "Changes in the Share of Wealth Held by Top Wealth-Holders, 1922–1956." *Review of Economics and Statistics* 41:379–392.

Lampman, Robert J. 1959b. *The Low Income Population and Economic Growth*. U.S. Congress, Joint Economic Committee, Study Paper no. 12. Washington, D.C.: GPO.

Lampman, Robert J. 1962. *The Share of Top Wealth-Holders in National Wealth, 1922–1956*. Princeton, N.J.: Princeton University Press, for the National Bureau of Economic Research.

Lampman, Robert J. 1963. "Income and Welfare in the United States: A Review Article." *Review of Economics and Statistics* 45:314–317.

Lampman, Robert J. 1966. "How Much Does the American System of Transfers Benefit the Poor?" In Leonard H. Goodman, ed., *Economic Progress and Social Welfare*. New York: Columbia University Press.

Lampman, Robert J. 1969a. "Expanding the American System of Income Transfers to Do More for the Poor." *Wisconsin Law Review* 2:541–549.

Lampman, Robert J. 1969b. "Nixon's Family Assistance Plan." Discussion Paper no. 57–69, Institute for Research on Poverty, University of Wisconsin–Madison.

Lampman, Robert J. 1969c. "Transfer and Redistribution as a Social Process." In Shirley Jenkins, ed., *Social Security in International Perspective*. New York: Columbia University Press.

Lampman, Robert J. 1970. "Transfer Approaches to Distribution Policy." *American Economic Review* 60:270–279.

Lampman, Robert J. 1971a. *Ends and Means of Reducing Income Poverty*. Chicago: Markham.

Lampman, Robert J. 1971b. "The Welfare Reform Provisions in H.R.1." Discussion Paper no. 105–71, Institute for Research on Poverty, University of Wisconsin–Madison.

Lampman, Robert J. 1974. "What Does It Do for the Poor? A New Test for National Policy." In Eli Ginzberg and Robert S. Solow, eds., *The Great Society*. New York: Basic Books.

Lampman, Robert J. 1975. "Scaling Welfare Benefits to Income: An Idea That Is Being Overworked." *Policy Analysis* 1:1–10.

Lampman, Robert J. 1976. "The Decision to Undertake the New Jersey Experiment." In David Kershaw and Jerilyn Fair, eds., *The New Jersey Income Maintenance Experiment*. Vol. 1. New York: Academic Press.

Lampman, Robert J. 1978. "Labor Supply and Social Welfare Benefits in the United States." Special Report no. 22, Institute for Research on Poverty, University of Wisconsin–Madison.

Lampman, Robert J. 1984. *Social Welfare Spending: Accounting for Changes from 1950 to 1978*. New York: Academic Press.

Lampman, Robert J., and Smeeding, Timothy M. 1983. "Interfamily Transfers as Alternatives to Government Transfers to Persons." *Review of Income and Wealth* (Ser. 29) 1:45–66.

Lancaster, Tony. 1979. "Econometric Methods for the Duration of Unemployment." *Econometrica* 47:939–956.

Lazear, Edward P., and Michael, Robert T. 1980. "Family Size and the Distribution of Real Per Capita Income." *American Economic Review* 70:91–107.

Lee, Lung Fei, and Maddala, G. S. 1983. "Sequential Selection Rules and Selectivity in Discrete Choice Econometric Models." Paper presented at the Econometric Society meetings, December.

Leigh, Duane. 1976. "Occupational Advancement in the Late 1960s: An Indirect Test of the Dual Labor Market Analysis." *Journal of Human Resources* 11:155–171.

Leimer, Dean R., and Lesnoy, Selig D. 1982. "Social Security and Private Saving: New Time-Series Evidence." *Journal of Political Economy* 90:606–629.

Leonard, Jonathan. 1979. "The Social Security Disability Program and Labor Force Participation." Working Paper no. 392, National Bureau of Economic Research, New York.

Lerman, Robert I. 1974. "JOIN: A Jobs and Income Program for American Families." In U.S. Congress, Joint Economic Committee, Subcommittee on Fiscal Policy, *Public Employment and Wage Subsidies: Studies in Public Welfare*, Paper no. 19. Washington, D.C.: GPO.

Lerman, Robert I. 1982. "A Comparison of Employer and Worker Wage Subsidies." In Robert H. Haveman and John L. Palmer, eds., *Jobs for Disadvantaged Workers: The Economics of Employment Subsidies*. Washington, D.C.: Brookings Institution.

Levin, Henry M. 1977. "A Decade of Policy Developments in Improving Education and Training for Low-Income Populations." In Robert H. Haveman, ed., *A Decade of Federal Antipoverty Programs: Achievements, Failures, and Lessons*. New York: Academic Press.

Levine, Robert A. 1969. "Policy Analysis and Economic Opportunity Programs." In U.S. Congress, Joint Economic Committee, *The Analysis and Evaluation of Public Expenditures: The PPB System*. Washington, D.C.: GPO.

Levine, Robert A. 1970. *The Poor Ye Need Not Have with You: Lessons from the War on Poverty*. Cambridge, Mass.: MIT Press.

Levitan, Sar A. 1969. *Programs in Aid of the Poor for the 1970's*. Baltimore: Johns Hopkins University Press.

Levitan, Sar A.; Rein, Martin; and Marwick, David. 1972. *Work and Welfare Go Together*. Baltimore: Johns Hopkins University Press.

Levitan, Sar A., and Taggart, Robert, III. 1974. *Employment and Earnings Inadequacy: A New Social Indicator*. Baltimore: Johns Hopkins University Press.

Levitan, Sar A., and Taggart, Robert, III. 1976. *The Promise of Greatness*. Cambridge, Mass.: Harvard University Press.

Lewis, H. Gregg. 1959. "Competitive and Monopoly Unionism." In Philip D. Bradley, ed., *The Public Stake in Union Power*. Charlottesville: University of Virginia Press.

Lewis, Oscar. 1965. *La Vida: A Puerto Rican Family in the Culture of Poverty— San Juan and New York*. New York: Random House.

Lidman, Russell. 1972. "Cost and Distributional Implications of a Credit Income Tax Plan." *Public Policy* 20:311–334.

Lillard, Lee. 1977. "Inequality–Earnings vs. Human Wealth." *American Economic Review* 67:42–53.

Lipset, S. M., and Bendix, R. 1959. *Social Mobility in Industrial Society*. Berkeley, Calif.: University of California Press.

Little, J. A. 1982. "Models for Nonresponse in Sample Surveys." *Journal of the American Statistical Association* 77:237–250.

Long, David; Mallar, Charles; and Thornton, Craig. 1981. "Evaluation of the Benefits and Costs of the Job Corps." *Journal of Policy Analysis and Management* 1:55–76.

Lurie, Irene. 1974. "Estimates of Tax Rates in the AFDC Program." *National Tax Journal* 21:93–111.

Lurie, Irene. 1975. "Integrating Income Maintenance Programs: Problems and Solutions." In Lurie, ed., *Integrating Income Maintenance Programs*. New York: Academic Press.

Lydall, Harold. 1968. *The Structure of Earnings*. Oxford: Clarendon Press.

Lynn, Lawrence, ed. 1978. *Knowledge and Policy: The Uncertain Connection*. Washington, D.C.: National Academy of Sciences.

Lyon, David W.; Armstrong, Philip A.; Hosek, James R.; and McCall, John J. 1976. *Multiple Welfare Benefits in New York City*. Santa Monica, Calif.: Rand Corporation.

MacDonald, Dwight. 1963. "Our Invisible Poor." *New Yorker*, January 19, pp. 82–132.

MacDonald, Maurice. 1977. *Food, Stamps, and Income Maintenance*. New York: Academic Press.

MacDonald, Maurice. 1983. "Multiple Benefits and Income Adequacy for Food Stamp Participant and Nonparticipant Households." Report to the U.S. Department of Agriculture, Food and Nutrition Service, Alexandria, Va., February. Mimeo.

MacDonald, Maurice, and Sawhill, Isabell. 1978. "Welfare Policy and the Family." *Public Policy* 26:89–119.

McClung, Nelson. 1970. "Estimates of Income Transfer Direct Effects." In *The President's Commission on Income Maintenance Programs: Technical Studies*. Washington, D.C.: GPO.

McFadden, Daniel. 1973. "Conditional Logit Analysis of Qualitative Choice Behavior." In Paul Zarembka, ed., *Frontiers in Econometrics*. New York: Academic Press.

Mahoney, B. S. 1976. *The Measure of Poverty*. Poverty Studies Task Force. Washington, D.C.: U.S. Department of Health, Education, and Welfare.

Maital, Shlomo. 1973. "Public Goods and Income Distribution: Some Further Results." *Econometrica* 41:561–568.

Mallar, Charles; Kerachsky, Stuart; and Thornton, Craig. 1980. "The Short-Term Economic Impact of the Job Corps Program." In Ernst W. Stromsdorfer and George Farkas, eds., *Evaluation Studies Review Annual*. Vol. 5. Beverly Hills, Calif.: Sage Publications.

Manski, Charles, and Lerman, Steven. 1977. "The Estimation of Choice Probabilities from Choice-based Samples." *Econometrica* 45:1977–1988.

Marin, Alan, and Psacharopoulos, George. 1976. "Schooling and Income Distribution." *Review of Economics and Statistics* 58:332–338.

Marmor, Theodore. 1971. "On Comparing Income Maintenance Alternatives." *American Political Science Review* 65:83–96.

Marmor, Theodore. 1971. *Poverty Policy*. Chicago: Aldine-Atherton.

Marmor, Theodore. 1975. "Public Medical Programs and Cash Assistance: The Problems of Program Integration." In Irene Lurie, ed., *Integrating Income Maintenance Programs*. New York: Academic Press.

Marshall, Ray. 1974. "The Economics of Racial Discrimination: A Survey." *Journal of Economic Literature* 12:849–871.

Marshall, Ray, and Christian, Virgil. 1978. *Employment of Southern Blacks*. Salt Lake City: Olympus.

Masters, Stanley. 1974. "A Note on John Kain's 'Housing Segregation, Black Employment, and Metropolitan Decentralization.'" *Quarterly Journal of Economics* 88:505–512.

Masters, Stanley. 1975. *Black-White Income Differences*. New York: Academic Press.

Masters, Stanley, and Garfinkel, Irwin. 1977. *Estimating the Labor Supply Effects of Income Maintenance Alternatives*. New York: Academic Press.

Mathematica Policy Research, Inc. 1983. *Final Report: Employment Opportunity Pilot Project: Analysis of Program Impacts*. Princeton, N.J.: MPR.

Matras, Judah. 1960. "Comparison of Intergenerational Occupational Mobility Patterns: An Application of the Formal Theory of Social Mobility." *Population Studies* 14:163–169.

Matras, Judah. 1980. "Comparative Social Mobility." *Annual Review of Sociology* 6:401–431.

Matza, David. 1966. "Poverty and Disrepute." In Robert Merton and Robert Nesbit, eds., *Contemporary Social Problems*. New York: Harcourt, Brace and World.

Maxfield, Myles, Jr. 1980. "Aspects of a Negative Income Tax: Program Cost, Adequacy of Support, and Induced Labor Supply Reduction." In Robert H. Haveman and Kevin Hollenbeck, eds., *Microeconomic Simulation Models for Public Policy Analysis*. Vol. 1. New York: Academic Press.

Merriam, Ida C., and Skolnick, Alfred M. 1968. "Social Welfare Expenditures under Public Programs in the United States (1929–1966)." Research Report no. 25. Office of Research and Statistics, Social Security Administration, Washington, D.C.

Merz, J. 1982. "Concept and Application of the Sfb3—Microsimulation Model." Frankfurt/Main: Department of Economics, J. W. Goethe University. Mimeo.

Michel, Richard C. 1980. "Participation Rates in the Aid to Families with Dependent Children Program, Part I: National Trends from 1967 to 1977." Working Paper no. 1387–02, Urban Institute, Washington, D.C.

Miller, H. P. 1960. "Annual and Lifetime Income in Relation to Education: 1939–1959." *American Economic Review* 50:962–986.

Mincer, Jacob. 1962. "On-the-Job Training: Cost, Returns and Some Implications." *Journal of Political Economy* 70:50–79.

Mincer, Jacob. 1970. "The Distribution of Labor Incomes: A Survey with Special Reference to the Human Capital Approach." *Journal of Economic Literature* 8:1–26.

Mincer, Jacob. 1974. *Schooling, Experience, and Earnings*. New York: Columbia University Press.

Mincer, Jacob. 1976. "Unemployment Effects of Minimum Wages." *Journal of Political Economy* 84:87–104.

Minimum Wage Study Commission. 1981. *Report of the Minimum Wage Study Commission* [to President Ronald Reagan]. Washington, D.C.: The Commission.

Mirer, Thad W. 1974. "Aspects of the Variability of Family Income." In James N. Morgan, ed., *Five Thousand American Families—Patterns of Economic Progress*. Vol. 2. Ann Arbor: Institute for Social Research, University of Michigan.

Mirer, Thad W. 1975. "Alternative Approaches to Integrating Income Transfer Programs." In Irene Lurie, ed., *Integrating Income Maintenance Programs*. New York: Academic Press.

Modigliani, Franco, and Brumberg, Richard. 1954. "Utility Analysis and the

Consumption Function: An Interpretation of Cross-Section Data." In K. K. Kurihara, ed., *Post-Keynesian Economics*. New Brunswick, N.J.: Rutgers University Press.

Moeller, John F. 1973. "Development of a Microsimulation Model for Evaluating Economic Implications of Income Transfer and Tax Policies." *Economic and Social Measurement* 2:183–187.

Moffitt, Robert. 1983. "An Economic Model of Welfare Stigma." *American Economic Review* 73:1023–1035.

Moffitt, Robert, and Nicholson, Walter. 1982. "The Effect of Unemployment Insurance on Unemployment: The Case of Federal Supplemental Benefits." *Review of Economics and Statistics* 64:1–11.

Moon, Marilyn. 1977. *The Measurement of Economic Welfare: Its Application to the Aged Poor*. New York: Academic Press.

Moon, Marilyn, and Smolensky, Eugene, eds. 1977. *Improving Measures of Economic Well-Being*. New York: Academic Press.

Mooney, J. D. 1969. "Housing Segregation, Negro Employment, and Metropolitan Decentralization: An Alternative Perspective." *Quarterly Journal of Economics* 83:299–311.

Morgan, James N. 1968. "The Supply of Effort: The Measurement of Well-Being and the Dynamics of Improvement." *American Economic Review* 58:31–39.

Morgan, James N. 1984. "The Role of Time in the Measurement of Transfers and Well-Being." In Marilyn Moon, ed., *Economic Transfers in the United States*. Chicago: University of Chicago Press, for the National Bureau of Economic Research.

Morgan, James N., and David, Martin H. 1963. "Education and Income." *Quarterly Journal of Economics* 77:423–437.

Morgan, James N.; David, Martin H.; Cohen, Wilbur J.; and Brazer, Harvey E. 1962. *Income and Welfare in the United States*. New York: McGraw-Hill.

Morgan, James N., et al., eds. 1974–84. *Five Thousand American Families— Patterns of Economic Progress*. Vols. 1–11. Ann Arbor: Institute for Social Research, University of Michigan.

Moynihan, Daniel Patrick. 1968. "The Crisis in Welfare." *The Public Interest*, no. 10 (Winter), pp. 3–29.

Moynihan, Daniel Patrick. 1969. *Maximum Feasible Misunderstanding*. New York: Free Press.

Moynihan, Daniel Patrick. 1973. *The Politics of a Guaranteed Income: The Nixon Administration and the Family Assistance Plan*. New York: Random House.

Moynihan, Daniel Patrick, ed. 1969. *On Understanding Poverty: Perspectives from the Social Sciences*. New York: Basic Books.

Muellbauer, John N. 1974. "Household Consumption, Engel Curves, and Welfare Comparisons between Households." *European Economic Review* 5:103–122.

Muellbauer, John N. 1977. "Testing the Barten Model of Household Composition Effects and the Cost of Children." *Economic Journal* 87:460–487.

Muller, L. Scott. 1980. "Receipt of Multiple Benefits by Disabled Worker Beneficiaries." Working Paper Series, no. 15 (May). U.S. Department of Health, Education, and Welfare, Social Security Administration, Office of Research and Statistics, Office of Policy, Washington, D.C.

Mullin, Stephen P., and Summers, Anita A. 1983. "Is More Better? The Effectiveness of Spending on Compensatory Education." *Phi Delta Kappan* 64:339–347.

Mundel, David S. 1985. "The Use of Information in the Policy Process: Are Social Policy Experiments Worthwhile?" In Jerry A. Hausman and David A. Wise, eds., *Social Experimentation*. Chicago: University of Chicago Press.

Murray, M. P. 1974. "The Distribution of Tenant Benefits in Public Housing." University of Virginia, Charlottesville. Mimeo.

Musgrave, Richard, et al. 1951. "Distribution of Tax Payments by Income Groups: A Case Study for 1948." *National Tax Journal* 4:1–53.

Muth, Richard. 1969. *Cities and Housing*. Chicago: University of Chicago Press.

Myrdal, Gunnar. 1944. *An American Dilemma: The Negro Problem and Modern Democracy*. New York: Harper.

Nathan, Richard, et al. 1981. *Public Service Employment: A Field Evaluation*. Washington, D.C.: Brookings Institution.

National Academy of Sciences. 1971. *Policy and Program Research in a University Setting: A Case Study*. Washington, D.C.: National Academy of Sciences.

National Academy of Sciences. 1978. *The Federal Investment in Knowledge of Social Problems*. Washington, D.C.: National Academy of Sciences.

National Academy of Sciences. 1979. *Evaluating Federal Support for Poverty Research*. Report of the Committee on Evaluation of Poverty Research, National Research Council. Washington, D.C.: National Academy of Sciences.

Newhouse, Joseph P., et al. 1982. *Some Interim Results from a Controlled Trial of Cost Sharing in Health Insurance*. Rand Report R-2847-HHS. Santa Monica, Calif.: Rand Corporation.

Nichols, Donald. 1982. "Effects on the Noninflationary Unemployment Rate." In Robert H. Haveman and John L. Plamer, eds., *Jobs for Disadvantaged Workers: The Economics of Employment Subsidies*. Washington, D.C.: Brookings Institution.

Nicholson, J. L. 1976. "Appraisal of Different Methods of Estimating Equivalence Scales and Their Results." *Review of Income and Wealth* 22:1–18.

Nixon, Richard M. 1969. "Welfare Reform: A Message from the President of the United States." House Document no. 91–146, *Congressional Record*, Vol. 115 (136), House of Representatives, 91st Congress, 1st Session, H7239–7241.

Novick, David, ed. 1965. *Program Budgeting*. Cambridge, Mass.: Harvard University Press.

Okner, Benjamin A. 1972. "Constructing a New Data Base from Existing Microdata Sets: The 1966 MERGE File." *Annals of Economic and Social Measurement* 1:325–342.

Okner, Benjamin A. 1975. "The Role of Demogrants as an Income Maintenance Alternative." In Irene Lurie, ed., *Integrating Income Maintenance Programs*. New York: Academic Press.

Olsen, Randall J. 1980. "Approximating a Truncated Normal Regression with the Method of Moments." *Econometrica* 48:1099–1105.

Orcutt, Guy H.; Glazer, Amihai; Harris, Robert; and Wertheimer, Richard, II. 1980. "Microanalytic Modeling and the Analysis of Public Transfer Policies." In Robert H. Haveman and Kevin Hollenbeck, eds., *Microeconomic Simulation Models for Public Policy Analysis*. Vol. 1. New York: Academic Press.

Orcutt, Guy H.; Greenberger, Martin; Korbel, John; and Rivlin, Alice. 1961. *Micro-Analysis of Socioeconomic Systems: A Simulation Study*. New York: Harper and Row.

Orcutt, Guy H., and Orcutt, Alice. 1968. "Incentive and Disincentive Experimentation for Income Maintenance Policy Purposes." *American Economic Review* 68:754–772.

Orcutt, Guy H., et al. 1976. *Policy Exploration through Microanalytic Simulation*. Washington, D.C.: Urban Institute.

Orr, Larry L. 1975. *Income, Employment, and Urban Residential Location*. New York: Academic Press.

Orr, Larry L. 1985. "Discussion." In Jerry A. Hausman and David A. Wise, eds., *Social Experimentation*. Chicago: University of Chicago Press.

Orshansky, Mollie. 1965. "Counting the Poor: Another Look at the Poverty Profile." *Social Security Bulletin* 28 (January):3–29.

Paglin, Morton. 1975. "The Measurement and Trend of Inequality: A Basic Revision." *American Economic Review* 65:598–609.

Paglin, Morton. 1977. "The Measurement and Trend of Inequality: Reply." *American Economic Review* 67:520–531.

Paglin, Morton. 1980. *Poverty and Transfer In-Kind: A Reevaluation of Poverty in the United States*. Stanford, Calif.: Hoover Institution Press.

Palmer, John L., ed. 1978. *Creating Jobs: Public Employment Programs and Wage Subsidies*. Washington, D.C.: Brookings Institution.

Parnes, Herbert S., et al., eds. 1970–81. *The Pre-Retirement Years* (4 vols); *Career Thresholds* (6 vols.); *Dual Careers* (4 vols.); *Years for Decision* (4 vols.); *Work and Retirement* (1 vol.). U.S. Department of Labor, Manpower R&D Monographs. Washington, D.C.: GPO.

Parsons, Donald. 1980a. "The Decline in Male Labor Force Participation." *Journal of Political Economy* 88:117–134.

Parsons, Donald. 1980b. "Racial Trends in Male Labor Force Participation." *American Economic Review* 70:911–920.

Patterson, James T. 1986. *America's Struggle against Poverty. 1900–1985*. 2d ed. Cambridge, Mass.: Harvard University Press.

Pechman, Joseph A. 1965. "A New Tax Model for Revenue Estimating." In *Proceedings of a Symposium on Federal Taxation*. Washington, D.C.: American Bankers Association.

Pechman, Joseph A. 1985. *Who Paid the Taxes, 1966–1985?* Washington, D.C.: Brookings Institution.

Pechman, Joseph A., and Okner, Benjamin A. 1974. *Who Bears the Tax Burden?* Washington, D.C.: Brookings Institution.

Pechman, Joseph A., and Timpane, Michael P., eds. 1975. *Work Incentives and Income Guarantees: The New Jersey Negative Income Tax Experiment.* Washington, D.C.: Brookings Institution.

Perloff, Jeffrey M. 1982. "Micro- and Macro-economic Effects." In Robert H. Haveman and John L. Palmer, eds., *Jobs for Disadvantaged Workers: The Economics of Employment Subsidies.* Washington, D.C.: Brookings Institution.

Perloff, Jeffrey M., and Wachter, Michael L. 1979. "The New Jobs Tax Credit: An Evaluation of the 1977–78 Wage Subsidy Program." *American Economic Review* 69:173–179.

Peterson, Paul E., and Greenstone, J. David. 1976. "Racial Change and Citizen Participation: The Mobilization of Low-Income Communities through Community Action." In Robert H. Haveman, ed., *A Decade of Federal Antipoverty Programs: Achievements, Failures, Lessons.* New York: Academic Press.

Phelps, Edmund S. 1972. "The Statistical Theory of Racism and Sexism." *American Economic Review* 62:659–661.

Piven, Frances F., and Cloward, Richard A. 1971. *Regulating the Poor: The Functions of Public Welfare.* New York: Pantheon.

Plotnick, Robert D. 1980. "The Redistributive Effects of Income Transfer Programs: A Better Measure." Institute for Research on Poverty, University of Wisconsin–Madison, Mimeo.

Plotnick, Robert D. 1982. "The Concept and Measurement of Horizontal Equity." *Journal of Public Economics* 17:373–391.

Plotnick, Robert D. 1985. "A Comparison of Measures of Horizontal Inequity." In Martin David and Timothy Smeeding, eds., *Horizontal Equity, Uncertainty, and Economic Well-Being.* Chicago: University of Chicago Press, for the National Bureau of Economic Research.

Plotnick, Robert D., and Skidmore, Felicity. 1975. *Progress against Poverty: A Review of the 1964–74 Decade.* New York: Academic Press.

Plotnick, Robert D., and Smeeding, Timothy. 1979. "Poverty and Income Transfers: Past Trends and Future Prospects." *Public Policy* 27:255–272.

Podell, Lawrence. 1967. "Families on Welfare in New York City." Preliminary Report. Center for Social Research, City University of New York.

Pollak, Robert A., and Wales, Terence J. 1979. "Welfare Comparisons and Equivalence Scales." *American Economic Review* 69 (May):216–221.

Prais, S. J. 1955a. "Measuring Social Mobility." *Journal of the Royal Statistical Society* 118 (Ser. A):56–66.

Prais, S. J. 1955b. "The Formal Theory of Social Mobility." *Population Studies* 9:72–81.

President of the United States. 1964. *Economic Report of the President.* Washington, D.C.: GPO.

President of the United States. 1965. *Economic Report of the President.* Washington, D.C.: GPO.

President's Commission on Income Maintenance Programs. 1969. *Poverty amid Plenty: The American Paradox.* Washington, D.C.: GPO.

Projector, Dorothy S., and Weiss, Gertrude S. 1969. "Income–Net Worth Measures of Economic Welfare." *Social Security Bulletin* 32 (November):14–17.

Proxmire, William. 1969. "PPB, the Agencies, and the Congress." In U.S. Congress, Joint Economic Committee, *The Analysis and Evaluation of Public Expenditures: The PPB System.* Vol. 1. Washington, D.C.: GPO.

Rainwater, Lee. 1974. *What Money Buys: Inequality and the Social Meaning of Income.* New York: Basic Books.

Rea, Samuel. 1974. "Incentive Effects of Alternative Negative Income Tax Plans." *Journal of Public Economics* 3:237–249.

Rees, Albert. 1974. "An Overview of the Labor-Supply Results." *Journal of Human Resources* 9:158–180.

Reich, Charles A. 1965. "Individual Rights and Social Welfare: The Emerging Issues." *Yale Law Journal,* Vol. 75.

Reynolds, Morgan, and Smolensky, Eugene. 1977. *Public Expenditures, Taxes, and the Distribution of Income: The United States, 1950, 1961, 1970.* New York: Academic Press.

Ribich, Thomas I. 1968. *Education and Poverty.* Washington, D.C.: Brookings Institution.

Ribich, Thomas, and Murphy, James. 1975. "The Economic Returns to Increased Educational Spending." *Journal of Human Resources* 10:56–77.

Rieken, Henry W., and Boruch, Robert. 1974. *Social Experimentation: A Method for Planning and Evaluating Social Intervention.* New York: Academic Press.

Rivlin, Alice. 1971. *Systematic Thinking for Social Action.* Washington, D.C.: Brookings Institution.

Robins, Philip; West, Richard; and Lohrer, Michael. 1980. "Labor Supply Response to a Nationwide Negative Income Tax: Evidence from the Seattle and Denver Income Maintenance Experiments." SRI International, Stanford, California, September. Mimeo.

Rogin, Leo. 1956. *The Meaning and Validity of Economic Theory.* New York: Harper.

Rogoff, Natalie. 1953. *Recent Trends in Occupational Mobility.* Glencoe, Ill.: Free Press.

Rolph, Earl R. 1967. "The Case for a Negative Income Tax Device." *Industrial Relations* 6:155–165.

Rose, Stephen M. 1972. *The Betrayal of the Poor: The Transformation of Community Action.* Cambridge, Mass.: Schenkman.

Rosen, Harvey. 1985. "Housing Behavior and the Experimental Housing Allowance Program: What Have We Learned?" In Jerry A. Hausman and David A. Wise, eds., *Social Experimentation.* Chicago: University of Chicago Press.

Rosen, Sherwin. 1977. "Human Capital: A Survey of Empirical Research." In Ronald Ehrenberg, ed., *Research in Labor Economics.* Vol. 1. Greenwich, Conn.: JAI Press.

Rossi, Peter H., and Freeman, Howard. 1982. *Evaluation: A Systematic Approach.* Beverly Hills, Calif.: Sage Publications.

Rossi, Peter H., and Lyall, Katharine C. 1976. *Reforming Public Welfare: A Critique of the Negative Income Tax Experiment.* New York: Russell Sage Foundation.

Rossi, Peter H., and Wright, Sonia R. 1977. "Evaluation Research: An Assessment of Theory, Practice, and Politics." *Evaluation Quarterly* 1:5–51.

Rossi, Peter H.; Wright, James; and Wright, Sonia R. 1978. "The Theory and Practice of Applied Social Research." *Evaluation Research* 2:171–191.

Schieber, S. J., and George, P. M. 1981. *Retirement Income Opportunities in an Aging America: Coverage and Benefit Entitlement.* Washington, D.C.: Employee Benefit Research Institute.

Schiller, Bradley S. 1976. "Relative Earnings Mobility in the United States." *American Economic Review* 67:926–941.

Schorr, Alvin. 1968. *Explorations in Social Policy.* New York: Basic Books.

Schorr, Alvin. 1971. "A Family Allowance Program for Pre-School Children." In Theodore Marmor, ed., *Poverty Policy.* Chicago: Aldine-Atherton.

Schultz, T. W. 1963. *The Economic Value of Education.* New York: Columbia University Press.

Schwartz, Edward E. 1964. "A Way to End the Means Test." *Social Work* 9:3–12.

Sen, Amartya. 1973. *On Economic Inequality.* Oxford: Clarendon Press.

Sen, Amartya. 1979. "Personal Utilities and Public Judgements: Or What's Wrong with Welfare Economics?" *Economic Journal* 89:537–558.

Sepanik, R.; Hendricks, G.; and Heinberg, J. D. 1975. "Simulations of National Housing Allowances: An Application of the TRIM Model." Working Paper no. 216–13, Urban Institute, Washington, D.C.

Sewell, William H. 1971. "Inequality of Opportunity for Higher Education." *American Sociological Review* 36:793–809.

Sewell, William H., and Hauser, Robert H. 1975. *Education, Occupation, and Earnings: Achievement in the Early Career.* New York: Academic Press.

Shell, Karl; Fisher, Franklin; Foley, Duncan; and Friedlander, Ann. 1968. "The Educational Opportunity Bank: An Economic Analysis of a Contingent Repayment Loan Program for Higher Education." *National Tax Journal* 21:2–45.

Shorrocks, A. F. 1980. "The Class of Additively Decomposable Inequality Measures." *Econometrica* 48:613–625.

Shoven, John. 1972. "A General Equilibrium Calculation of the Effects of Differential Taxation of Income from Capital in the U.S." *Journal of Public Economics* 1:281–321.

Shoven, John, and Whalley, John. 1984. "Applied General Equilibrium Models of Taxation and International Trade." *Journal of Economic Literature* 22:1007–1051.

Shriver, Sargent. 1973. "Testimony before U.S. Senate Subcommittee on Intergovernmental Relations," Washington, D.C., March 15. Mimeo.

Sirageldin, Ismail. 1969. *Non-Market Components of National Income.* Ann Arbor: Survey Research Center, University of Michigan.

Smeeding, Timothy. 1975. "Measuring the Economic Welfare of Low-Income Households and the Antipoverty Effectiveness of Cash and Non-Cash Transfer

Programs." Ph.D. diss., Department of Economics, University of Wisconsin–Madison.

Smeeding, Timothy. 1977. "The Antipoverty Effectiveness of In-Kind Transfers." *Journal of Human Resources* 12:360–378.

Smith, James D., and Morgan, James N. 1980. "Variability of Economic Well-Being and Its Determinants." *American Economic Review* 7 (May):286–295.

Smith, James, and Welch, Finis. 1977. "Black-White Male Earnings and Employment: 1960–1970." In F. Thomas Juster, ed., *The Distribution of Economic Well-Being*. Cambridge, Mass.: Ballinger, for the National Bureau of Economic Research.

Smith, Marshall. 1972. "Equality of Educational Opportunity: The Basic Findings Reconsidered." In Frederick Mosteller and Daniel Patrick Moynihan, eds., *On Equality of Educational Opportunity*. New York: Random House.

Smolensky, Eugene; Stiefel, Leanna; Schmundt, Maria; and Plotnick, Robert. 1977. "In-Kind Transfers and the Size Distribution of Income." In Marilyn Moon and Eugene Smolensky, eds., *Improving Measures of Economic Well-being*. New York: Academic Press.

Solmon, Lewis. 1970. "A Note on Equality of Educational Opportunity." *American Economic Review* 60:768–771.

Somers, Gerald, and Stromsdorfer, Ernst W. 1972. "A Cost-Effectiveness Analysis of In-School and Summer Neighborhood Youth Corps: A Nationwide Evaluation." *Journal of Human Resources* 7:446–459.

Somers, Gerald, and Wood, W. D., eds. 1969. *Cost-Benefit Analysis of Manpower Policies: Proceedings of a North American Conference*. Kingston, Canada: Industrial Relations Centre, Queens University.

Sørensen, Aage B. 1977. "The Structure of Inequality and the Process of Attainment." *American Sociological Review* 42:965–978.

Sorokin, Pitirim. 1927. *Social Mobility*. New York: Harper.

Spence, Michael. 1974. *Market Signaling: Information Transfer in Hiring and Related Screening Processes*. Cambridge, Mass.: Harvard University Press.

Speth, James, Jr., et al. 1968. "A Model Negative Income Statute." *Yale Law Journal* 78:269–288.

Spilerman, Seymour. 1970. "Careers, Labor Market Structure, and Socioeconomic Achievement." *American Journal of Sociology* 83:551–593.

Spilerman, Seymour, and Elesh, David. 1971. "Alternative Conceptions of Poverty and Their Implications for Income Maintenance." *Social Problems* (Winter):358–373.

Stafford, Frank. 1985. "Income Maintenance Policy and Work Effort: Learning from Experiments and Labor Market Studies." In Jerry A. Hausman and David A. Wise, eds., *Social Experimentation*. Chicago: University of Chicago Press.

Staines, Verdon. 1982. "Seven Events' Effects on Family Earnings, Transfer Incomes, and Economic Well-Being." Ph.D. diss., Department of Economics, University of Wisconsin–Madison.

Stein, Bruno. 1971. *On Relief*. New York: Basic Books.

Steiner, Gilbert. 1966. *Social Insecurity: The Politics of Welfare*. Chicago: Rand-McNally.

Steiner, Gilbert. 1971. *The State of Welfare*. Washington, D.C.: Brookings Institution.

Steiner, Gilbert. 1974. "Reform Follows Reality: The Growth of Welfare." *The Public Interest*, no. 34 (Winter), pp. 47–65.

Steiner, Peter, and Dorfman, Robert. 1962. *The Economic Status of the Aged*. Berkeley: University of California Press.

Stiglitz, Joseph E. 1973. "Approaches to the Economics of Discrimination." *American Economic Review* 63:287–295.

Stiglitz, Joseph E. 1975. "The Theory of 'Screening,' Education, and the Distribution of Income." *American Economic Review* 65:283–300.

Storey, James R.; Cox, Irene; and Townsend, Alair. 1973. "How Public Welfare Benefits Are Distributed in Low-Income Areas." In U.S. Congress, Joint Economic Committee, Subcommittee on Fiscal Policy, *Studies in Public Welfare*, Paper no. 6. Washington, D.C.: GPO.

Straszheim, Mahlon. 1974. "Housing Market Discrimination and Black Housing Consumption." *Quarterly Journal of Economics* 88:19–43.

Stromsdorfer, Ernst W. 1979. "The Impact of Social Research on Public Policy." In Kenneth J. Arrow, Clark C. Abt, and Stephen J. Fitzsimmons, eds., *Applied Research for Social Policy*. Cambridge, Mass.: Abt Books.

Stromsdorfer, Ernst W. 1985. "Social Science Analysis and the Formulation of Public Policy: Illustrations of What the President 'Knows' and How He Comes to 'Know' It." In Jerry A. Hausman and David A. Wise, eds., *Social Experimentation*. Chicago: University of Chicago Press.

Stromsdorfer, Ernst W., and Farkas, George, eds. 1980. *Evaluation Studies Review Annual*. Vol. 5. Beverly Hills, Calif.: Sage Publications.

Suchman, Edward A. 1967. *Evaluative Research: Principles and Practice in Public Service and Social Action Programs*. New York: Russell Sage Foundation.

Summers, Anita, and Wolfe, Barbara. 1977. "Do Schools Make a Difference?" *American Economic Review* 67:639–652.

Sundquist, James L., ed. 1969. *On Fighting Poverty: Perspectives from Experience*. New York: Basic Books.

Svalastoga, K. 1959. *Prestige, Class and Mobility*. Copenhagen: Gyldendal.

Taeuber, Karl, and Taeuber, Alma. 1965. *Negroes in Cities: Residential Segregation and Neighborhood Changes*. Chicago: Aldine.

Taggart, Robert. 1981. *A Fisherman's Guide: An Assessment of Training and Remediation Strategies*. Kalamazoo, Mich.: Upjohn Institute for Employment Research.

Taubman, Paul. 1976. "Earnings, Education, Genetics, and Environment." *Journal of Human Resources* 11:447–461.

Taubman, Paul, ed. 1977. *Kinometrics: Determinants of Socioeconomic Success within and between Families*. Amsterdam: North-Holland.

Taubman, Paul, and Wales, Terence. 1974. *Higher Education and Earnings: College as an Investment and Screening Device*. New York: McGraw-Hill.

Taussig, Michael K. 1969. "Research on Income Maintenance." Paper presented at the Conference on Research on Urban Poverty, Princeton University, May 22–23.

Taussig, Michael K. 1973. *Alternative Measures of the Distribution of Economic Welfare*. Princeton, N.J.: Industrial Relations Section, Princeton University.

Taussig, Michael K. 1980. "Discussion." In Robert H. Haveman and Kevin Hollenbeck, eds., *Microeconomic Simulation Models for Public Policy Analysis*. Vol. 1. New York: Academic Press.

Ten Broek, Jacobus. 1964–65. "California's Dual System of Family Laws: Its Origin, Development, and Current Status." *Stanford Law Review* 16:257–317, 900–981; 17:614–682.

Theobald, Robert. 1963. *Free Men and Free Markets*. New York: C. N. Potter.

Thurow, Lester. 1972. "Education and Economic Equality." *The Public Interest*, no. 28 (Summer), pp. 66–85.

Thurow, Lester. 1975. *Generating Inequality: Mechanisms of Distribution in the U.S. Economy*. New York: Basic Books.

Tinbergen, Jan. 1975. *Income Distribution: Analysis and Policies*. Amsterdam: North-Holland.

Tobin, James. 1958. "Estimation of Relationships for Limited Dependent Variables." *Econometrica* 26:24–36.

Tobin, James. 1970. "Raising the Incomes of the Poor." In Kermit Gordon, ed., *Agenda for the Nation*. Washington, D.C.: Brookings Institution.

Tobin, James; Pechman, Joseph A.; and Miezkowski, Peter. 1967. "Is a Negative Income Tax Practical?" *Yale Law Journal* 77:1–27.

Tobin, James, and Wallis, W. Allen. 1968. *Welfare Programs: An Economic Appraisal*. Washington, D.C.: American Enterprise Institute for Public Policy Research.

Tuma, Nancy B.; Hannan, Michael T.; and Groeneveld, Lyle P. 1979. "Dynamic Analysis of Event Histories." *American Journal of Sociology* 84:820–854.

Tuma, Nancy B., and Robins, Philip K. 1980. "A Dynamic Model of Employment Behavior: An Application to the Seattle and Denver Income Maintenance Experiments." *Econometrica* 48:1031–1052.

U.S. Advisory Council on Public Assistance. 1960. *Report*. Senate Doc. no. 93, 86th Congress, 2d Session. Washington, D.C.: GPO.

U.S. Advisory Council on Public Welfare. 1966. *Having the Power, We Have the Duty*. Report to the Secretary of Health, Education, and Welfare. Washington, D.C.: GPO.

U.S. Bureau of the Census. 1982. *Alternative Methods for Valuing Selected In-Kind Transfer Benefits and Measuring Their Effects on Poverty*. Technical Paper no. 50. Washington, D.C.: GPO.

U.S. Comptroller General, General Accounting Office. 1978. *Federal Evaluation Programs*. 1st ed. Washington, D.C.: GPO.

U.S. Congress, Congressional Budget Office. 1977. *Welfare Reform: Issues, Objectives, and Approaches*. Washington, D.C.: GPO.

U.S. Congress, Joint Economic Committee. 1968. *Income Maintenance Pro-*

grams. Hearings before the Subcommittee on Fiscal Policy, 90th Congress, 2d Session, Vol. 1. Washington, D.C.: GPO.

U.S. Congress, Joint Economic Committee. 1969. *The Analysis and Evaluation of Public Expenditures: The PPB System*. 3 vols. Washington, D.C.: GPO.

U.S. Congress, Joint Economic Committee, Subcommittee on Fiscal Policy. 1972. *Studies in Public Welfare*. Paper no. 1, "Handbook of Public Income Transfer Programs" (October 16). Washington, D.C.: GPO.

U.S. Congress, Joint Economic Committee, Subcommittee on Fiscal Policy. 1974. *Income Security for Americans: Recommendations of the Public Welfare Study*. Washington, D.C.: GPO.

U.S. Department of Health, Education, and Welfare. 1969. *Toward a Social Report*. Washington, D.C.: GPO.

U.S. Department of Health, Education, and Welfare. 1974. "The Changing Economic Status of 5,000 American Families: Highlights from the Panel Study of Income Dynamics." Washington, D.C. Mimeo.

U.S. Department of Health, Education, and Welfare. 1976. *The Measure of Poverty: A Report to Congress as Mandated by the Education Amendments of 1974*. Washington, D.C.: GPO.

U.S. Department of Health, Education, and Welfare, Office of Assistant Secretary for Planning and Evaluation. 1976. *Income Supplement Program: 1974 HEW Welfare Replacement Proposal*. Technical Analysis Paper no. 11. Washington, D.C.: GPO.

U.S. Senate, 96th Congress, 2d Session. 1980. *Department of State, Justice and Commerce, the Judiciary and Related Agencies Appropriation Bill, 1980* 16:33–34.

Vadakin, James. 1968. *Family Allowances*. Miami, Fla.: University of Miami Press.

Van der Gaag, Jacques, and Smolensky, Eugene. 1980. "Income, Consumption, Household Composition and True-Household-Equivalence Scales." Paper presented at the World Meeting of the Econometric Society, Aix-en-Provence, France, August/September.

Van der Gaag, Jacques, and Smolensky, Eugene. 1981. "True Household Equivalence Scales and Characteristics of the Poor in the United States." *Review of Income and Wealth* 28:17–28.

Vroman, Wayne. 1974. "Changes in Black Workers' Relative Earnings: Evidence from the 1960s." In G. von Furstenberg, B. Harrison, and A. Horowitz, eds., *Patterns of Racial Discrimination*. Vol. 2. Boston: Heath.

Wachtel, Howard, and Betsey, Charles. 1972. "Employment at Low Wages." *Review of Economics and Statistics* 54:121–129.

Wachter, Michael. 1974. "Primary and Secondary Labor Markets: A Critique of the Dual Approach." *Brookings Papers on Economic Activity*, no. 3, pp. 637–680.

Wallace, Phyllis, ed. 1975. *Equal Employment Opportunity and the AT&T Case*. Cambridge, Mass.: MIT Press.

Ward, Lester. 1906. *Applied Sociology: A Treatise on the Conscious Improvement of Society by Society*. Boston: Ginn.

Warlick, Jennifer L. 1981. "Participation as a Measure of Program Success." *Focus* (newsletter of the Institute for Research on Poverty) 5 (Summer):12–16.

Warlick, Jennifer L. 1982. "Participation of the Aged in SSI." *Journal of Human Resources* 17:236–260.

Watts, Harold W. 1967. "The Iso-Prop Index: An Approach to the Determination of Differential Poverty Income Thresholds." *Journal of Human Resources* 2:3–18.

Watts, Harold W. 1969. "An Economic Definition of Poverty." In Daniel Patrick Moynihan, ed., *On Understanding Poverty*. New York: Basic Books.

Watts, Harold W. 1986. "Have Our Measures of Poverty Become Poorer?" *Focus* (newsletter of the Institute for Research on Poverty) 9 (Summer):18–22.

Watts, Harold W., and Peck, Jon K. 1975. "On the Comparison of Income Redistribution Plans." In James D. Smith, ed., *The Personal Distribution of Income and Wealth*. New York: National Bureau of Economic Research.

Watts, Harold W., and Rees, Albert, eds. 1977. *The New Jersey Income Maintenance Experiment*. Vol. 2, *Labor-Supply Responses*. New York: Academic Press.

Weisbrod, Burton A. 1962. "Education and Investment in Human Capital." *Journal of Political Economy* 70:106–123.

Weisbrod, Burton A. 1965. "Preventing High School Dropouts." In R. Dorfman, ed., *Measuring the Benefits of Government Investments*. Washington, D.C.: Brookings Institution.

Weisbrod, Burton A. 1968. "Income Distribution Effects and Benefit Cost Analysis." In Samuel Chase, ed., *Problems in Public Expenditure Analysis*. Washington, D.C.: Brookings Institution.

Weisbrod, Burton A. 1969. "Collective Action and the Distribution of Income: A Conceptual Approach." In U.S. Congress, Joint Economic Committee, *The Analysis and Evaluation of Public Expenditures: The PPB System*. Vol. 1. Washington, D.C.: GPO.

Weisbrod, Burton A. 1970. "On the Stigma Effect and the Demand for Welfare Programs: A Theoretical Note." Discussion Paper no. 82–70, Institute for Research on Poverty, University of Wisconsin–Madison.

Weisbrod, Burton A., and Hansen, W. Lee. 1968. "An Income–Net Worth Approach to Measuring Economic Welfare." *American Economic Review* 58:1315–1329.

Weiss, Carol H. 1977. *Using Social Research in Public Policy Making*. Lexington, Mass.: Lexington Books.

Weiss, Leonard, and Williamson, Jeffrey G. 1972. "Black Education, Earnings and Interregional Migration: Some New Evidence." *American Economic Review* 62:372–383.

Weiss, R. O. 1970. "The Effect of Education on the Earnings of Blacks and Whites." *Review of Economics and Statistics* 52:150–159.

Welch, Finis. 1973. "Black-White Differences in Returns to Schooling." *American Economic Review* 63:893–907.

Welch, Finis. 1974. "Minimum Wage Legislation in the United States." *Economic Inquiry* 12:285–318.

Welch, Finis. 1975. "Human Capital Theory: Education, Discrimination, and Life Cycles." *American Economic Review* 65 (May):63–82.

Wertheimer, Richard, II, and Zedlewski, S. 1978. "Demographic Changes and the Distribution of Income in the United States: 1975–1985." In Martin Pfaff, ed., *Problembereiche der Verteilungs- und Sozialpolitik*. Berlin: Duncker and Humblot.

Wickenden, Elizabeth, and Bell, Winifred. 1961. *Public Welfare: Time for a Change*. New York: Project on Public Services for Families and Children.

Wildavsky, Aaron. 1979. *The Politics of the Budget Process*. Boston: Little, Brown.

Wildavsky, Aaron. 1985. "The Once and Future School of Public Policy." *The Public Interest*, no. 79 (Spring), pp. 25–41.

Wilensky, Gail R. 1970. "An Income Transfer Computational Model." In *The President's Commission on Income Maintenance Programs, Technical Studies*. Washington, D.C.: GPO.

Willis, Patricia. 1977. "Determinants of Intra-jurisdictional Variation in the AFDC Program in California." Ph.D. diss., University of California.

Willis, Patricia. 1980. "Participation Rates in the Aid to Families with Dependent Children Program, Part III: Eligible Families' Decisions and State Participation Rates." Working Paper no. 1387–04, Urban Institute, Washington, D.C.

Willis, R. J., and Rosen, Sherwin. 1979. "Education and Self-Selection." *Journal of Political Economy* 87:57–536.

Wirtz, W. Willard. 1966. "A Report on Employment and Unemployment in Urban Slums and Ghettos: Memorandum for the President." In U.S. Congress, Senate Subcommittee on Employment, Manpower and Poverty, 92nd Congress, 2d Session, *Comprehensive Manpower Reform*. Washington, D.C.: GPO.

Wiseman, Michael. 1976. "Public Employment as Fiscal Policy." *Brookings Papers on Economic Activity*, no. 1, pp. 67–104.

Wiseman, Michael. 1977. "Change and Turnover in a Welfare Population." In *The Income Dynamics of the Poor Project Report*. Berkeley: Institute of Business and Economics Research, University of California.

Wohlstetter, Albert, and Coleman, Sinclair. 1970. *Race Differences in Income*. Santa Monica, Calif.: Rand Corporation.

Wright, Erik O. 1980. *Class Structure and Income Determination*. New York: Academic Press.

Wright, Erik O., and Perrone, Luca. 1977. "Marxist Class Categories and Income Inequality." *American Sociological Review* 42:32–35.

Yarmolinsky, Adam. 1969. "The Beginnings of OEO." In J. L. Sundquist, ed., *On Fighting Poverty: Perspectives from Experience*. New York: Basic Books.

Yett, Donald E. 1979. *A Forecasting and Policy Simulation Model of the Health Care Sector: The HRRC Prototype Microeconomic Model*. Lexington, Mass.: Lexington Books.

Yett, Donald E.; Drabek, Leonard; Intriligator, Michael; and Kimbell, Larry J. 1980. "The HRRC Health Care Sector Simulation Model." In Robert H.

Haveman and Kevin Hollenbeck, eds., *Microeconomic Simulation Models for Public Policy Analysis*. Vol. 1. New York: Academic Press.

Zeckhauser, Richard, and Schuck, Peter. 1970. "An Alternative to the Nixon Income Maintenance Plan." *The Public Interest*, no. 19 (Spring), pp. 120–130.

Zimmerman, Carle C. 1935. *Family and Society*. New York: Van Nostrand.

Zimmerman, Carle C. 1936. *Consumption and Standards of Living*. New York: Van Nostrand.

Zucker, Albert. 1973. "Minimum Wages and the Long-Run Elasticity of Demand for Low Wage Labor." *Quarterly Journal of Economics* 87:267–277.

Index

299

COMPOSED BY MODERN TYPE & DESIGN, INC., CLEARWATER, FLORIDA
MANUFACTURED BY CUSHING MALLOY, INC., ANN ARBOR, MICHIGAN
TEXT AND DISPLAY LINES ARE SET IN TIMES ROMAN

Library of Congress Cataloging-in-Publication Data
Haveman, Robert H.
Poverty policy and poverty research
Bibliography: pp. 259–297.
Includes index.
1. Poverty—Research—United States. 2. Economic
assistance, Domestic—United States. 3. United
States—Social policy. I. Title.
HC110.P6H38 1987   362.5'8'0973   86-40453
ISBN 0-299-11150-4